9108

Water Policy for
Sustainable Development

Published in association with the Center for American Places
Santa Fe, New Mexico, and Staunton, Virginia
www.americanplaces.org

Water Policy for Sustainable Development

DAVID LEWIS FELDMAN

The Johns Hopkins University Press
Baltimore

© 2007 The Johns Hopkins University Press
All rights reserved. Published 2007
Printed in the United States of America on acid-free paper
2 4 6 8 9 7 5 3 1

The Johns Hopkins University Press
2715 North Charles Street
Baltimore, Maryland 21218-4363
www.press.jhu.edu

Library of Congress Cataloging-in-Publication Data
Feldman, David Lewis, 1951–
Water policy for sustainable development / David Lewis Feldman.
p. cm.
"Published in association with the Center for American Places, Santa Fe,
New Mexico, and Staunton, Virginia."
Includes bibliographical references and index.
ISBN-13: 978-0-8018-8588-4 (hardcover : alkaline paper)
ISBN-10: 0-8018-8588-4 (hardcover : alkaline paper)
1. Water-supply—Government policy—United States. 2. Water resources
development—Environmental aspects—United States—Case studies.
3. Watersheds—United States—Case studies. 4. Water-supply—Management.
5. Sustainable development. I. Title.
HD1694.A5F458 2007
333.91′150973—dc22
2006030066

A catalog record for this book is available from the British Library.

Contents

Preface

This book has its genesis in two sets of experiences. The first was the opportunity to undertake research with colleagues at the University of Tennessee and other institutions on the problems faced by the Southeast in providing an abundant, dependable water supply to sustain its frenetic pace of growth *and* peerless ecological bounty. Started in the late 1990s, this research has encompassed the study of conflicts involving Alabama, Florida, and Georgia over the allocation of water from three river basins; Mississippi and Tennessee over groundwater withdrawals; and North Carolina and Virginia over interstate water diversion, among others. This work was an offshoot of my longstanding interests in global water policy harking back to the 1980s.

In the late 1990s, to imply that a traditionally water-rich region like the Southeast was confronting water conflicts potentially as severe as those experienced in the Far West was to invite ridicule—or at the very least, astonishment. Yet such conflicts were not only possible, some of them had already begun to reach an impasse that promised federal court showdown, or worse. While these disputes have afforded my colleagues and me the opportunity to apply our multidisciplinary abilities to the task of helping public officials amicably resolve them, it has often seemed that our intervention was too late. The issues besetting their protagonists had, in many instances, already come to a head.

For Alabama, Georgia, and Florida, the central issue remains how to divide and jointly allocate three interstate river systems that support diverse activities ranging from irrigated agriculture in rural Georgia, fisheries along Florida's Gulf Coast, power generation in Alabama, and household uses in Atlanta—the region's largest and fastest-growing metropolitan area. While this conflict continues to simmer, the one between North Carolina and Virginia appears to have been settled, at least for now. In the early 1990s, these states engaged in a legal battle over a proposed project by the city of Virginia Beach to divert water from Lake Gaston, a reservoir on the Roanoke River that traverses the western portions of both states. Despite intervention by the courts and the Environmental Protection Agency (which largely sided with Virginia) the project was eventually completed—although lingering resentments remain on the part of many North Carolinians.

Finally, as this book went to press, Mississippi has filed suit against Memphis, Tennessee, over the latter's groundwater withdrawals which, the plaintiffs claim, are causing long-term injury to neighboring residents in the northern part of that state. It would not be a stretch to insist that these three conflicts epitomize the growing and frequently contentious competition over high-demand water resources, which are in short supply in some parts of the region and relatively abundant in others. Such competition is unfortunately all too familiar to students of water policy from *every* corner of our globe.

In my effort to understand these disputes better, their origins and their consequences, I came to the conclusion that, in many ways, they shared much in common with the historically momentous battles over the competing values of preservation and development, environmentalism and economic growth, and rural versus urban development fought in the American West in the nineteenth and early twentieth centuries (and which are currently being fought in many parts of the developing world today). Simply stated: hard-to-reconcile policy objectives, differences in power among groups, inflexible decision-making institutions, and policymakers ill-equipped to render equitable as well as scientifically sound policies are problems that are not limited to particular regions.

The second set of experiences that influenced the writing of this book also began in the late 1990s. This was the opportunity to reflect back on the conclusions of my 1991 book *Water Resources Management: In Search of an Environmental Ethic.* This reflection was prompted by changes in water and other environmental policies that had transpired in the decade since the book's publication. These changes continue to influence my research as a political scientist interested in the social construction of risk, global environmental change, and energy policy—as well as water issues.

The thesis of that book, drawing on examples from several regions, was that disputes over how natural resources should be managed, utilized, and allocated are fundamentally conflicts over divergent values held by government agencies, nongovernmental stakeholders, and the general public. Such conflicts could be resolved, I argued, if we systematically entertained moral principles in policy deliberations, and if we found the political will to incorporate such principles on a regular, sincere, and consistent basis.

In my reflections—helped along by the opportunity to work with policy-makers in Tennessee and the larger region to identify alternatives for dealing with challenges such as the threat of inter-basin diversion of water from Tennessee to Atlanta, the unprecedented growth of rural areas in the region through so-called green migration from the north and the Midwest, and the potential for growing conflicts between urban and rural residents over water supply—I was forced to consider whether my convictions were still warranted. More importantly, I was given the opportunity to test their realism in the light of practical experience and the adversity faced by public officials managing the disputes.

During this period, I was asked to help my own state draft legislation to regulate the inter-basin transfer of water and to manage water withdrawals better, and in 1998 and 1999 I organized two stakeholder forums attended by over three hundred federal, state, and local officials and representatives from water user groups, environmental organizations, and educational and research institutions from throughout the region. These forums, funded and supported by the Tennessee Valley Authority, the EPA, the U.S. Geological Survey, the Appalachian Regional Commission, the Oak Ridge National Laboratory, the University of Tennessee, and the Southern States Energy Board, afforded participants the chance to discuss impediments to resolving water conflicts both generally in the specific region. They also generated a number of recommendations that helped build some modest bridges among protagonists on how these conflicts might be amicably resolved.

I found the experience of participating in these forums to be especially instructive about the practical challenges in turning a "good" principle into a workable practice. For a political scientist long engaged in studying environmental policy, it was like "going back to school."

During this same period, I also began to work on a number of projects that taught me still more about the impediments to—as well as the opportunities for—achieving the goals set out in my first book. I examined the growing phenomenon of state and local environmental priority-setting activities in the United States, also called "comparative risk assessments." These pioneering activities resulted in the growing need to combine environmentally sound and socially just solutions to environmental threats to community and public health. These assessments revealed much about the difficulty of reconciling public preferences with environmental science. For example, could states really play an effective role in averting global warming? Could cities really make an impact in reducing regional air pollution? These were precisely the questions citizen activists and scientists engaged in these efforts were asking.

In the area of water policy, I developed a growing interest in "watershed initiatives"—citizen-based efforts founded on the principle that drainage basins could effectively serve both as planning units and as "environmental systems" that could be restored to health and ecological vitality through locally empowered community activism undertaken with a willingness to break from traditional forms of political-jurisdictional cooperation.

Other water policy reforms—international in scope—also caught my attention, including a growing number of efforts to examine and reform the patterns of ownership and control of the water supply in developing nations. These efforts are broadly concerned with such issues as the impact of large dam projects on the welfare of the politically disenfranchised and the widening gap between the haves and have-nots with respect to access to clean and affordable water supply and water treatment infrastructure—both of which remain luxuries in many parts of the third world.

The opportunities to study regional water problems in the South and to reflect on the conclusions of my first book in light of other experiences led me to see some common threads of hope *and* despair. If my book was an optimistic appraisal of *how* such conflicts *could* be amicably resolved, the water conflicts brewing in my own backyard were an obvious reminder of *why* they are not often resolved in such a manner.

I came to realize that while the incorporation of sound moral principles in policy deliberations may be necessary to resolve environmental conflicts, such principles are not, in and of themselves, sufficient to bring about change without an *institutional* setting that fosters such discourse. I also came to understand that in those instances where conflicts have been amenable to amicable and environmentally effective resolution, certain political, administrative, and communication factors tended to be present. These factors are the subject of *this* book.

Four common factors seem to be to be of paramount importance. The first is an approach to addressing transboundary resource problems that starts from the premise that *everything* we do when we intervene in the natural environment is characterized by some degree of uncertainty and risk. It seems reasonable to suggest that this is one of the lessons of current debates over how our use of fossil fuel sources may be affecting the global climate, for example. Thus, whenever we institute a practice, decision, or program to regulate, manage, or exploit a resource, we should seek policy innovations that are modest in scope, as scientifically sound as we can make them, and reversible in their impact. This approach, sometimes referred to as *adaptive management,* is based on the premise that natural resource decisions should be made and modified in light of new information we acquire about natural systems *and* human needs.

Second, to permit adaptive management, environmental and natural resource policy innovations should be designed as *social learning experiences.* Organizations charged with managing resources over large (or even not-so-large) geographic areas—including river basins, coastal zones, air sheds, parklands, or habitat protection regions—should be structured to permit their officials to learn from mistakes (including those brought about by previous decisions) and to adopt "mid-course" policy corrections. This requires, as we shall see, not only *institutional* flexibility but also some sort of allowance for the interpretation, application, and implementation of laws, rules, regulations, and prior agreements—*legal* flexibility—in order to amend imperfect decisions and adjust to the peculiar demands of the situations and settings we find ourselves in.

Third, such an organizational design assumes that policymakers are willing and able to acknowledge error—which leads to another vital factor explored in this book: officials must operate in an organizational and political setting that permits them to acknowledge their fallibility. Moreover, they must be willing to adopt a humble attitude toward the environment that makes them amenable to correcting mistakes before they become irreversible. This further assumes a high degree of *trust* among officials and between officials and the constituents and stakeholders whom they serve and who expect to be consulted on decisions. It also presumes a high degree of *confidence* among these constituents toward the organizations that manage these resources. How such trust and confidence are fostered is a topic of extensive discussion in our case studies.

Finally, there must be a shared vision about what an organization charged with managing natural resources is supposed to be doing. There will always be divergent values that arise over how to manage water and other resources. In a democracy, the problem is *not* divergence or disagreement per se but rather finding ways that we can systematically and fairly balance, weigh, prioritize, and choose among the arguments advanced by environmental advocates who seek, for example, to preserve scenic rivers, pristine waters, and the ecological resources that depend on them against the goals of regional development proponents who demand additional water to support economic growth and larger populations. This requires a willingness to reach accord for the sake of the common good, to embrace wide-scale participation in an effort to reach just outcomes, and to consider the interest of future generations in order to achieve environmental stewardship.

As we shall see, some of the more successful river basin and watershed initiatives explored in this book—initiatives that have sought to manage water supply and quality issues—have struggled with precisely these questions. Among the lessons they have learned is that once the means to address these challenges have been found, decision-makers must learn to do it all over again in a never-ending cycle of acquiring knowledge about the limitations and constraints their decisions confront in the face of implementation problems and then making *new* decisions in light of this knowledge. This last step provides a kind of "feedback" mechanism that makes stewardship possible.

If the concept of sustainable development, so often used to describe the goals of policymakers who seek to reconcile economic growth with environmental protection, has any real meaning, its achievement requires that we embrace these four factors—adaptability, humility, willingness to learn from mistakes, and enthusiasm over a shared vision about the obligations of stewardship. Achieving sustainable development requires a fundamental change in the values people hold toward the environment—that conviction from my first book still remains true, I believe. Attaining this value change requires that we embrace humility regarding what we know, stewardship in how we act, and fallibility toward what we are willing to admit about the consequences of our actions upon nature, other species, and one another—this is the theme of the present volume.

This book is aimed at social scientists, public officials, environmental professionals charged with managing water and other resources, and environmental advocates who work in nongovernmental organizations. Its aim to help all these experts find common ground where we can draw upon the expertise of everyone. This effort will be a success, I feel, if it helps to bridge the gap separating academics who study these issues and policymakers concerned with their management. By working together, we can address such problems in ways that are just, fair, effective, and protective of future generations.

In a project such as this, where issues are analyzed, problems dissected, and solutions reflected upon, an author accrues an enormous debt of gratitude to a great many people. I wish to especially thank Patrice Cole, former graduate assistant in the Department of Ecology and Evolutionary Biology at the University of Tennessee for her enormous help in analyzing the five cases discussed in chapter 3 and for undertaking the brief survey of protagonists in these cases. My faculty colleagues in the Southeastern Water Policy Initiative at UT—Bobby Jones, Carol Harden, Forbes Walker, and Rob Freeland—have been especially helpful in helping me understand the enormous challenges faced by those with the audacity to suggest that water problems can be judiciously managed through a combination of good science and effective public involvement. Together with former graduate students Aaron Routhe, Emily Heinrich, Lyndsay Mosley, and Jennie Caissie, the work of this initiative also helped me to grasp the multidisciplinary challenges facing adaptive management of water resources.

I am also grateful to George F. Thompson at the Center for American Places for supporting my interest in this project, as he has my previous ones published by the Johns Hopkins University Press. As a department head, I owe an enormous debt not only to those who helped directly but also to those whose conscientious attention to a million other tasks allowed me to complete this project. In this category I thank Sue Howerton and Debby McCauley of the political science department for their good deeds.

A number of friends and colleagues reviewed parts of this manuscript, referred me to additional sources, discussed and shared ideas on these issues, and greatly assisted in learning about environmental issues from different perspectives, including the local and state level. In the former category I include Helen Ingram of the University of California at Irvine and, in the latter, from the Tennessee Department of Environment and Conservation, Dodd Galbreath (formerly director of policy), Alan Leiserson (general counsel), and Paul Sloan, (deputy commissioner). As in any such project, all errors in fact or interpretation remain mine alone.

Finally, I thank Jill for her encouragement, support, friendship, love, and patience. Her confidence and understanding in my ability made it possible for me not only to complete this project but also—perhaps—to produce a far better book than would otherwise have been the case. This book is dedicated to her son, Justin Paul: may he and his children inherit the kind of world depicted in this book as an ideal worth striving for.

Water Policy for Sustainable Development

CHAPTER 1

Water and Sustainability

Facing the Challenges

> In the short term, at least, humans will be able to manage water
> scarcity. . . . Solutions will be found. The questions are how
> much damage and dislocation will occur in the process, and
> whether the resulting arrangements will be sustainable.
>
> —*Malcolm Scully*

Water is the economic, social, and cultural lifeblood of humanity. Clean, abundant water provides the basis for agriculture, industry, commerce and transportation, energy production, and recreation. More importantly, it is the basis for life itself, as the great diversity of our planet's flora and fauna attests. Despite its vital significance to our lives, however, population growth, urban development and sprawl, and growing competition among users worldwide, exacerbated by periodic drought and possible climate change, are raising concerns over the continued availability of a stable, dependable supply of freshwater for our nation and the world, now and for the foreseeable future (Solley, Pierce, and Perlman 1998; World Resources Institute 1999).

There is a growing appreciation that water—like energy, forests, rare aquatic and terrestrial species, and clean air—is a finite and increasingly threatened resource. There is also increasing recognition that water *supply*—the assurance that freshwater will be available when and where it is needed and in a quality suitable to support off-stream activities as well as instream habitat—is a critical environmental issue with political, economic, and strategic implications (Beach et al. 2000). In the past decade alone, many books, ar-

ticles, and reports have pointed to an impending global crisis over water supply. Terms like *intractable, disputed, scarcity, dislocation, stress, damage, de-*
pletion, regional conflict, and *grave* are used to describe the discord caused by
the competition for water in a manner reminiscent of how economists and others described the oil crises of the 1970s (e.g., Feldman 1996).

Disputes over water are not limited to poorer, less developed countries.
There are growing controversies over water supply in many industrialized societies, including the United States. In some respects, the sources of these disputes are comparable to those generating conflict in less developed societies,
including population growth, changing values toward water use, urbanization,
and divergence between aspirations for economic development on the one
hand and environmental protection—especially preserving endangered and
threatened species and their habitat—on the other (Cody 2000; Cody and
Hughes 1999, 2000).

This book's purpose is to illuminate how the management of freshwater has
become a global political, social, economic, and environmental problem and
to suggest ways we might soberly and equitably address it. Its premise is that
access to water is not only a basic human need—it is also a fundamental requirement of all forms of life. Thus, democratic societies should protect the
water supply through ensuring that allocation and management is fair, open,
honest, and flexible. By focusing on the United States, I argue that this objective is the essence of a democratic and environmentally sound approach to
management. Examples from other countries (chapter 2) are employed to illuminate lessons that can be adopted to improve water management *anywhere.*

ADAPTIVE MANAGEMENT AS SOLUTION:
CHANGE VIA SOCIAL LEARNING

The fundamental source of most water disputes is disregard for the links
connecting water quality, quantity, and human use. Reconciling water's natural distribution with the needs of nature *and* society's demands requires understanding the environment's carrying capacity, a commitment to policies
that cement quality-of-life concerns with those for economic growth, and dedication to promoting participation, fairness, and ecological protection concur-
rently (Ascher 1999a). These constitute the essence of *sustainable develop-*
ment. The latter, in turn, requires devotion to the *watershed principle*—an
effort to harmonize institutions that manage water with the natural character

of surface and groundwater—and adaptation through *social learning*. As James Burson notes, "Any regional water plan must attune itself with the institutional restraints of the water management system. International treaties and interstate compacts limit the amount of water available for consumption. . . . Without a doubt, forming a regional water plan that conforms to the physical and institutional limitations of the region while protecting the diverse interests of multiple stakeholders present many challenges" (2000: 562).

This claim is consistent with international efforts to achieve sustainability, including the UN's Conference on Environment and Development's *Agenda 21,* which encourages reforms to environmental decision-making to permit better integration of social, economic, and ecological considerations in policies; broad political participation in development and environmental protection decisions; and integrated watershed and related land development practices (Grubb et al. 1993). Given continued growth in population and water demand, the alternative to sustainable development is worsening and intractable competition over freshwater.

Sustainable development requires a distinctive set of political and institutional changes that revolve around *adaptive management,* an approach that builds accord among stakeholders, agencies, and nongovernmental organizations (NGOs) by formulating plans by which "decisions are made and modified as a function of what is known and learned about the (natural) system" (Haas 1988, 1990; Ingram 2001). This approach requires: (1) an organizational design that permits policymakers to recognize mistakes; (2) an ability to monitor and measure change, especially environmental change brought about by prior decisions; (3) a capacity to adopt mid-course corrections; and (4) an ability to apply what's been learned to more complex challenges.

Learning from previous mistakes is easiest when water managers adopt a decision-making structure that permits broad ethical and policy debate, accept a kind of "humble anthropocentrism," and make tentative and reversible decisions. Monitoring and measuring change requires gathering and disseminating good data and rejecting "advocacy science"—that is, science designed to promote a specific policy at the outset of a process. This is hard because agency staff whose role is analytical and dispassionate sometimes view themselves as policy advocates. A decision-making process that promotes clarity and coordination by inviting scientists and the public to come together to identify problems facilitates adopting mid-course corrections. Other stakeholders must also be welcome to evaluate in a systematic way structural and nonstructural alternatives for solving problems (e.g., Western Water Policy Review Advisory Commission 1998). Finally, an adaptive process seeks innovative solutions that consciously move the locus for decisions to watersheds or river basins.

Not only are these findings practically sound, as exemplified by the experience of the Delaware River Basin Commission (whose staff closely cooperate to share findings and collaborate across jurisdictions—see chapter 3), they are also theoretically sound (Weston 1984). In many entities charged with managing natural resources, adapting to changing conditions is impeded by the fact that staffs hold divergent analytical perspectives that make it difficult to collaborate without feeling threatened (Meltsner 1976; Jenkins-Smith 1982; Weimer and Vining 1998). Overcoming distrust requires melding many management perspectives.

A river basin commission, watershed management authority, or other entity may be said to be *adaptively managed* if it: has a well-developed feedback process that permits institutional change in the light of new information; permits policy analysts as well as citizens and decision-makers to find common ground in identifying and defining problems and solutions; and, encourages social learning—the ability to process new information about the natural and social environments while decisions are being made and implemented (feedback). The latter permits organizations, and the people in them, to adapt to new circumstances quickly and effectively.

Adaptive management results not only in transformed policies and programs, but transformed and *reformed* management organizations. From the standpoint of promoting sustainable development, this is one of its most important benefits. Traditionally, water resources management, and the organizations that undertake it, have been driven by linear, engineering-dominated approaches to problem-solving that embrace structural solutions; exalt regional economic development despite its adverse environmental impacts; and, inhibit broad participation due to an emphasis on programmatic speed, efficiency, and dominance of experts in decision-making (Lowi 1979; Mann 1993; McGinnis 1995: 2). By contrast, adaptable regimes develop mechanisms for collaborating across diverse groups, learn from mistakes by instituting elaborate feedback mechanisms and participatory innovations, and can reverse flawed decisions, in part because they choose nonstructural solutions. Moreover, adaptively managed organizations recognize that most problems are too complex and ill structured for single-discipline answers. Thus, they respond to problems by aiming for comprehensive solutions that avoid incompatible objectives (Ellis 1998; Blatter and Ingram 2001; Ingram 2001).

TABLE 1.1
Sustainability Criteria for Water Resources Planning

Criterion	Definition
Maintaining human health	A basic water requirement will be guaranteed to maintain human health.
Maintaining ecosystem health	A basic water requirement will be guaranteed to maintain and restore the health of ecosystems.
Minimum standards of quality	Water quality will be maintained to meet minimum standards. These standards may and will vary depending on the location of the water, and how the water is to be used.
Long-term freshwater renewability	Human activities will not impair the long-term renewability of freshwater stocks and flows.
Data collection and accessibility	Data and other information on the availability, use, quality, and quantity of water will be collected and made available and accessible to everyone.
Institutional mechanisms for resolving conflict	Institutional mechanisms will be established to prevent, alleviate, and resolve conflicts over water.
Democratic decision-making	Water planning and decision-making will be democratic, ensuring representation of all affected parties and fostering the direct participation of affected interests.

Source: Adapted from Gleick (1998).

Gleick (1998) suggests seven criteria for sustainable water planning, depicted in table 1.1. These are used as the basis for our own theoretical framework. What makes these criteria important is that they emphasize water supply as well as quality to sustain various activities. They can also be used to evaluate the effectiveness of schemes to manage water resources.

WATER: THE NEXT GLOBAL ENVIRONMENTAL PROBLEM?

According to the World Resources Institute (1999), "the world's thirst for water is likely to become one of the most pressing resource issues of the 21st Century." Pointing to the fact that global water consumption "has risen six-fold between 1900 and 1995—more than double the rate of population growth—and continues to grow rapidly as agricultural, industrial, and domestic demand increases," they suggest that global water conflicts will worsen as surface and groundwater supplies become overstressed. The single greatest stressor on freshwater supplies, the report states, is growing use of water for agriculture. In fact, the production of food and fiber account for fully 70% of current global water consumption (WRI 1999).

Even so moderate an organization as the World Bank reported nearly a decade ago that many developing nations face a "water crisis" as a result of growing reliance on irrigation for crop production, rapid urbanization and attendant growth in water consumption, and diminishing supplies due to stream and aquifer depletion and deteriorating and/or poorly maintained urban water infrastructure (World Bank 1996b). Journalist Jacques Leslie underscored some of the worst fears about this coming crisis in an article in *Harper's* magazine: "We face an unassailable fact: we are running out of freshwater. . . . In the last century we humans have so vastly expanded our use of water to meet the needs of industry, agriculture, and a burgeoning population that now, after thousands of years in which water has been plentiful and free, its scarcity threatens the supply of food, human health and global ecosystems" (Leslie 2000).

Recent statistics bear Leslie out. A 2003 report issued by UNESCO predicts that as many as seven billion people in half the world's countries will face shortages of potable water by 2050 and that "the average supply per person will have dropped by one-third" (Weiss 2003). Worldwatch Institute's Sandra Postel, an observer of disputes, describes the problems facing water supply management in less calamitous—but no less urgent—terms. In *Troubled Waters,* she asserts that water scarcity, especially in the Middle East, constitutes a national security challenge and a source of internecine conflict. Disputes over water rights in that region have become pitched battles over national sovereignty and, to some degree, the conditions for political and economic independence. Such conflicts "have the potential to incite civil unrest, impoverish already poor regions, and destabilize governments—as well as ignite armed conflict" (Postel 1999).

Preventing competition over water supply—particularly given its roles as a necessary ingredient for life and an "economic commodity"—is a common theme in Postel's writings, in which she focuses on water scarcity as a source of developing country conflict (Postel 1997, 2000). At the root of any viable solution to scarcity, she states, is a regard for *sustainability*—which she defines as avoidance of practices that deplete or overexploit the world's aquifers and rivers (for example, overpumping groundwater, irrigating crops in arid regions, and constructing large-scale, inefficient hydraulic infrastructure that destroys habitat and disrupts the instream functioning of aquatic and riparian ecosystems). Pleading for "new ways of thinking about, using and managing water, as well as new and creative approaches that draw upon many disciplines—not just engineering," Postel hints at the need for an adaptive management paradigm that encourages demand-side management, cooperation rather than competition, and a willingness to live with—rather than oppose—

nature: "Developing and implementing these options will require new partnerships and alliances that draw upon the expertise of professionals from
many disciplines. . . . It will also require a willingness of professionals to cross
not only disciplinary boundaries but professional boundaries; for academics
to join with practitioners, for example, and for both these groups to interact
with policy makers. Water management practices that protect natural capital
rather than depleting it will be critical to the . . . sustainability of agricultural
and economic activities" (Postel 2000: 946).

Some authors are more pessimistic. Thomas Homer-Dixon argues that
while water conflicts are unlikely to generate major wars, they may produce
low-intensity conflicts such as regional wars and violence. Like Postel, he cites
the Middle East as a region exemplifying the potential for such low-intensity
conflict. The continuing unsettled political dispute between Israelis and West
Bank Palestinians is partly the result, he argues, of Israeli efforts to allocate
groundwater in ways favoring Jewish, as opposed to Arab, settlers (Homer-
Dixon 1999).

Others concur with this assessment and suggest that unequal power, conflicting moral values, recourse to resource nationalization and political secrecy
in managing ground and surface water supplies, and, on occasion, religious
doctrines that define water rights and the meaning of environmental stewardship in radically divergent ways have all contributed to water conflicts. The
Jordan River and other areas of the Middle East are often cited as examples
where this has occurred. Moreover, these factors are viewed as a continuing
source of friction impeding permanent peace between Arabs and Israelis (e.g.,
Morris 1992, 1993; Elmusa 1995; Hassoun 1998; BBC 2003).

Finally, the Pacific Institute's Peter Gleick observes that growing disen-
chantment with large-scale water projects (for example, China's controversial
Three Gorges Dam) is leading to a "new paradigm" for water management
based upon conservation, water reuse, recycling, and other remedies designed
to reduce water use and hasten sustainable use (Gleick 2000). A source of this
new paradigm is the realization that older technical solutions to water resource management problems (flood control, power generation, navigation)
are not only environmentally damaging but economically and socially disruptive and politically unjust—sparking questions about what constitutes equitable control of and access to water. Almost two million Chinese have been
relocated as a result of the recently completed Three Gorges Project (Karasov
2000).

Some acknowledge the explicit political and social dimensions of this new paradigm, including managing of quality and quantity holistically, embracing watersheds as planning units, and encouraging interjurisdictional cooperation (Blatter and Ingram 2001). As Gilbert White noted many years ago in reference to water disputes in the Columbia, Danube, and Arax basins, "It is possible for nations to meet each other at some roughly halfway point in order to satisfy the needs of one generation without jeopardizing the interests of future ones" (White 1977: 17). When different polities share a common river basin, there is a high incentive to cooperate since no one party can hope to control all of the water in the shared basin by itself (Otchet 2001).

This is an important and overlooked point: many writers are inclined to paint water disputes in bleak terms—not necessarily because this is a good way to sell books but because these conflicts often appear intractable. For example, while Israelis and Palestinians have not yet agreed on conjoint management of the Jordan River or of the shared aquifers straddling both nation's territories, there is some evidence that both are aware of the need to resolve this problem peaceably—without waiting for the prior resolution of other, larger cultural or political problems (BBC 2003). That they cannot resolve their differences, however, is due partly to unequal power. Such inequality breeds mistrust and makes compromise for the sake of future generations impossible. Mistrust also outweighs the motive that drives societies to manage water problems amicably: mutual need.

Population Pressures, Growth in Demand, and "Water Stress"

Embedded in much of the literature on water conflict is the view that anthropogenic and naturally occurring pressures on water supply constitute *stressors* that overcome a society's ability to manage water. In recent years, several international organizations, nongovernmental entities, and academic researchers have tried to develop credible indicators to measure stress. According to the World Bank, a "commonly accepted measure" of stress is when a nation's water availability falls below 1700 cubic meters per person per year (Hirji 2002). The World Resources Institute adds that "stress" is a situation in which "disruptive water shortages can frequently occur" because of pressure on (its) availability (WRI 2002).

Employing this definition, several countries in the Middle East, North Africa, South Asia, sub-Saharan Africa, and Latin America fall into the categories of being "under stress" or, if below the figure of 1700 m^3/person/year, "water scarce." In areas where annual water supplies drop below 1,000 m^3/

TABLE 1.2
Countries of the World Undergoing Water Stress or Scarcity, 2002

Water stress (less than 1,700 but more than 1,000 meters^3 per person)	*Europe* Poland		*Asia* Afghanistan India
			Bangladesh
	Latin America Peru		Republic of Korea
	Africa		
	Nigeria	Uganda	
	Tanzania	Zimbabwe	
	Madagascar	Burkina Faso	
	Togo	Ghana	
Water scarcity (less than 1,000 meters^3 per person)	*Latin America* Haiti		*Middle East* Saudi Arabia
			Iran
	Africa		Syria
	Morocco	Kenya	Yemen
	Libya	Somalia	Jordan
	Tunisia	Egypt	Oman
	Ethiopia	South Africa	United Arab Emirates

Source: WRI (2002).

person/year, the consequences can be even more severe and lead to grave difficulties in producing adequate food or achieving satisfactory levels of economic development unless new technologies that promote more efficient water use, water conservation, or reuse of wastewater can be introduced (WRI 2002; see also table 1.2).[1]

Table 1.2 shows these countries by world region. Countries in both categories have long faced severe challenges obtaining adequate water for agriculture and public supply due in part to their location in arid desert climates (in the case of the Middle East) or as a result of long-term drought (North and sub-Saharan Africa). Recently, all of these countries have begun to experience pressures on water supply due to population growth and urbanization. Surprising, perhaps, are Poland and Bangladesh—the latter the victim of *too much* water due to periodic floods. Both nations share a long history of severe water quality problems that stem from a lack of adequate water treatment capacity, insufficient supplies of potable water in areas where heavy industry and intensive agriculture directly compete for available supply, and, in some regions, lack of potable water. In Bangladesh, these problems are exacerbated by poverty and water management practices that discriminate against women and the poor (e.g., Crow and Sultana 2002).

One criticism of the World Bank's formulation of stress is that "per capita water supply calculation does not take into account the coping capabilities of different countries to deal with water shortages" (WRI 2002). For example, while some less developed countries with large energy resources (for example, Saudi Arabia) can afford to adopt desalination or even reclaimed wastewater technologies, other developing nations cannot do so. Moreover, as the PAGE analysis used by the World Bank notes, while many developing countries have access to so-called fossil water sources (deep underground aquifers not recharged), these sources of water should be actively discouraged because their use is "unsustainable in the long term."

Water stress may also be functional—for example, financial difficulty in providing infrastructure or adverse ecological conditions affecting water quality. A 1997 UN assessment of freshwater resources found that fully one-third of the world's population lives in countries experiencing moderate to high stress. To arrive at this estimate, the UN used a methodology called a use-to-resource index based on each country's ratio of water consumption to total water availability. Moderate to high stress translates to consumption levels exceeding 20% of available supply (Raskin et al. 1997). A problem with this classification system is that it assumes every country is self-dependent for filling its needs. However, if a country shares a basin or aquifer with another, shortages in one nation may be caused by shortages in another, making a domestic ratio of use to resource problematic. Moreover, water demands may result from pressures for food or fiber originating *in other countries.*

Still others define the problem of stress as a *proportional imbalance* between supply and demand due to growing demand outstripping supply or supplies being depleted by lengthy droughts outstrippng steady or moderately growing demand. In short, population growth alone does not explain water use—the type of demand is a more credible predictor. Ohlsson (1999) has developed a Social Water Stress Index, derived by calculating freshwater availability per capita divided by the UN Development Program's Human Development Index (which is then divided by two). While a useful methodology, it does not incorporate the percentage of a country's population without access to freshwater or water treatment (Yoffe and Ward 1999) and only looks at per person water availability. Thus, it does not really assess the degree to which water is unevenly distributed—even though distributional equity is an important sustainability criterion.

There are four lessons embedded in this debate over how to define stress important to adaptive management. First, patterns of migration are important determinants of stress. When a nation's population migrates from widely scattered rural areas to urban centers, stress often results. The migration of millions of people to cities has had a dramatic impact upon water supply stress, principally because the majority of *megacities* (those whose populations exceed ten million) are in countries with a per capita gross national product (GNP) of $10,000 U.S. per year or less (Ezcurra and Mazari-Hiriart 1996). In 1994, the World Resources Institute compiled a list of the world's 21 largest cities. If one subtracts those located in highly developed countries with per capita incomes greater than $10,000 U.S. per year, that leaves 17 cities with populations ranging from 11.5 to 22.6 million. Of these, seven (over a third) are located in countries included in table 1.2.[2] Few of these countries can support large population concentrations with adequate freshwater supply without demanding sacrifice from other regions or inflicting severe pain.

Second, countries experiencing rapid population growth *and* a low GNP lack the capacity to augment water supply or adaptively respond to shortages. Exacerbating their lack of resources, megacities in poorer countries are growing at a faster rate than cities in developed nations. This growth contributes to degradation of water quality and promotes the rapid exhaustion of supply through overdrafting of aquifers and stream depletion—a dilemma highlighted in the quotation by the International Water Management Institute's director at the beginning of chapter 2 (page 33).

Third, regardless of how we define stress, many of the countries listed in various stress indices suffer from *other* problems adversely affecting their supply, including devoting a considerable portion of their water to food and fiber production (for example, Afghanistan). As they continue to grow, water demands from agriculture will grow as well, while changes in climate will only worsen efforts to provide adequate water to support their burgeoning populations.

Finally, demands to transfer water from where it is found to where people live is likely to become an even greater source of internal—and international—friction among regions, ethnic groups, and entire countries. Inter-basin diversion of water is a significant source of political friction among countries with high rates of population growth and the presence of megacities.

OUR OWN BACKYARD: WATER DISPUTES
IN THE UNITED STATES AND CANADA

A perusal of scholarly and popular literature might leave the reader with the impression that water supply conflicts are not really global at all but rather local concerns of those who live in water-short regions in less-developed nations or in water-rich pockets in otherwise arid regions (for example, the Jordan River valley between Israel and Jordan). These unfortunate populations are disadvantaged, at least partly, by the happenstance of climate: low precipitation, high runoff, and high average temperatures.

Some argue that these climatic disadvantages, characteristic of poorer, developing countries, are exacerbated by politics: their governments lack the ability to manage water—just as they cannot manage other environmental problems due to widespread poverty, dependence on a limited pool of commonly shared resources, economic globalization and preemption of local resource control, growing resource demand, corrupt leadership, eagerness to resort to command-and-control rather than market-based remedies, and low state capacity to implement change (Ascher 1999b; Barbosa 2000). This ignores the fact that difficulties in managing one's way out of water conflicts are not unique to developing nations, nor to those living in arid or semi-arid regions.

While water shortages and conflicts over how to allocate supplies have led to regional disputes throughout the developing world, disputes of comparable contentiousness, if not (yet) of comparable severity, have erupted in the United States and Canada. At their source, these disputes are exacerbated by similar institutional problems, including low governmental capacity to resolve conflicts, outmoded management philosophies, and antiquated problem-solving approaches.

Until a few years ago, not many would have thought that the Great Lakes—the world's largest freshwater basin—would be facing serious threats to its water *supply*. Yet in 1998 a company called the Nova Group received permission to ship over 150 million gallons of Lake Superior water overseas, mostly to the Middle East. Although the province of Ontario eventually withdrew permission for this action, the interstate and interprovince controversy the proposed withdrawal generated resulted in the matter being referred to the International Joint Commission (IJC), a conflict-resolution mechanism formed by the governments of the United States and Canada in the early twentieth century largely to manage issues of water *quality*. Significantly, the IJC concluded that neither state/provincial laws nor national laws in either the United States or Canada could ensure that large-scale withdrawals of water for out-of-basin diversion could be regulated in a manner that would prevent economic and environmental harm.

This potential threat is especially worrisome because it arose, in part, from fears that international trade agreements make more likely the commodifica-

tion of freshwater worldwide, while weakening existing environmental protections, codified in law, to prevent transboundary diversion. Many proposals
for diverting Great Lakes water were first given impetus following ratification
of the North American Free Trade Agreement in the mid-1990s and by the formation of the World Trade Organization (WTO). One California-based corporation, Sun Belt, Inc., concluded an agreement with British Columbia to export Canadian water by tanker and was issued a license. The agreement, filed
under NAFTA, would have been worth $1.4 billion and was only prevented
through public outcry that forced the government of British Columbia to ban
water exports—a decision that resulted in the payment of compensation to
Sun Belt (Leahy 2001: 15).

To understand the underlying threats posed by such contemplated actions
and to build institutional capacity to deal with them, the governments of the
United States and Canada requested an analysis of existing and potential consumptive water uses in the boundary-inhibited and transboundary basins and
shared aquifers of both nations. That is, they agreed to examine existing and
potential diversions of water in and out of the transboundary basins, including withdrawals of water for export; the cumulative effects of existing and potential diversions and removals of water, including bulk removals for export;
and the adequacy of current federal and state/provincial policies in terms of
their effect on the sustainability of the water resources in basins unique to single provinces or states, as well as the entire Great Lakes basin (International
Joint Commission 2000: 3). The purpose was to determine what the environmental and other consequences of diversions and consumptive uses would be
on the region.

Canada has implemented policies to prohibit out-of-basin exports from waters along its border with the United States. These regulations are permitted
under the International Boundary Waters Treaty Act. They require licensing of
any water-related projects affecting the flow or level of waters on either side
of the border, limit and regulate "bulk removals" of water, and allow court in-
junctions to protect boundary waters at their source, not just along the border.
According to Canada's foreign affairs minister William Graham, "The amendments coming into force . . . will protect the Great Lakes and other boundary
waters from such removals . . . thereby preserving critical freshwater resources" ("Canada Implements" 2002). As this action shows, prospects for diverting the Great Lakes are not idle threats but potential hazards with adverse
implications—even if no major diversions or export proposals are pending
(Leahy 2001).

This dispute is all the more urgent because the Great Lakes, by one count, have endured at least five crises since the early twentieth century, including widespread death from cholera and typhoid in the early 1900s due to drinking water contaminated by raw sewage; the collapse of fisheries in the 1950s due to invasive species, overfishing, and water quality and habitat degradation; eutrophication in the 1960s and 1970s from municipal and industrial waste discharges; shoreline property damage in the 1980s from inappropriate land use coupled with extremely high water levels; and the health and environmental effects from wastewater and airborne discharges of persistent toxic substances (Kiy and Wirth 1998). So prospects for diverting large volumes of water from the basin and its tributaries are one in a long line of anthropogenic threats to the Great Lakes basin ecosystem. Diversion may not only cause new problems but also exacerbate existing ones.

Lest one assume that this problem is a "local" issue without larger implications, consider that the Great Lakes ecosystem covers 765,990 km^2 (295,750 mi^2), about a third of which is covered by water. The states and provinces that surround it have a combined annual gross state/provincial product of $1.9 trillion—a figure roughly twice the GDP of the United Kingdom and fully three times that of Canada (Kiy and Wirth 1998: 75).

A no less controversial water supply dispute has been brewing for several decades among the states of Alabama, Florida, and Georgia—discussed in chapter 3. The focus of this dispute is the continuing effort to manage and allocate water supplies in two river basins: the Apalachicola-Chattahoochee-Flint (ACF) and Alabama-Coosa-Tallapoosa (ACT) systems. Conflicts among the three states over water rights started in the late nineteenth century and accelerated with metropolitan Atlanta's spiraling population growth in the 1960s. As of this writing, a negotiated solution to this dispute has not yet been reached.

SIMPLE DIAGNOSIS, COMPLEX SOLUTION: THE INSTITUTIONAL DIMENSION

As with many environmental controversies, solutions of various types and scales have been proposed. Disputes over water supply have led to debate among policymakers over such issues as how transboundary resources should be fairly allocated among stakeholders and how economic development interests should be balanced against environmental concerns about water management, but they have also rekindled debate among nongovernmental organizations, academics, and international aid and development agencies over how best to design and structure institutions, policies, and economic incentives to manage water sustainably.

Proposed remedies include satisfying competing demands for water through allocation schemes based on marketing and tradable rights; encouraging conservation and reuse through technical and economic innovation; spurring the integrated management of surface and groundwater sources through the introduction of geographic and other information systems; peaceably resolving disputes through mediation and arbitration; and reconciling instream and off-stream uses through legally binding compacts, basin commissions, or watershed authorities (Teerink and Nakashima 1993; World Bank 1996b; Marino and Kemper 1999).

Compounding this proliferation of solutions, many scholars focus their attention on the problems of rapidly growing areas in developing nations and on arid or semi-arid regions within industrialized countries (for example, the western and southwestern United States), thus ignoring the consequences of water shortages in traditionally water-rich regions such as the eastern United States, which, as we have seen, are experiencing user conflicts as a result of population growth, urbanization, and drought (Kilgour and Dinar 1995; Hassoun 1998; World Bank 1993, 1996a; Serageldin 1995; Abu-Zeid and Biswas 1996; Faruqee and Choudhry 1996; Feitelson and Haddad 1998). As a consequence, it remains unknown whether and to what extent solutions proposed for developing nations can be applied to the United States.

Even focusing on a limited set of approaches does not abate controversy. Advocates of water allocation rarely agree on the best avenue for reform. Often, those who endorse command and control remedies (for example, regulation) philosophically oppose economic, incentive-based ones. For instance, water marketing, a tool for buying and selling water rights used extensively in parts of the western United States by ranchers and farmers, has recently come into favor as a remedy for protecting instream flow, recreational amenities, and fish and wildlife habitat—and as a way to reduce wasteful, inefficient, and environmentally inappropriate water use.

In parts of the West, special markets negotiated by environmental groups have attempted to reduce the volume of water diverted off-stream for agricultural irrigation in favor of maintaining stream flows for fish and for other environmental purposes (Landry 2000: 14). In Oregon, Washington, California, Montana, Texas, and Nevada, environmental organizations, local and state governments, and private property owners have "brokered" various deals, of-

ten with the support of the agricultural community, which perceives marketing as an attractive alternative to intrusive regulation (NRLC 1997; Western
Water Policy Review Advisory Commission 1998: 5–11). These efforts are innovative and have proven to be effective.

What makes these efforts especially impressive is that they have been negotiated in the context of a major institutional constraint, the law of prior appropriation, based on the "first in time, first in right" principle. In effect,
whosoever came into first use of a watercourse acquired the right to use virtually all the water in a stream or river. Historically, this doctrine has favored
off-stream, socially beneficial uses by the first user of a water source as opposed to conservation or instream protection. Under a prior appropriation
regime, to "conserve" water is to risk losing the right to later use of it (Pearson
2000; Fleming and Hall 2000).

Despite limited success in working within this doctrine, however, it is not
yet clear how effectively such deals will withstand the pressures of a growing
population and competing agricultural and urban uses. Nor is it clear whether
such schemes can remain durable in the face of growing demands for water
that are likely to increase the price well-heeled users will be willing to pay to
obtain water rights, thus raising the ante on markets as a tool for preserving
water, as opposed to consuming it (Anderson and Leal 1988; Shabman 1994).

Experts concur that adopting water marketing on a large scale in order to
address the problems of the eastern United States would require a major
change in riparian rights doctrine. This doctrine generally does not recognize
rights to a specified amount of water, nor does it allow for the possibility of
"excess" water. So it is difficult to contract delivery of a specific amount of water for a precise period of time under a riparian system. Moreover, to promise
delivery of a precise amount through, say, state statute could be seen as an un-
justified property "taking" (for example, Frederick 1998) and might require
compensating current water rights holders for damages.

Finally, water marketing can be politically contentious, particularly among
residents of an exporting region. A study of California's San Joaquin Valley of
California and the Grand Valley of western Colorado found that residents of
exporting areas are more likely to oppose marketable water transfers than residents of importing areas. The reservations of the former group are due to concerns over fairness, the permanence of contracts, and the likelihood of recov-
ering rights once sales are negotiated (Keenan, Krannich, and Walker 1999). In
Australia, similar findings have emerged from studies of water marketing in
agricultural regions (for example, Tisdell and Ward 2003). Having said this, it

must be kept in mind that the potential value of markets for addressing *some* problems of water *quality* has only begun to be explored (see chapter 4). In short, to solve global water problems, we must contend not only with the in-stream flow (the natural or optimal amount of water flowing past a given point in a watercourse necessary for supporting fish and wildlife and protecting the habitat) and growing human demands but with a more complicated set of fac-tors—water laws and institutions and the underlying values and attitudes that support them.

There are two quandaries that help explain why institutional solutions to disputes over the management of water supply do not receive the attention they deserve, and why efforts to reconcile various proposed solutions have thus far met with little success. First, most policymakers think of *quality* as the most urgent environmental problem associated with water: ensuring that supplies are safe, clean, and usable—despite the increase in water shortages and depletion, and despite the many conflicts generated by plans undertaken to resolve these problems (for example, building more dams). This misper-ception is partly to blame for the inability of decision-makers to address wa-ter conflicts in a comprehensive manner. In fact, water *quality* and *quantity* are fundamentally inseparable.

Traditionally, planners, water managers, and other decision-makers in the United States have treated water *quality* (assuring that public water supply and waters for fish and wildlife are clean, safe, and protected) as a separate and distinct issue from that of water *quantity* (ensuring that there is an ade-quate, abundant supply of water for all needs in a region). This distinction is a misleading one when water supplies are abundant, few worry about some waters being less than fit for human consumption—or, in the language of the Clean Water Act, as "fishable and swimmable." Most public drinking water supplies are treated, and many accept that, say, urban creeks are unsafe for children to play in. The real point is that the amount of available water says nothing about its quality. Public officials must address both the quality of the available supply and the abundance of that supply to ensure that there is enough clean water. This is a point underscored by a United Nations Univer-sity report on transboundary water disputes and their potential for amicable resolution. Addressing the seemingly intractable difficulties in managing wa-ter conflicts in developing countries, the report noted:

> Water not only ignores our political boundaries, it evades institutional classifica-
> tion and eludes legal generalizations. Interdisciplinary by nature, water's natural

management unit, the watershed—where quantity, quality, surface and ground-water all interconnect—strains both institutional and legal capabilities often-past capacity. Analyses of international water institutions find rampant lack of consideration of quality considerations in quantity decisions, a lack of specificity in rights allocations, disproportionate political power by special interests, and a general neglect for environmental concerns in water resources decision-making. (Beach et al. 2000: 13–14)

A U.S. Geological Survey report on nonpoint water pollution, part of a series conducted under the National Water Quality Assessment Program, provides a good example of the problem identified in the UN University report in a developed-country context. Nonpoint pollution is one of the most severe water quality problems in the United States. Over 40% of rivers fail to meet current standards because of runoff containing pesticides, automotive fluid residues, and other toxins. The report finds that the impact on water quality from farm and paved-over area runoff are related to the *size* (volume) of a stream and the characteristics of the watershed in which it is contained: "Hydrologic and basin characteristics, including size of basin and amount of stream flow, affect the timing of, and magnitude of exposure to contaminants in the environment. Small streams respond quickly to rainfall or irrigation and, therefore, pulses of contaminants reach higher concentrations and rise and fall more quickly than in larger rivers" (USGS 2002: 17).

Effectively managing water *quality* requires an understanding that water pollution is a variable affected by water *quantity* and that managing *both* requires understanding the physiographic context (that is, the watershed) within which water quality problems occur.[3] Chapter 4 examines some emerging models for how institutions can be structured, drawing on economic and political innovations to foster sustainable development for quality *and* quantity within river basins and watersheds. These models exemplify an adaptive management approach in that they foster collaboration, encourage public participation, measure and monitor progress and change, and seek multidisciplinary nonstructural and behaviorally based solutions.

A second quandary noted in the UN University report is the lack of harmony between political institutions governing water quality and water quantity. In the United States, each is managed under its own set of laws—a series of federal statutes regulating emissions and designated water uses for quality (largely enforced at the state level) and a series of state laws (buttressed by vague common law) for water supply. Moreover, the legal regime for supply is further fragmented into separate doctrines, with distinct rationales, for states east and west of the 100th meridian. This is not only inefficient; it also inhibits comprehensive national management.

AGREEING ON THE CHALLENGES

There are three critical drivers that constitute common denominators of contemporary water disputes. They also constitute the principal challenges that must be dealt with if we are to protect the planet's supply of freshwater, now and in the future.

- *Economic Growth versus Environmental Protection.* There is a widespread desire in developing and developed societies to promote economic growth. Many assume that water supply is inimical to this objective. At the same time, the quality of that water supply must be protected in order to make it usable for development. These goals are difficult to reconcile.

In the American West, user conflicts and controversies over various water allocation schemes are also brewing in and around such rapidly growing metropolitan areas as Las Vegas, Denver, and Phoenix. All are involved in conflicts between upstream and downstream users within a shared drainage. In Israel, the Palestinian West Bank, India, Pakistan, Syria, Iraq, Turkey, Vietnam, Cambodia, and Thailand, water supply conflicts have become the nexus for numerous transboundary disputes. While opinions vary as to whether these disputes are likely to increase chances for armed conflict, there is little doubt that at a minimum, they place increasing demands upon public water infrastructure in nations that can ill afford to satisfy such demands. These disputes are difficult to resolve because they require not only cooperation among users from different countries with diverse systems of governance but also a high level of technical cooperation in order to apportion the burden of water resource development costs equitably and to create manageable economies of scale (Morris 1992, 1993; Grigg 1996; Dunphy 1997; Kundell and Tetens 1998; Hassoun 1998; Browder and Ortolano 2000).

As communities, regions, and entire nations experience burgeoning population growth, efforts to protect surface water, groundwater recharge areas, and riparian areas become harder to conciliate with that growth. In the United States, cities such as Memphis, Tennessee, and greater Miami, Florida, have been experiencing such conflicts—in the former case, over stewardship of an aquifer shared with Mississippi and Arkansas; in the latter, over efforts to refocus the management of the Everglades from intensive agricultural water use to greater balance between agricultural and municipal needs with those of wildlife (Vogel 1998; Charlier 1999). One question prompted by the Everglades Restoration Project is: can we restore the natural conditions as they existed prior to human disruption, return a river basin or entire eco-region to its previous state?

The Memphis case is little recognized even though it is one of the largest cities in the world that relies solely on groundwater. The city's water is provided from the Memphis Sand Aquifer. This underground reservoir lies underneath a region of nearly 7400 mi^2 stretching over western Tennessee and parts of Mississippi, Kentucky, and Arkansas. While Memphis is now the aquifer's largest user, DeSoto County, Mississippi, an area experiencing rapid economic and population growth—in part due to suburbanization of Memphis—views the aquifer as a potential source of future supply (Brahana, Parks, and Gaydos 1987; Parks and Carmichael 1990a, b; Ground Water Institute 1995).

Management of the aquifer currently faces three interrelated challenges. First, an increase in the current rate of water withdrawal in and around Memphis could have various "recharge" effects—that is, it could impede the aquifer's ability to become replenished with rainwater. Increased withdrawals might lower the water table even further. On the other hand, they might actually accelerate groundwater recharge by downward leakage from nearby surface water tables. This is problematic because the quality of the groundwater varies between different aquifers and even within the same aquifer. Second, as DeSoto County and other areas of northwestern Mississippi continue to grow, competition over available groundwater and debate over what entity properly "owns" it will grow. Finally, increased withdrawal and improperly managed land use may threaten both aquifer recharge and even lead to possible contamination. Such problems are not locally confined. Increasingly, decision-makers are coming to recognize that protecting drinking water supply means paying greater attention to source water protection—and that includes guarding the quality of water supplies far upstream within a watershed (EPA 1999).

In short, urban "sprawl" and other land use patterns clearly affects stream water quality, aquifer quality and quantity, and public supply. The effects of land use development are not only dramatic but diverse. Urbanization and sprawl, for example, affects the amount of stream flow after rain events (storms), the amount of pollutants in streams, and the health of aquatic and terrestrial life in the immediate stream vicinity (USGS 2002).

- *Climate Change and Meteorological Uncertainty.* Increases in temperature are likely to be accompanied by greater water demand at the same time that surface water supplies are subject to depletion. Less precipitation results in reduced stream flows, and increased evaporation from the surface of reservoirs occurs (Schaake and Tisdale 1997; Mahlman 1997).

While many scientists believe that the world's climate is changing due to emissions of carbon dioxide and other "greenhouse" gases, many policymakers (and the American public at large) remain largely unconvinced. There is an emerging body of research that has begun to examine the long-term implications of global climate change on water resources. Its findings are anything but certain, and this uncertainty compounds the problem of adaptive management by making it nearly impossible to predict how water resources will be affected *in specific places.*

For example, while there is widespread agreement that the frequency and duration of heavy rains and drought are likely to be exacerbated by climate change, and that evaporation *and* precipitation rates are *both* likely to increase, little is known about the *spatial* distribution of these impacts at scales smaller than an entire continent. Likewise, there is broad agreement that higher surface temperatures are likely to be experienced at mid-latitudes, and that during midwinter, the consequence of this temperature differential should be increased rainfall that, in turn, is apt to produce higher rates of runoff and wintertime soil moisture—leaving less runoff for the summer. If true, faster spring snowmelt may aggravate flooding, and increased summer heating may cause greater evaporation. Again, however, *where* this will take place is unclear.

In general, climate models predict larger increases in evaporation than precipitation in mid-latitude regions like southern Europe and North America, with more severe flooding as well as more severe drought (Hamburg et al. 2000: 15; see also UCAR 1997). According to the Intergovernmental Panel on Climate Change—the most important international collaborative scientific effort in climate change impact assessment—those regions that are currently arid or semi-arid are likely to experience above-average runoff. Moreover, these effects may follow a period of "widespread periodic and chronic shortfalls in those same areas caused by population growth, urbanization, agricultural expansion, and industrial development that are expected to manifest themselves by 2020" (Watson et al. 1996).

Uncertainty is also a theme in comprehensive studies of the possible impact of climate change in the United States. A study produced by the Water Sector Assessment Team of the U.S. Global Change Research Program (GCRP) attempted to identify U.S. vulnerabilities by examining impacts to precipitation, runoff, and water supply (Gleick and Adams 2000). The GCRP's report concentrates on snowpack changes in the western United States and concludes that because some areas actually experienced precipitation increases and decreases in temperature over the past century, calculating the possible impacts of global climate change on water is profoundly difficult.

Among its key findings, the GCRP concludes that higher amounts of nutrient runoff into lakes and streams and higher rates of pollutant intrusion into aquifers might increase water supply in some places and degrade quality in others. sea-level rise may also threaten coastal aquifers in regions such as the Carolinas (see Parmelee 2001: 46). More intriguing are the report's policy recommendations, which include moving away from exclusive reliance on surface water by integrating surface and groundwater management, communicating the results of climate change research to local water managers, and improving conservation and water reuse. One implication of these recommendations is that adaptive management of climate change means taking prudent action now that we are in a more resilient position to deal with problems later. Such actions may be thought of as "no regrets" strategies, as they make sense even if climate change does not occur. This implication resonates with other studies of the impacts of climate change in the United States that focus on state-level effects.[4]

Finally, a growing body of research on the possible effects of climate change on water quality, agricultural use, and domestic supply has tried to simulate important climate functions in various regions under higher temperatures (Cruise, Limaye, and Al-Abed 1999; Hatch et al. 1999; Frederick and Schwarz 1999). Although their findings are subject to uncertainty, they nonetheless amplify those of other studies and include the likelihood of increased nitrogen levels in streams adjacent to farms—leading to greater water quality degradation; decreased production of some row crops (corn, peanuts); more intense competition not only over water supply but also over runoff treatment, storage and control; and increased water costs. This last set of studies is especially

significant for sustainable development and water management for three reasons.

First, while the uncertainty of climate change impacts is high, should
change occur, its consequences will exacerbate other stressors on supply, including population growth, urbanization, demands for food and fiber, and
"normal" year-to-year meteorological perturbations like droughts or floods.
This is especially true if warming affects precipitation, runoff, and evaporation rates. Thus, it is altogether likely that effective adaptation will require institutional changes and innovations currently beyond the capacity of most developing nations.

Second, climate change is likely to compound the difficulty of establishing
stable, durable institutions that can equitably allocate and distribute water and
manage its quality to satisfy the instream needs of fish and wildlife. The same
basins responsible for producing food are also experiencing the highest rates
of population growth and, in many instances, are among the most productive
repositories for fish and aquatic life on the planet. A changing climate in these
watersheds means not only less food but also more stress on their resident populations.

According to the World Resources Institute, global water consumption rose
sixfold during the previous century, largely due to the production of food and
fiber. Agriculture accounts for fully 70% of world water consumption (WRI
1998). According to the World Resources Institute, the annual renewable water supply per person suggests the problem's seriousness in light of climate
change. In basins where projected population is expected to be higher than 10
million by 2025, six basins will go from having more than 1,700 m^3 to less than
1,000 m^3 of water per capita per year. These heavily agricultural basins include
the Volta, the Farah, the Nile, the Tigris and Euphrates, the Narmada, and the
Colorado River basin in the United States.[5] Each lies in regions of the world
already suffering from aridity, drought, and severe competition over supply as
well as high susceptibility to adverse impacts from a warmer climate (Gleick
and Adams 2000).

Finally, while adaptive management can fortify water resource institutions
against the adverse effects of climate change, many proposed adaptations
may generate further adverse consequences unless they are carefully thought
through. This problem has led some analysts to describe climate change as an
example of a "wicked problem": a tribulation that is "poorly structured for the
application of straightforward, disciplinary-based rational science" (Ingram

2001: 1). In short, adaptations implemented to address one goal (for example, protecting endangered species) may be incompatible with others (maximizing water supply for human use).

Climate change is also wicked because dramatic responses to it may produce "feedback effects" that produce unanticipated consequences (Newson 1997: 267). For example, substituting drylands crops or drought-resistant crops may harden a region against the effects of warming and less precipitation—arguably a beneficial change. However, changes in land cover brought about by crop switching may alter local meteorological conditions, leading to less rainfall or even greater evaporation rates (Newson 1997). As one analyst notes, "there is no firm guidance on the regional variability of . . . changes, the timing of change and the importance of extreme conditions, the effects of the response to change in the atmosphere or by natural plant covers, crops or water management systems" (Newson 1997: 267).

In short, "no regrets" policies are difficult to implement because there are "fundamental linkages between physical and biological systems and human uses of land and natural resources." These linkages compound the challenges in solving parts of a problem in isolation from others (Miller, Rhodes, and Mac-Donnell 1996). Solutions must acknowledge the "multiple-purpose" character of water use. As the Intergovernmental Panel on Climate Change's "Report on Impacts, Adaptation, and Mitigation of Climate Change" notes, water resources management is a "continuously adaptive enterprise" because it responds not only to changes in demand, hydrology, and technology but to behavioral and societal factors as well—including "society's perspective on the economy and environment" (Watson et al. 1995: 471). In essence, climate change reinforces the urgent need for an effective system of regional collaboration in water supply planning (Miller, Rhodes, MacDonnell 1996; Chang, Hunsaker, Draves 1992). Good science can be instructive about how to define and resolve wicked problems. However, reaching a political consensus over management goals and objectives to deal with them requires agreement on the values that stakeholders wish to pursue—a subject we take up in chapter 5.

- *Control and Ownership of Water: Dispute or Polemic?* Growing debate over fragmented water institutions and needs for better policy coordination, the growing privatization of water, and widespread demand for investing in new or expanded infrastructure have sparked discussion over who should "own" water. Much of this debate is polemical and

spurred by deeper questions about the compatibility of democratic accountability with for-profit ownership.

The issue of the privatization of water partly revolves around *economic development*: when we invest in new water supply infrastructure, create jobs,
and grow personal income, is it better, some ask, for water resource decisions
to be made by investor-controlled markets rather than governments? Privatization also prompts questions of *social justice* by directing our attention to the
charge that private ownership leads to centralized, monopolistic control of
natural resources. This centralization, many believe, displaces people from
productive livelihoods by building large dams or diverting rivers, threatens resource rights by closing off public access to water and transforming it into a
commodity sold to high bidders, and erodes democracy by shifting decision-
making authority for resource management and investment into the hands of
global NGOs such as the World Trade Organization (WTO) and the World
Bank, whose commitment to ideals of fairness and participation are suspect
(see, for example, Shiva 2002; Barlow and Clarke 2002).

While these are serious charges with some basis in fact, the privatization
critique is as much polemical as analytical, reflecting generalized frustration
with the globalization of environmental amenities, a presumed loss of national
sovereignty over resources, and anxiety over outright economic exploitation
of the poor in developing nations. It is also a debate characterized by strongly
polarized views. Many environmental organizations believe that access to water is a basic human right and that water should never be controlled by private, profit-making entities (see, for example, Barlow and Clarke 2002; *U.S.
Water News* 2003b). In the words of one official, this belief has transformed the
debate over privatization into a "religious dispute . . . long on ideology but
short on counter-proposals to improve existing [water infrastructure] systems"
(*U.S. Water News* 2003b).

For example, while critics of privatization often cite examples of adverse
river basin development and ascribe policy failures to private ownership of
water resources, the alleged market "failures" are often the result not of private ownership but rather of misguided government decisions to dam rivers,
divert water, and buy and sell water rights in order to "move" water from uses
deemed low in value to those deemed to be more advantageous for economic
development. Water development failures cited by critics in river basins as diverse as the Colorado, the Tigris and Euphrates, and the Indus have actually

been public projects that profited private interests and in some instances led to the unfair enrichment of certain groups.

Moreover, while private entities are often vigorous boosters of these projects, complicity between the state and powerful nonstate entities can occur in planned and socialist economies as well, where resources are regarded as the property of the state (e.g., Ascher 1999b). Moreover, when it occurs in market economies, the cause is not secretive conspiracy between corporations and government, but open collaboration between private interests and government during debates over river basin development (e.g., see discussion of the Colorado River in chapter 2).

Critics' arguments stand on a surer footing when they attack services and utilities that supply water to the public—and when they focus on management structures that impede public participation, inhibit accountability, and restrict decision-making to a few. Here, the issues they raise resonate strongly with international forums that warn against private sector cooptation of water management institutions—which may lead to decisions that price water beyond the average person's ability to pay—especially in developing nations (see, for example, Barlow and Clarke 2002; 84ff.). They also resonate with empirical studies of water access in developing countries.

Growing evidence from countries like Bangladesh, Zimbabwe, Honduras, and Bolivia confirms the hazards of privatization and its potentially adverse impacts on sustainable water management. These studies underscore the synergies connecting restrictive land tenure systems, affluence-friendly water rights, and rights of entry to markets for using water (such as irrigation equipment). They also point to ways that ethnicity and gender may affect access to land and water rights and the ability to determine one's use of both (Derman 1998; Loker 1998; Crow and Sultana 2002). Finally, they conclude that traditional institutions and mores, coupled with bureaucratic norms of control and allocation, may produce inequitable and insecure access to water—especially in the absence of civil and political rights guaranteeing participation.

In Bangladesh, gender and social class have been identified as significant determinants of access to water for both agriculture and personal use. In Zimbabwe, the dominance of large-scale commercial farms owned and managed, in many cases, by the nation's white minority has been identified as a factor inhibiting structural reform of the country's water supply system—a system in which water pricing favors those with political power. In Bolivia, efforts encouraged by the World Bank and the International Monetary Fund to allow private companies to compete for ownership of the country's water utilities has generated dramatic price hikes, accusations of monopoly and corruption, and massive rural protests (Olivera and Viana 2003). And in Honduras, the building of a large dam in the country's northwest has displaced thousands of people and denied the displaced subsistence rights as well as rights of access to land and traditional cultural amenities (Derman 1998; Loker 1998; Crow and Sultana 2002).

These cases raise legitimate questions about the extent to which the volatile combination of poverty, underdevelopment, chronic water shortage, inadequate private markets, and decentralized, un-coordinated political and legal institutions—all of which tend to exist in developing nations—invite opportunistic corporate investment in water by placing these nations in a position of strategic vulnerability (see, for example, Finnegan 2002).[6] International forums have begun to address these issues by recommending the adoption of broad water management principles. The 2002 World Civil Society Forum in Geneva, Switzerland, convened a water management working group that encouraged countries to adopt several lofty objectives, including achieving "universal access" to drinking water, sharing water resources among different users to avoid conflict, and bolstering a civil society sector to manage water equitably and efficiently through "encouraging investment in water management, conducting studies, and ensuring that water management and conservation become everyone's business" (World Civil Society Forum 2002).

The forum did more than simply articulate lofty goals. It also pondered impediments to achieving these objectives and how they might be overcome. Conferees concluded that, worldwide, "water management is divided between numerous unrelated institutions." They also acknowledged that a number of international meetings have been convened in an effort to seek greater coordination among these institutions, but to little avail. One notable coordination example they recommended as worthy of emulation, however, was Green Cross, established by former Soviet leader Mikhail Gorbachev in 1993 following the Rio Summit. Its purpose is to support sustainable development projects in large river basins related to the provision of water and "to educate the general public on water-related issues" (World Civil Society Forum 2002).

The forum also considered how the privatization of water supply can advance or retard the ability to bring potable water to rural populations and how to encourage a civil society. Among the reforms it suggested was finding ways to organize citizens to articulate their concerns on the local level and to seek redress for their problems through institutions adhering to principles of representation and due process. We shall revisit this issue in chapter 6.

The forum's themes resonated with those articulated a year earlier at the 11th Stockholm Water Symposium, attended by over 1000 water resource professionals from 150 nations. Organized by the World Water Council in conjunction with other NGOs, the symposium stressed the integration of water science, practice, policy, and "citizen involvement." A recurring theme in its discussions was the financing of water infrastructure "for those in need of such development throughout the world" (Delfino 2001). While attendees agreed that public-private partnerships are needed to achieve this goal, as at the World Civil Society Forum, privatization and the control of water resources were vigorously debated. In his address before the closing session of the 11th Symposium, Rene Coulomb, vice president of the World Water Council, warned that while "involving the private sector in providing services for people, irrigation, and electric power, and in financing investments is an absolute necessity for the future," participation of the private sector can only be helpful "if there is a predictable, transparent regulatory framework that protects the interests of investors and consumers alike" (Coulomb 2001: 9–10).

Finally, the 2002 World Summit on Sustainable Development held in Johannesburg, South Africa, adopted as one of its central themes water resources development. Delegates boldly committed themselves to building "a humane, equitable and caring global society cognizant of the need for human dignity for all" and to reducing by half the proportion of people unable to afford or obtain access to safe drinking water and basic sanitation by 2015. The summit was unique among international forums on water problems in putting forth a series of integrated principles regarding the normative and economic bases of water management. Unlike the other forums we cited, however, delegates rejected outright privatization, demanding that all governments "commit to public sector delivery of water services" and that "water and water services [be kept] out of GATT and the WTO." They boldly asserted that *local* production of water is the "key to sustainability" (World Summit on Sustainable Development 2002).

At their base, these forums remind us of three important lessons in sustainable water management. First, debates by policymakers, NGOs, and international aid and development institutions over how best to balance public and private interests in the design of institutions, policies, and incentives to manage water sustainably must embrace a number of difficult-to-separate issues. These include the needs to satisfy competing demands for water through marketing and tradable water rights, to encourage conservation through technical and economic innovation, to spur integrated management of surface and groundwater through geographic and other information systems, to resolve peaceably stakeholder disputes through mediation, and to reconcile instream and off-stream uses through compacts or commissions (Teerink and Nakashima, 1993; World Bank 1996b; Marino and Kemper, 1999).

Second, regardless of what international forums urge or preach, real decisional change will only occur within river basin entities and governments. Decisions over water pricing, distribution and access, and water rights will be fought out in courts, legislatures, bureaucracies, and international organizations. The case studies we examine in chapters 3 and 4 will show how key drivers of water disputes not only raise questions about control, access, and accountability within specific regions but offer practical answers to these questions. Further, they illuminate the difficulty in instituting reforms to achieve sustainable management objectives.

Finally, the privatization debate reminds us that water management decisions are made at multiple spatial levels. Even a local water service entity may be influenced by a multinational, global enterprise—making efforts to define the locus of decision-making and needed reform difficult. We must be open to the possibility that privatization can, within the constraints of sustainable development, offer a positive means to amass capital to improve water supply and quality—as has been the case in the United Kingdom and in a number of American cities hard-pressed for money to pay for infrastructure improvements (Lavelle and Kurlantzick 2002: 26).

IMPROVING WATER RESOURCES MANAGEMENT: THE REST OF THE BOOK

Chapter 2 provides a historical overview of river basin management, including previous federal initiatives such as interstate river basin commissions and refinements to federal-interstate compacts. I examine the evolution and effectiveness of institutions. Between the emergence of comprehensive river basin initiatives in the nineteenth century to the advent of severe problems of development, environmental protection, and social justice in the late twentieth century, a major change in management philosophy arose: a recognition of the need to respond to unforeseen challenges. This change underscored the need for institutional innovations that were not only scientifically sound but also bureaucratically flexible enough to respond to unexpected problems. While better science was required, so were changes to institutions and their management.

Chapter 2 also examines international efforts at comprehensive, coordinated management of rivers. This review is not definitive—the cases are much too varied, and most are still evolving quite rapidly. Rather, the goal is to synthesize and distill from these cases lessons applicable to the principles of sustainability—as well as to derive insights concerning barriers to its practical achievement. Among the lessons of chapter 2 are that, despite problems in achieving environmental protection and restoration, additional supply, and equitable allocation of water for regional development, virtually all initiatives have avoided open warfare—no mean feat. One major reason for this is that no country or province can completely control an international river basin, watershed, or aquifer without incurring enormous costs. This is a powerful incentive for countries to cooperate. Nonetheless, "low-intensity" conflict persists among many nations, especially in the Middle East, Africa, Southeast Asia and Latin America.

A number of impediments to sustainable development persist around the world. These include continued nonpoint as well as industrial pollution; degraded shorelines and river channels; threats to adequate in stream flow due to overutilization of rivers, especially for agricultural irrigation and needed food supplies in developing states; prospects for climate change; continued population growth and in-migration pressures, which place stress on water supplies; and drought. New developments may impose cumulative effects on management initiatives that are already overtaxed (and undersupported).

Despite these problems, water management institutions can be open, inclusive, and sensitive to stakeholder needs. Australia's innovative Murray-Darling River Basin commission is one of the world's most successful initiatives in promoting sustainable development and embracing community sentiments. It takes democracy seriously and tries to foster a true civil society characterized by a literate, highly involved public with a commitment to promoting the well being of one's fellow citizens—all keys to adaptive management.

Chapter 3 examines five U.S. river basin initiatives: the Apalachicola-Chattahoochee-Flint (ACF) Compact (Alabama, Florida, Georgia), the CALFED Bay-Delta Initiative (California), the Delaware River Basin Commission (Delaware, New Jersey, New York, Pennsylvania), the Susquehanna River Basin Commission (Maryland, Pennsylvania), and the Northwest Power Planning Council (Oregon, Idaho, Washington). These initiatives reveal the importance of meaningful citizen participation in embracing sustainability and empowering stakeholders. Other lessons include the need for initiatives to conform to ecosystem management principles by employing watershed boundaries broad enough to encompass all relevant issues. Sound scientific information is crucial to enabling effective decisions, and quality and quantity concerns must simultaneously be embraced to manage problems adaptively. While federal financial support is desirable, it is neither a necessary nor a sufficient condition for effectiveness. Commitment of state level officials, however, is important to hasten negotiation and conjoint management, heighten public awareness, and encourage hands-on management.

Effective dispute-resolution tools are also essential. At their base, such tools require intra-state policy reforms such as drought protection acts, conservation programs, and water withdrawal and anti-diversion regulations that not only put a state in the position of being able to protect its water but also strengthen its bargaining position relative to others with whom it is in conflict. Without reforms, bargaining from a position of strength is difficult because a state cannot really demonstrate that it has a need for the amount of water it is using and that it is managing its water well. In this vein, reliable verification and compliance approaches are also important. All these dispute resolution tools hasten the development and cultivation of an adaptively managed organization that is able to respond to change constructively.

Chapter 4 discusses the relationship between water quality and water supply. We show that quality and quantity must be jointly managed for sustainable development. Where decision-makers have tried to fuse these concerns, particularly in the areas of nonpoint pollution control and instream flow protection, their lessons may be applicable to other communities seeking to balance economic development, environmental protection, and social justice. This is shown by recent efforts of the EPA and states to protect water quality through the Total Maximum Daily Load (TMDL) program and efforts by these same entities to protect stream flow.

We also examine innovative partnerships that seek to address water quality issues through citizen monitoring, pollutant trading, best management practices, and state-local-federal partnerships. Central to successful innovation are a better linking of land-use planning with water quality issues and a greater commitment to preventive measures. Some effective tools include conjoint land purchases around reservoirs and streams to reduce encroaching development, discouraging impervious surface, and reducing runoff. Water marketing can also be part of the mix, although reform of riparian law is also required. Resistance to change is likely to arise unless measures are taken to compensate users and to protect their long-term needs. Critical land use controls preventing or restricting overdevelopment along shorelines and collaboration with agencies and scientists are also important tools in achieving this objective.

Chapter 5 discusses the ethical basis of reform—essential for achieving a civil society. Unsustainable water policies are based on narrow, acquisitive values that discourage a broad consideration of alternatives and that make it difficult to justify wide public participation or to consider equity. Three dominant approaches have been used to overcome these values in the past: covenantal thinking, which assumes that there are reciprocal obligations to care for nature and to look after the welfare of others; categorical imperatives, which assume that there are intrinsic moral obligations to keep promises and commitments; and stewardship ethics, which assume that we are responsible for nature and other humans to fulfill our ethical calling.

To be fully effective, these approaches must embrace the needs of watersheds and the demands of democratic theory. I suggest four strategies: inclusiveness and ethical eclecticism, democratic decision-making that permits a conscious weighing of alternatives, clear and transparent ethical assumptions, and collaboration with one's adversaries through stakeholder-engagement processes that encourage respect, integrity, and teamwork in the development of solutions to the management of resource problems (Daniels and Walker 2001).

Finally, chapter 6 discusses how to develop an adaptive management framework that encourages social learning, draws on local and indigenous knowledge as well as independent scientific information, conforms itself with place-based decision-making principles, and resolves conflict. It also discusses challenges to sustainable water resources management, including the potential effects of global climate change on water resources, growing competition over water supplies, prospects for better conservation, and reform of management institutions.

CHAPTER 2

U.S. and International Water Resource Management Efforts

Legacy and Lessons

If current trends continue, the shortage of water will extend well beyond the semi-arid and arid regions. Expanding demand for water will drain some of the world's major rivers, leaving them dry throughout most of the year.

—*Professor Frank Rijsberman, director general of the International Water Management Institute*

HISTORY OF U.S. FEDERAL RIVER BASIN PLANNING EFFORTS

Kenney and Lord (1994) have identified several coordinating mechanisms for managing interstate streams in the United States on a comprehensive basis. These include compacts, interstate commissions, and semiprivate/semipublic innovations (for instance, government corporations such as Tennessee Valley Authority, or TVA). Some of these innovations are utilized on intra-state rivers as well. Four coordinating mechanisms are worthy of special attention: federal interstate compacts (for instance, the Colorado River and ACF compacts), interstate commissions (Delaware and Susquehanna River Basin Commissions), Title II River Basin Commissions established by the Water Resources Planning Act of 1965, and federal regional corporations.[1]

For much of the nineteenth century, water resources planning, in particular river basin management, meant efforts by states and communities to develop engineering-based solutions to specific stakeholder needs such as flood control, water for municipal use, and water treatment (Kundell, DeMeo, and Myszewski 2001). These piecemeal efforts were single-purpose in their goal. They sought to identify possible sites for hydropower projects, ascertain likely methods for navigational or other improvements, and evaluate ways to mitigate flooding (see Merritt 1979: 48; Holmes 1979). While producing site-specific solutions to the problems of particular communities, they did not set broad priorities for regional sustainable development.

During the twentieth century, what is now termed "water resources planning" came to embrace multiple policy objectives undertaken by *all* levels of government. Such planning is now generally conceived to be a comprehensive effort to harmonize environmental, economic, and other concerns within a single region (Grigg 1996). Five distinct periods in the evolution of federal water planning are discernible: *a formative period* of federal intervention in response to specific regional needs beginning in the early nineteenth century and extending until about 1865; a *federal-state cooperative planning* era following the Civil War, the focus of which was navigation; a *multi-program era* beginning in the 1930s, characterized by the establishment of national priorities; an effort to federalize water planning through *presidential-level coordination;* and a *federal-state partnership* embracing greater sensitivity to environmental protection and restoration.

Sustainability Objectives at the Republic's Inception

The earliest federal water supply planning efforts coincided with exploration of the mountainous West. Often led by Army engineers, these expeditions had the purpose of determining the feasibility of improving water resources. While the journeys of Lewis and Clark (1804–05) and Zebulon Pike (1806–07) in the upper Missouri and Arkansas River basins, respectively, are the best known of these, Stephen H. Long's Central Rocky Mountain–Yellowstone expedition (1819–20) also surveyed regional water resources.

In 1824, the Corps of Engineers was officially designated the steward of the nation's water resources. The Corps began through the establishment, under President Thomas Jefferson, of a military engineering school at West Point, New York, in 1802—the beginning, also, of the U.S. Military Academy (NAS 1999). Between this time and the Civil War, the Corps identified mill sites and needs for navigational improvements and engaged in channel-widening and other flood hazard mitigation activities (Merritt 1979; Holmes 1979).

It is significant for later debates regarding sustainability that, for the first half-century of its existence, the Corps was at the center of controversy regarding the role of federal agencies in water resources development—a controversy only partly abated by the U.S. Supreme Court's decision in the 1824 case *Gibbons v. Ogden,* in which Chief Justice John Marshall ruled on behalf of the majority that the federal government had the power to control navigable rivers as a function of its constitutional authority to regulate interstate commerce (NAS 1999: 10). That same year, the Corps received a $75,000 appropriation from Congress to "investigate and improve navigation on the Mississippi and Ohio rivers." The result of the these two actions was legislation designed to encourage economic development through navigation improvements: "The President . . . is hereby authorized to take prompt and effectual measures for the removal of all trees, which may be fixed in the bed of said rivers [and] to raise all such trees, commonly called 'planters, sawyers, or snags'" (Clarke and McCool 1985: 15).

The Corps' first large-scale efforts in river basin planning began in 1850 when Congress directed it to "determine the most practical plan" for flood prevention on the Mississippi River (Clarke and McCool 1985: 16). Its efforts were generally deemed to be successful in producing site-specific solutions to local problems. While its remedies often generated fierce engineering debates, particularly over proposals to harness the Mississippi River for navigation and flood abatement (Barry 1998), they failed to meet what we now would regard as sustainability objectives because they did not set forth broad, consistent development priorities, nor did they anticipate how solutions imposed at this time might later have to be modified in light of new information.

The Advent of Federal-State Cooperative Planning: The Watershed Approach

In the late nineteenth century, *water resources planning* began to embrace multiple goals, public input, and varied approaches to meeting societal demands. The changes instituted at that time led to the contemporary notion of planning as a *comprehensive* effort to identify water supply needs and to harmonize and address environmental, economic, public acceptance, financial, and legal concerns to satisfy them (Grigg 1996: 89).

The phrase *comprehensive planning* refers to an approach ideally characterized by the inclusion of all relevant stakeholders, the pursuit of consensus-based solutions, the balancing of competing uses, the coordination of activities across political jurisdictions, and the continuous updating and revision "in light of new problems and opportunities" (Kundell, DeMeo, and Mys-zewski 2001: vi). It embraces many spatial levels and functions (legal or program mandates, agency agendas) that are to be pursued simultaneously (Kundell, DeMeo, and Myszewski 2001: 4–5, 22).

At this time, some suggested that comprehensive water planning needed to go even further, especially in the West, due to that region's water scarcity and the expectation that population migration might lead to conflict. The way to do this, they argued, was to reconcile human needs with hydrological principles through the adoption of the *watershed principle* as a planning approach. Conceptually, a watershed is an area of land from which surface and groundwater drain to a stream, river, lake, or other water body (Brown 1997). Such an area of land is also often called a *basin, drainage basin,* or *catchment.*[2]

As early as 1843, Joseph Nicollet, while surveying the Upper Mississippi River basin, suggested that the boundaries of new territories should follow river basin boundaries (Getches 1998b). Despite his recommendation, such practice was followed only when it was convenient to do so. It was left to the Western explorer John Wesley Powell to become this principle's greatest advocate. Powell appreciated that river basins link resources and people together in direct ways, offering a natural unit for integrated management (Powell 1879; McNamee 1994).

Powell is best known for his voyages, in 1869 and again in 1871–72, along the Colorado River and, in the process, through the Grand Canyon. The opinions Powell formed about water policy through these voyages remain the subject of speculation. We know that through "personal narrative" he became one of the first explorers to provide Americans with a holistic and incisive view of the Colorado River—and, by implication, of western water problems in general (Pyne 1999: 57–62). Ironically, his voyages contributed to greater westward exploration and settlement—the latter he discouraged by noting the formidable challenges in trying to create a bountiful society in an arid region with low precipitation and high extremes of temperature.

In 1879, Powell wrote the *Report on the Lands of the Arid Regions of the United States,* prepared while he was director of the forerunner to the U.S. Geological Survey. While skeptical about western settlement, Powell proposed what he felt was a sustainable model. Two-fifths of the nation—the portion west of the 100th meridian—could not support agriculture without irrigation. Even with irrigation, only 1 to 3% of that territory could yield a dependable harvest (Farmer 2000: 129).

Powell proposed scrapping the Land Ordinance of 1787 as a vehicle for dividing land among western settlers; the ordinance had been developed in an era when settlement west of the Alleghenies was beginning in earnest. Instead, the West's arid lands would be subdivided into irrigation districts, with each farmer allotted 80 acres "with water rights" (Farmer 2000: 130). These districts would be drawn to conform to watershed topography, with larger drainage basins serving as state boundaries. An economic survey would classify unclaimed lands according to their highest potential use (for instance, rangeland, timberlands, farmland; see Farmer 2000: 12). This was Powell's unique contribution—a combination of prescribed use and the employment of watersheds as political units, he felt, would compel farmers, ranchers, and others to work together to form irrigation districts replete with canals, diversion systems, and dams. Not only would land uses be balanced against available water, but immediately affected communities would also collectively make management and allocation decisions (Powell 1879; McNamee 1994; Farmer 2000).

Although he intended to discourage migration—in the process drawing the ire of Congress and land settlement interests—Powell's plea that the government support irrigation to make settlement economically feasible hastened efforts to build large-scale reclamation projects (Farmer 2000: 130), plans justified (and subsidized) by their flood control and hydropower benefits. This pattern characterized U.S. water policy through the twentieth century.

In exchange for broad support (and via the efforts of organizations such as the "irrigation congresses" formed by William Smythe and other boosters), a reciprocal system of large, publicly financed water projects was built. The apex of this movement was the establishment, in 1902, of the Reclamation Service (later the Bureau of Reclamation) sponsored by Senator Francis Newlands of Nevada. The Newlands Act established a revolving fund for the construction of reclamation projects, replenished by repayment of low-interest loans to farmers who purchased mortgages for 160-acre tracts and were then provided irrigation water via the Reclamation Service (Farmer 2000: 131). A similar system was provided to eastern states, principally for navigation, hydropower, and flood abatement (Foster and Rogers 1988; Wilkinson 1992; Mann 1993; Pitzer 1995).

In 1879, shortly after Powell's "arid lands" report, Congress established the Mississippi River Commission (MRC), one of the first efforts to coordinate water supply planning efforts in a single basin. The MRC was formed to deepen and widen the Mississippi's navigable channel and to provide flood abatement measures. Significantly, the Corps of Engineers, an agency with considerable engineering prowess, directed the MRC. This gave the Corps added authority for navigational improvements *and* flood abatement by investing it with greater authority for intergovernmental coordination of these functions (Clarke and McCool 1985).

During this period, little regard was paid to the growing problem of water *pollution* in the nation's lakes and rivers. Reflecting the growth of public health concerns in the late nineteenth century, however, Congress passed the River and Harbor Act of 1899, which gave the Corps the authority to "monitor, control, and/or prohibit the dumping of dredged material and other debris into the nation's navigable waters" (NAS 1999: 11). While a weak approach to abating pollution, the act was the first major water pollution law, and its approach underscores the then-limited appreciation for how degraded water quality affects economic growth and public health.

Efforts to bolster intergovernmental coordination in water planning occurred under President Theodore Roosevelt, who "was interested in securing state cooperation and assistance in his program" to develop comprehensive management of the nation's rivers (Caldwell 1947). These efforts were largely unidirectional: federal agencies, having greater fiscal and technical resources, continued to make most decisions regarding what projects should be built, and where.

A key goal of Roosevelt's—reducing the power of private interests to harness regional water resources for their own gain—was not seriously tackled until the 1930s. However, with the passage of the Federal Water Power Act in 1920—which established the Federal Power Commission (forerunner of the Federal Energy Regulatory Commission)—Congress took a bold step toward this goal. This act "established a uniform process for licensing private hydroelectric power projects," including the introduction of the systematic engineering evaluation of projects and the hydrological assessment of power potential and other water resource implications. Environmental protection concerns were only minimally addressed, as was the case generally during this period, and planning funds sufficient for undertaking systematic assessment of river basins were not made available until the mid-1920s (NAS 1999: 11).

Until the turn of the century, the notion that planners should seek to manage water resources "sustainably" and that economic demands on water must be balanced against the limitations of watersheds were viewed as exceedingly strange ideas. Lawyer and historian Charles Wilkinson notes, for example, that in the West, the *prior appropriation doctrine,* first legitimized by the California Supreme Court in 1855, diminished sound ecosystem management and ig-

nored the need to conform legal practice to stream flow or watershed characteristics: "Water developers have been allowed to tap into any . . . stream without charge and extract as much water as desired, so long as the water is put to
beneficial use. . . . Under [this] doctrine, western water users can, with im-
punity, flood deep canyons and literally dry up streams. . . . Until recently, no
consideration of any kind was given to the needs of fish, wildlife, or the
streams and canyons themselves" (Wilkinson 1992: 21–22).

Of special significance for sustainable development, however, is that the
initial licensing process for hydroelectric dams led to what one scholar has
termed "the first comprehensive river basin development plans for the nation"
(Moreau 1996, cited in NAS 1999: 11). The passage of the River and Harbor
Act of 1927 requested the Corps and the Federal Power Commission to examine the feasibility and cost of developing hydroelectric projects—in combination with other functions, including navigation, flood control, and irrigation—
on all the country's navigable rivers. These surveys later became known as
"308 Reports," after House Document 308, which listed the basins recommended for study (NAS 1999: 11), and they indirectly contributed to later river
basin planning efforts, including those of the Tennessee Valley Authority, to
which we now turn.

The Advent of the Federal Regional Corporation: The TVA

With the establishment of the Tennessee Valley Authority (TVA) in 1933,
the first truly comprehensive multipurpose federal water planning effort began. Ironically, a "308 plan"—intended to depict opportunities for *private* as
well as public hydroelectric development in the Tennessee basin—became the
basis for TVA's establishment (NAS 1999: 12).[3]

From its inception, the TVA was granted broad power over a seven-state region to engage in water supply planning, flood control and flood mitigation,
hydropower production, navigation, and economic development. In President
Franklin Roosevelt's words, it was to be a "corporation clothed with the power
of government but possessed with the flexibility and initiative of private enterprise" (Selznick 1966: 5; see also TVA 1934). Local entities were incorporated into its economic development and water and power programs, and political alliances were formed to ensure programmatic and funding stability.
Most importantly, the TVA not only "supplanted" other federal water resource
agencies in its operating region, but the absence of large private power companies also helped it achieve comprehensive breadth over the activities for

which it was responsible (Selznick 1966: 5). This was in marked contrast to the typical pattern of previous federal initiatives to manage river basins, and these characteristics represented potentially significant opportunities for promoting sustainable water management.

The political conditions that permitted the TVA to do these things were uniquely characteristic of American politics during the 1930s. Some contend that these conditions may no longer exist, which may explain why no TVA-like entity has been established anywhere else in the United States. The TVA has enjoyed two invaluable assets that make it a distinctively powerful entity. First, from its inception, the TVA was granted almost unlimited powers to engage in regional planning. Not only was this mandate wide-ranging and inclusive, but, some feel, it was also vague and imprecise—granting the agency a "blank check" under its charter to engage in various water-related programs and alter their priority whenever its board deemed it necessary.

Vagueness and imprecision also encouraged involvement by regional stakeholders ("grassroots" entities) in the TVA's programs by broadening the agency's mandate to include unconventional economic development programs such as fertilizer distribution, contour plowing, electricity distribution to rural cooperatives, and other programs that appealed to lower-status rural populations (see Selznick 1966). This not only endeared the agency to these entities, it also bolstered the TVA's legitimacy in bundling economic development and natural resources programs. Indirectly, it also helped the agency promote environmental justice through the distribution of tangible benefits to those who were economically and socially disadvantaged. It did this by providing cheap electricity, making cheap fertilizer available for farmers, and making available consumer and household education, particularly in rural areas.

Second, because the TVA supplanted the Corps of Engineers and the Soil Conservation (now the Natural Resources Conservation) Service in the Tennessee basin, it was able to assume authority for all the functions these agencies performed. Moreover, because these agencies' missions in the Tennessee Valley were meager in scope prior to 1933, there was little resistance to the TVA's takeover of these functions. And since there was no large private power entity in the region to challenge the TVA's dam-building efforts, the agency was able to become a major power producer.

Despite the TVA's success, the agency is not a fully optimal model of sustainable water management for three reasons. First, the TVA experiment has not been replicated elsewhere. In the 1940s, the Roosevelt and Truman administrations proposed TVA-style corporations with broad authority to manage other major river basins. Generations of political scientists and historians have amply documented how attempts to develop a Missouri Valley and Columbia Basin Authority were defeated due to resistance by federal water resource agencies, state water commissions, and local interests, all of whom enjoyed close relationships that engendered the support of key members of Congress and made the entry of any "monolithic" federal entity with broad planning authority all but impossible (Conkin 1986; Pitzer 1995; see also Hart 1957).

Second, despite the considerable powers the TVA enjoys, in areas outside its traditional authority (for instance, water supply) it has had to enter into creative partnerships. The TVA's authority and legitimacy to manage disputes —a problem not really anticipated when the agency was formed—is sharply limited. For one thing, it lacks the explicit authority to regulate water withdrawals. This inhibits its ability to be a player in long-term water supply planning and could become a serious problem if regional water demands increase as forecast.

The TVA can regulate individual state practices regarding surface water withdrawals—*if* they affect its statutory operations. Under Section 26a of the TVA Act, for instance, the agency can approve or reject construction of structures on, in, or along the Tennessee River or its tributaries that affect navigation or flood control or that could be hazardous to health or otherwise interfere with TVA operations—including water supply or intake lines. This authority provides some control over instream flow, discussed in chapter 4 (Kelley 2000; 16 U.S.C., sec. 831y).

Third, the TVA has no actual authority for water *quality,* even though nonpoint pollution from farms and urban areas, including construction sites, parking lots, and lawns, has become a major regional problem.[4] Because diminishing water quality affects the TVA's operations, it has had to employ nonregulatory approaches to abate it. TVA's "Watershed Teams" employ a unique strategy to enhance local community and citizen capacity to implement projects to help improve water quality. Key elements of this approach include encouraging dialogue among water users and forming partnerships among government, nonprofit, and private sector entities that cut across political boundaries in an effort to identify potential sources of federal and private funding for cleanup efforts and public education (see Poppe, Hurst, and Burks 1997; TVA 1999). The initiative exemplifies a move toward a more bottom-up approach that emphasizes articulation of stakeholder views, public input in setting priorities, and adaptive management.

The TVA has also completed a two-year reservoir operations study (ROS) designed to assess policies for operating the river system and its 49 impoundments for navigation, flood control, power, recreation, economic development, public land use, and water quality and supply. The genesis for this study was a recommendation by the TVA's Regional Resource Stewardship Group—an advisory panel—that the agency explore whether its current reservoir operations should be changed to optimize all of these functions and to assess whether changes "would result in greater overall public value." As a result of the ROS, the TVA has adopted a new operating policy or preferred alternative that leaves reservoir levels higher later in the summer, ensures that flood prone areas are not exposed to greater flood risk, and shifts the focus from achieving specific summer pool elevations to "managing the flow of water through the river system" (TVA 2004a: 1).

The ROS offers two reforms. First, it provides the opportunity to develop a basin-wide water budget in order to determine how surface waters managed by the TVA are currently allocated among diverse off-stream (and instream) demands. This is important for anticipating and developing the means to manage the growing demands for domestic supply, agriculture, and thermoelectric power. About 12 billion gallons of water are taken from the river system each day. In 2000, 84% of that was used for cooling at power plants (more than 99% of the cooling water was returned to the river). The other withdrawals were for industrial use (10%), public supply (5%), and irrigation (1%) (TVA 2004b: 1). Withdrawals are anticipated to increase as population and economic growth increase (TVA 2002a: 8; 2002b).

Second, the process by which the TVA conducted the ROS is instructive for water resources planning in the region and beyond. In the public scoping process the TVA undertook as required by the National Environmental Policy Act (NEPA), efforts were made to elicit broad input. Concerns expressed by the public were used to establish objectives for river system operation. A range of alternatives was generated and discussed in public meetings throughout the region (TVA 2002a: 6; see also TVA 2003a, b), in effect embracing a type of adaptive management approach to assess public concerns and gauge their importance. Early feedback suggests that the process yielded positive results. One issue that gave rise to the ROS—criticism by lakefront property owners along the Holston River that the TVA's seasonal drawdowns for flood storage were lowering property values by making shoreline use problematic—has largely been placated. Whether the TVA can reconcile these stakeholders, as well as navigation interests and environmental groups, to a single plan for reservoir operations while also meeting its statutory obligations remains to be seen.

Federal Interstate Compacts

Compacts are, in effect, legally binding contracts negotiated by sovereign states to formally allocate interstate waters, regulate water quality, or manage interstate bridges or ports (Caldwell 1947; Curlin 1972). There are approximately 22 interstate compacts dividing the waters of western rivers and several eastern compacts that address water pollution, flood control, or multiple water resource issues (McCormick 1994; Sherk 1994; see table 2.1).

The oldest and perhaps best known of these is the Colorado River Compact, which allocates the waters of the Colorado River and its tributaries among seven western states: Arizona, California, Colorado, Nevada, New Mexico, Utah, and Wyoming. While the compact was concluded in 1922, Arizona, due to resentment over what it considered to be an inequitable division of its share of the lower Colorado basin, refused to ratify it until 1944. When it finally did ratify the compact, it tried to use its ratification to leverage federal funds to build the long-coveted Central Arizona Project, designed to divert Colorado River water by aqueduct to Phoenix, Tucson, and surrounding rural communities (Stevens 1988; Sheridan 1998).

Typically, western-state compacts were formed for the purpose of allocating both claimed and "unused" water based on present and future state needs and water-use priorities (Tarlock 1990; Sheridan 1998; Grant 1998; *Arizona v. California* 373 U.S, 1963). The Colorado River Compact allocates claimed and unused waters based on future needs and priorities.

Other early compacts include the Red River Compact among Minnesota and North and South Dakota (1937) and the Potomac River Compact approved by Maryland, Virginia, West Virginia, Pennsylvania, and the District of Columbia (1941). In general, interstate compacts are most effective in resolving conflict when they serve as "vehicles for solutions," not solutions in themselves. Unlike economic tools, such as water markets, or court decisions that allocate water volumes or otherwise mandate some partial remedy to a dispute, compacts provide an ongoing mechanism for consultation and negotiation among various parties (Sherk 1994; see also Weston 1984). However, even when compacts articulate solutions, they may prove difficult to implement because of weak enforcement mechanisms or political barriers to that enforcement—for instance, popular resentment toward the solution (see Bennett and Howe 1998).

TABLE 2.1
Previous and Current River Basin Initiatives

River/Compact	Member States
Animas–La Plata	Colorado, New Mexico
Arkansas	Colorado, Kansas
Arkansas River Basin	Kansas, Oklahoma
Arkansas River Basin of 1970	Arkansas, Oklahoma
Belle Fourche	South Dakota, Wyoming
Bear	Idaho, Utah, Wyoming
Big Blue	Kansas, Nebraska
Canadian	Oklahoma, New Mexico, Texas
Colorado	Arizona, California, Colorado, New Mexico, Nevada, Utah, Wyoming
Costilla Creek	Colorado, New Mexico
Klamath	California, Oregon
La Plata	Colorado, New Mexico
Pecos	New Mexico, Texas
Red	Arkansas, Louisiana, Oklahoma, Texas
Republican	Colorado, Kansas, Nebraska
Rio Grande	Colorado, New Mexico, Texas
Sabine	Louisiana, Texas
Saco	Maine
Snake	Idaho, Wyoming
South Platte	Colorado, Nebraska
St. Croix	Maine and New Brunswick, Canada
Upper Colorado	Colorado, New Mexico, Utah, Wyoming
Upper Niobrara	Nebraska, Wyoming
Yellowstone	Montana, North Dakota, Wyoming
Wabash	Indiana, Illinois
Wheeling Creek	Pennsylvania, West Virginia
Merrimack	Massachusetts, New Hampshire
Thames	Connecticut, Massachusetts
Connecticut	Massachusetts, Connecticut, New Hampshire, Vermont
New England Interstate Water Pollution Control Commission	New York, New England states
New York Harbor	New York, New Jersey
Ohio	Illinois, Kentucky, Indiana, Ohio, West Virginia
New England	Connecticut, Massachusetts, Rhode Island, District of Columbia, Maryland, West Virginia, Virginia, Pennsylvania
Potomac	New York, New Jersey
Delaware	Pennsylvania, Delaware
Susquehanna	New York, Pennsylvania, Maryland
Chesapeake Bay	Maryland, Virginia
Great Lakes	Illinois, Indiana, Michigan, Minnesota, New York, Ohio, Pennsylvania, Wisconsin
Apalachicola-Chattahoochee-Flint	Georgia, Alabama, Florida
Alabama-Coosa-Tallapoosa	Georgia, Alabama

Sources: Curlin (1972), Bennett and Howe (1998), and personal correspondence.
Note: Partial listing.

Although interstate compacts vary in intent, scope of activity, and structure, all derive their legal authority from the compact clause of the U.S. Constitution (Art. I, Sec. 10, clause 3).

This endows compacts with the right to embrace within their jurisdiction public, as well as private, facilities and projects. It also binds the actions of signatory states *and* federal agencies and authorizes the allocation of interstate waters in accordance with the doctrine of equitable apportionment (that is, in ways that do not impair rights awarded to parties under Supreme Court decree without their consent). In effect, their decisions have the force of national law. As discussed in chapter 5, compacts often employ a type of covenantal language that assumes that consenting parties agree in perpetuity to dividing waters. This creates a built-in impediment to renegotiating a compact when conditions warrant—an obstacle to adaptive management. The Colorado River Compact exemplifies this problem, one brought about, in part, because negotiations toward an agreement among Wyoming, Colorado, New Mexico, Utah, Nevada, Arizona, and California to develop a "law of the river" for the Colorado actually focused on a particular remedy—a huge dam in Boulder Canyon near present-day Las Vegas. This dam heralded the triumph of the "Reclamation dream" (Farmer 2000: 130).

In 1905, a canal constructed by irrigationists in the Imperial Valley failed due to severe flooding on the Colorado River. Also used by Mexican farmers, the canal had no head gate; when flooding occurred, the river broke through and filled the below–sea level Salton Sink, creating, after two years, a 50-mile-long lake called the Salton Sea (Farmer 2000: 131). The flood and its aftermath helped generate regional cooperation over how to manage the river and led, in 1917, to an organized effort to compel the federal government to develop a comprehensive management plan. The Reclamation Service's director, Arthur Powell Davis (nephew of J.W. Powell) had an engineer's dream—to restrain the river through a huge impoundment. He convinced farmers in the Imperial Valley that a canal by itself was impractical; harnessing the river required an upstream storage dam to prevent floods, trap silt, and provide a dependable year-round water flow for power, irrigation, and municipal supply.

Davis acquired a second ally in 1920 when the city of Los Angeles expressed interest in the proposed dam. Having already grown 600 percent in the first two decades of the century and having virtually depleted the Owens Valley through water diversion via a vast aqueduct system, the city sought new sources of water and power (Farmer 2000: 132). When the Colorado River Compact was consummated and when Davis's dream of an upstream im-

poundment, Hoover Dam, was finally completed, the "reclamation dream"—
that "the water . . . be used"—was fulfilled. "In the mind of reclamationists, it
was better to use and be wasteful than to not use at all" (Farmer 2000: 135).
Sound, sustainable management was construed as *utilization* of the river, not
adaptively seeking to *conserve* it.

This reclamation dream was also promoted by irrigation booster William
Smythe (mentioned earlier), who believed it would further the cause of
democracy. With the "miracle of irrigation," he predicted that the West would
"become the egalitarian domain of small, prosperous farmers," fulfilling the
Jeffersonian ideal of the independent yeoman (Farmer 2000: 130). Supporters
turned to the compact as a vehicle for resurrecting irrigation's promise: thus,
the compact was sought not as a vehicle for future planning but to aggrandize
utilitarian and practical needs.

The most important figure in this endeavor proved to be Secretary of Commerce—and civil engineer by training—Herbert Hoover. Hoover, who served
as the federal representative to the compact negotiations, proposed that the
basin be arbitrarily divided into upper and lower sub-basins. The objective
was to "avoid the sticky issue of state-by-state allocation," a clever compromise in light of the seeming intractability of state positions on allocation
(Stevens 1988: 18). With each sub-basin allocated a portion of the river's estimated flow of 18 million acre-feet on an annual basis each portion equaling
7.5 million acre-feet—individual state allocations could be deferred until
later. Meanwhile, the lower basin was permitted to take an additional million
acre-feet, while the remaining 2 million acre-feet were left "un-apportioned"
as a reserve for Mexico.

This was the clincher that sealed the deal for the compact—with only Arizona dissenting due to fears that California, led by the Los Angeles Water and
Power Department's mercurial William Mulholland, would seek to acquire an
extra share later on—Los Angeles had in fact proposed to construct a 240-mile-
long aqueduct from the Colorado River near Parker, Arizona, to supply Los Angeles County (Stevens 1988; Sheridan 1999).

Within seven years of the compact's ratification, Congress approved the
Swing-Johnson Boulder Canyon Act, authorizing the Bureau of Reclamation
to construct a massive dam to abate downstream flooding for the benefit of
Imperial Valley farmers, to provide water for irrigation and public and municipal supply, and to supply power for Southern California—kilowatts that
would fuel economic growth *and* amortize the dam's $165 million cost (Ste-
vens 1988). Arizona also opposed passage of this act, and it was joined by rep-

resentatives from eastern states, who saw the dam as an unnecessary waste of tax dollars and without national benefit. Private power interests were also opposed to the competition Hoover Dam would provide.

After repeated attempts to block passage of the Boulder Canyon Act, it became law on June 25, 1929, and provided for "a dam, power plant, and the All-American Canal" (Stevens 1988: 27). Hoover, now president and one of the project's most ardent supporters, championed a full appropriation for building it despite congressional opposition in early 1930 due to the Great Depression. He effectively argued that, rather than save money, cutting the project's appropriation would delay repayment of power revenues to the treasury and forestall job creation (Stevens 1988: 170). Early in its development, the project was known as the Hoover Dam. However, in the Swing-Johnson Bill that authorized construction, the project was referred to as the Boulder Dam.[5] Given Hoover's important role in the negotiations and compromises involved in the Colorado River Compact and in promoting the project, the final name given to it in 1947, Hoover Dam, was neither unexpected nor undeserved (Stevens 1988: 174).

During the early years of the Great Depression, the Boulder Canyon project took on a life of its own as a symbol of what a large public works project could do to energize a nation suffering from massive economic dislocation. It also revealed the difficulty, during times of economic hardship, of convincing the public and elected officials of the value of adaptive management. The immediate need for jobs and demands for regional development preempted any reservations held toward the implications of the Colorado River Compact or of plans to harness a great river by building a great dam.

Federal Interstate Water Commissions

Unlike traditional compacts, the federal interstate commission (also called a compact: see Cairo 1997) is empowered to deal with interstate conflicts over water supply and quality and management issues and has the U.S. government as a member. The Delaware and Susquehanna River Basin Commissions (DRBC and SRBC), the nation's oldest federal interstate water commissions, have been granted a broad scope of authority in all matters relating to the water resources of their respective basins, ranging from flooding to fisheries to water quality. The DRBC was the first such commission to include the federal government as a partner—a model later followed by the SRBC (Weston 1995, 1999; DRBC 1998).

These commissions emerged out of debate over a number of water quality and supply concerns that first emerged in the Great Depression and accelerated in the post–World War II boom. In the 1930s, FDR's interior secretary, Harold Ickes, formed several basin study groups with staffs, planning funds, and some powers of program review. These groups had little access to Congress and lacked the ability to initiate new projects or to overrule what they deemed uneconomical or environmentally damaging decisions by established agencies. They also had no control over planning objectives, which were left to the Corps and other construction agencies (Derthick 1974). Unlike the initiatives that began in the postwar period—which embraced water pollution and drought management—these seminal efforts were largely driven by a desire to harness federal authority to express regional resource development aspirations and to provide a less ambitious surrogate for what the Tennessee Valley Authority was doing in the Appalachians.

During the 1960s, largely in response to deteriorating water quality and serious droughts in the Northeast, multipurpose planning efforts began to consider innovative ways to combine the talents of state and federal agencies to develop long-term water supply strategies. Interstate commissions established for the Delaware and Susquehanna basins were empowered to allocate interstate waters (including groundwater and inter-basin diversions), regulate water quality, manage interstate bridges and ports, and exercise broad authority over water resources (DRBC 1998; Weston 1999). The commission formed for the Potomac basin was only given authority over water quality—a power preempted by the states after passage of the Clean Water Act.

A characteristic of these agreements is that parties must be willing to settle disputes over water through negotiation and alternative means of dispute resolution rather than litigation or Supreme Court petition. This provides a built-in flexibility to respond to grassroots concerns and to revisit solutions in the light of new pressures and issues. Reliance on regular, intensive, face-to-face negotiations; careful coordination among politically neutral technical staffs; sharing of study findings among partners; willingness to sacrifice institutional independence when necessary; and authority of commissions to implement decisions are all of inestimable importance in bringing about equitable compromises and long-term strategies for river basin management that transcend short-term pressures to act expediently (Weston 1984; Cairo 1997).

Since 1997, most compacts have functioned without federal appropriations as a result of congressional adoption of a Heritage Foundation recommendation that urged "defunding" programs whose benefits were viewed as more regional than national in scope. The DRBC and SRBC have since sustained themselves without federal appropriations. (In 1997, DRBC's executive director advised Alabama, Florida, and Georgia officials during negotiations for the ACF and ACT compacts.) The structures of the DRBC and SRBC compacts were explicitly adopted as models by the framers of the ACF and ACT compacts (DRBC 1998). We discuss three of these compacts in chapter 3.

"Federalizing" Water Supply Planning

In the early 1960s, Congress embarked on an effort to provide greater coordination of water supply planning, both by itself and through better interagency cooperation. It also sought to enhance the role of public input in water supply planning by drawing on greater stakeholder involvement in decisions. In part, this effort was undertaken in response to emerging controversies in both the East and West that required a more holistic and less piecemeal approach to river basin planning. In the West, there arose an important controversy over the continuing efforts by the Bureau of Reclamation and its interest group allies to construct impoundments on the Green River in Wyoming and, more controversially, in Marble Canyon and other sites within the Grand Canyon (Farmer 2000). In the Northeast, continuing drought served as a catalyst in the formation of the DRBC (Derthick 1974) and gave rise to a greater federal planning role.

The apex of these coordinating efforts was the U.S. Water Resources Council (WRC), established by the Water Resources Planning Act of 1965 (PL 89–80) and charged with comprehensive planning.[6] Composed of representatives from the Departments of the Army, Agriculture, Commerce, Housing and Urban Development, Interior, and Transportation as well as the EPA (starting in 1970) and other agencies and commissions, the WRC's mission was to "encourage the conservation, development, and utilization of water and related land resources of the United States on a comprehensive and coordinated basis" and "maintain a continuing study of the nation's water and related land resources and to prepare periodic assessments to determine the adequacy of these resources to meet present and future requirements" (WRC 1968, 1978).

The Water Resources Planning Act also encouraged states to establish "Title II" River Basin Commissions (RBCs) charged with integrating and harmonizing state assessments of water supply problems and encouraging regional supply planning. RBCs were staffed by state *and* federal representatives and could receive funds furnished by Congress and distributed by the WRC through a competitive process. These were to be used to gather basic water data, identify local problems, and develop long-term programs for "comprehensive, coordinated management of water resources" (WRC 1978: x). RBCs also coordinated the efforts of the Corps, the Bureau of Reclamation, and other agencies in providing assistance to states and communities in drawing up their own plans.

The WRC's assessments were intended to provide a "nationally consistent database" to assist in this planning (WRC 1978). Unfortunately, despite the WRC's formal powers to foster adaptive management, meaningful citizen participation was not incorporated into the planning process, unified planning was opposed by traditional beneficiaries of water projects, and many agencies continued to adhere to their own plans and to bypass instruments that would encourage public involvement. The failure to achieve an adaptive management paradigm can best be appreciated in the WRC's failure to undertake comprehensive planning.

In 1973, the WRC introduced a series of "Principles and Standards for Planning Water and Related Land Resources." These prescribed that agencies consider nonstructural alternatives to water resource problems; undertake rigorous, systematic benefit-cost assessments that considered all viable options for achieving the same resource management objectives; and incorporate the views of states and the general public in plans and programs. They were not initially mandatory, although they were later made so, as we shall see.

In effect, the initial planning process instituted under the Water Resources Planning Act was a two-level approach—federal data collection, standard setting, and financial support coupled with regional (watershed-based) planning, implementation, and assessment. The WRC conducted two national assessments, in 1968 and 1978. Both thoroughly depicted the nation's current and projected water needs; analyzed water-related problems from national, regional, and major river basin vantage points; and provided a wealth of data on water quality, quantity, and land-use trends and problems so that others could undertake their own studies based on WRC findings (WRC 1968, 1978). The 1968 and 1978 assessments embraced issues related to water quality, water supply, and related land-use considerations. Stakeholder views were elicited through broad inter-agency and federal-state cooperative efforts.

As long as the WRC's efforts remained limited to preparing broad sets of recommendations for others to weigh and adopt, they garnered little public attention. All this changed in the late 1970s during the presidency of Jimmy Carter, when the Office of Management and Budget charged the WRC with mandating the use of these principles and standards in the evaluation of water projects as well as mandating state cost-share guidance. In order to enforce "principles and standards" as administrative rules, the WRC was granted the authority to discourage projects of dubious economic value or potentially adverse environmental impact.

Carter actively sought to diminish Congress's tradition of using water projects as a vehicle for aggrandizing local interests in dams, navigational improvements, and other water projects by developing "omnibus" authorization bills, which were little more than collections of local public works projects. These pork barrel projects, Carter charged, were wasteful of public expenditures, economically unjustifiable, and, in many cases, ecologically harmful. Criticism grew in Congress that the WRC was exercising an "anti-dam" agenda through budget-cutting and fiscal impoundment in order to eliminate locally popular projects which the administration alone found wanting (see Fradkin 1996).[7]

In a 1981 report to Congress, the comptroller general of the General Accounting Office concluded that the Title II river basin commissions chartered by the Water Resources Planning Act had made meaningful contributions toward enhancing water resource planning and development. However, the report noted that the law gave commission chairs little authority for policy, that commission membership was voluntary, and that incentive for membership was minimal. Federal and state water plans and programs continued to be prepared independent of commission influence, and commission members "chose not to use their collective authority." Furthermore, less than half the nation was under the umbrella of the six river basin commissions established under Title II.

Finding that the commissions did not perform any function or service that the states were not able to accomplish themselves, the Department of the Interior requested no funds for river basin commissions beyond 1981. The elimination of federal funding effectively eliminated the Water Resources Council and the Title II river basin commissions (Cody 1999a), and in 1993, Congress decided that principles and standards were no longer rules that had to be followed.

As a result of these criticisms and its eventual demise in 1981 under President Reagan—whose administration "zeroed-out" the agency's budget—the WRC has become widely regarded as a failure.[8] Critics charge that it did not ensure meaningful citizen participation at the inception of federal agency planning; overcome disagreements among states, communities, and other traditional beneficiaries of "pork-barrel" projects; or overcome the perception that its planning efforts were perceived as top-down in nature. Moreover, it failed to find "an appropriate ideological basis for policy" (Goslin 1978; Robie 1980). In fairness, it must be acknowledged that the WRC was a controversial planning effort from its inception because it sought to overcome the inertia of established agency agendas, despite wide input into its recommendations from those very agencies.

Stepping back from these criticisms, however, the WRC's failure may hold lessons for advocates of sustainable water resources planning through adaptive management. The WRC lacked legitimacy in instituting practices that could have led to an adaptive management framework. This lack of legitimacy stemmed from three problems: a lack of meaningful participation, a lack of leadership, and the absence of an overall philosophy for water resources management able to rally people around a long-term cause. First, the technical assistance WRC provided to states and river basin commissions did not ensure *meaningful citizen participation* at the inception of federal agency planning. Most agencies undertook plans with little input from the public and only involved stakeholder groups after initial plans were formulated—thus inhibiting the opportunity for truly structuring plans and programs around adaptive principles early on. Second, many agencies *did not look to river basin commission plans as guideposts* for their own efforts—in part because Congress and many interest groups did not urge them to do so. In effect, agencies formulated legislation and initiated projects by themselves—as they had long done—without feeling that they had any particular obligation to look toward commission aspirations as a sort of benchmark around which these plans and projects should be evaluated. Finally, the WRC failed to find "an appropriate ideological basis for policy" (WRC 1968; see also Goslin 1978; Robie 1980; Feldman 1995). Since the 1980s, most water supply planning efforts have revolved around river basin compacts and, increasingly, individual states.

Before leaving this subject, we should mention the National Water Commission (NWC), which lasted from 1967 to 1973. This entity grew out of controversies surrounding proposals to dam the lower Colorado River in the 1960s. Its chief legacy was the attempt to impose fiscal discipline on federal water supply efforts and to identify ways to improve the coordination of federal agency water supply planning and pollution control activities (NWC 1974; Western Water Policy Review Advisory Commission 1998).

The NWC did succeed in placing species diversity, riverine protection, and other environmental issues on an equal policy footing with traditional economic development drivers associated with federal water resources policy. Moreover, the NWC's final report provided a "penetrating critique of water resources decision making" (Western Water Policy Review Advisory Commission 1998: p. 4–24). That these issues are now part of virtually all water supply discussions in policy circles owes something to this effort. Its recommendations to improve groundwater management, to liberalize instream flow protection, to urge greater wastewater reuse, and to increase agricultural water efficiency remain a part of many recent water resource planning efforts and are all recommendations that embrace adaptive management strategies such as water conservation, nonstructural approaches to addressing flood mitigation and floodplain management and avoiding strategies that pose irreversible damage to the environment as well as to regional economies.

The New Paradigm: Federal-State Partnership and Environmental Sensitivity

Since the 1980s, a new paradigm for federal water supply planning has evolved that stresses greater stakeholder participation in formulating policy alternatives, explicit commitment to environmentally sound and socially just management, greater reliance on drainage basins as planning units, and state-federal cost sharing for projects—in part to reduce costs borne by any single jurisdiction and in part to encourage greater fiscal responsibility in identifying what is an actual need (Hartig et al. 1992; Landre and Knuth 1993; Cortner and Moote 1994). This sustainable development framework promotes management approaches that are accountable to *varied* interests by being amenable to "regionally and locally tailored solutions" (Western Water Policy Review Advisory Commission 1998); protective of fish, wildlife, and flora; focused on drainage basins; and willing to embrace "ecological, economic, equity and social considerations" in a single framework (May et al. 1996: 6). In short, this paradigm emphasizes adaptive management via spatial and managerial flexibility, collaboration, participation, and sound, peer-reviewed science. It is an approach that ironically became legitimized through declining federal interest in water supply (exemplified by Congress's 1997 "zeroing-out" of funding for river basin commissions) and a general decline in the support for dams (Reuss 1991; Long 1993; Stine 1993; McGinnis 1995; Miller, Rhodes, and MacDonnell 1996; Cody 1999b). A good example of this new paradigm's values is articulated by the Western Water Policy Review Advisory Commission's 1998 report, which stated, "Part of the impetus for our Commission's formation was the Congress's finding that current federal water policy suffers from unclear and conflicting goals implemented by a maze of agencies and programs. . . . Lack of policy clarity and coordination resulting in gridlock was a consistent theme of public testimony and . . . research. . . . We have concluded that these problems cannot be resolved piecemeal but, rather, must be addressed by fundamental changes in institutional structure and governmental process" (1998: xiii).

The Northwest Power Planning Council (NPPC) exemplifies this new paradigm. NPPC is a multi-state, multi-agency partnership comprised of the Bonneville Power Authority; the Pacific Northwest Electric Power and Conservation Council; representatives from Washington, Oregon, Idaho, and Montana; several federal agencies; 13 tribes; eight utilities; and numerous fish, forest, and environmental NGOs. We discuss the NPPC further in chapter 3.

The NPPC was established in 1980 when Congress passed the Pacific Northwest Electric Power Planning and Conservation Act. The act's purpose was to restore salmon spawning runs on the Columbia and Snake Rivers by making salmon a "coequal partner" with hydroelectric power in the operation of the Columbia Basin's more than 150 dams (Blumm 1998).

While the NPPC is not a compact, it has compact-like powers to develop plans and combine the operations of state and federal management entities. This has helped it pursue adaptive management—its operational and engineering innovations intended to restore salmon stocks are the product of data management tools refined in the light of experience.

As we shall see, the NPPC's record with regard to salmon restoration is, at best, mixed. Nevertheless, it has forced environmental issues onto the agenda of water and power agencies in the Pacific Northwest, and it has emphasized ecological imperatives, aesthetics, and demands for equity that "have given rise to a greater consciousness of the ethical implications of water use" (Getches 1998c: 190). Unlike previous federal efforts in the region, the NPPC has encouraged extensive public involvement and planning for long-term threats by incorporating local community and tribal concerns (Getches 1998a). It is not only a major departure from previous federal water planning efforts, it may also be a window into the future of *adaptive management.*

Another example of the new paradigm is the current effort to revisit the Colorado River Compact. As noted earlier, the compact was negotiated to allocate water among seven states and to promote economic development through dams and irrigation projects. For many years, it could be said that the compact promoted development at the expense of the environment.

Since 1964, critics of Glen Canyon Dam have insisted that its impact on the upper basin has been injurious almost from the moment it was completed. The most frequently cited problems are the flooding of one of the West's most beautiful canyons under the waters of Lake Powell, increased rates of evapo-transpiration and other forms of water loss (for instance, seepage of water into canyon walls), and the eradication of historical flow regimes. The latter problem has been the focus of recent debate. Prior to Glen Canyon's closure, the Colorado River was highly variable. Flows ranging from 120,000 cubic feet per second (cfs) to less than 1,000 cfs and a temperature range of 65 degrees Fahrenheit to below freezing exemplify this variance.

When the dam's gates were closed in 1963, the Colorado River above and below Glen Canyon was altered by changes in seasonal variability. Once characterized by muddy, raging floods, the river changed into a clear, cold stream. Annual flows were stabilized and replaced by daily fluctuations of as much as 15 feet. A band of exotic vegetation colonized a river corridor no longer scoured by spring floods, five of eight native fish species disappeared, and the broad sand beaches of the pre-dam river eroded away. Utilities and cities within the region came to rely on the dam's low-cost power and water, and in-stream values were ignored.

Attempts to abate or even reverse these effects came about in two ways. First, in 1992, under pressure from environmental organizations, Congress passed the Grand Canyon Protection Act, which mandated that Glen Canyon Dam's operations coincide with protection, migration, and improvement of the natural and cultural resources of the Colorado River. Second, in 1996 the Bureau of Reclamation undertook an experimental flood to restore natural flow and turbid conditions to the river ecosystem. Planners hoped that additional sand would be deposited on canyon beaches and that backwaters—important rearing areas for native fish—would be revitalized. They also hoped that the new sand deposits would stabilize eroding cultural sites while high flows would flush some exotic fish species out of the system (Moody 1997; NRLC 1997). In fact, the 1996 flood did create over 50 new sandbars, enhance existing ones, stabilize cultural sites, and help to restore some downstream sport fisheries.

What made these changes possible was a consensus developed through a six-year process led by the bureau that brought together diverse stakeholders on a regular basis. This process developed a new operational plan for Lake Powell, produced an environmental impact statement (EIS) for the project, and compelled the Bureau, in conjunction with the National Park Service, to implement an adaptive management approach that encouraged broader discussion over all management decisions.

While some environmental restoration has occurred, improvement to backwaters has been less successful. Despite efforts to restore native fisheries, the long-term impact of exotic fish populations on the native biological community and the potential for the long-term recovery of native species remain uncertain (NRLC 1997). In effect, efforts to restore the Colorado River's normal flows were products of an innovative, fortuitous set of circumstances. The Grand Canyon Protection Act forced the National Park Service and the Bureau of Reclamation to work together toward the common objective of restoring historical flows on the river, while citizen-driven efforts to restore historical flows (at least in part) made legislative change possible. Finally, an "interdisciplinary partnership" (Pringle 2000) led to the trial flood in the Grand Canyon implemented in 1996. The use of instream flow management tools, together with NGO (for example, the Grand Canyon Trust) encouragement of their use—and extensive lobbying on behalf of the new act—all contributed to policy change (Moody 1997).

Whither Federal Water Supply Planning?

As we have seen, U.S. water supply planning efforts first began as attempts to promote support for regional power, reclamation, or flood control projects or to thwart the influence of private interests who wanted to develop such projects themselves. For much of their history, these efforts limited public involvement to a consultative role, failed to provide adequate interagency coordination, and fell short of being truly comprehensive because they emphasized single-purpose problem-solving. We now know that effective federal water supply planning must overcome agency turf wars by pursuing objectives defined by regional stakeholders, replace fragmented political authority vested in several agencies with a single management framework to set priorities (as with the TVA), and manage multiple needs in an integrated manner (for instance, DRBC and SRBC have mandates over water quality *and* supply). The record of federal planning further suggests that the most effective efforts are those perceived as economical, efficient, fair, and able to generate public support (ASCE 1984).

Finally, effective efforts encourage collaboration among those stakeholders most directly affected by water supply problems. Collaboration overcomes resistance to change, facilitates new opportunities for funding, and stimulates resilient policies (Chrislip and Larson 1994). Collaboration must take place at several jurisdictional levels to be truly effective.

As we enter a new millennium, two questions remain to be answered: How do we determine what objectives plans should pursue? And what should the federal role be in their implementation? Two answers can be offered. First, water supply planning should aim to *optimize choices in an uncertain future.* A formidable challenge decision-makers face is reconciling actions mandated by law or environmental conditions, on the one hand, with the goals and objectives of communities, on the other (see, for example, U.S. National Water Commission 1972). In effect, if planning is a sort of insurance policy against the severity of unforeseen problems, then planning efforts should seek to meld local needs and national priorities. This is also one lesson of successful water planning efforts in other countries.

Second, planning should *hasten adoption of proactive policies* in order to foster the most economical, efficient, fair, and supportable projects and programs to meet unforeseen problems (see, for example, ASCE 1984). In short, planning permits foresight into the best means to prevent problems from arising in the first place.

A GLOBAL PERSPECTIVE:
RIVER BASIN PLANNING ELSEWHERE

In May 2002, the Secretary-General of the United Nations Kofi Annan publicly acknowledged the importance of of water problems to development, stating, "More than one billion people are without safe drinking water. Twice that number lack adequate sanitation. More than three million people die every year from diseases caused by unsafe water. Unless we take swift and decisive action, by 2025 as much as two-thirds of the world's population may be living in countries that face serious water shortages" (United Nations 2006).

River basin planning efforts designed to integrate water, land use, economic development, and environmental protection are practiced around the world. These efforts are motivated by problems comparable to those found in the United States. We now examine eight efforts in order to discern the challenges in creating a sustainable management regime. Efforts to manage water resources by basins and watersheds—and to cross political boundaries within *and* among countries—are attempts to bridge divergent values and foster adaptive policies.

River Basin Management: The French Approach

France has long been regarded as one of the world's leaders in developing novel, innovative means for managing water resources, having first established river basin organizations in 1964. Its experience offers an interesting example of the challenges a highly developed society faces in managing water resources when it must also reconcile disparate interests whose priorities include water supply, water quality, and social justice.

Six river basin agencies, embracing France's major drainage basins, are empowered to assist municipalities and industries in meeting national water quality standards.[9] Although these agencies are primarily concerned with the prevention of water pollution and the provision of water supply, they also address the development of water resources when that development affects either water quality or supply issues. These agencies employ several methods to achieve their goals, including regulations and economic incentives such as loans, grants, and fines.

Under French law, basin organizations are considered "administrative public corporations" under the supervision of the Ministère de l'Aménagement du Territoire et de l'Environnement (Ministry of the Environment). Each basin organization is responsible for a single major watershed (MATE 1999). The process for establishing, enforcing, and implementing these incentives is complex. Figure 2.1 depicts the various participants and their roles and relationships. The Ministère de l'Aménagement du Territoire et de l'Environnement issues pollution and water withdrawal standards. Inspectorates appointed by the ministry implement and enforce those standards. Commissars, elected by local residents, work with national inspectorates to discover breaches of law and levy fines and other penalties established by the ministry (Feldman 1995).

The role of the basin agencies is to establish a system of charges for consumers and polluters of water in proportion to the amount of water drawn or degraded in order to reduce the ultimate costs of pollution control to society and, thus, to make the ministry's task easier. Charges are paid by all water users in a basin and are levied by a complex formula based on the mass of pollutants discharged, the estimated costs of decomposition, and the actual water used (that is, withdrawn). These charges, which function as a form of economic inducement, are intended to alleviate the need for the ministry to have to resort to more formal penalties (Feldman 1995; MATE 1999). In effect, basin organizations employ a sort of marginal cost pricing system in which user fees sus-

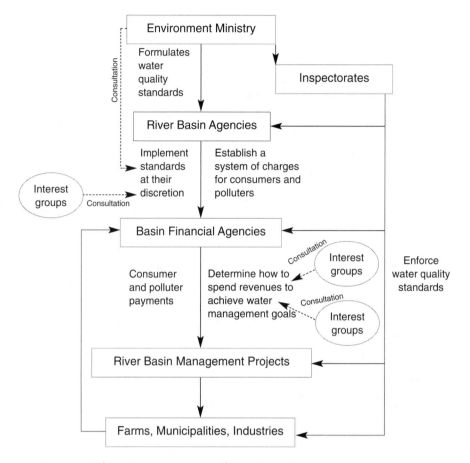

Figure 2.1. Schematic Representation of River Basin Management in France

tain the operation of each organization. Moreover, fees are based on the economic impact of a user's actions, that is, water withdrawn or diverted, amount of water polluted, and so on.

Revenues collected by the agency belong to that basin to spend on pollution abatement and water supply projects according to prearranged, multi-year plans for meeting water resource objectives. In effect, they are redistributed in the form of free loans or "subsidies intended to encourage . . . end users to improve the way they use the resource" (UNWWAP 2003: 339). Some indication of the relative cost of water under the French system may be gauged by comparing prices for one cubic meter of water in the Seine-Normandy basin with that of other nations, including the United States. In 1999, the average Seine-

Normandy water user spent about US $2.70/m³ of water compared with $1.91 in Germany, $1.23 in the remainder of France, $1.18 in the United Kingdom, $0.51 in the United States, and $0.40 in Canada (UNWWAP 2003: 338–339).[10]

Multi-year plans are developed with the assistance of *comités de bassin* (basin committees)—advisory boards made up of equal numbers of water users and local government representatives from the same watershed. Nature protection and environmental interest groups, as well as local and regional councils, have also been invited to participate in plan formation, and they often function as investigative arms of Environment Ministry inspectorates by reporting violations of water pollution standards to the government (Feldman 1995). In essence, each basin committee convenes representatives of all water users and authorizes charges.

This devolution of water resources planning and decision-making to local and regional entities appears to have worked well. Since 1980, organic waste discharges in France have declined an average of 4.4 percent per year, and 50 percent of toxic waste discharges have been eliminated through an aggressive pretreatment program. Recognizing that basin agency decisions are often arrived at after all parties make concessions, commissars rarely exercise their veto authority. Opposition to government policy is disarmed by making interest groups part of the decision-making process—a feature that is possible only because basin agencies are self-managed authorities that can utilize a variety of economic incentives (Feldman 1995).

In January 1992 the French parliament authorized for local political authorities in France (for instance, municipalities and departments) powers and responsibilities over management and upkeep of watercourses and sanitation facilities. This legislation, the Water Act of 1992, also mandated a "Master Water Development and Management Plan" to be developed by each watershed (MATE 1999). The act was an attempt to hasten the trend toward devolution of political authority to local levels of government—introduced by the government, then controlled by the Socialists. It required basin agencies to work with established elected jurisdictions in drafting plans for the management and development of water resources.

In essence, river basin agencies now share authority with private companies, government departments, and environmental organizations for planning. Moreover, within each basin agency, a SAGE (Schema d'Amenagement et de Gestion des Eaux) must be prepared for "significant individual basins"—those facing serious water quality problems (Newson 1997: 342). Above this framework, a Water Resources Department in the Ministry of the Environment oversees the planning process and ensures that plans are formulated and implemented in conformance with the spirit of devolution and that "water . . . is recognized as an integral part of the national assets" (MATE 1999).

One of the biggest challenges to the sustainable management of France's river basins is exactly how much authority for their management should be delegated to local authorities versus how much should be left in the hands of national ministries. The strongest advocates for *national* water quality goals are national regulatory agencies whose constituencies include scientists and environmental NGOs and European Community (EC) peers, whose collective regulations and prescriptive standards provide a sort of benchmark for environmental quality.

One criticism of the French system is that water management plans are driven by water quality interests and concerns instead of "ecosystem protection" goals. The latter favor greater decentralization and emphasize not only human water consumption concerns but preservation of endangered and threatened species. Since the basis for the devolution of authority previously discussed is "political, not environmental," fragmentation of political authority, in the view of one scholar, may inhibit a more holistic and sustainable approach to water management (Buller 1996). In effect, political fragmentation, while making public participation and access to decisions easier, may make the comprehensive management of watersheds more difficult. This balance between access and coordination is important in adaptive management.

Another debate in France is the issue of privatization, discussed in chapter 1. Three companies dominate the public water supply in France: Vivendi Environnement, which controls nearly half the country's waterworks, Suez Lyonnaise des Eux (25%), and Saur, a subsidiary of the Bouyages conglomerate (10%). The remainder is municipally owned. Critics note that France is the "birthplace of water privatization" and that the influence of its water companies extends beyond the country's borders (Suez has 115 million customers in over 130 countries, while Vivendi serves 110 million customers in over 100 nations). Moreover, private companies charge more for the same water services and exercise inordinate political and economic power.

This political clout exists because the French government has resisted allowing foreign competition within France—granting to its three domestic giants what, in effect, amounts to an oligopoly over water services. Moreover, as the global reach of these companies has grown, more nations hoping to become part of the European Community will almost have to hire them to provide municipal water services in order to comply with the European Bank for Reconstruction and Development's (EBRD) environmental standards (ICIJ 2003a, b).

The influence of France's private water providers has several implications for sustainable water management. First, the EBRD "fosters the transition toward market-oriented economies" in Eastern and Southern Europe (ICIJ 2003a). This philosophy benefits the large water companies but may make it difficult for the developing nations dependent on the private companies hired to provide supply and treatment services to hold them accountable—or to permit broad-scale public participation in decisions over pricing, level of service, or access. Second, these companies have proven difficult to examine in part because, as private entities, their internal operations are less transparent than those of public utilities.

Third, these and other private companies have long lobbied for trade laws to force cities to privatize their water operations and, many fear, monopolize water operations so that they can drive up prices. Because these companies operate in over 100 countries, they also serve as striking examples of the global reach of privatization. Finally, France's private water companies remind us that reconciling the efficient management of water supply with equity concerns is a challenge that must be met on many spatial levels—river basins, municipalities, and corporations—with the latter operating within elaborate, interconnected, globally powerful networks.

Within France, private water companies work closely with local governmental entities called "inter-municipality drinking water associations." The latter serve the needs of over two-thirds of the country's population and work through public-private partnerships to provide potable water infrastructure and sanitation services. These associations retain actual ownership of the system while private providers supply the services. According to a UN Report, "This system allows a clear delineation of roles and exchanges of experience, as private operating companies manage the water services of many different communities. Delegation is also favorable to efficiency, because of the technical expertise and the economic constraints of the private companies" (UNWWAP 2003: 380).

In comparing the experiences of privatized water services in France with services outside the country, there seem to be two implications for adaptive management. First, privatization seems to bode well for delivery efficiency within France—but conjures up criticisms of the potential for exploitation elsewhere. This raises the question: to what extent is efficiency a function of institutional capacity? In France, local water authorities and basin agencies co-manage water supply, ensuring that private enterprise is subject to check and balance. Such an institutional balance of power is notably absent in many developing nations.

Second, the relationship between private and public water sectors in France is a mutual partnership based on political accountability. The input of civil society (the nongovernmental sector, including rate-payers and elected associations) ensures that public and private entities are answerable for their acts (UNWWAP 2003: 380). Again, where criticisms arise over the power of private entities in the arena of water services, these usually take the form of disparagement over a lack of political accountability and a lack of public review of decisions.

The International Commission for the Protection of the Rhine against Pollution

The Rhine is the longest river in Western Europe, flowing over 1200 kilometers (about 770 miles) from Switzerland to the North Sea. Six countries—Switzerland, Liechtenstein, Austria, Germany, France, and the Netherlands share it (Wessel 1997)—and its tributaries pass through Belgium and Luxembourg. A century ago, the Rhine was one of Europe's most productive sources of salmon, with annual catches of 150,000 fish. By 1958 salmon catches had disappeared entirely, 90% of the river's floodplain had been cut off through development, and severe chemical pollution of the Rhine had led to such ecological consequences as the local extinction of the river otter in the Netherlands, the high mortality of seals in the Wadden Sea, and the low survival of cormorant chicks in the Rhine delta. Fully 20% of the world's chemical plants line the banks of the Rhine, and the river is one of the most channelized streams in the Western world (Newson 1997: 45; Barlow and Clarke 2002: 31).

The first attempt to manage the basin through international treaty occurred in 1816—at the conclusion of the Napoleonic Wars—with the establishment of the Central Commission for Rhine Navigation. The treaty guaranteed free and unregulated international navigation by countries bordering the river. An 1868 agreement was consummated over fisheries and additional navigation concerns (Newson 1997: 313). Water quality issues were not adequately addressed for some time after, even though the basin embraces a number of industrial and mining activities, many of which pollute the river (for instance, potash mining in Alsace contributes fully one-third of the river's salt load; see

Newson 1997: 313). Riparian uses vary widely among up- and downstream portions of the basin, with agriculture dominant downstream and industry upstream. Moreover, Switzerland, a headwaters country, is not a European Union (EU) member and thus not subject to the EU Directives on the Control of Water Pollution (Newson 1997: 313).

Beginning in the early twentieth century, a number of regional conventions and other arrangements were established to protect water quality. The most notable of these are the Ruhr Agencies (1904), which manage water pollution, water supply distribution, and hydropower; the Lake Constance convention (1960), which commits Austria, Switzerland, and two German states (*Länder*) to protect the lake from pollution; and the Moselle and Saar Commissions (1956, 1960), which regulate navigation and water (Wessel 1997).

To address declining water quality in the Rhine, the Netherlands, Germany, France, Luxembourg, and Switzerland created the International Commission for the Protection of the Rhine against Pollution in 1950. The ICPR received official status through the Berne Convention in 1963. Two additional conventions, for chemical and chloride pollution, were adopted in 1976 and are enforced by the ICPR. These conventions follow EU environmental practice in establishing lists of chemicals whose discharge is discouraged or, in some cases, forbidden. The conventions also urge adoption of "best available technologies" for water treatment and place quantitative limits on discharges (Wessel 1997: 226).

The commission conducts research to determine the nature, degree, and origins of pollution. It can advise the European Union and national governments on pollution prevention measures, and it is charged with coordinating the efforts of individual member nations. In 1988, the commission adopted the Rhine Action Plan. The plan has four goals: to create conditions conducive to the return of large vertebrates, including protecting habitats for migratory fish; to safeguard drinking water supply; to eliminate sediment pollution by hazardous substances; and to protect the ecology of the North Sea (Newson 1997; Milich and Varady 1998).

In recent years, the ICPR has undertaken a series of efforts to accommodate the concerns of environmental NGOs in the basin's management and to address other environmental threats facing the basin. The 1998 ICPR-Plenary Assembly "officially granted observer status" to nine NGOs who now are able to participate in ICPR's working groups. These organizations are Birdlife International/NABU, the European Association of Chemical Industry (CEFIC), the International Syndicate of Waterworks in the Rhine Catchment Area (IAWR), the World Wide Fund for Nature (WWF), Greenpeace, the "Re-naturation of the High Rhine" syndicate, the European Association of Water Suppliers and Waste Water Treatment Plants (EUREAU), Alsace Nature, and the "Hoch-wassernotgemeinschaft Rhein" organization (ICPR 2002).

Meeting in France in 1998, the 12th Conference of Rhine Ministers adopted a new Rhine Convention, which granted observer status to a number of inter-governmental organizations (IGO) concerned with issues of environmental protection, such as commissions dedicated to the protection of the Saar and Moselle (IKSMS), Lake Constance (IGKB), the North Sea (OSPAR), the Scheldt (CIPE), the Meuse (CIPM), the Elbe (IKSE), the Danube (ICPD), the Odra (IKSO), and Lake Leman (CIPEL), as well as the Central Commission for Navigation on the Rhine (ZKR). Allowing greater NGO and IGO collaboration and participa-tion strengthens the ICPR in its efforts to implement its "Programme on Sus-tainable Development of the Rhine" (ICPR report No. 97) by involving a greater number of key stakeholders.

Launched in 1999, the "Programme on Sustainable Development" targets improvements to water quality, flood mitigation, ecosystem protection, and groundwater protection and permits close cooperation between government agencies and the aforementioned NGOs and IGOs in implementation. Flood mitigation efforts are centered on a new program titled the "Action Plan on Flood Defence," adopted by the Conference of Rhine Ministers in January 1998. Its goals are to reduce damage risks by 10% by 2005 and by 25% by 2020, to reduce extreme flood stages by up to 30 cm by 2005 and by up to 70 cm by 2020, to increase public awareness of flood hazards, and to improve flood fore-casting. Strategies focus on improving national coordination in these four ar-eas as well as sharing information better and reporting data more consistently (ICPR 2002). As in the Columbia basin in the northwestern United States, ecosystem restoration efforts focus on enhancing the ability of salmon to re-produce in fisheries. Moreover, to provide further impetus to salmon fisheries, fishing in important spawning areas and "juvenile fish habitats" is banned. De-spite the adoption of all of these strategies, none has yet succeeded in restor-ing stocks to prior levels or in providing a sustainable salmon fishery on the Rhine.

Severe challenges to sustainable development persist, including a lack of effective transnational political and legal authority for enforcing antipollution norms, a lack of integration in the management of different water uses and ac-tivities, and a lack of political will to make the Rhine Commission a strong multinational entity with robust enforcement functions. The commission has no independent power or primary responsibility for water pollution. Each nation continues to exert primary authority over water resources issues within its own borders, and, as noted, EU influence does not extend to Switzerland. In effect, conformance with the Rhine and other conventions is nonbinding and largely voluntary (Wessel 1997).

Although many national laws and pollution cleanup plans have been adopted in response to directives from the European Union, their implementation is often hampered by a lack of coordination among responsible authorities. One major weakness of the ICPR is that an older, transnational commission that is responsible only for navigation has authority over it. Since the two commissions have entirely different mandates, their actions can easily conflict (for instance, maintenance of instream flow for navigation has a very different meaning than for supporting healthy fisheries). To date, this attempt at international coordination of management of the Rhine has failed to overcome problems of fragmentation, duplication, and inter-agency conflict among the many domestic agencies active in water issues. While the riparian countries of the basin do not struggle with the task of providing sufficient water for agriculture as well as municipal use, their advanced industrial infrastructure and intensive land uses take a toll on water quality and ecosystem health. Moreover, as in the United States, nonpoint pollution (phosphorous and nitrates) from agriculture and urban runoff remains a growing, intractable problem (Wessel 1997).

Finally, for adaptive management, the Rhine experience provides still another lesson. In an era of globalization, where environmental policies are widely diffused globally (see Hoberg 2001), failure to address problems adequately within the basin may retard efforts to export or diffuse innovations to developing countries that could benefit from the NGO-government partnerships pioneered in the Rhine basin.

The Danube Declaration: Linking Public Participation and Sustainability

The Danube, Europe's second-longest river after the Volga (2,857 km) connects Eastern and Western Europe. Its basin includes parts of 17 countries, including Germany, Austria, the Czech Republic, Slovakia, Slovenia, Croatia, Bosnia-Herzegovina, Serbia, Hungary, Romania, Bulgaria, Moldova, and Ukraine. Portions of Poland, Albania, Italy, and Switzerland also lie within the

Danube basin, constituting less than 2 percent of the total catchment area (Milich and Varady 1998). The river transects the capitals of Austria, Hungary, Serbia, and Slovakia (Vienna, Budapest, Belgrade, and Bratislava) (Beach et al. 2000: 84).

Prior to World War II, a relatively loose accord, the European Commission of the Danube, dating back to the 1856 Treaty of Paris, regulated river navigation. In 1948, a new navigation accord called the Danube Convention created the Danube Commission. The original parties to this accord were the Soviet Union, Hungary, Romania, the Ukrainian SSR (now Ukraine), Czechoslovakia (now the Czech Republic and Slovakia), and Yugoslavia (now represented by Serbia). Austria joined in 1965, and Germany, Croatia, and Moldova joined in 1998 (Milich and Varady 1998). The accord was a compromise of sorts between Soviet-bloc countries and non-Communist riparian states. The former wanted navigation authority to be the exclusive province of each riparian state. It was not until the 1980s that water quality issues rose to the forefront of negotiations and eventual policy intervention in a unified basin-wide manner.

The Danube has long undergone environmental abuse. Phosphate and nitrate loads have increased sixfold since the 1970s, and cross-national rivalries over control of the river and its tributaries persist even though many countries sharing the river cooperate on a number of environmental issues. In 1985, the riparian states issued the Bucharest Declaration, which articulated the principles that the Danube's water quality depended on an integrated, holistic view of the basin and that each state must commit to a basin-wide "unified monitoring network" and an ecosystem-based management approach (Beach et al. 2000: 85).[11] This was a major step forward because the Danube Commission's original focus was limited to safe navigation, flood control, and hydroelectric power generation—not unlike the Tennessee Valley Authority in the United States.

In 1991, after a meeting of riparian states at Sofia, a coordinated plan was launched to create an interim task force charged with encouraging and supporting "national actions for the restoration and protection of the Danube." (Beach et al. 2000: 86). Under this "Environmental Program of the Danube River Basin," each member country appoints two officials to serve on a basin "coordination unit." The first of these sets of officials serves as liaison between the basin program and one of the 11 member countries, while the second serves as a "country focal point" responsible for coordinating a nation's work plan. Subsequent meetings among coordinators, focal points, and donor agencies have met to produce agreement over criteria for national reviews of water quality data availability, to decide on issue priorities, to develop funding priorities, and (in 1993) to develop a "strategic action plan" for the basin.[12]

In 1994, riparian countries in the basin adopted the Convention on Cooperation for the Protection and Sustainable Use of the Danube River, also known as the Danube River Protection Convention. Actions agreed to under the convention include "sustainable and equitable water management, including the conservation, improvement and rational use of surface and groundwater in the catchment as far as is possible," taking all "appropriate legal, administrative and technical measures" to improve water quality, and setting priorities for action at the national and international level "aimed at sustainable development and environmental protection" (Beach et al. 2000: 87). As noted in a UN University report, the Environmental Program of the Danube River Basin is the first basin-scale international body that "actively encourages public and NGO participation throughout the planning process" (Beach et al. 2000: 87).

Unfortunately, as with other international conventions lacking subsequent protocols specifying the obligations of the signatories, there is little agreement among the states on the criteria for water quality and compliance. Some critics contend that claims for the convention's openness may be overrated and that basin management suffers from a longstanding tendency to forge agreements behind closed doors, ruling out any form of public participation and the involvement of other governmental bodies with an stake in the water quality. As a result, management of the Danube will continue to be a contentious issue, with the commission's achievements limited to a series of nonbinding resolutions (Milich and Varady 1998). The reality of cooperation among basin parties probably lies somewhere between these assessments—exemplified by the fact that while serious bi-national problems remain, strenuous efforts to address them are being pursued.

The persistence of serious problems leading to bi-national conflict is illustrated by a 1992 case: Slovakia (then part of Czechoslovakia) decided to begin operating the recently completed Gabcikova Dam along the border with Hungary, despite the objections of environmentalists in both countries—Hungary had withdrawn from the project in 1989 (Barlow and Clarke 2002: 70). In 1993, the two countries referred their differences to the International Court of Justice in The Hague. Meanwhile, fish catches in the lower Danube (below Gabcikova) declined by 80%, and wetlands and bottomland forests were also diminished (Barlow and Clarke 2002: 70).

From the standpoint of sustainable management, the Danube experience offers four lessons. First, it reveals the importance of addressing institutional and ethical concerns in achieving sustainability by embracing broad public and NGO input. Second, it underscores the continuing difficulty in reconciling economic development and environmental protection concerns. Third, it shows that transjurisdictional water management schemes must build trust and confidence among participants by sharing information. Attempts at cooperation that are limited to instruments of agreement and compliance without the civil society amenities necessary for ensuring that compliance are likely to fail. We shall return to this issue.

Finally, the Danube basin experience also offers anecdotal evidence of the importance of adaptive management in the newly emerging democratic states of Eastern Europe. Prior to the fall of Communism, gross economic inefficiencies, high rates of government subsidy, and highly centralized water management decision-making institutions were commonplace in Hungary—as it was in other countries in the region. As of this writing, few durable solutions to these problems have emerged, and considerable debate continues over the modalities needed to manage the country's water resources effectively.

Since the mid-1990s, Hungary has undertaken an evaluation of state subsidies for water services, the advantages and disadvantages of privatization, greater decentralization and stakeholder participation in decisions pertaining to river basin development and watershed protection, and adoption of Western European quality standards (Nemeth 1994; UNDP 2004). According to one water official, Hungary has adopted a number of reforms that have important implications for transnational cooperation. These reforms, which are gradually being introduced across the region, include reevaluation of state subsidies for expensive water services, a movement away from "one sided, extensive quantity-oriented development," a reduction of state-owned water utilities, greater consultation and coordination with local interests in adoption of river basin and water supply decisions, and a proliferation of private, nongovernmental water utilities and irrigation providers (Nemeth 1994).

As of 2004, these reforms have met with mixed success. Less than 60% of homes are connected to a centralized sewage treatment system, and wastewater services are not expected to reach all settlements over 2000 people until 2015. On the other hand, 98% of Hungary's population is publicly supplied with water, flood safety has been improved along the Tisza, Hungary's second most important river, and—slowly—the percentage of the population whose water quality meets EU standards continues to improve yearly (UNDP 2004). Other transitional economies in the region are receiving assistance under the

Global Environment Facility (GEF), funded by the World Bank and UNCED, to identify major manufacturing enterprises posing the greatest threat to transboundary nutrient and organic pollution, to assist in developing a regional approach to nutrient reduction, and to transfer abatement technologies for these persistent compounds (UNWWAP 2003: 239, 297).

What is perhaps most important about these developments is that they hasten managerial flexibility and administrative openness and transparency while also embracing environmental and social justice issues. Problematically, however, they also exacerbate uncertainties of control, political accountability, and sufficiency of economic resources for long-term water infrastructure improvement. Clearly, these reforms have led to greater technical and policy-level exchanges between professional water managers in the Danube basin and those in Western Europe, more grants and other forms of funding to enhance managerial capacity, a lessening of some water demands—especially for inefficient agricultural practices—and greater effort to accommodate a larger number of societal concerns in water management decision-making (Nemeth 1994). While future trends are impossible to predict confidently, water planning is becoming more adaptive due to greater emphasis on compromise, deliberation, and democratic decision-making.

Ironically, however, tragedy has tested the efficacy of this adaptive management framework. In January 2000, an accident occurred in Baia Mare, Romania, when an earthen dam was breached on the Szamos River, impounding gold-mine tailings. A tributary of the Tisza, which flows into the Danube and thence to the Black Sea, the Szamos took in tons of cyanide-contaminated slurry (UNWWAP 2003: 232). After this accident, the UN Industrial Development Organization (UNIDO) implemented a pilot project to "promote an integrated approach to risk management in the Tisza River basin." Drawing on principles first articulated in the late 1990s by the European Union's Water Framework Directive and OECD directives on minimizing industrial contaminant transport into the environment, UNIDO is helping Tisza basin states apply precautionary (that is, pollution minimization) principles to industrial pollution, to improve emergency preparedness and risk communication programs, and to refine emergency response measures such as warning systems, quantitative risk assessment at selected sites, and first responder training (UNWWAP 2003: 232).

Sub-Saharan Africa: The Zambezi River Basin Commission

The Zambezi River basin comprises all or part of eight countries: Zambia, Angola, Namibia, Zimbabwe, Mozambique, Tanzania, Botswana, and Malawi. These countries and three others outside the basin (Lesotho, South Africa, and Swaziland) adopted an action plan and legally binding protocol in 1995 to co-ordinate the use and development of the basin's resources. The plan focuses on activities in 36 economic sectors, with the overall goal of harmonizing na-tional development policies through the implementation of integrated proj-ects. Its mandate extends to several environmental concerns, including water pollution and drought. The Zambezi River Basin Commission (ZRBC) is the body created to implement the plan.

The ZRBC consists of the member nations' heads of state (who meet bian-nually to set policy), a council of ministers (which meets annually to monitor operations), an executive directorate responsible for day-to-day operations, and a unit responsible for coordinating inter-country activities on the river and its tributaries. Unfortunately, the ZRBC lacks adequate funding and has other administrative drawbacks. It is structured as a top-down agreement and is thought to be overly ambitious, especially given its inadequate funding base ("Other River Basin Accords" 1998). It also shares authority with the Zambezi River Authority (ZRA).

As in other regions, the Zambezi and its tributaries are governed by a series of related agreements negotiated to manage hydropower, irrigation, water sup-ply, fishing, and instream flow (Beach et al. 2000: 218–219). The earliest of these dates to 1953, when many of the riparian states were still colonies of the United Kingdom and Portugal. So far as is documented, these agreements, many of which are bilateral—for instance, between the United Kingdom and Portugal or between northern and southern Rhodesia (now Zimbabwe and South Africa and Portugal)—have been effective in limited management func-tions. Few actual conflicts among parties have arisen over management issues.

The ZRA was established in October 1987 by parallel legislation in the Par-liaments of Zambia and Zimbabwe following the reconstitution of the Central African Power Corporation under the Zambezi River Authority Acts (Act No. 17 and 19 in Zambia and Zimbabwe, respectively). The governments of Zam-bia and Zimbabwe jointly and equally own the power corporation. The ZRA was created principally to manage the Kariba Dam and to provide hydroelec-tric power to both countries. A four-member council of ministers manages it, and it is heir to the Inter-Territorial Hydro-Electric Commission established in 1946 by the Central African Council to promote "coordinated development" of the Zambezi Basin. In accordance with this mandate, the ZRA is responsible for "investigation and development of new sites on the Zambezi River" and "analyzing and disseminating hydrological and environmental data and monitoring environmental conditions" on the river and the Lake Kariba (Zambezi River Authority 2002).

One unique feature of the Zambezi River Basin Commission and Authority is the relatively high level of cooperation displayed among states that remain poor and impoverished and are deficient in their capacity for resource management. There are three reasons this high level of cooperation has occurred. First, it is possible that the agreements themselves have preempted disputes from forming. Second, relations among these countries were generally amicable to begin with—as the existence of these entities confirms. Finally, as mentioned earlier, conflict over water resources is the last thing these nations can afford. Mutual self-reliance for management of the basin makes sense. Amicable resolution of shared water resource disputes is more desirable as a course of action since—regardless of a country's level of economic development—when it shares a river basin, it has every incentive to divide the resource in an amicable way precisely because it cannot control it alone without great sacrifice (Otchet 2001).

There is some evidence for this supposition in the context of the Zambezi. The parties to these agreements receive hydropower and water supply (Malawi, certainly) and are thus dependent on these entities for their livelihood. Moreover, in at least one instance, consummation of an agreement was required for building a dam whose benefits were shared (Beach et al. 2000: 218). Nevertheless, the agreements are far from perfect, and the capacity of member states to operate as a coherent entity remains limited by funds and lack of grassroots participation. While the 1995 protocol on shared water resources "has laid down the foundation for coordinated and integrated development of transboundary water resources development in the region" (UN Division for Sustainable Development 1999), member countries have not yet begun work on the various aspects of integrated development the agreement has aspired to promote.

Discussions led by the Economic Commission for Africa in the late 1990s produced a set of objectives and a "work programme" to hasten greater cooperation among member states of several basin initiatives on the continent—including the Zambezi, the Nile, and the Congo. Among other things, this program is aimed at hastening the preparation of various technical studies, hosting seminars on water resource management problems, and providing secretariat services to member countries in order to "assist member states in the building of capacities for international negotiations on trans-boundary water resources" (Economic Commission for Africa 2000).

Despite these ambitious goals, intra-country barriers, including antiquated systems of property rights and water rights, make achievement of sustainable development difficult. In Zimbabwe, an important water use and allocation issue is the powerful role wielded by the country's large-scale commercial agricultural sector, which pays nearly nothing for water, produces most of the nation's food, and is owned by a prosperous elite that is mostly white. Without a commitment to price reform that makes water more accessible to the average person and to an equitable water allocation system, effective collaboration with neighboring countries will be difficult to initiate. Countries do not cooperate well over water when they view compromise as a threat to entrenched economic power. Clearly, a foundation for cooperation between Zimbabwe and its riparian neighbors is at least recognized as important within the region. Paradoxically, its importance may not be as appreciated by its own political elites.

Southeast Asia: The Mekong

The Mekong is the world's seventh-largest river in volume of water discharged and the tenth-largest in total length. Originating in South Central China, it flows for some 4,200 kilometers through Myanmar (formerly Burma), Thailand, Laos, Cambodia, and Vietnam on its way to the South China Sea. Principal issues in its management revolve mostly around protecting and restoring water quality. Allocation of supply has not historically been a major problem, in part because of the high annual average precipitation found in the basin (Beach et al. 2000: 108). One of the basin's remarkable features is that, even though all of the riparian states are developing nations with relatively weak resource management infrastructure, a comprehensive and integrated planning regime has been developed and implemented.

Conjoint management of the river has not been easy, however, chiefly because of the widely diverse governments and divergent cultures in the basin. Those who have studied the Mekong's management report that the problems caused by this diversity are exacerbated by the high level of technical cooperation among countries that effective conjoint management requires in order to apportion the costs of environmental restoration and water quality abatement equitably and to create economies of scale (Browder and Ortolano 2000). How the Mekong countries have achieved such cooperation is an important case study—especially for the lessons it may offer other developing countries seeking to manage river basins sustainably.

In 1957, shortly after the French withdrew from Indochina following their defeat at the hands of the Vietminh forces in Vietnam, the UN Economic Commission for Asia and the Far East (UNECAFE) determined that harnessing the main stem of the Mekong could bring about hydropower production, greater irrigation acreage, extended navigation, and reduced flood threats, all of which could generate stable, robust regional growth and, by implication, peaceable development. Acknowledging that greater cooperation among riparian states would be required to bring about such plans, the UNECAFE suggested "an international body for exchanging information and developing plans" (Beach et al. 2000: 108).

Later that year, a series of coordinating committees were convened and a draft charter among the lower riparian states was concluded. Beginning in fall 1957, several countries, led by France's donation of the equivalent of $120,000, contributed to the formation of a coordinated effort, the Mekong Committee, to investigate the water resources of the basin and to propose water development projects able to achieve these objectives. Contributions grew to $14 million by 1961 and $100 million by 1965, eventually involving pledges and various financial and in-kind contributions from over 20 nations, various international organizations, and NGOs. Member states Kampuchea (Cambodia), Laos, Thailand, and Vietnam directly support the organization, and China and Myanmar provide indirect support.

The Mekong basin initiative's history may be divided into three periods. The formative years were 1957 to 1965. Rapid progress was made to establish networks of monitoring stations for hydrology and meteorology, riverine surveys, and navigation improvement. Remarkably, these data-gathering efforts continued amidst violent turmoil in the region—both between countries (North and South Vietnam) as well as within them (Laos). Many of these efforts were facilitated by multinational cooperation (UNECAFE) as well as bilateral foreign assistance (for instance, the U.S. Bureau of Reclamation undertook many of these studies).

A second period emerged in 1965 (lasting until about 1978) with the signing of an agreement between Laos and Thailand to develop a hydropower project along the Nam Ngum—a major Mekong tributary within Laos whose power would mostly be sold to Thailand. The project was funded by an international effort and was successfully completed. Moreover, in 1975, the riparian states agreed to "reasonable and equitable use" principles, allowing allocation issues to be resolved amicably (Beach et al. 2000: 107). These principles were based on the so-called Helsinki Rules of 1966 and were a logical follow-up to a 1970 "Indicative Basin Plan" that attempted to move the basin initiative from planning and data-gathering efforts to the large-scale implementation of needed projects. A number of large-scale hydroelectric projects were proposed during this period but never built—largely because of environmental opposition and the failure to acquire international funding.

The third period in the initiative's evolution may be termed a time of tribulation caused, in large part, by political unrest and full-scale war in the region. The basin committee formed in 1957 by all four lower riparian states became a three-member "interim committee" in 1978 during the Cambodian civil war. Cambodia/Kampuchea did not rejoin until 1991 (Beach et al. 2000: 110). U.S. assistance to the Basin Committee was cut off, and few significant projects were implemented. Projects pursued during this time were undertaken by individual countries that led, for the first time, to allocation conflicts among states (Browder and Ortolano 2000).

The basin committee was re-ratified as the Mekong Commission in 1995, after Cambodia rejoined the fold in 1991. Overall, the initiative's achievements are modest. Institutionally, the committee/commission structure has endured rather well and has remained relatively intact through war and political strife as well as peace, and a considerable amount of planning activities and infrastructure development have taken place—all of which are important for sustainable development and its prospects. On the other hand, integrated basin development through joint projects—the original objective of the initiative— failed to be achieved largely due to the Vietnam War and its "geopolitical changes" (Browder and Ortolano 2000).

The Mekong Commission experience shows that while developing countries can cooperate on water resources planning and pursue sustainable development objectives even in the midst of war and civil strife, regional conflict will eventually take its toll on the ability of such regions to manage water resources adaptively. The reason for this is that the factors producing such conflict create a vicious cycle of noncooperation that erodes funding, a capacity to plan jointly, and, ultimately, trust in other countries. When conflict arose, the first result was that funding fell off from the United States and international organizations, as they were deterred by continued strife and fearful that monies would not be well spent. This created a kind of "one step forward, two steps back" phenomenon where it may take years to recover early initiatives generated before various civil wars in the region take their toll on infrastructure development. The consequences of this enmity may take years to reverse, exemplified by the last of these problems—funding. Second, as resources declined, each Mekong basin country has sought an advantage by developing the river's resources on its own, worsening relations among the countries by lessening trust and further cooperation.

Latin America: The Plata River Treaty

The Rio de la Plata (Plata River) is shared by Argentina, Bolivia, Brazil, Paraguay, and Uruguay. It has a drainage area of more than 3 million km² and encompasses the Parana (35%), Paraguay (35%), Uruguay (12%), and the Plata (4%) rivers. It also includes the Pantanal, one of the world's largest wetlands with a drainage area of 400,000 km² (Beach et al. 2000: 115; Day 1977: 134). Three of the world's largest mega-cities are located in or near the basin: Rio de Janeiro and Sao Paulo, Brazil (estimated populations of 12.2 and 23 million), and Buenos Aires, Argentina (12.8 million) (WRI 1995).

In 1969 these countries adopted the Plata Basin Treaty as a coordinating mechanism for promoting joint development of the basin—particularly hydropower development. A secondary purpose of the treaty was to establish a framework for resolving conflicts. Treaty objectives include improved navigation, rational use of water resources, conservation of plant and animal life, improved infrastructure and communications, region-wide industrial planning, "economic complementarity" (a term in vogue during this period that means spin-off development), natural resource development, and the attainment of comprehensive knowledge of the basin. In short, the treaty embraces several factors in an effort to achieve "balanced and harmonious basin development and [to] accelerate regional economic advances" (Day 1977: 123).

The treaty requires "open transportation and communication along the river and its tributaries" and prescribes cooperation in areas as diverse as education, health, and riparian resource management for soils, forests, wildlife, and the like (Beach et al. 2000: 116). In effect, it serves as a sort of "affirming" mechanism underscoring the longtime willingness of these states to cooperate with one another in managing the Plata.

In 1989, parties agreed to extend the treaty's authority by consummating the "Hydrovia" (which translates to "water-way") project designed to improve barge transportation and other river development. Historically, transportation has been the most important economic activity associated with the river (Day 1977: 132). Some contend that the sheer size and the economic as well as ecological impacts of the project are straining cooperation among the treaty's partners. In the late 1990s, the Inter-American Development Bank funded a number of technical and environmental studies in order to address these concerns.

As of the late 1990s, one component of the Hydrovia project—the Paraguay-Parana Waterway, a 2100-mile shipping channel between Caceres in Brazil's Mato Grasso state and Nueva Palmira, a port city in Uruguay—has been on hold. This project would have doubled and in some places tripled the depth of the Paraguay River and led to removal of over 29 million cubic yards of river sediment (Gomes 1997). Another project would involve dredging and straightening the Parana's channel and partial draining of the Pantanal to allow year-round barge traffic. Both projects have tested the efficacy of the Plata treaty framework and angered many environmental organizations, scientists, and even residents of traditional communities in the basin who fear that the waterways would interfere with riparian flow, turn the Pantanal into a large floodplain, and increase the flow and speed of the Paraguay River, thus significantly reducing the size of the wetlands and threatening rare and unique wildlife habitat.

Some ranchers and environmentalists are also concerned that threats to various birds in the region from draining swampy areas could threaten the health of the thousands of head of cattle raised here. In effect, the birds help prevent the spread of pests affecting their welfare (Gomes 1997; Beach et al. 2000: 115–116). While the original plan for a waterway in the region was foiled by the Inter-American Development Bank on the grounds of being too ambitious and ecologically risky, an EIS has been prepared for a downsized version claiming "small to moderate harm." As of this writing, the debate continues, with many environmental organizations remaining unconvinced that a smaller project would not be harmful.

The foreign affairs ministers of all five countries meet annually to set policy and guide implementation. A permanent intergovernmental coordinating committee maintains a secretariat that promotes and administers multinational efforts. A financial institution funds programs consistent with the treaty's objectives. In theory, projects agreed to by parties are supposed to be prioritized, although there is some debate over how well this priority-setting process works.

Critics have identified four major problems with planning under the treaty. First, the treaty organization lacks a "supra-legal body" (Beach et al. 2000: 116) to manage its provisions. Every proposed project must go through each member country's legal system, which frequently results in decisional delay. Second, the treaty is said to rely on a top-down, diplomatic approach for negotiation—the lack of a strong coordinating body necessitates bilateral and multilateral negotiations for each treaty modification or project. There are few mechanisms for "bottom-up" policy innovation, an important component of adaptive management. For this reason, too, the treaty is said to be institutionally weak, despite the long history of generally amicable relations among the signatory nations over Plata basin issues. Moreover, while the treaty has been successful at avoiding open conflict among the riparian states and eased the construction of hydroelectric dams on international rivers ("Other River Basin Accords" 1998), whether this is the direct result of the treaty or simply an affirmation of the general amity between basin states and their dependence on one another is difficult to determine.

Third, there is a lack of basic hydrological and other information available for the basin, despite many years of cooperation under terms of the Plata Basin Treaty. As we have seen, this is a characteristic of river basin management in many developing nations. Prior to consummation of the Plata Basin Treaty, little detailed hydrological, biological, geographical, or social information was available. A regional development branch of the Organization of American States, together with the Institute for Latin American Integration of the Inter-American Development Bank, undertook detailed inventories of the basin's resources beginning in the late 1960s through synthesis and analysis of existing data as well as a review of aerial photography and other remote sensing information. A special effort was made to compile information on soils, geology, vegetation, groundwater, agriculture, population, energy, and transportation (Day 1977: 134).

Policy reforms initiated by these data collection efforts include the expansion of hydrological and climatological monitoring networks, regional development studies of particular sub-basins, and, with the assistance of the United Nations Development Program (UNDP), a series of navigational and water quality improvements on the Parana and Paraguay Rivers (Day 1977: 134). Studies were also undertaken of fishery resources, human health conditions (including measures to prevent the spread of communicable disease among peoples of the basin) and improvements to general basin infrastructure, including electricity demand and power generation potential (rivers in the basin are major sources of hydroelectric power).

From the standpoint of sustainable development, the Plata Basin Treaty underscores the importance of institutional capacity to reconcile economic and environmental issues and improve the basic level of existence of the region's inhabitants. As a vehicle for improving cooperation among basin countries, the treaty enhanced the collection of basic information and in the process helped improve the welfare of the entire region, especially in regard to the monitoring of baseline environmental conditions and the funding of infrastructure improvements. In addition, several pressing issues among riparian states have been addressed, in part due to the presence of a political framework that facilitates discussion and cooperation, including improvements to hydropower generation and distribution systems and development of an "open" transportation system throughout the navigable portions of the basin's major rivers. On these matters, cooperation has been relatively easy, if not completely free of impediments.

The basin continues to face a number of serious environmental and economic challenges that impede progress toward adaptive management. Upstream dams have reduced the size of downstream fisheries—a problem we have noted in other regions—and resettlement of native populations as a result of the building of dams, together with the in-migration of workers and their families for the construction of hydroelectric projects have produced dislocations, the spread of new diseases, and increased pollution in the more populous, urbanized portions of the basin.

Finally, the aforementioned Hydrovia project makes accord between groups in the region arduous while inhibiting consensus over a framework for basin-wide sustainable development (Day 1977: 138). What makes Hydrovia especially contentious is that it is forcing treaty states and NGOs into difficult choices between economic development and ecological protection that may be irreconcilable unless the scope of proposed navigational improvements on the Parana and Plata Rivers is limited. Whether basin treaty states can agree to such limits remains to be seen.

Australia: The Murray-Darling Basin

Australia is one of the world's most arid continents, which makes most of the country's territory ill-suited for farming and helps explain why nearly 80% of its population is clustered along a narrow coastal zone (Newson 1997). Thus, it is somewhat ironic—but, given the need to adapt its environment, by no means surprising—that Australia's southeast corner features one of the world's most ambitious river basin schemes: the Murray-Darling Initiative.

The Murray-Darling is fed chiefly by mountainous headwater streams and receives little input along the remainder of its path. Nonetheless, the region encompassed by the basin is a major contributor to Australia's agriculture. The region contributes a quarter of the country's cattle and dairy farms, half of its sheep and cropland, and three-quarters of its irrigated acreage (Newson 1997: 135). The basin also occupies 14% of the continent, and the city of Adelaide draws over 40% of its water from the Murray—up to 90% during drought (MDBC 2002).

Prior to the country's independence from the United Kingdom, the River Murray was largely managed by the Australian colonies of New South Wales, Victoria, and South Australia. Unclear political and hydrologic boundaries, together with heavy reliance on the river as a transportation artery and, beginning in the 1880s, a source of irrigation water, made cooperation across jurisdictions imperative yet difficult (Wright 1978; MDBC 2002). Initial attempts at cooperation began in 1863 when representatives from the three states convened in Melbourne to consider building locks on the rivers to improve their navigability. Conferees agreed that navigation improvements to the Murray, Edward, Murrumbidgee and Darling Rivers could benefit the economic development of the entire nation but approved no specific projects (Eastburn 1990).

Despite many investigations over the next four decades, it took a seven-year drought beginning in 1895 to provide "the catalyst that eventually resulted in a workable agreement between the states," which was concluded at an NGO conference in Corowa in 1902 (Powell 1993; MDBC 2002). In 1915, the River Murray Waters Agreement was concluded among Australia, New South Wales, Victoria, and South Australia, and a management entity (the River Murray Commission) was formed two years later. The commission was charged with "regulation of the main stream of the Murray to ensure that each of the riparian states . . . received their agreed shares of the Murray's water" (MDBC 2002).

In support of this mission, the First Agreement for Regulation of the Murray provided for the construction of a dam on the upper Murray, storage at Lake Victoria, and a series of weirs and locks between Blanchetown, South Australia, and Echuca, Victoria, and on the lower Murrumbidgee River. Various amendments have been made over the years "reflecting shifts in community values and changes in economic conditions" (MDBC 2002). In the late 1960s, the River Murray Commission conducted salinity investigations in the Murray Valley. This ultimately led to the further amendment of the River Murray Waters Agreement in 1982 and broadening of the commission's role to include water quality issues.

Increasing evidence of how land use was affecting the quality of the basin's water resources led to further amendments to the agreement in 1984. Finally, in 1987, the Murray-Darling River Basin Commission (MDRBC) was formed and signed by the governments of the Commonwealth, New South Wales, Victoria, and South Australia in 1987. The agreement was revised in 1992. In 1996 Queensland became a signatory; the Australian Capital Territory was added in 1998. The Murray-Darling Basin Agreement (MDBA) has the goal of promoting and coordinating "effective planning and management for the equitable, efficient and sustainable use of the water, land and environmental resources" of the basin (MDBC 2002). A depiction of the evolution of a comprehensive management regime for the River Murray is shown in table 2.2.

By the early 1980s, it became clear that the first River Murray Waters Agree-

TABLE 2.2
Evolution of the River Murray Waters Agreement, 1914–1981

(a) Matters beyond the powers of the commission in 1914
    Problems arising on tributary rivers.
    Problems caused by adjacent land use.
    Problems of flood mitigation and protection.
    Problems of erosion and catchment protection.
    Problems of water quality and pollution from agricultural and other sources.
    Problems of influent and defluent waters.
    The needs of flora and fauna.
    Possible recreational, urban, or industrial use.
    The environment or aesthetic consequences of particular proposals.

(b) Matters permitted by previous amendments and informal practice before 1976
    Limited powers of catchment protection.
    Power to initiate future proposals.
    Provision of certain dilution flows to maintain water quality.
    Lock maintenance work, improvements in navigability.
    Provision of recreational facilities.
    Expenditure on salinity investigations.
    Expenditure on redesigned works to protect fish life.
    Construction and operation of storages on tributaries.

(c) Principal innovations in agreement reached in October, 1981
    Power to consider any or all relevant water management objectives, including water
       quality, in the investigation, planning, and operation of works.
    Power to monitor water quality.
    Power to coordinate studies concerning water quality in the River Murray.
    Power to recommend water quality standards for adoption by the states.
    Power to make recommendations to any government agency or tribunal on any matter
       that may affect the quantity or quality of River Murray waters.
    Power to make representations to any government agency concerning any proposal that
       may significantly affect the flow, use, control, or quality of River Murray waters.
    Power to recommend future changes to the agreement.
    New water accounting provisions.

Source: Clark (1982).

ment was unable to address adequately the basin's environmental problems—rising water salinity and irrigation-induced land salinization that extended across state boundaries (SSCSE 1979; Wells 1994). In October 1985, a meeting of environmental ministers in Adelaide representing New South Wales, Victoria, South Australia and the Commonwealth discussed these and other problems and agreed to undertake a two-year round of intensive negotiations among the four governments. The outcome was the Murray-Darling Basin agreement—an effort to provide for the integrated and conjoint management of the water and related land resources of the world's largest catchment system.

There are six formal partner governments in the agreement as well as several departments and agencies. A schematic depicting the management structure of the MDBA is shown in figure 2.2. Three components are worthy of note: a basin ministerial council, which constitutes the principal decision-making forum for the agreement; a basin commission, which serves as the executive arm of the agreement and caries out its decisions; and a community advisory committee, which "provides the Ministerial Council with advice and provides a two-way communication channel between the Council and the community."

The basin authority established under the Murray-Darling Basin Agreement has the power to consider any or all relevant water management objectives, including overseeing investigations; planning and operating dams and impoundments; monitoring water quality and coordinating water quality studies in the River Murray; recommending water quality standards for adoption by the states; issuing recommendations to any government agency or tribunal on any matter that may affect the quantity or quality of River Murray waters; issuing new water quantity accounting provisions; and recommending future changes to the agreement.

According to commission sources, the substantive and process-oriented achievements of the initiative have been significant. Some of the more notable of these include programs to promote the management of point and nonpoint source pollution; the balancing of consumptive and instream uses (a decision to place a cap on water diversions was adopted by the commission in 1995); the ability to increase water allocations—and rates of water flow—in order to mitigate pollution and protect threatened species (applicable in all states except Queensland); and an explicit program for "sustainable management." The latter hinges on implementation of several issue-specific strategies, including a novel human dimension strategy adopted in 1999 that assesses the social, institutional, and cultural factors impeding sustainability as well as adoption of

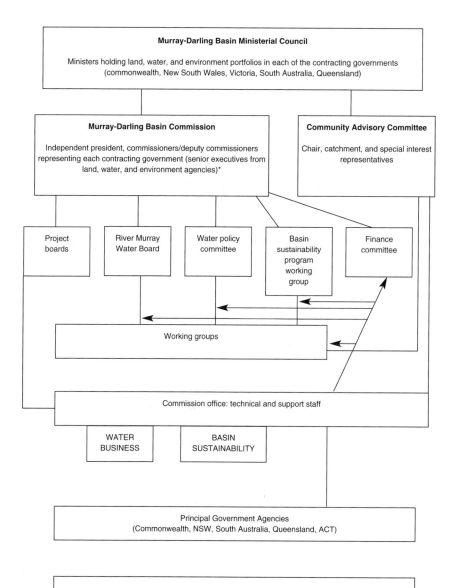

Figure 2.2. Governance and Structure of the Murray-Darling Basin Initiative (Participation of the Australian Capital Territory is via a memorandum of understanding.)

specific policies to deal with salinity, to manage wetlands, to reduce the frequency and intensity of algal blooms by managing the inflow of nutrients, to reverse declines in native fisheries populations (a plan which, like that of many river basins in the United States, institutes changes in dam operations to permit fish passage), and to prepare floodplain management plans.

Moreover, a large-scale environmental monitoring program is underway to collect and analyze basic data on pressures upon the basin's resources as well as a "framework for evaluating and reporting on government and community investment" efforts and their effectiveness. This self-evaluation program is a unique adaptive management innovation rarely found in other basin initiatives. To support these activities, the commission funds its own research programs and engages in biophysical and social science investigations. It also establishes priorities for investigations based, in part, on the severity of problems, and the knowledge acquired is integrated directly into commission policies through a formal review process designed to assure best management practices. A comparable process of priority setting is used in the CALFED initiative in the United States (see chapter 3).

From the standpoint of sustainability, the Murray-Darling Basin Agreement is one of the broadest and most far-reaching river basin management efforts found anywhere. It seeks to integrate quality and quantity concerns in a single management framework; has a broad mandate to embrace social, economic, environmental and cultural issues in decisions; and, perhaps most important, has considerable authority to supplant—even supplement—the authority of established jurisdictions in implementing environmental and water development policies. While water quality policies adopted by the authority are recommended to states and the federal government for approval, in general the latter defer to the commission and its executive arm.

Moreover, the agreement makes possible a truly integrated approach to water resources management. The commission have responsibility not only for functions as varied as floodplain management, drought protection, and water allocation but for coordinating them as well. For example, efforts to reduce salinity are linked to strategies to prevent waterlogging of floodplains and land salinization in the Murray and Murrumbidgee Valleys (MDBC 2002). Also, the basin commission's environmental policy aims to use water allocations not only to control pollution and benefit water users but also to integrate its water allocation policy with other strategies for capping diversions, governing instream flow, and balancing instream needs and consumptive (agricultural irrigation) uses. Perhaps the most notable of all innovations characterizing the MDBC's efforts, however, is its community advisory effort.

Community Partnerships: Public Involvement and Adaptive Management

Under the 1992 Basin Agreement, the Murray-Darling Basin Initiative created a special partnership between MDBA member governments and local governments in the basin. This partnership produced the Community Advisory Council, an instrument that employs "extension techniques" (Newson 1997: 135) to persuade farmers to prevent the salinization of soils and nutrient runoff pollution and to protect the water rights of aboriginal peoples. While the ministerial council and the commission contain representatives from each of the partner governments, the Community Advisory Committee represents the basin's wider community, and its chairperson attends meetings of both the ministerial council and the commission.

In 1990, the ministerial council for the MDBC adopted a "Natural Resources Management Strategy" that provides specific guidance for a community-government partnership to develop plans for integrated management of the basin's water, land, and other environmental resources on a catchment basis. In 1996 the ministerial council put in place a "Basin Sustainability Plan" that provides a planning, evaluation, and reporting framework for the management strategy and covers all government and community investment for sustainable resources management in the basin.

How these two initiatives are connected is somewhat vague. The community-government partnership component of the MDBA is considered one of two "pillars" of the "Natural Resources Management Strategy," the other being the concept of integrated watershed management. Currently, the advisory council has approximately 20 members—mostly regional organization representatives. It provides advice to the ministerial council on "community perceptions of and proposed solutions to the management problems of the Basin's water, land and other environmental resources." In 1992, representation of basin interests from Queensland and ACT was added "to empower communities" to provide advice to the council, and much of the advisory council's efforts since the early 1990s has focused on catchment management issues including instream flow, indigenous community involvement, biodiversity, capacity building, and implementation of the integrated catchment management program (MDRB 2002).

According to Newson, while the policy of integrated management has "received wide endorsement," progress towards effective implementation has fallen short—especially in the area of floodplain management. This has been attributed to a "reactive and supportive" attitude as opposed to a proactive one (Newson 1997: 137). Despite these criticisms, it is hard to find another initiative anywhere that has attempted to implement a sustainable management program based upon community involvement more actively than the Murray-Darling system.

Distant Neighbors: Free Trade, Water, Mexico, and the United States

While there has long been conflict between the United States and Mexico over transboundary water resources, there has also been uneasy cooperation over water management. Both underscore the challenges in developing an adaptive management framework that meets environmental protection, economic development, and social justice objectives *across* political boundaries between a developed and a developing nation. *Within* each country, conflicts between up- and downstream users, as well as unsustainable practices, have jeopardized cooperation in the past—a trend that may be changing due to reforms resulting from NAFTA.

To understand these challenges, we must first understand the sources of Mexico's water problems. Like other rapidly growing developing nations, Mexico faces a water crisis resulting in part from population growth, climate, pollution, and overall water stress. Especially in its northern portion, village wells are drying up, demand far exceeds supply, and there is a huge disparity between where most of the nation's water supply is located and where most of the needs are. Agriculture uses 80% of the nation's water, but laws dating to the 1910 revolution prohibit charging farmers for it—one of many antiquated features of the legal system. Households pay about one-third of the cost of its delivery—leaving industry paying up to five times more per gallon of water than household residents. This disparity is especially costly because industrial growth is considered key to Mexico's development. Finally, 85% of the country's economy and 75% of its population live in the north, while most of its water is in the southern portion of the country (Rosenbaum 2002).

The challenges facing Mexico's water are behavioral, not hydrologic. Public policies and consumption patterns have resisted reform despite rural-to-urban migration patterns and high birth rates. As stated by the deputy director of Mexico's National Water Commission: "We have lots of water in some places, but not where the people are. . . . We have to balance growth with the distribution of resources" (Mario Cantu Suarez, quoted in Rosenbaum 2002). Growth has also impelled inter-basin diversion. In pre-Hispanic times in the great Valley of Mexico, the Aztecs used water from artesian wells and were self-sufficient (Ezcurra and Mazari-Hiriart 1996). After independence and before the Mexican-American War, Mexico City began pumping water from two additional watersheds, the Lerma and Cutzamala basins, which now provide only one-third of the city's supply. Since the mid-1960s, water shortages and continued residential growth has led to exports from elsewhere (Ezcurra and Mazari-Hiriart 1996: 11).

While there are a number of technical approaches to encourage more sustainable water management, including aggressive conservation practices and reducing energy use, technical solutions alone will not work, because the metropolitan area's water demands are simply too great (Zoreda-Lozano and Casteneda 1998). Demands for more water from other parts of the country place additional pressures on the basin's overstretched supplies. Currently, Mexico City gets 40% of its water from outside the basin of Mexico. The social and ecological dimensions of Mexico City's water problems are exacerbated by transboundary competition over *alternative* sources that might satisfy a part of the demand generated in the regions outside the city's valley.

Transboundary Cooperation between Superpower and Non-Superpower

Following the 1849 Mexican War, during negotiations that led to the Gadsden Purchase (including areas now comprising parts of Arizona and New Mexico), an agreement was reached over division of waters between the United States and Mexico. This accord was vague at best. Both countries agreed that their interests at the time would be better served by permitting diversions for off-stream use rather than insisting that either the Colorado or Rio Grande basins—the two most significant transboundary waters—remain navigable (U.S. Bureau of Reclamation 1948: 135). For the Colorado River, both countries divert water at different points: California via the All-American Canal near Yuma, Arizona via the Central Arizona Project at Parker Dam, and Mexico through Alamo Canal, which draws water 1.5 miles north of the international boundary.

As noted earlier, the Colorado River Compact stipulates that Mexican rights are to be supplied via surpluses over and above the 16 million acre-feet allocated between the upper and lower portions of the basin contained within the United States. This allocation is reiterated in the 1944 treaty between the two countries and encompasses the Colorado, Rio Grande, and Tijuana Rivers. The treaty created the International Boundary and Water Commission (IBWC) and guaranteed Mexico 1.5 million acre-feet per year of Colorado River water (modifiable if drought make deliveries impossible). This guaranteed amount has been progressively and incrementally reduced to 375,000 acre-feet since 1980 (U.S. Bureau of Reclamation 1948: 50, 135).

IBWC was made responsible for "a broad range of sanitation and sewage problems along the border" and, later, for dispute resolution. However, as Stephen Mumme notes, IBWC, and the 1944 treaty that shapes its authority, are remnants of an "old regime" of transboundary management whose primary responsibilities have been "fundamentally allocative," concerned mostly with distributing off-stream supplies for agricultural users on both sides of the border. Environmental concerns were secondary in importance, and IBWC often deferred to each country's government to resolve disputes (1995: 829–830).[13]

Despite these agreements, conjoint management of boundary waters has never been free of conflict. As one study notes, irrigation evangelists such as William Ellsworth Smythe extolled development of a cotton empire in the Mexicali and Imperial Valleys and set the border region of the Colorado on a path of rapid agricultural development that transformed the ecosystem of the Sonoran Desert. This development eventually led to diversification of crops, including citrus, but it also produced a salinity crisis affecting soil fertility beginning in the 1960s and 1970s as well as diminishment of the Colorado's flow (Ward 2003).

Even today, farmers in Texas, Arizona, New Mexico, and Mexico accuse one another of using more water than they are entitled to, and many blame the dire effects of drought on the inefficient use of water on the *other* side of the border. Other social changes exacerbate these problems. Population density in the borderlands has quadrupled in Mexico and tripled in the United States since the 1950s (Mumme 1995: 827). Together with the difficulty in defining essential uses, differentials of power make amicable resolution of differences arduous.

The Border Environmental Cooperation Commission: An Adaptive Regime?

With adoption of the North American Free Trade Agreement (NAFTA) and its subsidiary conventions designed to equalize access to markets and coordinate environmental standards, changes in transboundary water management soon followed. Three new institutions were established in the 1990s: the North American Commission on Environmental Cooperation (NACEC), the North American Development Bank (NADBank) and the Border Environment Cooperation Commission (BECC). Moreover, a new model for solving problems has developed.

While the NACEC is responsible for overall environmental improvement, avoiding trade distortions in environmental decision-making, encouraging sustainable development, and imposing penalties to achieve compliance with its rulings, NADBank funds community adjustment needs related to NAFTA. Finally, BECC works in conjunction with the older IBWC to enhance the border environment by collaborating with public and private financial organizations to fund environmental infrastructure improvements and certifying projects, including those affecting water quality (Mumme 1995; Milich and Varady 1998).

The BECC has a six-member board of directors as well as ex officio members (the administrators of the U.S. and Mexican Environmental Protection Agencies, for instance). To encourage "bottom-up" accountability, the 10-member board includes nongovernmental organizations and state and local government representatives, including the Southwest Research and Information Center in Albuquerque, the Texas Parks and Wildlife Board, the city of Tijuana, and an environmental consulting firm. The Mexican counterparts are comparable (Milich and Varady 1998).

Project requests originate at the grassroots level. The BECC charter contains provisions for public input and participation, which have influenced the decision-making process on several occasions. For example, when the commission failed to adhere to self-imposed guidelines for a forthcoming meeting, e-mail protests were so numerous that the directors rescheduled the meeting. At another meeting attended by over 200 people, when the chair gaveled the proceedings closed before allowing public comment, the cascade of protests led to an apology and a binding modification of procedures allowing for future comment.

The BECC extols participation and openness. The board meets quarterly at various sites. Participants describe discussions as being remarkably free of hidden agendas or manipulation. Decisions are never final until publicly voted on, after questions and discussion (Milich and Varady 1998). The BECC and the IBWC work together in planning and implementing border sanitation and other projects. The decision-making approach stresses flexibility and capacity building rather than adherence to strict regulatory standards. Avoiding diplomatic-type decision-making, rejecting pure engineering solutions, and promoting equity embrace sustainable development objectives. Some argue that this approach could serve as a model for other transboundary schemes (Milich and Varady 1998), while Stephen Mumme, for one, claims that it significantly improves "the accessibility, responsiveness, and accountability of the water management agencies to a broadened constituency along the U.S.-Mexican border" (1995: 832).

Both countries continue to face challenges that make difficult the amicable resolution of conflicts. Recent clamor among farmers on both sides of the Rio Grande River over declining levels of water flow due to drought—and claims of over-irrigation—has not been resolved by the BECC or the IBWC. Mexico has consistently failed to deliver its required 350,000 acre-feet of Rio Grande water to the United States (Mumme 2003). Without dramatic reductions in groundwater withdrawals in the Great Basin of Mexico or slower population growth, Mexico City will come very close to exhausting its water supply (Ezcurra and Mazari-Hiriart 1996: 29).

There are some reasons to hope that this changing regime, coupled with growing awareness of the seriousness of water problems on both sides of the border, will lead to greater use of adaptive management principles. For example, there is growing recognition that safer and more potable water could be provided through adequately treated wastewater. Less than half of Mexico City's wastewater is treated. The majority sinks into underground lakes or drains to the Gulf of Mexico. And only about 27% of the country's surface water is clean enough for primary water treatment methods to ensure its usability. About half of the country's supply must be treated through complex secondary and tertiary methods (Rosenbaum 2002). This is where NAFTA's changes hold great promise.

Charged with funding "community adjustment needs," NADBank has begun to play an important role in helping to construct water and wastewater treatment projects. In 2002 over $119 million was spent—double the amount spent in 2001—on treating drinking water, increasing water supply capacity, and extending water services to households. Loans and grants totaling nearly $500 million have been allocated since 1995 on projects that typically focus on the needs of local communities and result from grassroots partnerships between public and private entities in Mexico and the United States.

Recently, both countries agreed to expand the area eligible for funding from 100 to 300 kilometers on either side of the border (Nagel 2002). Progress has also been made in developing a bi-national drought management/warning system using IBWC as the monitoring and reporting center (Mumme 2003), and there is talk of developing an international regime for the Colorado, Rio Grande, and Tijuana Rivers by incorporating government agencies and NGOs into a comprehensive management system. That both nations have agreed to use NAFTA tools for drought mitigation, conservation, and project development is an enormous step forward.

CODA: MAKING SUSTAINABILITY
INTO A PRACTICAL POLICY ANCHOR

In the context of water, *sustainability* refers to the ability to provide sufficient clean water to maintain essential economic activities while protecting the natural environment and human activities. A sustainable water management regime ensures a level of economic development that does not exceed a region's carrying capacity, protects ecological values by providing sufficient instream flow for flora and fauna, and ensures an equitable apportionment of water for various needs. Such a regime is flexible, amendable, participatory, and fair—not just efficient (Stoerker 1994).

While sustainability is often criticized as a highly idealized objective, the experiences we have discussed show how it can serve as a guiding principle by setting priorities, providing a crucible to determine if decisions are likely to resolve conflicts by embracing solutions to several problems at once (or to exacerbate them by promoting one objective at the expense of others), gauging if decisions will benefit an entire region, enhancing or impeding partnerships, and producing durable, publicly acceptable remedies (Ostrom 1990; President's Council on Sustainable Development 1996). We now focus on four factors pertinent to discussions of watershed and basin sustainability: (1) physical attributes; (2) ecological resources; (3) economic and social constraints; and (4) institutional and ethical issues. Figure 2.3 depicts how these factors relate to one another (Mederly, Novacek, and Torpercer 2002).

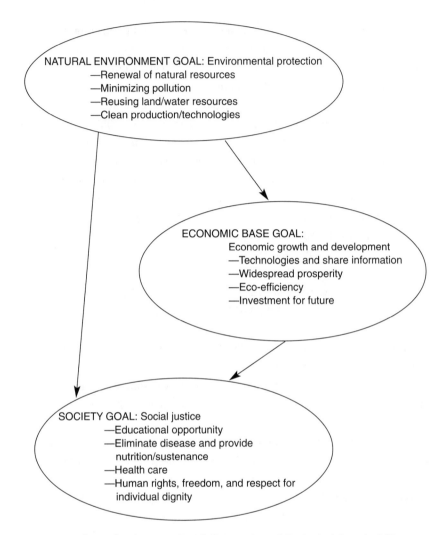

Figure 2.3. Relationship between Social, Economic, and Ecological Sustainability Factors

Embracing Physical Attributes and Constraints

Physical attributes of water pertinent to sustainability include hydrology, ground- and surface water quality, channel morphology, aquifer size and quality, geology and soils, and weather and climate. These attributes constrain carrying capacity and underscore the need for policymakers to identify physical indicators and track how human activities affect them.

Despite their widely varying sizes, hydrological characteristics, meteorological conditions, and surrounding terrain, the initiatives we have reviewed
share a number of problems. Many suffer from point and runoff pollution, depleted fisheries, growing off-stream uses, degraded shorelines and river channels (which affect communities and ecosystems dramatically—as with the
Plata basin), and the likelihood of climate change affecting future water quality and supply.

Perhaps the most profound effect of climate change is to exacerbate other
stressors, including population growth and the diversion of water to agricultural production. From the standpoint of adaptive management, however, climate change is not a policy priority in most initiatives, although the Murray-
Darling basin's recent drought management efforts were partly animated by
concern over whether climate change would exacerbate the problem.

Protecting Ecological Resources

Ecological resources include flora and fauna and the underlying hydrologic
features that sustain them. They are affected by decisions to modify or alter
physical attributes of streams as well as by other practices that increase demand or seek to augment or reallocate water. Such practices result in changes
in surface water quantity, quality, and sediment load, which affect aquatic
plants and animals, riparian vegetation, and terrestrial plants and animals.

Channelization, impoundment, and diversion or draining of wetlands,
streams, or other watercourses affect ecological habitats by changing species
composition, population size, age distribution, and diversity. This affects food
chain dynamics in a region. Significantly, few initiatives, despite widely varying innovations to address water quality and fisheries, have satisfactorily addressed these challenges. In the Columbia basin in the United States, diminishing salmon stocks and deleterious changes to the economy of Native
Americans have been attributed to the construction of major impoundments
in the early twentieth century—as we shall see in chapter 3.

The Rhine and the Danube continue to face dangers to their fisheries, while
industrialization threatens source water protection. In Africa and Latin America, hydropower and navigation projects have taken their toll on water quality
(sedimentation, turbidity) and affect the habitats of aquatic and terrestrial
species. Finally, in Australia, large-scale irrigation projects, together with
growing demands for public supply, generate salinity problems. A common
denominator is the importance of *cumulative* impacts: major basins have un-

dergone engineered changes for navigation, power, and flood control. Further engineering measures exacerbate prior impacts. Dams, canals, and diversion projects in the Plata, Zambezi, and Mekong basins, intended to foster more production of food and fiber and greater economic opportunities for navigation, mining, and industry, impose multiple ecological impacts.

Economic and Social Constraints

Economic issues pertinent to water sustainability include pricing structures, private versus public project funding, and the influence of water quality and supply on economic development. Monetary and nonmonetary values of clean, free-flowing rivers; controversies over how to assess and compare the value of municipal, industrial, and agricultural uses; and the role of market forces on behavior (for instance, how the price of water affects demand) are important considerations in decision-making (Liverman et al. 1988; Verbruggen and Kuik 1991). Finally, willingness to pay for sustainability initiatives, gauged by the acquiescence of polluters and water users to fee-paying innovations (for instance, France), are also controversial.

Our cases show that adequate funding is needed to accomplish an initiative's goals and objectives. Perhaps France's greatest success in this vein is the "user pays" principle incorporated into local project financing. Although the Environment Ministry enjoys exclusive authority over setting national quantity and quality standards, local basin committees set user charges. Likewise, the Murray-Darling has established a system of user charges and taxes to support its agenda. In contrast, the commissions established to protect the Rhine and Danube Rivers have limited fiscal authority, and the ZRBC suffers from inadequate funding—this prevents the mitigation of adverse impacts from poorly thought-out projects and impedes planning studies that might prevent such adverse outcomes from arising in the first place.

Privatization efforts exacerbate problems by shifting the locus of control from basin-scale to local entities that are, in effect, tools of global corporatism. On the other hand, the BECC and IBWC experiences show that it is possible to harness privatization efforts to cross-border infrastructure investment. What has made such reform possible in the U.S.-Mexican case is reform, ratified by NAFTA, that embraces grassroots input; broad community participation; and a public, transparent process of decision-making. While by no means flawless, such a system of decision-making offers the potential to harness private interest to public good.

Social aspects of water pertinent to sustainability include the perceived value of small versus large communities and their access to water, the equity of inter-basin transfers or changes in water use, and how the cultural heritage of a region is affected by changes in water demand, supply, and quality. Other social issues that have a bearing on sustainability include perceptions of water-related activities (for instance, recreation or residential shoreline development) and defining a desired quality of life as well as what constitutes a "natural" landscape (Chang, Hunsaker, and Draves 1992).

Institutional and Ethical Challenges

Institutional issues pertinent to sustainability of water resources include water law and water rights; policies and programs for the management of water resources and associated lands; and the roles, responsibilities, and relative effectiveness of private and public water management institutions. Key institutions include federal, state, local, intergovernmental, semipublic (TVA), and private agencies (for instance, water development districts, cooperatives).

Particular aspects of institutions to be considered in debates about sustainability include the ability of political boundaries to conform to hydrologic and ecological regions, assigned roles and responsibilities of different jurisdictions, and mechanisms for policy coordination, dispute resolution, and evaluation. Discussions about sustainability must inevitably weigh the feasibility of bringing about change within established legal and political institutions as well as the capacity of countries to institute adaptive management changes (for instance, how to heighten consideration of equity and biodiversity in decision-making; see Downing 1984; Biniek 1985).

In developing nations, poverty, a limited pool of shared resources, and weak administrative capacity to manage resources, coupled with the willingness of autocratic leaders to align themselves with elites in exchange for relinquishing control over resources, leads to unsustainable patterns of resource exploitation (see Ascher 1999b). Autocratic governments don't do well in achieving either economic development or social justice because their leaders rely on a small group of powerful elites to sustain power. Not surprisingly, such conditions not only retard development but also contribute to resource depletion and degradation, resistance to environmental innovations, and contempt for policies that protect nature, promote environmental stewardship, and foster social equity (Bueno de Mesquita and Root 2002).

Finally, ethics and institutions are connected—as we discuss in chapter 5.

Institutions governing water arise out of deep-seated values, traditions, and attitudes that emanate from philosophical, behavioral, and even spiritual norms. Adopting alternative values can help avoid adverse environmental and social effects that lead to unsustainable water management. However, achieving transparent policy objectives that are ethical and practical through a political process is always difficult: politics is the pursuit of power to exercise decisions—not a craft well suited to identify justice. And there are no ethical panaceas for achieving sustainability.

"Civil" Society and Resolving Water Conflict

A growing literature suggests that environmental and natural resource issues are increasingly likely to lead to armed conflict and political instability (see, for instance, Gleick 1993; Homer-Dixon 1999). As we have seen, international conflict over the management of shared water resources is clearly a ubiquitous problem. Domestically, water scarcity may contribute to civil unrest by decreasing food production, accelerating migration, and destabilizing political institutions (Dimitrov 2002).

The most common course of action a country takes when faced with *international* dispute over a shared watercourse, however, is peaceable resolution. A number of theories have been offered to explain this. One holds that, regardless of a nation's level of development, when it finds itself in conflict with another country over water it has every incentive to *share* the resource in some equitable manner precisely because no nation has the capacity to capture or control an entire resource by itself, *unless* it is willing to capture large amounts of territory and subjugate vast populations. It is far easier and less expensive to negotiate (Otchet 2001).

Another, taking as its point of departure incentives for cooperation, suggests that by focusing on war, we miss the less visible, but no less damaging, effects of low-intensity conflict. Despite numerous treaties and other instruments for cooperation, the scope and level of discord over water supply often takes the form of unarmed discord. While less violent, this conflict nonetheless leads to adverse consequences to human health and the environment, the food supply, poverty, and development: all important to a nation's welfare. Low-intensity conflicts also have few historical parallels, making them difficult to discern (Yoffe and Ward 1999; Dimitrov 2002).

International efforts to protect water sources and to allocate supplies often fail to achieve much beyond "paper" goals (the signing of treaties) in the face

of unequal political power. If one goal of sustainable water management is social justice across national boundaries, then means must be found to enhance
the capacity of domestic institutions responsible for water management while
strengthening international cooperation. This takes more than allocation tools.
It requires an infrastructure to manage demand, to provide equitable access,
and to empower citizens to voice their interests in order to monitor water problems, to fund local improvements, to build appropriate water works and treatment facilities, and to anticipate threats to water quality and supply. Efforts to
mitigate water conflicts across national boundaries, particularly in the Middle
East and in North America, illustrate this infrastructure's importance (see Morris 1992, 1993; Elmusa 1995; Hassoun 1998; Luterbacher, Schnellenhuber, and
Wiegandt 1998).

One of the most interesting themes to emerge from our global survey is the
effort to redesign water management institutions to be more open, inclusive,
and stakeholder-driven. In different ways, the approaches used by France and
the BECC appear to be effective largely because they both rely on local, grassroots participation by a wide array of stakeholders. The Rhine basin, meanwhile, has made genuine efforts to incorporate the scientific and environmental NGO sector in its constituent countries better. By contrast, the Danube
Declaration, the ZRBC, and the Plata Basin treaty suffer from a calculated "top-
down" decision-making process that generally excludes broad public participation as well as participation by local government agencies with a direct stake
in water resources management—although some reforms in the Danube basin
embrace greater economic discipline and public input. In many regions (for
instance, the Mekong River basin), poverty, underdevelopment, and a continuing tradition of political authoritarianism undoubtedly has had the effect of
retarding broad-scale public participation in basin-wide activities—although
this has been anything but easy to document.

While Australia's Murray-Darling initiative is comprehensive, it is also decentralized and responsive to the concerns and input of many organizations.
The sustainability initiatives it undertakes are notable for the manner in which
they embrace local community sentiment and outreach to farmers. Recent efforts by the Rhine basin authority to incorporate NGOs in developing fisheries
and floodplain management plans are also notable. The experience of these
initiatives lends credence to the claim that failure to overcome suspicion and
cultural differences can be a significant impediment to negotiation and the
achievement of policy change. For example, the Plata basin has long been
hampered by a history of political distrust among signatory nations. Con-

versely, the solidarity of cultural identity in France might well be an attribute that contributes to cooperation among local, regional, and private entities in river basin management. Likewise, the long history of state-to-state negotiations in Australia no doubt has played a part in the ability of the Murray-Darling system to innovate as well as it does.

Antiquated legal systems that encourage profligate water use persist in Mexico, and cultural perceptions toward water-related activities (for instance, navigation or residential shoreline development) play an important role in shaping conflicts in many initiatives—both in developing countries (for instance, the Plata basin) and even in the TVA. Similarly, the continued existence of dual management structures for the Rhine (navigation versus other functions) hampers comprehensive management of the basin.

Finally, the failure to conciliate basin authorities with watersheds may impede success. Those initiatives that are most effective in managing, anticipating, and responding to problems—in France, Australia, and the Rhine basin—conform fairly closely to this ideal. Ensuring that every relevant political jurisdiction and stakeholder can influence an initiative's decisions is more difficult (Rowe et al. 1978; McNeely and Pitt, 1985; Western and Wright 1994). In recent years, scholars have argued that local communities, drawing on *local* knowledge, are in the best position to know exactly what their most critical economic, social, and environmental concerns are—and to address them effectively. This "bioregional" point of view sees communities as united by their natural resources (McGinnis 1995). The one initiative that most nearly approaches this ideal is the Murray-Darling basin's community partnership strategy.

The New Frontier: Democracy as Independent Variable?

Sustainable water management requires engagement of an active, organized, and savvy public opinion sector that is permitted to operate freely. This sector must have a sense of obligation about the proper ends for its operation, and it requires a true civil society to promote a comprehensive and engaged water management system that can achieve the ideal of sustainable management. Such a civil society is a goal of democratic polities. It is characterized by public-spiritedness—a desire to promote the welfare of one's fellow citizens, to sustain the environment, and to embrace the welfare of future generations (Bellah 1996; Mansbridge 1996).

Civil society is difficult to bring about. Recent experiences in the Russian

Federation in environmental reform and water resources management demonstrate the importance of two preconditions.[14] First, the emergence of a genuine civil society requires a capacity among citizens and NGOs to gather environmental information independently and to monitor environmental conditions. Since 1991, there have been some encouraging developments regarding the ability of citizen groups to collect and disseminate information on Lake Baikal and elsewhere. NGOs have been instrumental in defining data-gathering responsibilities and in helping to hasten adoption of information technologies to monitor pollution independently (Dryukker 2001; Zakharov 2001). The Russian government has also been compelled to consult with interested publics in this effort.

The emergence of public participation in bureaucratic decision-making is also important. In Russia, bureaucracies have traditionally resisted public consultation. Since the early 1990s, there is evidence that in Russia, as in many Eastern European states, once guarantees of basic human rights became credible—and the threat of punitive actions against citizens less likely— the legal means for participation arose in the form of public interest law, civil suits, and protests (Mischenko 2001; Haliy 2001). Changes in bureaucratic behavior are necessary for these reforms to occur. In chapter 6, we will see that these challenges are not unique to developing nations. In mature democracies, citizen groups and government agencies struggle with instituting bona fide information-gathering efforts, independent monitoring, and a sense of public-spiritedness that transcends one state or region and extends to larger entities— such as a river basin authority.

CHAPTER 3

Five U.S. River Basin Initiatives

*Case Studies in Search of
Sustainable Development*

The Commission will be the leader in protecting, enhancing, and
developing the water resources of the Delaware River Basin for
present and future generations. In performing this leadership
role, the Commission will serve as a policy-maker, regulator,
planner, manager and mediator on behalf of the Signatories
to the Delaware River Basin Compact and the citizens of the
Basin. . . . We believe in: Serving the public; treating everyone
with fairness and respect; acting in an open, honest and professional manner; listening and responding to our constituents;
encouraging innovative, creative solutions to water management
problems; improving our expertise; enjoying and respecting the
magnificent resource that is the watershed of the Delaware River.

—*Delaware River Basin Commission, "Vision Statement"*

We have squandered a tremendous opportunity. Our children
and their children will say we were complete idiots.

—*Bob Kerr, Georgia's chief negotiator for the ACF compact,
after the failure of another round of negotiations
to agree on an allocation formula, March 18, 2002*

INTRODUCTION: USING CASE STUDIES
TO ANALYZE WATER POLICY

This chapter discusses five U.S. river basin management initiatives. These cases are used to assess various institutional, political, ecological, economic, and ethical conditions that lend themselves to or detract from sustainable water management. Three initiatives are formally chartered river basin commissions (RBCs), the Delaware RBC in Delaware, New Jersey, New York, and Pennsylvania; the Susquehanna RBC in New York, Maryland, and Pennsylvania; and the Apalachicola-Chattahoochee-Flint (ACF) RBC in Alabama, Florida, and Georgia.

The remaining case studies are innovative, one-of-a-kind initiatives established in response to unique regional sustainability problems that, for a variety of reasons, protagonists chose to resolve with unconventional methods and approaches. The first of these is the Northwest Power Planning Council (NPPC), an entity comprised of several agencies and interest groups that oversees the operation and management of the dams of the Columbia River basin. It encompasses the basin states of Idaho, Oregon, and Washington. The second is CALFED, a partnership comprised of several stakeholder groups, California state agencies, and several federal agencies. Its mission is to allocate and manage instream flows and off-stream water withdrawals in the Sacramento River–San Francisco Bay delta region.

While these initiatives are geographically diverse, encompassing river basins in the Northeast, Southeast, Pacific Northwest, and Far West, they are also different in other ways, as we shall see. Despite these differences, however, they exemplify a number of important challenges that must be overcome in order to achieve the sustainable development of managed river basins. These challenges include protecting and improving water quality—especially when faced with numerous sources of nonpoint as well as point source pollution; balancing instream flow to ensure the robust survival of fish and wildlife against off-stream withdrawals needed for public, municipal, industrial, and agricultural uses; allocating water—once a commitment to off-stream withdrawals are made—among divergent uses with varying political and economic clout; and reconciling competing uses of both surface and groundwater sources, which in many instances are shared by several political jurisdictions.

These initiatives also vary in age and, thus, experience. Two of them (the Delaware and Susquehanna RBCs) were established in the early 1960s and were among the first water management initiatives to be based on strong federal-state cooperation in the conjoint management of water supply and water quality issues in single, large interstate river basins.

Because they are older, they are widely thought to have overcome the organizational problems characteristic of attempts to foster interjurisdictional and inter-agency cooperation. These problems remain very much a part of the newer initiatives we will discuss. The newer initiatives (ACF, CALFED, and NPPC) range from one to nearly two decades old and still face major hurdles regarding building trust among stakeholders, developing the capacity to manage water resource problems effectively, and generating confidence among constituents about their ability to resolve major disputes over ecosystem protection, water allocation, and water quality. In the case of the ACF, it might be premature to even label the initiative an operational entity, since the protagonists have not actually agreed, as of yet, on an allocation formula for the three major rivers that fall under the compact's jurisdiction—the Apalachicola, Chattahoochee, and Flint Rivers. Formally, the compact does not take effect until such an allocation agreement is consummated, and—as we shall see— reaching accord over such a formula has been outright contentious.

The next section discusses how primary information from principal protagonists involved in the management and operation of these initiatives was collected. It also provides information about the decision-making framework that we used to analyze the primary and secondary source information collected for the five cases. Following this discussion, the remainder of the chapter is devoted to two subjects: a discussion of the background, history, operation, and achievements and impediments faced by each initiative and a discussion of the results of our interviews with the officials involved in each one. We conclude with a discussion of the significance of our findings for sustainable development and adaptive management. Before proceeding, a word about the use of a case study approach for our investigation.

The principal advantage of case studies is to increase our understanding of why and how decisions are made by generating insights about what the participants involved in such decisions thought about when they engaged in making them. Case studies also help us better understand what protagonists aspire toward—in other words, their goals, objectives, and other motivations for collaborating, negotiating, and agreeing to plans for water resources management. A unique strength offered by the case study approach is that "only when we confront specific facts, the raw material on the basis of which decisions are reached—not general theories or hypotheses—do the limits of public policy become apparent" (Starling 1989; see also 1979) In short, case studies put a human face on environmental decision-making. And if we are to understand the basis for adaptive management of water, we need to understand how institutional, ethical, economic, and scientific constraints and factors influence these decisions on a human level.

To make our analysis of these cases generalizable, we have adopted what is sometimes termed a "grounded theory" approach. This approach discerns general patterns (or principles of behavior common to decisions—as with the motives of decision-makers who collaborate on a common agreement). These patterns are not experimental—instead, they occur within real-world settings where decision-makers and the public relied on local knowledge. Thus, they produce more accurate insights into decision-making than theory or deduction alone (Glaser and Anselm 1967; Goffman 1974; Fischer 1995: 78–79). The use of grounded theory also has three other advantages. First, it helps us identify additional cases—at different geographic or temporal scales—to confirm or disconfirm initial findings. Second, by providing feedback on real-world conditions, it also allows us to rethink initial assumptions, thus providing a foundation for testing theories as well drawing lessons for decision-makers, citizens, and students about the conditions that promote—and inhibit—sustainable development.

Finally, while this approach is limited to a select number of cases that can only be investigated at one moment of time, its major strength lies in the many issues that can be studied in depth. For example, cases permit researchers to reason from analogy, to draw comparisons and render contrasts, and to capture subtle changes in decision-maker perceptions, attitudes, or beliefs over time (Yin 1984; Stone 1988; Babbie 1989: ch. 10). This, we feel, makes the approach we are using an apt tool for understanding adaptive management within the context of the aspiration for sustainable development.

METHODOLOGY: GATHERING INFORMATION
AND MAKING COMPARISONS

River basin initiatives are remarkably prolific generators of self-analyses, descriptions, and chronicles of their accomplishments. Primary documents, both in print form and on the Internet, were a major source of information on the activities of these initiatives. These were supplemented by a host of good secondary scholarly literature, which has described and analyzed specific aspects of these initiatives, ranging from how and why they were formed to the impediments they have encountered. A modest effort was also made to collect primary information on these initiatives independently of their own reports, as discussed below.

We employed a fourfold framework to compare our river basin management cases. This framework consisted of a description of the setting of the case (that is, the geographical, historical, and cultural setting of the case); a documentary account of how and why various stakeholders came together to manage the water resources in question (compared to how it had been previously managed); reported obstacles or impediments encountered in efforts to implement a comprehensive solution to water management problems (and the degree of success achieved in overcoming them); and, finally, documented resources that have been available to the initiative and the extent to which such resources might be applied to other cases.

Primary information was collected via a questionnaire that was mailed to key decision-makers in each initiative. The main purpose of these questionnaires was to acquire information on the interpersonal dynamics characterizing these initiatives—how well do they negotiate disputes? How do they use science in making decisions? Who participates in proceedings, and how do they do so? And, in the view of decision-makers, how well have they overcome the various impediments facing their efforts?

Specific survey questions were intended to elucidate many of the key features articulated in the comparative framework, including (1) the means by which stakeholders come together to formulate decisions, as well as their aspirations when entering into the process; (2) the inclusiveness of stakeholder involvement in these schemes—how many, and what types of stakeholders are involved; (3) how consensus over goals and objectives is achieved; and (4) how strategies are developed to implement goals and objectives.

The questionnaire was mailed to individuals (a minimum of six people per case study) who had been identified as having been among the key participants in a river basin initiative. This judgment was based on the appearance of their names in news media reports, documents generated by their respective initiative, or explicit reference by at least one other participant. These individuals included compact commissioners, former compact commissioners, as well as staff members (for the long-established initiatives) and key negotiators (for the ACF).

Respondents were asked their perceptions about the initial motivation for establishing the initiative; the reasons for its continuation; the processes used to negotiate major decisions, the acquisition of public input and its role in decisions, the use of scientific information in the initiative's undertakings, the influence of various interest groups on decisions, the adequacy of funding and other resources for carrying out the initiative's mandates, the overcoming of obstacles, and the measurement of the success of the initiative. The survey is provided in appendix A.[1]

In all, 14 completed questionnaires plus one partially completed questionnaire were returned. There were five responses from CALFED, four responses from the SRBC, three responses from the DRBC, two responses from the ACF, and one response from the NPPC. Overall survey findings, organized according to this framework, are depicted in table 3.1 below. A detailed discussion of the survey results is found at the end of the chapter.

CASE STUDY DESCRIPTIONS: DELAWARE
AND SUSQUEHANNA EFFORTS

This section provides an overview, based on documentary records and other sources, of all five cases. The overview consists of an examination of each initiative's physical setting, history, negotiations leading to the parties coming together to form an initiative, and discussion of each initiative's achievements—in the view of the major participants. It also includes discussion of the impediments and obstacles to fulfillment of their objectives, also in the view of the major participants.

Delaware River Basin Compact: Physical Setting

The Delaware River basin drains an area of 12,765 square miles. About 50% of the basin lies in Pennsylvania, with smaller portions in New York, New Jersey, Delaware, and Maryland (the latter does not border the river, however, and contributes only eight square miles to the entire watershed). The river begins as two streams, the East and West branches, on the western slopes of the Catskill Mountains in New York State. From the point at which the East and West branches join, the river flows 326 miles to the Atlantic Ocean, acting as a boundary that first divides New York from Pennsylvania, then New Jersey from Pennsylvania, and finally New Jersey from Delaware (Majumdar, Miller, and Sage 1988). On average, the river has a mean annual flow of less than 12,000 ft^3 per second (Durlin and Schaffstall 1997).

The Delaware's largest tributaries are the Schuylkill and Lehigh Rivers. Respectively, the former drains an area of 1,893 mi^2 with an average yearly flow

TABLE 3.1

Major Attributes of Five River Basin Initiatives: Summary of Principal Decision-maker Survey Findings

River Basin Initiative (RBI)	CALFED Bay-Delta Program	Delaware River Basin Commission	Susquehanna River Basin Commission	Northwest Power Planning Council	Apalachicola-Chattahoochee-Flint Compact
Principal members	CA state agencies, U.S. environmental-related agencies	DE, NY, NJ, PA, U.S.	PA, MD, NY, U.S.	WA, OR, MT, ID	AL, FL, GA, U.S.
Driver of stakeholders to come together	Fractious conflict between agricultural and urban users, as well as environmental interests over management options; failure of established water allocation and instream protection programs	Perceived need for comprehensive planning in light of water quality/inter-basin diversion issues; need for a mechanism for the peaceable allocation of water	Irreconcilable interstate water quality concerns; perceived need for a mechanism for the peaceable allocation of water	Federal court decision ordering reexamination of river operations in the region, as well as a congressional mandate to incorporate environmental concerns in river operations	Interstate, multi-user supply/quality conflicts, as well as a desire to avoid litigation; need for a mechanism for the peaceable allocation of water to promote continued economic growth
Negotiation process	Consists of facilitators; public advisory council; various stakeholder meetings among agencies/environmental and user groups; public referenda	Public hearings, larger public meetings, special-interest seminars; long-term basin-wide planning process	Advisory groups and public information meetings	Public meetings	Public meetings and workshops; team building retreats with formal facilitator; continued semi-secret negotiations
Soliciting public input	Public meetings, newsletters, workshops, presentations to schools, groups, stakeholders	Public meetings, newsletter, workshops, presentations to schools, groups, stakeholders	Public meetings, newsletter, workshops, presentations to stakeholders	Public meetings, newsletter, workshops, presentations to schools, groups, stakeholders	Public meetings, newsletter, workshops, presentations to schools, groups, stakeholders
Amount of public input	A great deal; increase over time due to growing public awareness and concerns over impending decisions	Same	Same	Same	Same

Uses of scientific data	Identify problems, set priorities, identify solutions	Same	Same	Same	Same
Proponents	Many groups	Many groups	Many groups	Many groups	Many groups
Opponents	Upstream counties	Industry, power companies, farmers, local government officials, recreational fishermen	Government officials	None	A few special interests
Most influential groups	Agriculture interests, environmental groups	Recreational fishing, power companies, environmentalists, manufacturing	Recreational fishing, power companies, environment groups	Commercial fishing	Municipal governments
Funding sources	State and federal funds, other fees	State and federal funds, user fees	State and federal funds, user fees	State and federal funds	State and federal funds
Adequacy of funding	Mission increases faster than funding	Mission increases faster than funding, recent withdrawal of federal support	Mission increases faster than funding, recent withdrawal of federal support	Mission increases faster than funding	Mission increases faster than funding
Obstacles	History of conflict, divergent stakeholder interests and needs	Parochial view of the states, lack of federal support	State government concerns over sovereignty	High costs of environmental restoration; court challenges to planning efforts	Mistrust of states self-interest
Means of overcoming obstacles	Stakeholder-driven collaborative process	Crisis (flooding, threats of litigation)	Strong leadership, aggressive support, "deft" work	N.A.	N.A.
Degree of success	Somewhat successful	Somewhat/very successful	Somewhat successful	Somewhat unsuccessful/ continuing court challenges	Too soon to evaluate
Factors contributing to success	Willingness to compromise	Political support, staff leadership	Political commitment, wide recognition	Keeping "players" at table	Science developed by comprehensive plan
Assessment of success	Comprehensive monitoring, assessment and research program	Formal progress review through public survey	Commission report, monitoring of conditions	None	None

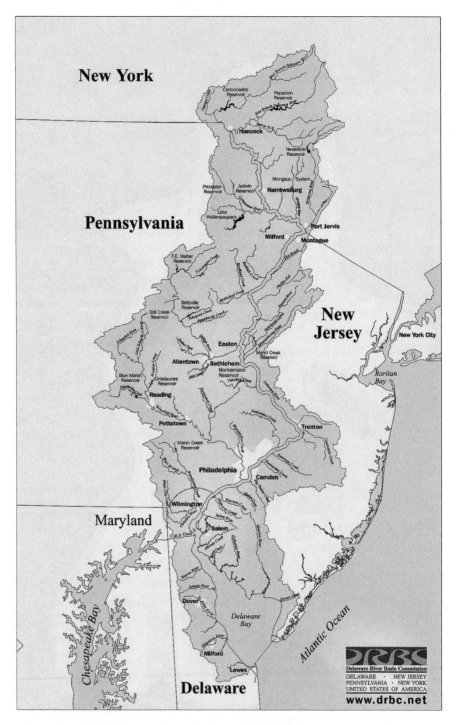

Figure 3.1. Delaware River Basin and Surrounding Region
Map courtesy of Sue Owens, graphic designer, Delaware River Basin Commission.

of about 2,720 ft^3/s, while the latter has a drainage of 1,359 mi^2 with an average yearly flow of about 2,890 ft^3/s. Whereas the Schuylkill drains to the Delaware at Philadelphia, the Lehigh connects to the Delaware at Easton, Pennsylvania. Larger tributaries joining the Delaware River in its upstream reaches include the Mongaup and Neversink Rivers of New York and the Lackawaxen River of Pennsylvania. From the Port Jervis area, the Delaware River flows to Trenton, New Jersey, where Trenton Falls limits the landward penetration of tidal waters. Figure 3.1 depicts the region encompassed by the Delaware River basin, with major towns and streams.

The Delaware and Lehigh Rivers are impounded at various places for water supply, power generation, flood control, flow augmentation, and recreation. Three reservoirs in the upper Delaware River Basin operated by the City of New York divert up to 800 millions of gallons of water a day (Mgal/d), principally for public supply (Parker et al. 1964), while others are used to maintain sufficient flow at Trenton, New Jersey, to control estuary salinity. During the summer, reservoir releases account for over 70% of the upper Delaware's tidal flow. New York City is the major beneficiary of inter-basin water transfers from the Delaware system (Parker et al. 1964).

In the last four decades, the basin has experienced major water quality and water supply problems. Although the basin's population has not increased significantly over the past 20 years, and although average annual precipitation tends to be abundant relative to other areas of the country (42 to 50 inches per year, with the higher figure in the upstream portion of the basin in the Catskills; see Jenner and Lins 1991), suburbanization surrounding Philadelphia, in particular, has imposed growing public water demands. In recent years, periodic drought has exacerbated efforts to provide a dependable public supply to major urban areas.

As regards other uses, power generation accounts for almost 70% of total water use in the basin, while public supply and industrial self-supply each account for 15%. Most of the water is returned to streams and aquifers in the basin, except for about 311 Mgal/d in consumptive uses within the basin and about 900 Mgal/d in out-of-basin diversions to the New York metro area.

Historical Overview: How the DRBC Came To Be

Water pollution problems in the lower Delaware River were documented over 200 years ago. For example, during the 1780s, epidemics of waterborne diseases occurred annually in Philadelphia, causing significant death tolls and even occasionally closing the federal government. Both the Congress and President George Washington fled the periodic epidemics from the nation's second capital city. Around the turn of the last century, low dissolved oxygen concentrations contributed to the decline of fish populations in the Delaware Estuary. With increased manufacturing, pollution problems in the river increased during World War II, resulting in frequent and massive fish kills (Majumdar, Miller, and Sage 1988). With the advent of the Clean Water Act and its amendments (see chapter 4), major improvements in reducing point source pollutant inflow occurred, especially in and around major urban areas in the basin. However, nonpoint pollutants have remained a serious management challenge.

According to the U.S. Geological Survey's National Water Quality Assessment Program (NAWQA), the principal water quality challenges being managed within the basin today are runoff from various nutrients, contaminants, and, of course, sediment generated by construction activities, farming, and other land uses. Moreover, polychlorinated biphenyls (PCBs), including trace elements in surface and ground water, have been found—these are probably legacy wastes from obsolete and discontinued industrial activities. However, other problems stem from more current activities. The presence of some human pathogens and pesticides in waters used for both public supply and recreation, coal mine discharges in portions of the basin, septic systems located on residential or commercial properties, and reduced streamflow caused by groundwater withdrawals all pose serious problems for water quality and the health of ecological communities. The NAWQA report also lists "natural radioactivity in domestic supplies" (radon) as a serious problem as well as "the continuing impact of large impoundments and diversions" (for instance, for providing water supply to New York City) on water quality and fish and benthic (that is, bottom-feeding) invertebrates (Fischer 2002). The same impoundments that affect waterborne species and their health are also supposed to provide storage to furnish water for all the uses chronicled in the previous section.

How the Parties Came Together

In 1936, the Interstate Commission on the Delaware River Basin (INCODEL) was created by the four basin states. INCODEL was only an advisory committee, and it paid primary attention to the cleanup of water pollution—an effort it was never very effective in carrying out, largely because of the difficulty of coordinating pollution control policies among the various states. INCODEL was also unable to prevent or resolve interstate conflicts caused principally by water supply. Such conflicts escalated in the 1920s when New York City announced plans to divert water from the headwaters of the Delaware. This amounted to an inter-basin transfer, because New York City is located in the Hudson River basin.

New York had already polluted the Hudson River to the point that it was no longer a suitable water supply source. New Jersey was concerned that New York's proposed diversion of Delaware River water would compromise its own industrial and agricultural use of the river. Philadelphia, on the other hand, was mostly concerned about the effect that this transfer would have on salinity levels in the portion of the Delaware River on which that city was wholly dependent for its water supply—an example of the difficulty in separating, and trying to manage independently, quality and quantity concerns, as discussed in chapter 1. The U.S. Supreme Court eventually settled the latter dispute. However, all the parties wanted a method for settling future disputes that would be less fraught with uncertainty than resort to the federal judiciary (Derthick 1974). Federal court solutions tend to remove control over water management decisions from the immediate protagonists by imposing rigid policies for water management and allocation.

As a result of investigations, surveys, and studies, it was recommended that an interstate compact with federal participation be created. Officials in the basin recognized that one of the major difficulties they would face would be getting binding federal participation. They also concluded that without such federal participation, a regional organization would be not be able to manage— or reconcile policies regarding—water quality and supply. Indeed, there was considerable resistance on the part of federal representatives to enter into a compact that could tie the hands of the federal government. Seven federal agencies opposed the compact, believing that it might be unconstitutional and involve a conflict of interests for federal agencies. There were also concerns that the federal government would be committed to expenditures decided on by a state-dominated commission. To allay these fears, the states agreed to give Congress the right to amend the compact and to give the president a veto over elements of the comprehensive plan that he believed to be against federal interests.

The Delaware River Basin Compact (DRBC) was approved by the four basin states and ratified by the federal government in 1961. The "Comprehensive Plan" for the basin is the key element of the compact and is "the yardstick against which all water resources programs and projects within the basin are measured" (Grigg 1996). Among the issues addressed by the comprehensive plan are drought, water management, estuary water quality, toxic substances control, groundwater overdraft, and flood losses. The Delaware River Basin Compact's governing commission is composed of the governors of the signatory states (or their appointed "alternatives") and a federal member representing the president (the secretary of the interior).

The commission essentially has a licensing authority over projects with a substantial impact on the basin's water resources. All federal agency activities must be consistent with the comprehensive plan unless the president or his appointed representative specifically finds that consistency is not in the public interest. A river master (an employee of the U.S. Geological Survey) supervises diversions from and releases to the river and makes an annual report to the U.S. Supreme Court—the court of final appeal for state vs. state suits and for determining if the interstate management of resources conforms with, and is not injurious to, federal interests.

Achievements: What the DRBC Has Wrought

The DRBC has broad powers to "acquire, operate and control projects and facilities for the storage and release of waters; for the regulation of flows and supplies of surface and ground waters of the basin; for the protection of public health, stream quality control, economic development, improvement of fisheries, recreation, dilution and abatement of pollution; [and] the prevention of undue salinity and other purposes" (Majumdar, Miller, and Sage 1988). It can also "formulate and adopt a comprehensive plan . . . for the immediate and long-range development and uses of the water resources of [their respective] basin[s] (Cairo 1997; DRBC, P.L. 87–328, 75 Stat 688). These plans include all public and private facilities and projects and carry "legal clout," that is, they bind the actions of commission members and signatory states.

The commission also has the authority to allocate interstate waters in accordance with the doctrine of "equitable apportionment," although it may not allocate water in any way that disturbs or impairs rights awarded to parties under Supreme Court decree without unanimous consent of the parties. In recent years, the DRBC has adopted numerical groundwater withdrawal limits and pumping regulations in areas where water demands outstrip available supply. The DRBC may also prescribe special surface water withdrawal and diversion regulations, declare drought emergencies, and force adoption of conservation strategies. It has even used water budgeting to manage depletive use (Weston 1995, 1999; DRBC 1997).

The DRBC's first real test came in the form of drought, which began in 1961 and lasted until 1966. The commission held a public hearing, declared an emergency, and worked out a temporary formula for diversions and releases, drawing on its powers over water resources throughout the basin and its links to other public organizations. The one success gained through this experience was in meeting its primary aim of settling water allocation disputes through an administrative process, without the use of litigation between the basin states.

Another early achievement of the DRBC was the improvement of dissolved oxygen levels in the Delaware Estuary through the issuance of wasteload allocations to approximately 90 dischargers in 1968. The commission set a national precedent in establishing water quality standards for the Delaware Estuary and adopting regulations to implement those standards through the wasteload allocation process. Subsequent water quality improvements led to the revival of shad fisheries on the nontidal Delaware River. More significantly, these standards and the policy for meeting them were issued shortly after Congress passed the Federal Water Pollution Control Act of 1965. This legislation empowered states to set water quality regulations for dischargers seven years before the more ambitious Clean Water Act. Problematically, as we shall see, while the DRBC was trying to be proactive in issuing these standards, its authority to enforce them was soon called into question.

Dissolved oxygen increases were also accompanied by decreases in fecal coliform, rendering the river safer and more attractive for recreation. The DRBC began publishing Delaware River recreation maps in 1966 and helped draft the enabling federal legislation that led to the inclusion of 107 miles of the river in the National Wild and Scenic Rivers System in 1978.

As early as 1973, the DRBC required metering customer connections for new, major water supply systems, launching a water conservation campaign that years later became fashionable with other agencies. To manage drought better, in 1985 the commission began construction of Merrill Creek Reservoir, designed to provide make-up water for riverbank electric generating plants during low-flow conditions on the Delaware. Having no resources of its own to build such an impoundment, the commission directed in-basin electrical utilities to build the $217 million impoundment or face cutbacks during droughts.

The DRBC undertook extensive floodplain mapping, adopted regulations restricting development in the 100-year floodplain, and prohibited development in the floodway. It also launched programs to develop ways to control the discharge of toxic substances to the river. One observer intimately familiar with both the DRBC and its sibling, the Susquehanna River Basin Commission (SRBC), states that one key to success is that the "parties in a basin need to recognize common problems" (Weston 1999). Further, such bodies must be willing to settle subsequent disputes surrounding the management of regional waters through negotiation and alternative means of dispute resolution rather than through litigation or Supreme Court petition.

DRBC disputes tended to be resolved, especially in its early years, through intensive, face-to-face negotiations on a regular basis (facilitated by getting signatories together several times a year); careful coordination among technical staffs who remained politically neutral; the sharing of study findings among partners; and a willingness to sacrifice institutional independence when necessary. In addition, the DRBC and the SRBC, as early prototypes of commissions, were given the power to implement, as well as to make, decisions (Weston 1984).

Obstacles and Constraints to Sustainable Development

Most commentators seem to agree that the DRBC has not met its full potential. For projects such as reservoirs that were planned, financed, and built after 1961 by federal and state agencies and utilities, the DRBC's role has been limited mostly to oversight—not actual management. The latter authority continues to reside in the federal agencies, including the Army Corps of Engineers. Furthermore, the headlong expansion of federal activity in the field of water pollution control beginning in the 1970s brought the commission into conflict with other agencies and left it struggling to protect its newly asserted claim to river basin management.

For example, the Federal Water Pollution Control Act of 1965 required states to set standards for interstate rivers, and the Federal Water Pollution Control Agency (FWPCA), a forerunner of the EPA, was given the authority to approve those standards. The FWPCA delayed action on the DRBC's proposed standards for the entire Delaware River—discussed in the previous section— and instead treated the states' individual submissions of proposed standards as legitimate. The FWPCA eventually approved the commission's standards as well as those proposed by the states, choosing the higher standard in cases of discrepancy. However, the DRBC's unique role in allocating the river's assimilative capacity among waste dischargers and administering pollution control programs was threatened by the Corps of Engineers, which began requiring discharge permits under the Rivers and Harbors Act of 1899, and by the Environmental Protection Agency, which was eventually charged with enforcing the Water Pollution Control Act Amendments of 1972—better known as the Clean Water Act.

The lack of federal commitment to the organization and the apparent tendency of some federal agencies to ignore the DRBC has been offered as primary reasons why the commission has failed to exercise the sweeping authority granted to it by the 1961 compact. It is said that even the individual states composing the compact rarely launch initiatives of any kind through the commission. Instead, initiatives typically originate with the staff, which must cajole the states into cooperation (Derthick 1974). Erosion of state support for the DRBC is evident in the gradual shift from attendance by the governors or cabinet-level alternatives at commission meetings to attendance by lower-level political appointees and agency staff designates.

Since FY1997, the DRBC and all other federal interstate compacts have functioned without federal appropriations as a result of congressional adoption of the recommendations of a report by the Heritage Foundation—a Washington-based policy institute that recommended that Congress "defund" certain programs and activities whose benefits were viewed as more regional than national in their scope (DRBC 1997).[2] Fortunately, because the value of the DRBC and the SRBC is deemed sufficiently high within their operating regions, both have been able to sustain themselves despite the absence of federal appropriations. Moreover, Congress did not vote to remove the federal government from the compacts.

Although the commission could have been used to influence growth and economic development in the region, it has been constrained to a more limited water management role. Clearly, the DRBC has so far been successful in settling interstate disputes over water allocation, the initial purpose for which the member states came together to form a compact. The most significant policy challenge facing the DRBC in recent years has been managing the serious droughts that have struck the region, most recently in 2001–2002. How the DRBC has intervened to address this issue exhibits both its strengths in promoting coordinative action among member states and its weakness—specifically its limited authority in achieving a comprehensive and coordinated policy vision for water management in the basin.

In late 2001, the DRBC passed a resolution designed to "preserve and protect water supplies in the . . . basin" by declaring a drought emergency. This basin-wide emergency declaration followed actions by New Jersey, New York, and Pennsylvania declaring drought warnings in their respective basin counties—and it followed a period of protracted low rainfall and high demand. While these initial warnings called for voluntary user cutbacks, however, the DRBC used its authority to require allocation of impounded water in reservoirs that were privately owned by electric power companies (Wallenpaupack Dam and Mongaup reservoir, located in Wayne and Sullivan Counties in northeastern Pennsylvania) in order to support instream flow needs as monitored in Montague, New Jersey (Delaware River Basin Compact Commission 2001). In effect, this added level of protection went beyond limited state powers to urge voluntary conservation.

Nevertheless, as an acknowledgment that the DRBC shares power with other federal entities, the drought declaration also noted the commission's policy to operate these and other reservoirs for optimal power production on a seasonal basis as well as to furnish instream flow protection. The declaration followed this acknowledgment with a *request* to the Army Corps of Engineers to retain storage in one of its projects (Walter Reservoir) and "provide releases of water upon the [Commission's] request . . . [to] maintain the Trenton flow objective," that is, instream flow protection. It also urged Pennsylvania to provide releases of water from the Nockamixon Reservoir "upon the request of the Commission" in accord with priority uses. Finally, in an action that confirms how its regulatory powers over water use are shared with member states, it required self-supplied users of ground and surface waters using 1 MGD or more to prepare contingency plans for water curtailment or reduction—if requested by a signatory state. Voluntary conservation by residents was also urged (Delaware River Basin Compact Commission 2001).

The significance of this declaration for drought policy in particular—and adaptive management more generally—is threefold. First, the DRBC has in place protocols for calling into action an array of administrative and management machinery to respond to region-wide emergencies. What is particularly important about the drought declaration of 2001, for example, is that it was partially triggered by a prearranged guideline—the storage requirements of New York City's Delaware River basin reservoirs prompted drought operations in accordance with DRBC guidance—an automatic and, in effect, routinized provision.

Second, it remains unclear what factors brought about the declaration that the drought emergency were at an end in 2002. Was the decision based on the occurrence of more precipitation; on additional supplies acquired through the

DRBC's regulatory policies and encouragement; both; or some other reason? This is an important issue because it is central to evaluating both external conditions and the effectiveness of internal decision-making. In fact, however, drought is probably one of the toughest challenges to assess in this way.

Finally, as an entity that shares authority for water management with an array of public as well as private entities, the DRBC can only act in areas in which it is able to forge a clear consensus—or in which it has been given jurisdictional power before the fact. These constraints on action need not necessarily be viewed as drawbacks: after all, DRBC members have historically followed commission recommendations regarding these and other water management issues, and the very commission officials who issue such recommendations—whether authoritatively binding or not—serve as members of the same agencies who compose the commission. In effect, this "dual role" strengthens the legitimacy of the commission's decisions at the very same time it underscores the commission's contingent authority. In effect, why would a Corps of Engineers official recommend that the agency operate a water project in a way that he or she knew would contradict the needs of the basin states comprising the compact? Shared authority is not necessarily weak authority—it is merely decentralized, dispersed, and collective.

Some suggest that the DRBC's best chance for future success is in promoting regional solutions to local pollution problems, such as the consolidation of waste treatment plants, the coordination of various federal projects in the Delaware River basin, and the coordination and integration of reservoir and groundwater withdrawal policies. Certainly, these are admirable objectives. While far from perfect, the commission's recent drought management policies illustrate that such aspirations are not impossible to achieve. It would be difficult to describe the commission as a full-blown model for integrated sustainable development of the Delaware River basin. However, if the political will for such integrated development and management were ever to arise, it is clear that the DRBC has the infrastructure in place to provide a sound foundation for such an effort.

Susquehanna River Basin Compact: Physical Setting

The Susquehanna River is the sixteenth-largest river in America and the largest river situated entirely in the United States that flows into the Atlantic Ocean. The river drains some 27,500 mi^2 of New York, Pennsylvania, and Maryland—about 76 percent of the basin lies within the state of Pennsylva-

Figure 3.2. Susquehanna River Basin and Surrounding Region
Map courtesy of Jeff Zimmerman Jr., GIS specialist, Susquehanna River Basin
Commission.

nia, with 23 percent in New York, and about 1 percent in Maryland. The 444-mile-long river discharges to the Chesapeake Bay, contributing half of the freshwater flow to the nation's largest estuary. The Susquehanna is also the subject of the nation's second federal-interstate river basin compact—one that confers regulatory authority over management of water allocation and quality. Patterned after the Delaware River Basin Compact, the Susquehanna River Basin Compact (SRBC) remains one of the few river basin compacts crafted in the 1960s that was not abolished or otherwise sharply deemphasized in the 1980s. Figure 3.2 depicts the region encompassed by the Susquehanna River Basin Commission.

The Susquehanna's first impoundments were built near Binghamton, New York, not far from the river's headwaters. Smaller milldams built on the river's tributaries were erected in the early to mid-1700s. Major impoundments since constructed were intended to assure dependable water supply for public, industrial, and other uses and to provide flood control, hydroelectric power, and instream flow. Historically, a major problem caused by these larger dams was the disruption of fish migration hundreds of miles from Chesapeake Bay. Prior to their construction, American and hickory shad, river herring, eels, alewife, and other anadromous species were able to complete their reproduction and life cycles in upstream portions of the Susquehanna, West Branch, and Juniata Rivers unobstructed. Such species were an important food source for Native Americans and, later, white settlers who learned their fishing skills from these same tribal nations in the 1700s (Pennsylvania Fish and Boat Commission 1997).

Efforts to restore these anadromous species, especially the shad, have constituted a major policy component of the SRBC since its establishment in the early 1960s. The engineering and scientific methods used to restore fish runs, including construction of fish passages, restocking, and other techniques, were actually introduced—but on a smaller scale—in the 1950s. Many of these early efforts concentrated on facilitating migration of shad upstream of one of the Susquehanna's largest impoundments—and the greatest single impediment to fish migration—the Conowingo Dam. We will examine these efforts in due course.

Other water quality and ecological problems facing the Susquehanna revolve around excess nitrogen and phosphorous from farming runoff, a problem particularly affecting Chesapeake Bay that originates in a handful of counties, principally in south central Pennsylvania. Sediment and siltation are also problems in the basin—and typically originate with farming as well as construction. These phenomena destroy fish spawning areas and affect fish species in other adverse ways. Spurred on by the cooperative framework of the SRBC, two of the three compact states, Maryland and Pennsylvania—together with the District of Columbia, Virginia, the EPA, and the Chesapeake Bay Commission—consummated a partnership, the Chesapeake Bay Agreement, committed to contributing to fisheries restoration efforts, including removing stream blockages, and most importantly, reducing nitrogen and phosphorous in the bay by 40% by the early twenty-first century (Pennsylvania Fish and Boat Commission 1997: 15). The principal methods that are being employed in this effort are promoting and cost-sharing so-called Best Management Practices (BMPs) among farmers in the basin. These practices include timing fertilizer application, employing runoff controls, and managing and properly disposing animal wastes (see chapter 4).

Historical Overview: Evolution of the SRBC

Water quality concerns, more than conflicts over consumptive withdrawals, motivated the formation of the SRBC. William Voight, a key player in the creation of the SRBC, wrote a detailed account of events leading up to the compact's drafting and a chronicle of the process through which it was signed into law by the three states and the federal government. Voight assessed water quality in the basin circa 1970 and concluded that it was grossly degraded in places, overdrawn in others, and haphazardly managed but even so "not yet fully overworked or progressively maltreated." He concluded that this relatively fortuitous condition was not likely to continue indefinitely and that pressures were more likely to increase rather than to decrease over time. In effect, his report—which contributed to the formation of SRBC—suggests that its creation at least partly resulted from foresight and a desire to take preemptive action to protect water quality.

It was Voight's contention that water quality problems in the Susquehanna River basin began, and were perhaps most pronounced in, its headwaters in the upper portions of West Branch in the Lackawanna and Wyoming valleys. According to Voight, pollution sources included domestic and industrial wastewater discharges: most especially acid drainage from coalmines. Coal mining began in those valleys in the 1830s, but laws did not prohibit acidic discharges from active mines until 1965. Regulation of active mining operations did not address legacy wastes—ongoing discharges from old, abandoned mines. Numerous subsurface seeps, including the 20,000 gallon-per-minute Duryea Gravity Outfall that began as a blowout on the Lackawanna in 1961 and continued to discharge vast amounts of acidic, metal-laden water to tributaries of the Susquehanna River. Voight stated that pollution from coalmine drainage was without question the largest and most difficult task facing water quality managers in the basin.

Pollution from inadequate municipal wastewater discharge treatment, especially in New York and Pennsylvania, was compounded by agricultural inputs of manure, pesticides, fertilizers, and silt, especially in the Pennsylvania portion of the basin. However, Voight concluded that there was still much in the way of water quality to conserve, develop, and protect against future unwise exploitation. In the midst of debate over these concerns, other issues— and actors—also intruded. In 1949, Congressman Daniel J. Flood, whose district represented the Wyoming Valley, first proposed a "Susquehanna Valley Authority" for the purpose of developing levees and other flood control projects. These projects would not only reduce property damage, they would also promote soil conservation and economic development (Stranahan 1993: 282).

Although water quality was the most obvious water resource concern in the Susquehanna basin, water shortages were also being experienced in the mid-1960s as a result of the same mid- 1960s drought that affected the Delaware basin. Water supply reservoirs for Scranton, Pennsylvania, were nearly dry in 1966. In that same year, tank trucks had to haul water 11 miles from the Susquehanna River to York, Pennsylvania, for rationed use by its residents. At that time there was already controversy between the city of Lancaster, Pennsylvania, and upstream farmers over use of the available water. As in most other agricultural areas, withdrawals for crop irrigation tended to coincide with seasonal low flows in the Susquehanna and its tributaries.

Several inter-basin diversions for public use were already in place by the late 1960s, and more were anticipated. For example, the New York metropolitan area was looking speculatively toward the upper Susquehanna River as a likely supplemental water source. Northern and central New Jersey, Philadelphia, Baltimore, Greater Washington, D.C., and Wilmington, Delaware, were among the rapidly growing metropolitan areas that were expected to vie for the Susquehanna's "surplus" water. Flood control, hydroelectric power generation, and recreational use of the Susquehanna's waters were additional issues that were being addressed by "duplicating, overlapping, uncoordinated, and in some cases conflicting jurisdiction and administration of a large number of federal, state, and local agencies" (Voight 1972).

How the Parties Came Together

As of 1960, conflicts generated by water quality and availability were less urgent in the Susquehanna basin than in the Delaware basin. Nevertheless, a few visionaries recognized an opportunity to follow the Delaware River Basin Commission's lead to coordinate planning and programming of water resources activities for the benefit of an entire region. Fred Zimmerman, a professor of political science at Hunter College in New York City and an expert on federal-interstate compacts, had been closely involved in the development of the interstate agreement for the Delaware River basin. Zimmerman first broached the subject of a federal-interstate compact for the Susquehanna River basin with Pennsylvania Congressman Harris G. Breth in early 1961.

Coincidentally, the Corps of Engineers had been directed to conduct a survey of the basin's water and related land resources. A "vigorous temporary instrumentality of the three basin states," the Interstate Advisory Committee on the Susquehanna River Basin (IAC), was soon organized with the basin states' governors' approval (Voight 1972). The purpose of the IAC was to oversee the drafting of the Susquehanna River Basin Compact, to facilitate the approval of the compact by the three states, and to ensure that it was signed into law. The IAC consisted of four members from each state and was jointly funded by the three states. Maurice Goddard, secretary of the Pennsylvania Department of Forests and Waters, was chosen permanent chairman. William Voight Jr., who had served as executive director of the Isaac Walton League of America and later headed the Pennsylvania Fish Commission, was made executive director.

The SRBC was patterned closely after the DRBC. Like its predecessor, the SRBC created an interstate river basin commission with strong decision-making and enforcement authority. However, there are significant differences in the scope of the commissions' authority and role in the management of water resources in their respective basins. The Delaware River Basin Commission sets water quality standards and allocations. It is also the permitting authority that must approve any project that potentially affects water quality or quantity in the river system. Conversely, existing state agencies in the Susquehanna basin establish their own water quality standards and maintain permitting authority, with the Susquehanna River Basin Commission having authority *only* over those projects that have interstate ramifications. The Susquehanna commission operates more as a coordinating body among the three states rather than a supervisory one.

New York's governor, Nelson Rockefeller, was in favor of the SRBC, and the New York legislature approved the compact in 1967 with little public attention or fanfare. Likewise, there was little opposition to the compact in Maryland, with the exception of concerns on the part of the City of Baltimore regarding its water supply intakes on the Susquehanna. For the most part, Maryland had more to gain than to lose from the compact, since the state contains only 1% percent of the regulated watershed. However, the state has an enormous stake in the health of the Chesapeake Bay, into which the Susquehanna discharges. The main sources of resistance to the compact were the Pennsylvania Farmers Association and certain representatives of the federal government. Then, as now, agricultural interests opposed anything that might place restrictions on their operations, including water use. The federal agency concerns had more to do with the appearance of an interstate compact abrogating the authority of the federal government—an issue comparable to one that first arose in the Delaware basin.

Pennsylvania was the last state to approve the compact, which was signed by Governor William Shafer in July 1968. There was considerable debate and negotiation over compact language, especially with regard to preserving federal rights and prerogatives, before Congress finally approved the compact in late 1970. Goddard, Voight, and a few others met with James Watt, assistant secretary for energy and water power and future secretary of the interior, and convinced him to not oppose the compact. President Nixon quietly signed the compact into law at Camp David on Christmas Eve of 1970. With little or no national publicity, the three states and the federal government thus became bound for a minimum of 100 years to the task of "planning, conservation, utilization, development, management, and control of the water resources of the Susquehanna River basin."

Some have credited the successful passage of the SRBC through the political maze to the leadership of Maurice Goddard and the confidence that he instilled in many U.S. senators and other political leaders. It has also been suggested by some of the participants in the creation of the SRBC that a change in the political climate shortly after the passage of the SRBC (for instance, growing opposition to ceding states' rights to a compact situation) made it more difficult for other compacts to be readily approved.

Voight provides a detailed account of the process used to overcome opposition to the compact. In effect, the IAC used sophisticated public information techniques and overt political maneuvering to sell the compact to the public, the Pennsylvania legislature, and Congress. The IAC recognized that several "publics" had to be enlisted, including elected officials, heads and certain personnel of state agencies with an interest in water resources, planners and local government officials, the news media, interested organizations and societies of various kinds, several segments of official Washington, and the lay public. Numerous public information meetings were held throughout the basin, especially in Pennsylvania (Voight 1972). The IAC produced several films that were distributed free of charge to various groups, including schools, to inform and gain the support of thousands of adults and students. News releases, speeches, magazine articles, and interviews were carefully prepared and timed to weaken the opposition's misinformation campaign. Tens of thousands of simple informational folders were printed and distributed by mail and at various announcement luncheons that were held for top media executives in strategic communities. Unlike the DRBC, the process of generating direct public support for the SRBC resembled that of a major election campaign or political referendum.

Achievements: What the SRBC Has Accomplished

How successful has the SRBC been in managing the basin's water resources? The answer to that question depends on the criteria to measure success. Development pressure on the Susquehanna River basin has not yet been as intense as in many other parts of the eastern United States, primarily due to constraints of topography and hydrology. Much of the basin is hilly or mountainous, and large stretches of the river are not navigable, so heavy industry and many other types of development that depend on commercial navigation or that would entail large withdrawals of water have bypassed the Susquehanna River basin. As a result, neither allocation nor water quality problems have increased much since the inception of the SRBC, so the ultimate ability of the commission to address user conflicts remains untested.

One observer of the SRBC's evolution over its first 21 years has observed that states used to send cabinet level members to the commission and that they "actually talked through some higher environmental policy issues" and jointly made decisions that would be carried out. He expressed concern that the commission has been reduced to a more "technical, technocrat level" in recent years, and he considered this to be a major step backward from the capabilities of the commission as originally envisioned (private survey response). Others suggest that the commission has done such a good job of facilitating cooperation that it is virtually invisible—as long as there is no controversy.

Others who have been involved in, or been observers to, the operation of the commission have expressed disappointment over the creation of "supplemental organizations" charged with promoting improvements to water quality through partnership and voluntary efforts such as the Chesapeake Bay Program. In their opinion, the SRBC could serve the same purpose these organizations are established to promote. This creation of supplemental entities has been blamed on the failure of the commissioners to sell the SRBC aggressively as the most appropriate vehicle for such initiatives. As one observer has put it, "High-minded goals also were reluctantly discarded, including . . .

preservation of the Susquehanna's natural beauty on an equal footing with development." (Stranahan 1993: 284).

In assessing accomplishments of the SRBC, two efforts should be considered. The first is the commission's ability to control water allocation, and the second is the efforts to restore shad species in the basin. Both should be focal points for measuring success. We will discuss the first of these in the next section, under constraints to sustainable development. The second is an issue for which the SRBC's management has become well known.

Efforts to restore shad and other fish have a long heritage in the basin. An agreement signed by SRBC members in 1977 to restore shad entailed restocking the river with shad eggs and developing a fish-trapping facility at Conowingo Dam, a major impoundment impeding upstream migration. The goals of this shad restoration plan were to reopen the river to natural migration and restore annual spawning populations of 2 million shad and 10 million herring within 25 years of fish passage development. The program has been a model of persistence, cooperation, and long-term commitment among resource agencies and private utilities, all of whom share the goal of restoring migratory fish runs (Pennsylvania Fish and Boat Commission 1997: 5).

The approach taken has been multifaceted and has involved a variety of structural and nonstructural measures, including restocking above blockages, constructing fish passage facilities, improving degraded habitat, and regulating the harvest of adult fish. In recent years, the emphasis has changed to providing greater and more efficient fish passage. Once a source of blockage is identified, the Pennsylvania Fish and Boat Commission works with the owner of the impoundment to determine the best and most cost-effective solution to providing fish passage, while the Chesapeake Bay Program provides matching funds on a 1:1 basis with nonfederal dollars spent on migratory fish restoration. The shad restoration program is popular with the general public, enjoys the consensus of several agencies, and is practical. On the down side, it does not really represent a change in instream flow policy as much as a series of engineering and ecological adjustments to the presence of dams.

Obstacles and Constraints to Sustainable Development

During the 1992 public forum on the first 21 years of the SRBC, Maurice Goddard asserted that the commission's effectiveness had been compromised by an erosion of state governments' commitment, due in part to the trend away from having cabinet-level individuals serve as commissioners. He emphasized the importance of direct communication between the commissioners and their respective governors to ensure that commitments, especially financial commitments, on the part of commissioners are honored by the states.

Perhaps the need for a stronger role for the Susquehanna River Basin Commission was thwarted, in part, by the passage of the federal Clean Water Act, the development of national water quality standards, the creation of the EPA, and the resultant maturation and consolidation of regulatory agencies and standards within each of the signatory states. The commission's recent activities include such projects as development of a flood forecasting system, negotiations with the City of Baltimore regarding plans to increase its withdrawals from the Conawingo Pool, review of numerous requests for out-of-basin diversions and groundwater withdrawals for consumptive uses such as bottling and irrigation, water quality and stream flow monitoring, and several technical reports and publications of general interest.

The issue of out-of-basin diversion is an important one for several reasons— not the least of which is that water transferred from one basin to another raises profound questions about equity and fairness. Historically, such diversions tend to generate concerns over low-flow management issues, ecological sustainability, and foregone economic development opportunities. The SRBC has considerable powers to regulate diversions—powers granted in 1978 in part due to concerns over future growth in the basin. The SRBC discourages interbasin transfers of water.

Before any diversion project is approved, the project sponsor must demonstrate to the commission "through clear and convincing evidence" that every effort has been made to avoid the need for the diversion through development and conservation of water resources in the basin for which the request for diversion is being made. Water conservation standards must be adhered to if the diversion request is granted, and the commission may consider a variety of environmental effects, the timing of diversions as well as of return flows to the Susquehanna basin, and economic effects (SRBC 1998). Most importantly, decisions to divert must be granted by the SRBC; common law principles historically used to guide diversion decisions—that diversions are de facto "unreasonable" and that basins of origin must be protected—must be followed.

From the standpoint of adaptive management, this policy is significant for three reasons. First, it emphasizes a "look before you leap" philosophy—efforts to discourage actions that may impose irreversible impacts, whether environmental or societal, should be made whenever practicable. Second, good science should guide decisions—and proponents of diversions are obliged to show why no adverse impacts will result. And finally, the policy seeks to protect future uses by giving priority to "reasonably foreseeable needs" of all off-stream users as well as instream demands (SRBC 1998). Clearly, while the SRBC's record of achievement is mixed, its inter-basin diversion policy, coupled with its efforts to restore shad and other fisheries, reveals a strong corporate aspiration of the commission to adhere to sustainability ideals and to utilize adaptive management principles.

THE APALACHICOLA-CHATTAHOOCHEE-FLINT BASIN: ACHIEVING THE COMPACT IDEAL IN THE SOUTH

The Apalachicola-Chattahoochee-Flint River Basin: Physical Setting

The Apalachicola-Chattahoochee-Flint (ACF) River Basin Compact—and its sibling, the Alabama-Coosa-Tallapoosa (ACT) Compact—are the newest interstate river basin compacts in the United States. The ACF's emergence probably best illustrates the growing complexity of user conflicts that have arisen in fast-growing regions, such as the American South, which have not traditionally worried about water supply. The controversy surrounding the ACF constitutes one of the region's first interstate water disputes of any magnitude.[3]

Some observers contend that the dispute, like the one that has erupted in the nearby Alabama-Coosa-Tallapoosa basins serving Alabama and Georgia, represent a turning point in the region's environmental history. This is so because the dispute revolves around satisfying growing demands for water in the region's largest city, Atlanta, while at the same time balancing off-stream demands of other users against instream needs to support fisheries and minimum flows for water quality (Hull 2000). While the basin is rapidly urbanizing, farming and the rural communities that depend upon farming remain important parts of the region's economy. Figure 3.3 depicts the region encompassed by the Apalachicola-Chattahoochee-Flint Compact.

The ACF system begins as a spring seeping out of the side of a mountain at Brasstown Bald in northern Georgia. A first-order stream at that point, it gathers tributaries and eventually becomes the Chattahoochee River. The Chattahoochee and Flint Rivers meet at the Georgia-Florida state line to form the Apalachicola River, which snakes across the Florida panhandle to the Gulf of Mexico. The uppermost impoundment on the Chattahoochee is Lake Lanier, a 38,500-acre reservoir north of Atlanta. After the construction of the Buford

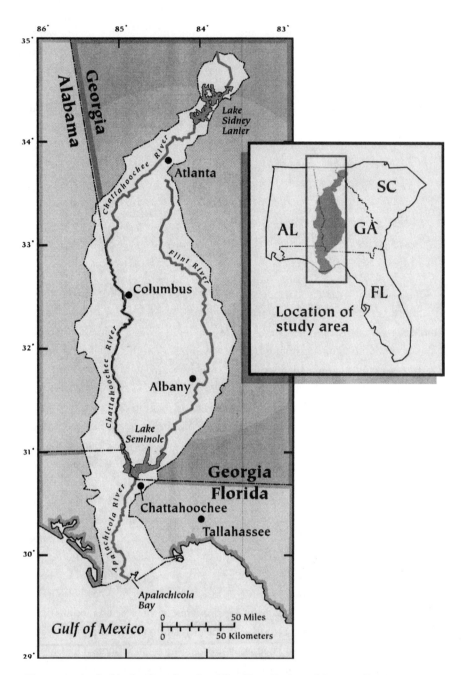

Figure 3.3. Apalachicola-Chattahoochee-Flint River Basin and Surrounding Region
Source: Lipford (2004)

Dam to form Lake Lanier in the mid-1950s, 12 additional reservoirs were developed along the river, making the Chattahoochee one of the most impounded waterways in the nation. The system has a total of 16 projects, five of which were built by the U.S. Army Corps of Engineers.

The Flint River begins just south of Atlanta's Hartsfield International Airport, traverses some of the most fertile cropland in Georgia, and then enters the Chattahoochee at Lake Seminole near Columbus, Georgia. It is at this point that the system becomes the Apalachicola River, which discharges into the Gulf of Mexico at Apalachicola Bay in the Florida panhandle, and thence to the Gulf. The entire ACF is operated by the Corps of Engineers, primarily for flood control, navigation, and power generation. The river's flow is also exploited for domestic and industrial water supply, hydroelectric power generation, assimilation of wastewater discharges, and irrigation of crops (Wangsness 1997).

The series of impoundments, channelization efforts, and other developments on the river system have generated numerous environmental effects— some of which, over time, have proven to be irreversible. Gulf and lake sturgeon used to inhabit the Chattahoochee-Flint and Coosa River systems, respectively. The former can no longer migrate into the Chattahoochee-Flint system due to the Woodruff Dam on the Florida-Georgia border. Likewise, American eels are no longer found upstream of dams on the Chattahoochee (Cowie et al. 2002: 10).

The ACF basin drains approximately 19,800 square miles of western Georgia, northern Florida, and eastern Alabama. An estimated 2.6 million people depend on the ACF for their water needs, 75% of whom live in and around the metropolitan Atlanta area, with most of that need satisfied by the Chattahoochee. Moreover, the ACF provides critical freshwater flows to Apalachicola Bay, an estuary system that provides a significant amount of the nation's seafood, including almost 90% of that consumed by Florida's and 13% of the nation's commercial oyster fisheries. The harvest is extremely sensitive to both water quality and instream flow.

While metro Atlanta's growth has had a profound effect on water quality and water supply in the basin, agriculture also remains important to the region's economy and way of life. Numerous livestock and poultry farms dot the upper and middle portions of the Chattahoochee and Flint River basins, while the southern portions of both basins are used for row crops and vegetables. In addition to being economically important, these agricultural activities also affect water quality throughout the region—all the way to the Gulf (Wangsness 1997).

Without adequate amounts of freshwater correctly timed to coincide with certain life stages of estuarine organisms, the nation's supply of oysters, crabs, and shrimp would suffer, along with the region's economy. The diversity and intensity of the uses of the ACF may make it the most important Southern watershed after the Mississippi River (Hull 2000: 2). Longstanding water quality problems in the basin include sediments, heavy metals, and pesticides and organic chemical runoff from farms (especially row crops and concentrated animal feeding operations like poultry farms) and cities (see Frick et al. 1998). In short, the ACF system serves many users and supports considerable off-stream demands.

Historical Overview: The Making of a Southern Water Dispute

Conflicts over water rights in the basin involving Georgia, Florida, and Alabama began in the late 1800s. Many of these conflicts revolved around local disputes over water for agriculture or public use and, in a few instances, navigation rights. As early as the 1960s, people in west and southwest Georgia, southeast Alabama, and northwest Florida began to worry about Atlanta's population growth, economic development, and ever-increasing water withdrawals from the Chattahoochee. Metro Atlanta currently draws more than 400 million gallons of water per day from the river and discharges into it more than 300 million gallons of wastewater each day.

The pollution of downstream river reaches from metro Atlanta's wastewater load is aggravated by urban runoff laden with silt, petroleum products, heavy metals, pathogens, and toxic chemicals as well as by passes of untreated sewage during rainstorms. This renders the remaining flow less usable for downstream communities as a source of domestic and industrial water supply and as a receiving stream for *their* waste. This is an unusual situation in that sensitive watersheds rarely bear the pollution from a metro area the size of Atlanta at their headwaters. As one commentator has stated it, "The Chattahoochee . . . is the smallest river basin providing the most water supplies for any metropolitan area in the U.S." (Hull 2000: 2). Most major American cities, such as Boston, New Orleans, or New York, are located at or near the mouths of major rivers closer to the sea. Thus, the ACF system represents an especially striking challenge for sustainable development because it is a battle between upstream users who claim first rights to the waters of the basin and downstream users who claim that upstream users are "robbing" them of their rightful share of water while also polluting what they do receive.

Droughts in the 1980s heightened downstreamers' concerns over growing water demands and the means to support them. Beginning in 1986, Atlanta area municipalities contracted with the Corps of Engineers to obtain water supplies from its facilities in the ACF system. In 1989, the Corps announced a plan to reallocate 20% of the water normally reserved in Lake Lanier to drive turbines for hydroelectric power generation to assure an adequate municipal supply for the metro Atlanta area through 2010. Almost immediately, downstreamers protested, demanding that the reallocation plan be suspended until its economic and environmental effects on downstream reaches could be assessed.

In 1990, Georgia asked the Corps for a permit to construct a 4200-acre reservoir on the Tallapoosa River (the so-called West Georgia Regional Reservoir) five miles upstream of the Georgia-Alabama state line. This project was intended to be the first of up to a dozen regional reservoirs to make Atlanta and northern Georgia "drought-proof." Alabama immediately filed suit against the Corps in federal court, alleging a violation of its water rights and the failure on the part of the Corps to assess the environmental effects of the project. Florida subsequently intervened on behalf of Alabama while Georgia predictably sided with the Corps. Table 3.2 provides a chronology and description of the principal events in this complex dispute.

While the precipitating causes of the conflict are fairly well known and easy to identify, the underlying causes of the dispute are more difficult—and far more important—to understand. This is because these long-term causes help us to understand why the dispute has remained intractable for more than a decade. A good place to begin is with population growth. Two of the three states embroiled in the dispute, Florida and Georgia, are among the nation's fastest-growing states. According to the 2000 census, for example, Georgia's population grew by 25% in a single decade—one out of four Georgians currently residing in that state did not live there in 1990! Likewise, Florida's growth rate has annually exceeded 20% for several years.

Attitudes toward water use—and the resistance of these attitudes to change—have also been important factors in the dispute—if sometimes difficult to measure precisely. For example, while more people in the region rely on publicly supplied sources of water for their needs, there remains a widespread belief that water supply is locally provided. According to the U.S. Geological Survey, between 1960 and 1995 the publicly supplied population in

TABLE 3.2

The ACF Dispute—A Case Study Timeline

- 1986—Due to drought, Atlanta contracts with the Corps for water supply from Lake Lanier and other projects; environmental NGOs push for management plan for Apalachicola Bay inflow, a move prompted by Atlanta's action.

- 1987—The Corps announces plan to reallocate 20% of power generation flow to municipal supply through 2010

- 1989—Alabama, Florida demand assessment of economic, environmental effects.

- 1990—Georgia asks the Corps for permit to construct reservoir on Tallapoosa River near Alabama border to make Atlanta "drought-proof"; JUNE: Alabama files suit in Northern District U.S. Court in Alabama against the Corps to stop project and Lake Lanier reallocation, charging water rights violation. Florida intervenes on behalf of Alabama; Georgia joins the Corps. The Corps undertakes comprehensive study of ACF/ACT basins to project needs (through 2050), evaluate alternatives.

- 1991—APRIL: Letter of Agreement (LOA) signed by governors of Alabama, Florida, and Georgia and the assistant secretary of the Army to address short-term issues in ACF.

- 1992—JANUARY: Governors of Alabama, Florida, Georgia agree to Memorandum of Agreement committing to work together as partners throughout the Comprehensive Study process undertaken by the Corps.

- 1997—Comprehensive study completed. Alabama, Florida, Georgia draft compacts for ACF and ACT basins, which are ratified by Congress, signed by president. *Purpose:* "promote interstate comity . . . (by) removing causes of present and future controversies, equitably apportioning surface waters, engaging in water planning, developing and sharing common data bases." Compacts go into effect when states agree on water allocation formulae, date for agreement frequently pushed back.

the states of Alabama, Florida, and Georgia has grown by 35%, 122%, and 59%, respectively (U.S. Geological Survey 2002). As we shall see, one aspect of the negotiations shaping the outlooks of parties has been their view on the sustainability of this public supply.

Finally, actual patterns of water use in the region have also begun changing in the last couple of decades, in important ways. For example, consumptive water uses—those uses of water that actually remove water from a basin or aquifer (through evaporation or transpiration) rather than return it immediately for the next downstream user—have increased considerably in recent years, primarily due to the growth of agricultural irrigation and livestock watering. While Alabama consumes only 7.5% of its water withdrawals as of 1995, Florida consumes over 38% and Georgia about 20%.[4] Consumption rates are important because each drop of water consumed or removed from the basin or aquifer places additional pressure on downstream users—particularly during periods of low flow or drought.

How the Parties Came Together

Following the eruption of controversy among Alabama, Florida, and Georgia in the early 1990s, some decision-makers in the three states dedicated themselves to avoiding lengthy and expensive litigation that likely would have led to a decision that would have pleased no one. In 1990, the three states began an 18-month negotiation process that resulted, first, in a letter of agreement (April 1991) to address short-term issues in the basin and then, in January 1992, a memorandum of agreement stating among other things that the three states were in accord on the need for a study of the water needs of the three states. The governors of the three states also agreed to initiate a comprehensive study of water demands (Kundell and Tetens 1998: 20).

Parallel with the negotiations and in support of these objectives, the U.S. Army Corps of Engineers, in cooperation with the three states, undertook a comprehensive study of the ACF, using 2050 as a planning horizon. The study assessed water demand, availability, and comprehensive management of the basin (U.S. Army Corps of Engineers 1996; Graham 1998). Not only did the study serve as a forum for ongoing dialogue in both basins (see Graham 1998), it also supported a follow-up National Environmental Policy Act (NEPA) scoping process to assess the environmental effects of potential water allocation formulas. This scoping process employed special models developed for the comprehensive study. It also incorporated a review of the tools previously used to manage natural resources in the basin, ample opportunity for input from the public, and a series of professionally moderated sessions among states and the Corps to elicit concerns. Importantly, the Corps' comprehensive study began *before* the governors actually agreed to support it—Congress authorized funding the study in 1990 (Kundell and Tetens 1998: 20; see also table 3.1).

An important tool the Corps employed in the study was the shared vision modeling approach developed by its Institute for Water Resources with assistance from the engineering faculty at the University of Washington.[5] Shared vision modeling is a disciplined effort to incorporate key stakeholders' views into linear models depicting various water resource activities within a single, integrated system (for instance, navigation reliability, power generation, recreation). The goal is to resolve conflicts by giving managers and system operators the opportunity to envision the effects of changes to river operations given various combinations of natural inputs, competing uses, and their own conflicting demands—clearly an adaptive management approach. Through an iterative process of tweaking various inputs—articulated as operational questions (for instance, what happens to x if we move y water through the system?)—alternatives to system operation can be evaluated and modified (Palmer 1998a, b).

From January 1995 to September 1996, the approach was instituted among officials from the three ACF states and other interested parties (for instance, Alabama and Georgia Power Company representatives). It consisted of a series of workshops (up to 80 participants), several model-generation efforts based on participant input, and subsequent modifications to water balance models. At the end, a "User Guide" was distributed to various parties to continue the process as negotiations toward a compact proceeded. However, little else was achieved. According to a key protagonist, while the effort sparked robust discussion and succeeded in accurately capturing current and past operating policies, the challenge of defining credible alternatives that could be used not only to evaluate future options but also to formulate new ones was not resolved.

Another set of problems arose because the approach was incorporated "into a long and extended debate on water management," leading to frustrations among negotiation participants. As one modeler stated: "During its development, the model had been both praised and criticized, for being too complex and . . . too simplistic, for attempting to do more than any model could do, and for not doing enough" (Palmer 1998a: 5). An accurate assessment of its value can only be achieved after state-line flow agreements have been established— a process still not completed.

Following completion of the comprehensive study and the shared vision modeling process, the three states concluded that interstate water compacts would be the most appropriate mechanisms to ensure equitable allocation of water in the ACF and the Alabama-Coosa-Tallapoosa (ACT) systems. Reflecting the initial optimism that accompanied the effort to negotiate a settlement amicably, former Alabama governor Guy Hunt stated, "There are no walls that separate Georgia, Alabama, and Florida, and the leaders of the three states cannot allow bureaucratic walls to stand in the way of the pursuit of the common good for all the people of the region" (*Atlanta Journal and Constitution* 1993). Despite the optimism, the agreement to enter into an interstate water compact was delayed until January 1997, as Georgia contended that a compact was unnecessary given the availability of water in the region. Georgia also stated that the comprehensive study should not be the basis for an allocation agreement.

Once the impasse over compact language was resolved, a process that succeeded largely because of the direct intervention of former Georgia congressman Newt Gingrich, who was very interested in the controversy, the legislatures of the three states approved compacts for the ACF and ACT systems within three months. Congress approved the two compacts, and President Clinton signed them into law later the same year. The governors of the three states signed the compacts in February 1998 (see H. J. Res. 91, 1997).

Both the ACT compact and the ACF compact have a three-voting member commission (formally state governors or their designated representatives) and one nonvoting federal commissioner appointed by the president. At the conclusion of the 1998 compact summit chaired by former representative Gingrich, the three states agreed to protect federal regulatory discretion and water rights, to assure public participation in allocation decisions, to consider the environmental effects in allocation, and to develop specific allocation numbers—in effect, guaranteeing volumes "at the state lines."

Water allocation formulas were to be developed and agreed-upon by December 31, 1998. However, negotiators for the three states requested at least a one-year extension of this deadline in November 1998, and several extensions have been granted over the past dozen years—often at the eleventh hour of stalemated negotiations.

Two recent opportunities for a breakthrough came in early 2002 and mid-2003. Both exemplify the dashed hopes and frustrations following eleventh-hour negotiating efforts for better than a decade. The 2002 incident occurred when a press release from the Georgia Department of Natural Resources reported that the three states had "agreed in principle on the numbers for a water allocation formula for the ACF." Georgia's chief negotiator claimed that the formulas posted by Georgia and Florida, while different, were similar enough to allow the former to "accept Florida's numbers (and to work to resolve language differences) in the terms and conditions of the formula." Alabama representatives concurred that the numbers were workable and that differences could be resolved. Nonetheless, within days of this tentative settlement, negotiations broke off once again (Georgia EPD 2002a). In August 2003, Governors Riley, Bush, and Perdue from Alabama, Florida, and Georgia, respectively, actually signed a memorandum of understanding detailing the principles for allocating water for the ACF over the next 40 years. An optimistic press release by Georgia Governor Perdue declared that "twelve years is far too long for these . . . issues to go unresolved," while Florida's Governor Bush declared, "I am hopeful we can achieve a fair and equitable water allocation for Florida"

(U.S. Water News 2003a). Despite this fanfare and a commitment by the three states to issue a draft agreement for a 60-day public comment period, as of this writing no agreement has been concluded, and negotiations again appear to be stalemated.

Assuming an agreement is eventually reached, within 255 days of an accord over a water allocation formula, the federal commissioner to the ACF must announce concurrence or nonconcurrence with the state commissioners' agreement. Likewise, the ACF compact commission is to be staffed and funded by the three states themselves, and a specific conflict resolution procedure relying on mediation is to be developed.

Obstacles and Constraints to a Sustainable Solution

Although reaching an agreement on water allocation has been difficult for several reasons, two issues appear to be paramount. First, the various demands imposed on the river system share a high intensity and, in the long run, may be incompatible: protecting instream flow while permitting varied off-stream uses are not easy objectives to reconcile. Second, many of the prominent user conflicts facing the three states are really up- versus downstream disputes— an issue endemic to many water conflicts around the world (see chapter 1). For example, Atlanta is a major user of the Chattahoochee. However, as previously noted, it is also a "headwaters" metropolis. The same water used by Atlanta for water supply and wastewater discharge is used by "upstreamers" for recreation and to provide shoreline amenities such as high lake levels for homes, especially along the shoreline of Lake Lanier, and provides downstream water supply to other communities. Without adequate drawdown from Lanier, for example, water quantity may be inadequate to provide for all of Atlanta's needs. Likewise, as many are quick to point out, water quality may be severely degraded because of the inability to dilute pollution discharges from point and nonpoint sources around Atlanta adequately. This is especially true if instream water volumes decline due to growing off-stream demands.

For their part, downstreamers south of Atlanta are concerned about the quality and availability of municipal and agricultural supply and, in Florida especially, about the ability to support a lucrative fishing industry currently threatened by degraded water quality; meanwhile, fishermen argue that there is insufficient flow to dilute pollution flowing into Apalachicola Bay. One theme that has emerged in the ongoing negotiations is the desire of Georgia to ensure that it has sufficient water for the next 30 to 50 years *without* limiting either agricultural consumption or Atlanta's growth. A distinct exception to this insistent demand was the 2000 decision by Georgia's legislature to pass the Flint River Drought Protection Act, a measure authorizing the purchase of water rights from southwest Georgia farmers in the Flint basin through use of an auction. The objective of this innovative legislation was to preserve a minimum instream flow in the Flint and to alleviate the effects of drought by lessening local reliance on the river for irrigation (Holliday 2002; Georgia EPD 2002b).

Alabama and Florida have also imposed strong conditions on the negotiations. Alabama wants sufficient flow for Birmingham's public supply now and into the future and support for navigation on the Coosa system. Finally, Florida wants sufficient high quality inflow to support fisheries in Apalachicola Bay—an important economic resource, as we have seen. In addition to upstream/downstream conflicts, there are also competing uses of the rivers that are closely juxtaposed and conflicting. For example, promoting navigation and protecting freshwater mollusks (or mussels) are two objectives at odds with one another. Mussels, which serve an important cleansing function for waterways by filtering large quantities of nutrients and organic matter, are disappearing from the Chattahoochee, due in part to dredging by the Corps of Engineers and various contractors to accommodate a nine-foot navigation channel.

Compounding the difficulties in reaching accord over how to protect water quality while ensuring navigation, barge operators and developers have criticized proposals to place certain mussel species on the endangered species list. For example, the head of the Tri-Rivers Waterway Development Association and the Tri-State Mussels Coalition, which represent barge operators, developers, and businesses in the ACF basin, has been quoted as saying, "People are important, and what good do these mussels provide?" However, Georgia officials have acknowledged the possibility of a navigation cutback, meaning that Georgians may have to make more frequent use of non-navigational means of transporting goods due to a less reliable ACF navigation channel. Taxpayers pay about $3.5 million annually to maintain the ACF channel. The majority of the commerce that moves on the rivers is sand and gravel dredged from river and lake bottoms (Seabrook 1998).

In attempting to understand the relationship between water quality and quantity issues in the three states, the Clean Water Act's importance to this dispute and its resolution cannot be overestimated. The EPA contends, as do many states, that protection of water quality entails not just assuring an "antidegradation" policy toward rivers but also a willingness to accept that states can select certain designated uses for streams under the Clean Water Act and then to establish criteria necessary to support those uses (see chapter 4). Alabama, Florida, and Georgia, for example, have supported designated uses for fish, wildlife, and other aquatic life on the ACF system—including tributary streams. Since the Clean Water Act predicates, as an interim goal, "the protection and propagation of fish, shellfish, and wildlife, and provides for recreation in and on the water be achieved,"[6] it is the obligation of the federal government and states to arrive at some kind of solution that protects not only water quality for human health needs—regardless of what type of allocation agreement is reached—but minimum instream flow as well.[7]

This is why the project of reconciling agricultural, industrial, and public supply activities constitutes such a significant challenge for reaching an amicable settlement to the ACF dispute. Agricultural activities can affect the health of aquatic life in these rivers. In addition to the commercial fisheries that depend on an adequate supply of freshwater at certain times of the year, low flows and waterborne pollutants jeopardize the survival of ecologically important aquatic biota. Southeastern waterways are some of the most biologically diverse places on earth. The basins at the center of this dispute are home to more than 170 species of fish. Some water experts consider farming in southwest Georgia to be a greater threat than metro Atlanta to fish and other aquatic life. Southwest Georgia has some 4500 irrigation systems that can collectively divert hundreds of millions of gallons a day from the Flint and Apalachicola Rivers.

Not only does agriculture account for 60 to 80% of all current water withdrawals in southwest Georgia, it is a historically important activity in the region. The history of much of the Flint River and Chattahoochee Valleys was bound up in cotton almost from the date of Georgia's founding. Following the introduction of Eli Whitney's cotton gin in 1793, the commodity became profitable to grow on smaller farms that used family labor—and not just large plantations dominated by slaveholding. In fact, by 1860, Georgia had become the world's largest cotton producer, and the Flint River Valley had become one of the major producing areas (Smith 2001: 29).

Even those farmers who withdraw water from the Floridian aquifer for irrigation affect flows in the Flint and Chattahoochee. According to a U.S. Geological Survey study, the two rivers lose about six-tenths of a gallon of flow for each gallon pumped from the aquifer (Seabrook 1998). Furthermore, very little of the water withdrawn for agriculture returns directly to the streams, whereas about 70% of the water used for human consumption *is* returned to the rivers as treated wastewater. Farmers currently face fewer regulations than

other major water users: their withdrawal permits do not expire after any specific period of time, and—as is common throughout southern states—they do
not need to report their usage. Moreover—and a special challenge from the
standpoint of adaptive management—the timing of agricultural use further ag-
gravates the potential damage to downstream ecosystems: farmers are most apt
to irrigate from May through August, precisely when Apalachicola Bay oysters
are most in need of fresh water.

Even upstream users near the Chattahoochee's headwaters are concerned
about an allocation formula that increases downstream flow. Lake Lanier landowners fear that Alabama's proposal that more water be released from the lake
would result in perilously low water levels, leaving many docks on dry land,
making boating dangerous, and interfering with the operation of marinas. A $2
billion recreation industry is at stake, as are waterfront property values.

Economic and lifestyle changes seem unavoidable for many of the users of
the ACF and ACT systems. Georgians may have to pay higher electricity rates
as hydropower production is reduced. Strict limits on water for irrigation may
be imposed on southwest Georgia farmers. Navigation at Georgia's inland ports
may be curtailed. Industries and municipalities (and the people they serve)
may have to pay more to treat wastes discharged into the rivers. Ultimately,
building restrictions and water rationing may be imposed on metro Atlanta—
but Atlantans are likely to demand that downstream communities control their
growth as well (see ARC 1997). One dire forecast of the growth control impacts
through 2010 for metro Atlanta and Georgia combined include over 1 million
in lost population, 680,000 in lost jobs, almost $127 billion in lost wages, and
over $8 billion in lost gross tax revenues. Whatever the substantive costs might
be for resolving this interstate water war, one thing is certain. It will change
the traditional attitude that water is free and plentiful in the South. As stated
by Harold Reheis, head of the Georgia Environmental Protection Division, "We
have to plan as if drought is always imminent."

In trying to get a handle on impediments to resolving the ACF controversy,
it is also necessary to understand the role of institutional deficiencies. From
the standpoint of adaptive management, this is key. All three states practice riparian doctrine—the dominant water law doctrine in states east of the Mississippi River. Under riparian doctrine, landowners have rights to "reasonable
use" of waters flowing past their lands subject only to the rights of downstream
riparians. During drought, water shortages are a "common loss," so all riparians expected to cut back proportionately. Riparian law is covered in more detail in chapter 4.

In riparian systems definitions of "reasonable" vary by location, court of law, circumstance, local custom, and local riverine priority. As the upstream riparian, Georgia argues that it is entitled to "reasonable" use and diversion of not only the Chattahoochee but the Coosa and Tallapoosa Rivers as well. As downstream riparians, Alabama and Florida argue that they are entitled to an "undiminished" flow in both quality and volume. Without long-term legal reform, it is doubtful that any real progress can be made. Since 1999, the conflict has become regionalized. Rumors of Atlanta purchasing water from Chattanooga's water company led Tennessee to pass the Interbasin Water Transfer Act. Unanimously passed by the state legislature in 2000, the act requires state approval for out-of-basin diversion (Feldman 2001).

Dispute Prognosis

The current phase of the dispute began in 1999 when momentum toward what appeared to be imminent agreement on a water allocation formula sputtered. While Georgia officials initially indicated an unwillingness to extend the deadline a second time if a water-sharing formula was not reached by year's end, the deadline for an agreement has repeatedly been extended. In fact, the three states have repeatedly imposed new deadlines and then exceeded them—only to agree to eleventh-hour extensions of negotiations. Georgia continues to want a reservoir on the Flint River in Pike County. The EPA and others have expressed concerns that implementation of the proposed project prior to an interstate allocation agreement would jeopardize the current negotiations (*Atlanta Journal and Constitution* 1998).

Inability to reach an ACF accord has also affected the ACT. In early 2000, Alabama and Georgia reached agreement, in principle, on a formula for water allocation in the Alabama-Coosa-Tallapoosa basin. Georgia proposed that water levels in three major federal reservoirs on the Chattahoochee (Lanier, West Point, and Walter F. George) be maintained at higher than historical levels to ensure metro Atlanta of enough water for future growth. Alabama wanted the reservoirs operated to meet all water needs, particularly hydropower and commercial navigation on the lower Chattahoochee. Alabama also demanded 40% of the annual daily flow from any new reservoirs to be built in Georgia (*Atlanta Journal and Constitution* 1999). Finally, Lake Allatoona on the Coosa River was to be kept higher in winter for Alabama's benefit. Georgia was also allowed to construct new reservoirs on the Tallapoosa—so long as 25% of the flow was guaranteed for Alabama's benefit. The agreement was contingent on an ACF accord with Florida, federal agency approval, and completion of a favorable public comment period. Moreover, environmental groups have charged that the agreement provides insufficient instream flows for fish and aquatic habitat.

As noted earlier, in 2002 Alabama, Florida, and Georgia came the closest they had ever come since the ACF compact was initially drafted in the late 1990s to concluding an allocation agreement for that basin (Georgia EPD 2002a), only to have the allocation formula rejected at the last possible moment by Florida. Claiming "irreconcilable differences" with Georgia over sharing the ACF's waters, Florida declared in March 2002 that continuing negotiations would be "pointless" (Seabrook 2002: A1). For several months, it was uncertain if Florida even wanted to continue in negotiations by participating in seeking an extension of the compact. Florida filed suit in the Eleventh Circuit Court for standing in regards to Lake Lanier operations. As of 2006, negotiations were expected to get back on track, with two of the three states (Alabama and Georgia) having new governors at the helm. And according to Alabama's chief deputy attorney general, discussions on how to allocate water from the Chattahoochee are progressing, so as to protect freshwater mussels in the Apalachicola while still leaving sufficient upstream supply for Alabama and Georgia (*Chattanooga Times Free Press* 2006). Also, the governors of Alabama and Georgia are continuing to seek a negotiated solution to the dispute—but without Florida's participation. In short, ad hoc measures to manage the basin are being implmented even though the three states do not appear to be on the verge of a major breakthrough to their impasse.

A remaining impediment appears to be the assurance that any allocation agreement can be flexible enough to be reopened in the future if conditions warrant (for instance, greater certainty over actual flow) and that any allocation formula can be independently verified. As noted earlier, the ability to revisit decisions is a key component of adaptive management. Florida and Alabama are uneasy about any agreement that would be based on a certain amount of water being delivered to their state boundaries. The uncertainty and variability in river flows from day to day, season to season, year to year would confound the downstream states' ability to determine if Georgia is violating an allocation formula. The downstream states have proposed an allocation formula that would limit consumption by municipalities and industry. Georgia has refused to negotiate based on consumption, arguing that such a water-sharing formula would jeopardize that state's ability to decide how to use water within its own borders (Seabrook 1999). Yet, as previously noted, some kind of agreement on what constitutes adequate instream flow is essential to any durable settlement.

Finally, water conservation has begun to emerge as an important factor in the negotiations toward an allocation formula. A reality facing all three states is that, with the possible exception of smaller impoundments devoted principally to local supply, there will be no new large impoundments built anywhere in the region. Most good sites for impoundments are already taken, and public opposition to building dams all but rules this option out. The Atlanta Regional Commission has been exploring long-term incentives that could modify water use, and consideration of ways to reallocate water "internally" in Lakes Allatoona and Lanier continue to be discussed. In 1995, per capita water use in Georgia was estimated at 195 gallons/day: higher than the figure for any neighboring state and higher than the national average. Annual per capita water use in states adjacent to Georgia was as much as 17% lower (Cowie et al. 2002: 17).

The ACF controversy is instructive with respect to the sustainable development of water resources and the prospects for adaptive management, for several reasons. First, it reminds us that water supply problems do not respect political boundaries. Problems generated in one jurisdiction ultimately affect up- and downstream jurisdictions. In short, if adaptive management assumes the capacity of political entities to incorporate what they have learned about political and environmental pressures in ways that feed back into more effective and collaborative decisions, then one barrier to its implementation is the limited means available for cooperating across jurisdictions. In short, if these states remain unable to resolve their dispute, the case would go to the Supreme Court as an "equitable apportionment" suit. Historically, the Court generally resolves such disputes by permanently "splitting the difference."[8]

There are other options for a settlement short of litigation that are equally onerous. Congress could step in and allocate the waters of the ACF system. Historically, Congress rarely does this (Hull 2000). And, of course, a negotiated settlement remains possible. As one observer notes, resolving the dispute through compact is preferable to other solutions because it would avoid legal costs, as well as further delay and uncertainty, and it provides the best chance of assuring that public and stakeholder comment are incorporated, in some constructive and meaningful way, into the allocation formula and its implementation (Hull 2000: 4).

Second, the ACF dispute teaches us that adaptive management requires a view of environmental problems—especially water allocation problems—as inextricably connected to decisions over economic development, water quality, population growth, and urbanization. Prior to this dispute, political leaders in the region tended to treat water problems as isolated issues that could be addressed in a piecemeal fashion. Such policy "isolationism" was generally characteristic of water resource management in the South prior to the droughts of the late 1980s. What protagonists are perhaps grappling with more than anything else is how to develop an integrated system for managing *all* of these issues simultaneously.

Third, the dispute teaches us that if one objective of adaptive management is to find means to establish amicable settlements permanently by ensuring a climate of trust and confidence, then an essential precondition for achieving these conditions is the ability of protagonists to verify and confirm that the strictures of any agreement are being met. Such verification also provides another means of feedback to decision makers and builds a sense of competence in their ability to monitor and anticipate problems. Aside from Alabama and Florida's need for assurance that Georgia will not siphon the Chattahoochee's headwaters to its own benefit, there is a longer-term need related to this issue of compliance and verification—one that can only be provided through institutional reform. This need is for each state to respect one another's water needs by putting into place a verifiable monitoring and compliance system to measure water use and withdrawal—not just instruments and equipment but an administrative capacity to collect data, to verify and validate its reliability, and to report and disseminate it objectively. If it is any consolation, this issue is not unique to the ACF. Water disputes across the eastern United States—in the Potomac, Delaware, and other basins—are becoming increasingly characterized by a lack of civility in their resolution. States and communities, fearing that their thirsty neighbors will seek to aggrandize all available water in the local vicinity, are becoming increasingly distrustful (Jehl 2003). That such distrust arises in the first place only serves to confirm the need for a civil society that fosters high levels of confidence, participation, and shared power (see chapter 2)—an important precondition for adaptive management.

NEWER INNOVATIONS: PLANNING,
PARTNERSHIPS, PANACEAS?
Northwest Power Planning Council: Physical Setting

The Northwest Power Planning Council (NPPC) is a water resources management innovation that encompasses the Columbia River basin. The Columbia River begins in the Selkirk Mountains of British Columbia, Canada. One of the most important rivers in North America, the Columbia first flows in a

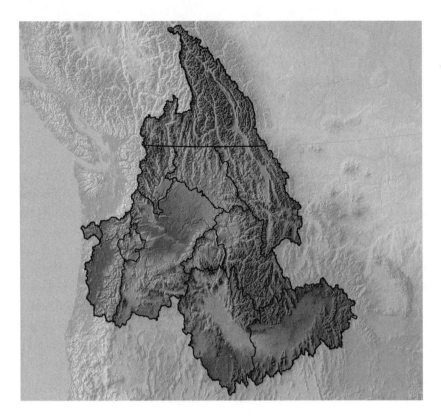

Figure 3.4. Columbia River Basin and Surrounding Region
Map courtesy of Stephen Sasser, creative director, Northwest Power and Conservation
Council.

northwesterly direction, then turns south and, after passing through a chain of
long and narrow lakes, enters the United States. It forms the boundary between
the states of Washington and Oregon on its way to the Pacific Ocean. The Snake
River, a major tributary to the Columbia, drains parts of Idaho and Montana.
The Columbia River is 1,214 miles long and drains 258,000 mi^2 of land. Only
three other rivers in North America travel farther and discharge more water
than the Columbia. Figure 3.4 depicts the region encompassed by the Northwest Power Planning Council.

Historical Overview: People, Salmon,
and the Search for Sustainability

In addition to its size, the Columbia is remarkable for its steep drop, a trait that led to its being harnessed for hydroelectric power generation early in this century. Fifteen large dams have been constructed on the mainstem of the Columbia (including three on the Snake River) since the mid-1930s, and more than a hundred smaller dams are on its tributaries. Grand Coulee, the first dam constructed on the Columbia, is still the biggest dam in North America. The Columbia is said to be America's most elaborately engineered electricity-irrigation-transportation "machine," with over 90% of its hydroelectric power potential exploited (Muckleston 1990; Harden 1997). Despite this success at resource exploitation in the region, its development has long been contentious and controversial.

One writer characterizes the history of water management in the Columbia and Snake basins as a "clash in values" between traditional and modern societies and their respective needs (Getches 1998c: 177). At the time of westward expansion, during the era of Lewis and Clark's expedition to the Columbia basin in 1805, at least five species of Salmon[9] flourished in the river and provided the dietary staple for an estimated 50,000 indigenous tribal members. Salmon represented not merely an economic base for the region's inhabitants but a cultural and religious way of life as well—providing the basis for many tribes' governmental and land use patterns and dictating how—and where—tribes resided throughout the year. Tribal activities coincided with the migration, harvest, preparation, and consumption of these species (Getches 1998c: 179).

Damming the Columbia dramatically altered the character and economy of the Pacific Northwest and had a huge impact on tribal traditions. In addition to providing abundant, inexpensive electricity to support industrial and residential development, federal development of the river system created a heavily subsidized irrigation project called the Columbia Basin Project (CBP). Originally authorized to irrigate 1,095,000 acres, the CBP is one of the nation's largest federally subsidized reclamation projects. Due to runoff, seepage, evaporation, and other losses, almost twice as much water must be delivered to the irrigation canal system as is actually used for irrigation. In the mid-1990s, it was reported that as much as 43% of the CBP's acreage is in low-value forage and pasture crops that account for over 60% of the water consumed on the project (Columbia River Basin Institute 1994).

The extensive agricultural development that resulted from the availability of cheap water for irrigation also created a demand for barge transportation of produce and other commodities on the Columbia. Abundant and inexpensive electrical power and water also stimulated the development of heavy industry, especially aluminum smelting. These industrial activities also increased barge traffic on the river, a form of transportation that depends on maintenance of relatively high pools of water throughout the navigable portion of the river.

There are two significant themes in the development of the Columbia for irrigation, power generation, and transportation that resonate throughout historical accounts of the region found in analyses by those who have carefully studied the river system and the people who live within it. First, efforts to develop the river system have deep and lengthy roots. Many of the most important political figures in the region, business and agricultural leaders and even media moguls, have long and avidly championed the development of large hydroelectric dams on the river and were convinced early on that such developments would dramatically transform the region—long called by its most evangelical boosters the "inland empire"—in a positive way.

As a result of their fervent promotion of dam development, they were neither easily deterred from their goal nor always cognizant of (or particularly concerned about) the deleterious environmental as well as economic changes on indigenous peoples, among others, that such development might impose (Pitzer 1995; Harden 1997). Compounding the conflict, advocates of dam development now face equally determined advocates of "un-damming" parts of the Columbia. The strident positions taken by these interested parties makes compromise in negotiations over salmon difficult.

Obviously, such strong emotions also impede adaptive management by deterring tentative or adjustable solutions to the river's conditions. Passions have long run high on both sides of the issue of sustainable development—economic advocates promoting irrigation and inexpensive power as boons to growth and prosperity, tribal nations and environmental supporters often from the western side of the Cascades defining sustainable development as the way to restore the region to a more pristine existence.

Second, there is also good evidence that advocates of the dams—in particular those who worked in agencies such as the Bureau of Reclamation and the Army Corps of Engineers—clearly did not know how severe the adverse impacts to salmon and other fish species from building dams could be. Little effort was expended to monitor environmental conditions caused by large main-stem impoundments such as Bonneville and especially Grand Coulee or to design water projects to accommodate specific flow demands. Furthermore, few measures were adopted to accommodate the needs for passage of spawning fish until much later because few people had any knowledge suggesting that it would be necessary to do so (Pitzer 1995). Not surprisingly, much later writing on adaptive water resources management often cited the Columbia basin as an example of how not to manage a riverine environment and as proof of the need for a new way of thinking about complex river systems so as to advance the underlying science governing their operation (see, for instance, Muckleston 1990; Ortolano and Cushing 2002; Blatter and Ingram 2001).

Until the 1980s, the economic interests represented by power generation, irrigation, and barge navigation were generally satisfied with how the Columbia River was managed by the Corps and the Bureau of Reclamation. Dam releases and water diversions could be managed to provide for these uses by timing them to coincide with power demands or drought. However, timing water releases in order to satisfy these demands would not necessarily be in sync with the needs of salmon, whose spawning habits and migration patterns require different sets of water flow demands to be sustainable.

Salmon are anadromous fish, meaning that they hatch in freshwater streams and travel to the ocean, where they reach adulthood, eventually returning to the freshwater stream to spawn and die. Dams are a formidable barrier to juvenile salmon trying to get to the ocean and to adults trying to return upstream to their spawning areas. Hydroelectric power-generating turbines physically damage the fish, killing between 7 and 32% of smolts at each dam. Furthermore, the "slackwater" behind the dams is warmer and lower in oxygen, reducing the survival of migrating juveniles. Timing is critical for juveniles in their journey to the sea, and the slower-moving slackwater is yet another source of mortality. These individual sources of mortality associated with the impoundment of the Columbia River system account for an annual loss of between 5 million and 11 million adult salmonids and by 1990 had cut annual fish runs from an estimated 10 to 16 million to fewer than 3 million (Muckleston 1990). This trend alarmed "fish interests," including anglers, ecologists, environmentalists, and Native American tribes whose culture and livelihood were centered on salmon. These interests were instrumental in forcing the advent of a new management regime for the Columbia River system.

How the Parties Came Together: Formation of the NPPC

A new direction in management of the Columbia River began in 1980. The Northwest's electric utilities thought they were running out of energy and saw no way to finance new energy development, so they asked Congress to allow the region to use federal power revenues from the Columbia River dams to finance new energy development. At the same time, tensions had come to a head over protecting the remaining anadromous species such as salmon whose stocks were becoming more depleted year after year. Congress provided authority to use power revenues to finance new developments through the Pacific Northwest Electric Power Planning and Conservation Act of 1980. The legislation also established the Northwest Power Planning Council (NPPC) to oversee federal energy development decisions. It was revolutionary in western water management in that it established the use of the Columbia River by salmon to be on the same footing as power production, navigation, and irrigation (Volkman 1992).

The NPPC is comprised of two governor-appointed members from the four basin states of Washington, Oregon, Idaho, and Montana. The council initially was responsible for developing a 20-year electrical power plan that will guarantee adequate energy at the lowest cost to the region and a regional program to protect and rebuild the fish and wildlife populations affected by hydropower development. It was also charged with exposing these plans to extensive public input. Early in its history, the NPPC was praised as an innovative and cooperative means of addressing complex transboundary problems, and some scholars suggested that the council was an intergovernmental model of "cooperative federalism" unique to the United States (McGinnis 1995). Perhaps one of the most obvious contrasts between the NPPC and the other initiatives is that it is really a power-related agency, not a water management authority.

The NPPC's more recent mandate has proven to be daunting. The ongoing decline of salmonid fisheries led to the listing of some species of Pacific Northwest salmon under the Endangered Species Act. Restoration and protection of endangered salmon and their habitat now lies with the NPPC. The council's fish and wildlife program strives to restore endangered species and critical habitats through promoting artificial salmon reproduction in hatcheries, limiting harvests, improving habitat, designating sanctuary streams to be protected from future hydroelectric development, and improving fish passage on the mainstem Columbia-Snake system. All restoration activities are carried out with extensive public involvement (Muckleston 1990).

NPPC's Achievements: Overcoming Obstacles on the Path to Adaptive Management

The NPPC has encouraged cooperation among utility systems, conservation and efficient power use, greater involvement of state and local governments in regional power planning, and oversight of electric power system planning and regional fish and wildlife recovery. It is also developing a long-range plan to ensure low-cost power for the region while protecting and rebuilding fishery and wildlife populations depleted by previous hydropower development. Because the NPPC represents a bold step toward adopting this new paradigm, its efforts have been heralded as an innovative means of bringing stakeholders together under an adaptive management umbrella. Its activities have even led to the creation of a regional "water budget" designed both to protect fisheries and provide for other services (over 4 million acre-feet for salmon, seasonally allocated on the Columbia and Snake Rivers), and the designation of 44,000 river miles of prime fish and wildlife habitat as free from new hydropower development.

Despite its enormous effect on regional electric policies and regional approaches to fish and wildlife protection and restoration, the NPPC has not prevented several species of Snake River salmon from being listed under the Endangered Species Act. By 1990, annual fish runs had been reduced from an estimated 10 to 16 million to fewer than 3 million, notwithstanding the more than $100 million in annual expenditures on environmental improvements at dams and decreased hydropower production. By 1995, many West Coast salmonid species had been driven to extinction, while others remain at risk of extinction to this day. Adding to its problems, in 1994 the Ninth Circuit Court of Appeals rejected the NPPC's "Salmon Strategy," criticizing the council's "sacrificing the Act's fish and wildlife goals" (Getches 1998c: 190). The NPPC has promulgated a new plan to provide for endangered salmon recovery and to ensure protection of other fish species.

By 1990, the NPPC had succeeded in changing the way the Columbia River system was managed, and salmon runs seemed to be improving. The council had created a water budget designed to anticipate instream and off-stream needs. This allowed for water that was stored upstream to be released to wash smolts through the reservoirs more quickly. The Corps of Engineers has been encouraged to retrofit mainstem dams with enormously expensive screens to guide fish away from turbines and into bypass channels that drop them into the water below spillways. Some dams have been fitted with fish ladders that facilitate the upstream migration of spawning salmon. About 44,000 river miles of prime fish and wildlife habitat have been set aside and protected from new hydropower development.

In chapter 2, we discussed the importance of understanding economic constraints on sustainable development. Of the cases we have thus far discussed, the NPPC may best exemplify these constraints. The effort to save salmon in the Columbia basin has been expensive as well as technically complicated. In fact, the biological restoration program in the Columbia River basin has been characterized as one of the most expensive environmental restoration programs ever undertaken.[10] Since 1980, approximately $100 million has been spent *annually* on fish hatcheries, turbine bypass facilities, and foregone hydropower. Extreme means have been employed to move fish around dams, including transporting salmon fingerlings in trucks and even on barges. Unfortunately, the salmon population continues to decline. Hatchery-raised fish are generally less fit than wild salmon for survival in the wild. Moreover, hatchery fish dominate the remaining wild stock. Ironically, genetic diversity, often considered a hedge against extinction, has been reduced through dependence on hatcheries—complicating the issue of sustainability.

By 1995, 106 populations of West Coast salmonids (salmon, steelhead, trout, and char) had been driven to extinction, and 214 additional populations were at risk of extinction (McGinnis 1995). Beyond the natural values associated with native species and habitat loss and the tremendous expenditure for restoration of these stocks, the losses of fisheries has also had an economic cost. Pacific Northwest salmon fisheries produce over $1 billion in personal income per year and provide more than 60,000 jobs (McGinnis 1995). However, an analysis of the cost-effectiveness of NPPC's proposals for future mitigation projects concluded that "this action is too expensive for its apparent limited efficacy" (Paulsens and Wernstedt 1995).

According to David Getches, another complication faced by NPPC's efforts to restore salmon and other species is a transactional cost issue. Since 1994, the council has promulgated a plan to replace the earlier one criticized by the court. While estimated to cost power users $171 million per year, it provides for endangered salmon recovery and ensures water for protecting other species and values (Getches 1998c: 190). While from a technical standpoint a major step forward in sustainable development has resulted from this decision, institutional issues associated with implementing these technical fixes remain unsettled. Among the latter are the issue of public involvement in the management of the salmon restoration strategy and whether or not the public can accept the implicit values embraced by its cost.

Complicating this debate over the benefits and costs of restoring salmon and other species is a recent spurt of regional economic analyses of the region's energy needs. These analyses have numerous implications for environmental programs as well as for economic development policies. Their conclusions, moreover, would appear to bolster the views of avid environmentalists who argue that the only lasting way to restore salmon stocks is through tearing down many of the large hydroelectric power projects that impound the Columbia river system. One of these recent analyses was produced by the RAND Corporation and boldly stated that tearing down four dams on the lower reaches of Oregon's Snake river to restore the region's salmon could create up to 15,000 new jobs and leave the region's economy "unharmed" ("Studies Show" 2003). The study also claimed that by diversifying its energy sources and not relying so heavily on hydropower, the basin could become less vulnerable to drought—a problem expected to become exacerbated by climate change (Pernin et al. 2002)—and, thus, better able to adapt to future environmental conditions.

As if echoing the findings of the RAND study, a Tellus Institute report released at nearly the same time claims that a combination of greater energy efficiency measures and increased reliance on renewable energy could provide two benefits. First, such a move would provide enough new electricity to more than make up for the removal of the lower Snake River dams. Second, dam removal coupled with renewable energy sources would adequately meet the region's growing need for power. The report's authors advance the proposition that aggressive household and industrial and commercial sector conservation, an effort that could yield a net addition of nearly 2400 MW of new capacity— together with new developments in biomass, wind, and geothermal power— could add nearly 13,000 MW of capacity to the entire basin (Lazarus, Von Hippel, and Bernow 2002).

While the assumptions on which the economic and engineering arguments of both reports are based are generally clear and logical, a problem common to both studies is the absence of any serious consideration of policy constraints. Neither report contemplates how such ambitious economic objectives can be achieved; how elite opinions can be influenced and actually changed; and how past energy investment patterns may be altered and modified. Answers to such questions would seem to be a key to adaptive management. After all, if previous patterns of behavior cannot be altered and opinions modified, then what prospects are there for such a drastic change from the status quo to improve environmental quality and achieve continued economic growth?

Neither study says much about the potential adverse impacts to the environment from many of the supposedly benign technologies advocated. For example, while the Tellus study asserts that 6000 MW of wind energy can be added to the region using sites that "pose [no] environmental risks or intrude on culturally sensitive areas" (Lazarus, Von Hippel, and Bernow 2002), this claim ignores the fact that in other regions of the country where efforts to introduce wind power have been introduced, opponents of such projects have often not been animated by concerns with protecting culturally or environmentally sensitive areas but with preventing noise pollution or aesthetic alteration of the landscape, both common problems associated with wind generation.

While the RAND study is far more equivocal in recognizing the environmental tradeoffs associated with all energy sources, the economic assumptions it posits for future fossil energy costs and the long-term effects of shifting the economy away from other hydropower-associated benefits (for instance, the transition away from an irrigation-intensive economy) are also not infallible. The debate prompted by both studies, however, is important for adaptive management because in the context of longer-term concerns with sustainable development and the NPPC, they elucidate the complexity associated with efforts to array in mathematical terms the economic benefits to salmon and people from realigning energy consumption and use patterns. They also reveal the uncertainty surrounding future employment and other social and economic patterns in the region. Unfortunately, where one stands in these debates is often influenced as much by ideology as by economics or other pragmatic arguments. For this reason, economic logic alone cannot dictate future policy in the region.

As McGinnis (1995) points out, the Endangered Species Act places species preservation above economic considerations as a matter of law. Likewise, industrial, commercial, residential, and recreational use values of a regional ecosystem are also second to listed species preservation under the Endangered Species Act. Thus, the Northwest Power Planning Council's attempts to balance multiple uses of natural resources in the Columbia River basin might be inconsistent with ESA requirements. Yet restoring natural salmon to the Columbia bioregion will require cooperation among stakeholders who hold conflicting values. McGinnis contends that the long-term effectiveness of regional cooperation in this case is likely to be a function of (1) the amount of federal authority that Congress granted to the compact; (2) the level of regional efficacy and trust among regional stakeholders; and (3) the extent to which there is an allegiance to an ecocentric—as opposed to a mostly economic—worldview in decision-making.

Each of these conclusions has implications for adaptively managing the resources of the Columbia basin. Without sufficient authority within the region to develop policy alternatives, regional stakeholders will have little responsibility for environmental and other outcomes and may over time become passive or at the very least cynical. Likewise, without sufficient trust among regional stakeholders and between federal agency officials and state and local NGOs, there will be little confidence in whatever institutional means are established to verify compliance, to monitor environmental improvements, and to acquire information about human activities that degrade and improve ecological conditions. Such institutional measures must be commonly respected as legitimate across political jurisdictions.

On balance, the NPPC's successes show that water resource stakeholders in the region at least seem to be learning to work together across large geographic, political, and economic boundaries to address common resource problems (Volkman 1992). This holds important lessons for sustainable development. In addition to the NPPC itself, no less than 11 state and federal agencies, 13 Native American tribes, eight utilities, and numerous fish, forest, and environmental groups count among the stakeholders in the project of restoring the Columbia River system (McGinnis 1995). The capability of these stakeholders to cooperate and restore critical aquatic habitats and protect endangered species is predicated on their collective and shared values about the landscape, their sense of place in it, their perceived relationship to nature, and their faith and allegiance to the ability of science and technology to restore ecosystems.

One author has observed that the NPPC case exemplifies the importance of ethical as well as institutional constraints in the management of water disputes. According to Michael McGinnis, if the river system of the Columbia is ever to be genuinely restored, fundamental value changes among both decision-makers and citizens must come about. Among these values are reverence, humility, responsibility, care, and respect for the natural world—"fundamental prerequisites in the pursuit of restoration" (McGinnis 1995). Moreover, as another observer has noted, the changes in policy pursued by the NPPC are at least "animated by a broader range of values" than just economics. Ecological

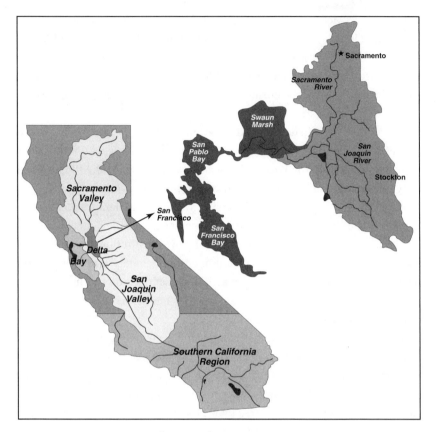

Figure 3.5. CALFED Project and Surrounding Region
Source: CALFED website, calwater.ca.gov/Regions/DeltaRegion.shtml

imperatives, aesthetics, and demands for equity "have given rise to a greater consciousness of the ethical implications of water use." (Getches 1998a). Clearly, as we shall see in chapter 5, the attainment of adaptive management requires a social learning context that is predicated on ethical imperatives such as the obligation to protect the environment and other forms of life. We will return to the example of NPPC in our discussion of this role of ethics in adaptive management.

The California Bay–Delta Accord/CALFED: Physical Setting

The California Bay–Delta is the largest estuary on the western coast of the Americas, and it once produced an abundance of Dungeness crabs, shrimp, and oysters. Today, the delta itself supports over 130 fish species. The Bay-Delta is formed by the confluence of the San Joaquin and Sacramento Rivers. These two rivers drain the 450-mile-long, 50-mile-wide Central Valley in the heart of California and encompass 47% of that state's surface water. The river system comprised of these major streams provides 60% of California's water supply; more than 20 million Californians derive at least a part of their supply from this system. Recipients include residents of Northern California and a good part of Southern California—as far south as San Diego. Moreover, the elaborate plumbing system now constituting the CALFED Bay-Delta system has over 700 miles of sloughs and waterways (Jacobs, Luoma, and Taylor 2003: 32).

The Sacramento River rises on Mt. Shasta, a 14,162-foot quiescent volcano. As it flows southward toward the delta, it receives almost all its water from tributaries in the Sierra Nevada Mountains to the east. The San Joaquin River drains the southern Sierra Mountains and flows northward. The San Joaquin was once the southernmost salmon river in the world, while the Sacramento was the second-largest Chinook salmon river in the world. Figure 3.5 depicts the geographic scope of the CALFED Bay-Delta Program and its major features.

Historical Overview: California as a Hydrologic Republic

In 1849, gold was discovered on the American River, a tributary of the Sacramento. Hydraulic mining, whereby water was funneled under high pressure into hoses that enabled miners to wash mountainsides down to bedrock, sent tens of millions of tons of soil and rock into the waters of the Sacramento River. This practice was prohibited in 1884, but further assaults on the rivers continued in the form of railroad construction, extensive logging, and overfishing.

The state began allowing the formation of irrigation districts in 1887, and small dams were constructed on numerous streams in the Central Valley. In 1933, the state legislature approved the Central Valley Project for the export of "surplus" water from the north to the more populous south, which is mostly arid. The Central Valley Project called for the construction of a series of dams and canals, starting with the Shasta Dam on the upper Sacramento River and the Friant Dam on the San Joaquin. In 1935, the U.S. Bureau of Reclamation took charge of the project.

Completed in 1944, the Shasta Dam prevented salmon and steelhead from reaching their spawning grounds on the upper Sacramento. Meanwhile, 98% of the San Joaquin's water was diverted for irrigation, virtually destroying the river's fisheries. Drastic reductions in freshwater delivery to the Bay-Delta resulted in increased salinity of the estuary, disrupting the biological processes that had supported a diverse ecosystem and important commercial fisheries.

CALFED traces its origins to these disruptions, their societal impacts, and the reactions of stakeholders to both. In the early 1990s, efforts to protect endangered species led to the allocation of 800,000 acre-feet of water under the Central Valley Project Improvement Act of 1992 to instream flow. Serious droughts occurring simultaneously forced a series of actions by diverse agencies and stakeholders that were intended to ensure the enforcement of various legal mandates. The intercession of high-level political leadership was also instrumental in bringing matters to a head.

While the EPA pressured the state's Water Quality Control Board to safeguard endangered fish in the Bay-Delta (in support of the Endangered Species Act), leading to limits placed upon water exports, Governor Pete Wilson and Secretary of the Interior Bruce Babbitt shepherded state and federal agencies in an effort to establish a coordinated federal-state management plan to manage the Bay-Delta water resources (Jacobs, Luoma, and Taylor 2003: 32).

How the Parties Came Together

By 1993, two fish species indigenous to the Bay-Delta system were listed under the Endangered Species Act, and petitions to list other species had been filed. These listings resulted in restrictions on the state's major water projects, significantly affecting the amount of water they would be able to export. Subsequently, fractious debate among California's agricultural, urban, and environmental interests regarding management options for multiple uses of the Bay-Delta system led to what some regarded as a virtual state of panic—and political stalemate. In some ways this policy impasse allowed political leadership to step up and cajole the parties toward a solution. While Governor Pete Wilson arranged for a state management framework to share responsibility for the Bay-Delta in June 1994, Secretary Bruce Babbitt compelled relevant federal agencies with environmental management responsibilities to form the "Federal Ecosystem Directorate" (thus, the "FED" in CALFED).

A series of joint state-federal "Principles for Agreement" was signed in late 1994, and the CALFED Bay-Delta Program embracing these principles was formally initiated in 1995. In essence, these principles provide guidance as to how federal and state agencies shall function together in formulating and implementing water quality standards, protecting endangered species, and determining how Central Valley water projects shall be operated to balance environmental and economic needs (Jacobs, Luoma, and Taylor 2003: 32).[11]

The overall mission of the CALFED Bay-Delta Program is "to develop and implement a comprehensive, long-term plan that will restore ecological health to and improve water management for beneficial uses of the Sacramento-Bay Delta system" (Jacobs, Luoma, and Taylor 2003: 31–32). The principles for agreement guaranteed reliable supplies of water both for the environment and for cities over a period of three years. To protect Bay-Delta water quality and endangered fish species, the agreement called for enhanced freshwater flows through the delta and into the bays: 400,000 acre-feet of additional flows in normal years and 1.1 million acre-feet of additional flows in critically dry years. To appease agricultural interests fearing the impact of additional endangered species listings on their claims to irrigation water, the agreement also stipulated that additional needs for water to protect threatened or endangered species recently added to the list of those protected by the Endangered Species Act must be met by water purchases financed with federal funds. These funds would be used to buy water rights from farmers, ranchers, or other willing sellers.

The Bay-Delta accord institutionalized state-federal collaboration in the form of a new entity—CALFED, composed of fifteen state and federal agencies and charged with overseeing the collaborative effort. CALFED's official mission is to "develop a long-term comprehensive plan that will restore ecological health and improve water management for beneficial uses of the Bay-Delta." A new planning entity under CALFED's authority, the CALFED Bay-Delta Program endeavors to develop a plan to manage the Central Valley Rivers, the delta where they merge, the San Francisco Bay, the Sierra foothills, and the needs of Southern California water users while balancing competing environmental, urban, and agricultural interests (Gomez 1997). The Bay-Delta program is managed by an "interdisciplinary, interagency staff" and lacks any permanent bureaucratic structure of its own (Jacobs, Luoma, and Taylor 2003: 33). Technical experts from state and federal agencies and consulting organizations assist the staff.

Early on, CALFED embarked upon a unique three-phase process to address problems it was charged to resolve. First, in order to define more clearly how the various problems facing the region were to be addressed, a range of alternatives were first generated and then discussed through an extensive public involvement–public meeting process. This process not only obtained public input but helped narrow the range of viable alternatives to be pursued. The second phase, beginning in 1996, entailed a comprehensive programmatic environmental impact review. Phase III involves implementation of a preferred alternative for managing the delta and is expected to take longer than 30 years (CALFED Bay-Delta Program 1999b).

While much of the frenetic activity associated with public participation during Phase I was undertaken in obvious compliance with both NEPA and the California Environmental Quality Act, it went beyond mere legal conformity in its operation (CALFED Bay-Delta Program 1999b). By 1996, a range of alternatives was identified for achieving long-term solutions, and an innovative public participation program was under way. Some measure of how innovative the participation program has been is illustrated by its structure. Overseeing the program is a 32-member advisory committee chartered under the Federal Advisory Committee Act. More than 500 meetings have been held to establish goals and objectives, and there was a strong, personal commitment by both Governor Wilson and Secretary of the Interior Babbitt to adopting a "stakeholder-driven process" for decisions (Jacobs, Luoma, and Taylor 2003: 37).

Independent assessments of this component of CALFED concur that the success of the public participation effort can be confirmed by several measures. Not only were all key early decisions on funding, research, and policy adopted in public meetings within the CALFED Bay-Delta Advisory Council mentioned above, but meetings also took place throughout the state and in different venues to permit the broadest possible input. Moreover, several key NGOs—ranging from agricultural and large water user groups to environmental organizations and urban water agencies—played advisory roles throughout the process of identifying issues and problems (Jacobs, Luoma, and Taylor 2003: 37). Perhaps most importantly, however, all of this public and stakeholder collaboration resulted in revisions to environmental documents, new studies of various aspects of problems not originally anticipated (for instance, greater consideration of the effects of changes in water management on endangered and threatened fish species), and refinement of agency-directed objectives. In fact, having all relevant stakeholders at the table resulted, according to a NOAA-sponsored forum, in a process that was "powerful but agonizingly slow" (NOAA 2002, quoted in Jacobs, Luoma, and Taylor 2003: 37). What made all of this participation viable, aside from the commitment of high-level decision-makers, was adequate funding to support statewide meetings and travel—totaling $16 million per year from 1994 to 1999; this budget was split 50–50 by the federal government and the state of California (Jacobs, Luoma, and Taylor 2003: 37).[12]

Six months after the Bay-Delta accord was announced, Betsy Reike, who had participated in its development as assistant secretary for water and science in the Department of the Interior, offered these observations about its lessons, stating that such accords need (1) open, collaborative, inclusive processes; (2) external incentives for water users to collaborate and negotiate (for instance, federal mandates or federal dollars); (3) recognition that there is no one-size-fits-all process or paradigm for watershed protection efforts; and (4) the requirement that government continue to have a role in natural resource decision-making—markets and private, voluntary partnerships cannot achieve durable agreements alone.

In addition to the federally chartered Bay-Delta Advisory Council (BDAC), other mechanisms are used to elicit stakeholder input. BDAC has an "Ecosystem Roundtable" that provides input on the coordination of CALFED's ecosystem restoration projects. Other public involvement mechanisms include a website, a 24-hour public information telephone line, and various media outreach programs (CALFED Bay-Delta Program 1999a: 6). While ambitious in their scope, the full effect of these mechanisms remains open to debate.

Obstacles and Constraints in Sustainable Management

In mid-1998, the Natural Resources Defense Council invited representatives of environmental and fishing groups in California to critique CALFED's efforts to date and to share their perspectives on the Bay-Delta's future for a report. One representative's comments echoed the Pacific Institute's conclusion that CALFED underestimated the potential for demand management and water use efficiency in forecasting that Southern California's water demand will rise dramatically, by as much as 2 million acre-feet, by the year 2020. Others accused CALFED of the "same tired old thinking," claiming that its proposals still look like more water-development activities—this despite the far-reaching and innovative scope of the initiative's public involvement and public participation efforts. There seemed to be a pervasive sentiment among those interviewed that if the Bay-Delta is to be restored and protected, it will be due to reliance on laws such as the Clean Water Act and the Endangered Species Act.

Somewhat ironically, this report followed by a few months the release of a draft environmental impact assessment (EIS) released by CALFED that identified a series of management options for improving water supply reliability, water quality, and levee protection (Jacobs, Luoma, and Taylor 2003). The draft EIS proposed over 600 ecosystem restoration projects as well as a water budget to ensure that fish are protected "from operations that increase the reliability of urban supplies" and greater water conservation (Jacobs, Luoma, and Taylor 2003: 33).

Overall, CALFED's achievements and failures must also be assessed in a larger context—that of California's water problems as a whole. California continues to undergo water stresses that make compromise and long-term solutions difficult. The state continues to use more water from the Colorado River than it is entitled to draw,[13] and, beginning in 2003, the federal government will reduce that amount by a volume that could serve the needs of 1.5 million families. Currently, the Colorado river supplies 30% of coastal Southern California's water, even though the Colorado River's spring flow has run at only 14% of the normal rate (Kasindorf 2002: 12A). Possible long-term solutions entertained as of this writing include greater conservation, an increased rate of underground water storage, desalination, and elimination of the state water law favoring farms in order to give cities precedence (Kasindorf 2002: 12A).[14]

Also as of this writing, the effort to forestall conflict among the seven Colorado River compact states—including California—has reached a serious impasse due in part to the refusal of a rural irrigation district in Southern California to sell water to San Diego County for public and municipal use for fear of increasing demands for its water rights. The recent vote by the Imperial Valley Irrigation District to reject the sale of a small portion of its share of the Colorado River's water has set off a chain reaction of events that almost immediately led U.S. Secretary of the Interior Gale Norton to cut off California's share of the Colorado River (Murphy 2002; U.S. Water News 2002).

Part of the complex series of agreements on river reallocation depended on the valley's 400 or so farmers relinquishing a portion of the Colorado's water that they use so it can be used by the Southern California Metropolitan Water District's 17 million customers—this was termed the Quantification Settlement Agreement. Farmers were reluctant to agree to this for fear that they might never reacquire rights to the water *and* because of the possibility of reduced runoff to the Salton Sea. This might ironically increase the sea's salinity levels and harm aquatic species sensitive to changes in salinity (Murphy 2002).[15] Refusal to reverse the decision not to sell the water forced the Interior Department to reduce the state's use of the Colorado beginning in 2003 to levels originally agreed to in 1929 (U.S. Water News 2002). Moreover, the continuing plague of drought in the region keeps the issue in the news.[16]

There are three main lessons of this ongoing conflict. First, sustainability is impossible to achieve without mechanisms in place—and the supporting community attitudes—to permit the sharing of a common resource for the long-term benefit of all, even if short-term sacrifice is required. Second, management systems that are unable to change with evolving conditions may not only produce new conflicts but also engender a breaking of covenants formerly agreed to under different conditions. In effect, an inflexible, permanent, and flawed agreement is worse for the management of natural resources than no agreement at all—from the standpoint of sustainability. An adaptive management framework that permits change, flexibility, and the reopening of existing agreements when conditions warrant would be a far better way of managing— indeed, preventing—such conflicts. As an official with the San Diego County Water Authority recently stated, "The days of water wars is a place where nobody wanted to return, particularly when we had a agreement that provided for something the Colorado River has never experienced, which is 75 years of peace on the river" (Murphy 2002).

Finally, regardless of the long-term prognosis for this conflict, it—and similar conflicts—have already resonated throughout the West in one *positive* sense: by encouraging renewed dialogue among western states and communities over the need for long-term planning and "locally driven solutions" ("Interior Secretary Kicks off Dialogue" 2003: 1345). A measure of how well such dialogue has enabled new programs to be developed is the November 2002 approval, by California voters, of a $3.4 billion bond measure to provide new water supply and quality management measures to the state. Nearly 25% of this bond measure—$825 million—is going to support CALFED projects revolving around ecosystem protection, levee restoration, and additional studies (Whetzel 2002).

CALFED Achievements: Can Sustainable Development Be Learned?

If there is one area where CALFED has made remarkable inroads, it is in explicitly using adaptive management principles. As one observer notes, CALFED is based on "an iterative learning and management process (that) requires ongoing monitoring and evaluation of management actions." (Jacobs, Luoma, and Taylor 2003: 39). While far from perfect, CALFED exemplifies the adaptive management paradigm in several ways. For one thing, science and policy are linked in virtually all decisions—from restoring salmon to determining riverine flows. While program objectives are fixed and relatively unchanging (due to court-ordered policies), CALFED has the ability to adjust its actions to changing circumstances. In some instances, this has led to actions that critics have labeled overly expedient—too quick to cut deals to placate powerful interests instead of being based on the best science, especially in the initiative's early stages. Fair or not, such criticisms miss a larger point: some scientific agendas chosen early on were justifiable because they led to early political agreement—and thus were viewed as legitimate by participants—even if they were less technically ambitious. Such successful agreements are important to the long-term effectiveness of any new political entity (Jacobs, Luoma, and Taylor 2003: 38).

Another aspect of CALFED that exemplifies the adaptive management paradigm is the initiative's embracing of partnership with nongovernmental organizations committed to sustainability, including corporations. In 1999, Pacific Gas & Electric and CALFED signed a memorandum of understanding (MOU) to restore more than 40 miles of northern California's Battle Creek— "the largest restoration of migratory fish habitat (Steelhead trout and Chinook salmon) in the state's history," according to the Nature Conservancy (Calhoun 1999). Five small hydroelectric dams will eventually be removed, fish ladders and diversion screens will be installed on the stream's remaining dams, and the utility will forego $20 million in revenue. CALFED has paid $28 million for the dam removal portion of the project thus far. As of 2006, however, the project has been stalled due to what CALFED calls "delays and increased costs" (Battle Creek background, CALFED website, www.calwater.ca.gov). In 2005, CALFED's ecosystem restoration program called for renewed efforts to model Chinook salmon and steelhead migration, assess reintroduction of these species in some streams, and monitor program outcomes once various strategies are introduced (CALFED 2005).

The Nature Conservancy's role in this project is twofold. First, by coincidence, Battle Creek is located in its Lassen-Foothills's project area in northern California, where the Nature Conservancy is seeking to monitor and restore fish habitat. The Nature Conservancy has a longstanding interest in adaptive management and species restoration, particularly in this region, and it so happens that one of the small hydro dams to be removed is in this region. Second, it has used a $3 million grant to establish an "adaptive management fund" for the project, the purpose of which is to monitor the effects of dam removal and "fine-tune" the project as needed (Calhoun 1999).[17]

PG&E benefits by receiving indirect compensation for the loss of hydropower revenues, CALFED benefits by being able to achieve a restoration of habitat for threatened and important fish species, and the Nature Conservancy has the opportunity to use the project as a sort of test-bed for its efforts at adaptive management and sustainability. Most important of all, CALFED itself does not take on sole responsibility for managing restoration—not only a difficult task but, from the standpoint of adaptive management—an undesirable task as well, since the objective should be to change attitudes and practices at the grassroots level over the long run so as not to be dependent on a single agency to impose or enforce a policy.

CALFED's experience thus far exemplifies another important lesson about adaptive management: we have now entered an era in which water disputes will increasingly confront different users of the same water source, often in the same region or even in the immediate vicinity. As we shall see in chapter 5, this mandates the need for agreements that make it possible for an ethic of sustainability to prevail. Such an ethic must make it practical for people within a given watershed or water use region to manage all uses of water in a way that is efficient, equitable, and economically affordable.

For example, while it would be easy to blame Imperial Valley farmers for refusing to give up some of their water to support urban users, it must also be kept in mind that those same farmers—and their families—would be legally responsible for paying to protect the Salton Sea's endangered species, which could be further threatened with extinction if the sea became even "saltier" as a result of a reduction in runoff due to selling water to San Diego (*U.S. Water News* 2002). In effect, it is easier to assign blame than to come up with sustainable solutions that require equitable sacrifice and fair contributions from everyone—and that acknowledge that it may be possible to violate a law in the spirit of obeying an ethical principle.

As in the NPPC case, ethical change is not merely an abstraction—partnering NGOs are making tangible efforts to achieve it. Currently, the focus of these efforts in CALFED is environmental justice: meetings with community groups and others on the impact of Bay-Delta issues on the welfare of communities as well as on reforming the process by which community decisions related to water resources management (conservation, water pricing, water quality protection) should be made (Gomez 1997).[18] How much long-term impact these efforts will have remains open to question. What is certain is that the object of these efforts—to bring water management issues in CALFED down to the level of local communities—especially communities of color—represents a major change in the manner in which water resources policies have been made in the United States, as we discussed in chapter 2. Clearly representing a departure from the old model of policymaking, these efforts also are consistent with CALFED's goal to avoid and redress the environmental mistakes of the past by not engaging in fractious and divisive conflict and encouraging educated debate instead.

HOW DECISION-MAKERS VIEW THEIR INITIATIVES:
SURVEY FINDINGS

This section examines the findings of our survey of a handful of key decision-makers, which we discussed at the beginning of this chapter. In our assessment of these findings, we begin by examining the motives for forming these initiatives. The questions alluded to in this discussion are contained in appendix A.

Overview of Survey Results: What Drives the Formation of an Initiative?

The CALFED responses to the question of motivation were noteworthy in that most respondents indicated several motivations for establishing and continuing the initiative. A desire to achieve more local or regional flexibility in decision-making was the only choice that was not indicated as an initial or current motive for CALFED. Ensuring peaceable allocation of water supply was the choice selected most often (that is, by three of the five CALFED respondents) as the single most important motivator for CALFED. The other two CALFED respondents indicated that the failure of established programs to address an environmental problem was the single most important motivator, and one of those respondents stated that this motive was linked to another concern—enabling continued economic growth by reducing uncertainty. Another CALFED respondent added reversing a long decline in ecosystem health to the list of choices.

On the other hand, SRBC and DRBC respondents most often noted ensuring peaceable allocation of water supply as a motive for establishing and continuing these initiatives. A desire to be proactive and to achieve more local or regional flexibility in decision-making were also frequently indicated motives for the SRBC's establishment, and both motives were offered along with peaceably allocating water supply as the single most important motivation for the initiative. Interestingly, only one DRBC respondent offered the avoidance of litigation as the single most important motivation for the initiative's formation.

One ACF respondent indicated that ensuring peaceable allocation of water supply was the single most important motivation for establishing the initiative, whereas a desire to be proactive in addressing a potential future river basin problem was said to be the primary reason for *continuing* the initiative. The other ACF respondent suggested that avoiding litigation and enabling continued economic growth were the initial and current motivations, respectively, for the initiative. As we saw, avoiding litigation was an important incentive in the desire of ACF negotiators to extend "eleventh-hour" discussions to agree on an allocation formula. The lone NPPC respondent alluded to a crisis (the decline of salmon stocks in the Columbia basin) as the primary initiating and sustaining concern for the initiative.

Establishing Consensus, Making Decisions

Survey responses appear to confirm what secondary accounts of CALFED's experience indicated—the CALFED Basin Advisory Committee appears to use the greatest variety of tools for negotiating decisions and developing consensus, including meeting facilitators, a public advisory council, stakeholder meetings, technical and scientific review panels, and even public referenda. SRBC is likewise said to use advisory groups and public information meetings, but "good, competent, professional staff and dedicated commissioners" were also highlighted in SRBC responses as being instrumental to establishing consensus.

In addition to public hearings, meetings, and seminars, DRBC respondents referred to the current basin-wide, comprehensive planning process as a means of defining the elements of the DRBC's vision as well as a way to identify challenges and introduce solutions. ACF respondents alluded to technical and public policy meetings, workshops, and team building retreats with facilitators as important tools designed to build agreement. The NPPC respondent cited public meetings as the dominant instrument for consensus-building and decision-making.

Soliciting Public Input and Using Science in Decision-Making

All respondents cited the fact that public meetings, newsletters, and workshops are used to solicit public input. Only ACF respondents did not cite the use of presentations made to schools and other organizations for the purpose of disseminating information and soliciting public comments and concerns. All the initiatives surveyed agreed that television and radio advertising was not a common means of soliciting public input. CALFED respondents referred to the initiative's website and a public service video, while the DRBC respondents cited a recent conference on watershed management issues as an example of how public input was solicited.

Respondents concurred that current decisions garnered the greatest amount of public input. Most respondents also indicated that there has been a significant increase in public input over time. When asked for the reasons for this increase in public input, the most common reason given was growing public concern over impending decisions growing out of an initiative. Exemplifying such impending decisions is this statement by the sole NPPC respondent who corresponded with us via survey: "The Endangered Species Act is forcing tough decisions to be made; some can seriously affect people's livelihood." The increasing visibility and public awareness of programs was also frequently offered as a reason for increased public input.

Respondents also indicated that public input is considered in every aspect of their respective initiative's actions, especially with regard to the content of planning documents and reports. Respondents also stated that scientific information is used to identify problems, to set priorities, to model the dynamics of river systems, and to identify solutions to problems. One DRBC respondent added that scientific information is used for monitoring existing environmental problems and conditions. While not explicitly mentioned by any other respondent, one suspects that this use of scientific information would also characterize other initiatives as well.

Stakeholder Roles in River Basin Initiatives: Supporting and Opposing the Status Quo

Many groups were said to be proponents of the initiatives, including environmental organizations and farmers. CALFED respondents were the most likely among all respondents to suggest the virtual absence of opposition to the initiative, although in reality virtually every aspect of the CALFED initiative has garnered some opposition from some group. One CALFED respondent stated that "area-of-origin" interests (upstream counties) have expressed the most opposition to the initiative.

For their part, SRBC respondents characterized government officials as being initiative opponents: Congress for recently withholding funding; state and federal agencies, who have expressed concern over a loss of authority; and local officials whose projects are subject to regulation by the basin commission. Industry and farmers were also listed as *initial* opponents of the SRBC. DRBC respondents cited industry, power companies, farmers, local government officials, and "grassroots" activists as initial opponents of the basin commission.

The sole NPPC respondent indicated that there were no opponents to that initiative—a surprising response.

There is no clear consensus among initiatives with regard to the level of influence various interest groups have had on key decisions. CALFED respondents seemed to have the greatest difference of opinion. SRBC respondents suggested that electric power generators, recreational fishing interests, and environmental/ecological concerns held the greatest sway. Recreational fishing interests, environmental/ecological concerns, and electric power generators scored high with DRBC respondents also, although the manufacturing sector and nonfishing recreationalists were also said to be influential in key decisions. One ACF respondent indicated that Native American groups had the greatest influence, while municipal government had the least—but there may have been a misunderstanding with regard to how to rank influence. Indeed, the other ACF respondent ranked Native Americans as having the lowest influence, with municipal governments having the most. The NPPC respondent stated that commercial fishing interests had the most influence while electric power production interests had the least.

Most respondents felt that the relative influence of all these special interest groups had changed over time. Environmental groups, agricultural interests, and Native Americans were said to be more active, vocal, and inclined to use the judicial system in recent years. Electric utilities were variously characterized as having become "greener and more public minded," in the case of SRBC, and less cohesive and organized, in the case of DRBC.

Funding and Obstacles to Goal Achievement

Respondents cited a variety of state and federal government-funding sources. CALFED, SRBC, and DRBC respondents cited user fees as a major source of funding. Although there were differences of opinion, even within an initiative, with regard to funding adequacy, staffing, and other resources, a recurring theme was that available resources are not keeping up with expanding missions, even when funding increases. SRBC and DRBC respondents cited recent reductions and even the elimination of federal support as an important fiscal constraint.

When asked what had been the most significant obstacle to establishing the initiative, SRBC respondents most often referred to state government concerns over sovereignty. DRBC respondents also mentioned the "parochial view of the states" as well as the resistance of the federal government to enter into an agreement as one party among five equal partners. ACF respondents cited mistrust, positional attitudes, and self-interest on the part of the member states as impediments to cooperation. CALFED respondents cited a history of conflict over California water resources and diverging stakeholder interests and needs as a recurring issue.

CALFED respondents indicated that collaboration through an open, stakeholder-driven process was the primary way that this obstacle of mistrust was overcome. Strong leadership, aggressive support, and "deft work" at the state and federal levels were said to have overcome initial opposition to the SRBC. Crisis (a flood and the threat of litigation) was said to have underscored the need for the DRBC, while allowing Congress to add the "federal effectuation section" to the compact (the section which provided for a federal agency veto over compact actions not in accord with federal law and practice) helped overcome federal resistance to the Delaware compact. One ACF respondent stated that the biggest single obstacle to the establishment of a successful initiative— agreement on an allocation formula for water—had not been overcome, whereas the other ACF respondent answered this question with one word: "science" (implying that the absence of science had impeded agreement).

Survey respondents were asked about significant obstacles to the achievement of goals. CALFED respondents stated that some parties refused to relinquish their traditional positions, believing their interests would ultimately fare better in the courts or with the legislature. A critical shortage of developed water supply was also cited as a major obstacle. Inadequate resources, limited public awareness, lack of support from federal agencies, and fragmented staff goals were offered as the major obstacles to the SRBC's success. DRBC respondents cited similar obstacles: inadequate funding, inadequate political attention and commitment, and institutional resistance to change. One DRBC respondent stated that it was difficult to maintain a high level of interest while doing a good job and having no major problems. ACF respondents pointed to "state staff level power plays" as a major obstacle to success, while the NPPC respondent cited a lack of consensus in the region over major water management issues.

Measuring Success: Have Impediments Been Overcome?

Each of the CALFED respondents had a different perception of how the obstacles cited—the obstinacy of parties and critical water supply shortages—

could be overcome. One expressed doubt that these obstacles would ever be overcome, while others suggested the need for high-level government leadership and better development, conservation, and allocation of water resources. One CALFED respondent offered the particularly interesting strategy of making funding for all programs contingent on their success in achieving their objectives.

SRBC respondents felt that their past record of successes, an active current program of public outreach, restoration of federal funding, and strong leadership in the White House would help overcome the obstacles to achieving their goals. DRBC respondents were most likely to suggest that drought or other "natural disasters" would overcome the obstacles to success. The NPPC respondent suggested that keeping all parties involved was the key to success, while one ACF respondent made the curious comment that the "necessity of Georgia water supply demands" would overcome the obstacles to that initiative's achievement of its goals. Another ACF respondent stated, as before, that the obstacle of mutual mistrust among the member states had not been overcome and that this impedes change.

CALFED respondents were evenly split between "somewhat successful" and "too soon to judge" in their assessment of the success of their initiative. SRBC respondents judged their initiative to be somewhat successful, with one respondent indicating that it had been very successful on some issues and less successful in dealing with others. DRBC respondents variously reported that their initiative had been very successful, generally successful, and somewhat unsuccessful. The ACF was judged by one respondent to be somewhat successful, whereas the other respondent thought it was too soon to judge. The NPPC respondent was the only one to characterize the initiative as somewhat unsuccessful.

Within most of the initiatives there was an even split of opinion regarding whether formal means have been developed to assess effectiveness. Two CALFED respondents referred to a comprehensive monitoring, assessment, and research program. Two SRBC respondents mentioned regular reports on commission activities and achievements as well as continuous monitoring of the impact of regulations promulgated by and through the initiative. Two DRBC respondents noted the existence of a formal progress review undertaken via public surveys. ACF and NPPC respondents indicated there are no formal means of assessing initiative effectiveness.

There was strong consensus among CALFED respondents that willingness to compromise was the factor that would most contribute to the success of that initiative. Broad-based recognition of the SRBC as the primary stewards of the basin's water and related resources as well as a political commitment to using SRBC as the primary device for planning and managing these resources were said to be the factors that would most contribute to the success of that initiative. Political support, staff leadership, restoration of full funding, and the recognition of the need for unified regional management were offered as the factors that have already most contributed to the success of the DRBC or would eventually do so. The ACF respondent who judged that initiative to be somewhat successful stated that "the science developed through the comprehensive plan" was the most important factor leading to success. The NPPC respondent said that "keeping everyone at the table" was a critical factor.

Finally, we asked initiative respondents if the effort they were involved in created a new certification or other formal mechanism for approval of projects that affect water quality or supply. CALFED respondents indicated that such details were still being worked out. SRBC respondents referred to section 3.10 of the compact, which provides the authority to approve or disapprove certain projects involving water withdrawals and consumptive uses. Likewise, DRBC respondents pointed to enabling statutory authority (that is, section 3.8 of their compact and 18 CFR Parts 410 and 430), which state that all projects having a substantial effect on water resources must be applied for and approved by DRBC prior to starting construction. Under the DRBC compact, as stated in Section 3.8, projects must be approved by the commission before being undertaken. One ACF respondent alluded to "approval of increased water supply allocation," while the other ACF respondent indicated that there was no formal approval mechanism associated with that initiative. The NPPC respondent stated that there was no formal mechanism for project approval.

ASSESSMENT: TOWARD A MODEL
OF SUSTAINABLE MANAGEMENT

Our principal research objectives in undertaking this survey were twofold: (1) to determine the conditions necessary for making comprehensive river basin/watershed management schemes acceptable to major parties involved in their development and operation; and (2) to ascertain whether or not these initiatives have thus far met the conditions for sustainable management. The second of these objectives can best be assessed, we feel, by combining our earlier literature survey with the decision-maker survey results. We hypothesized that there are four principal conditions necessary for success:

- Overcoming mutual suspicion;
- Synchronizing basin authorities with the natural/ecological region;
- Enmeshing activities with the cultural context of the region; and
- Addressing environmental problems with the greatest salience to the region.

In assessing the degree to which the survey results support these hypotheses, the first observation to make is the difficulty in drawing strong conclusions from the few responses that were received. We must appreciate that responses do more in the way of suggesting than indicating what is going on. However, we might be able to glean additional insight into the nature of these initiatives based on the level of response. For example, the low level of ACF and NPPC response might be due to the high degree of contention that has characterized both initiatives so far.[19]

Many of the news media accounts of events related to ACF compact negotiations, as we have seen, have characterized the underlying conflict as a "water war." Alabama, Florida, and Georgia remain far apart in reaching accord over how to divide up the waters of their shared rivers. Radical concessions may need to be made by each side (see, for instance, *Atlanta Journal and Constitution* 1999). It is possible that potential ACF respondents were concerned that candid responses to a survey might aggravate an already tense situation. It is also possible that they found it difficult to anticipate or judge the answers to our questions, given the brief history of the compact. A similar situation may characterize the NPPC.[20] We surmise that the political sensitivity of the initiative may have inhibited candid responses from questionnaire recipients. While we discuss the single response from the NPPC, we do not in any way consider its content to be definitive or to reflect any consensus among the larger group.

The initiatives we examined meet at least two of the four principal conditions necessary for success. Each basin authority has been synchronized with the appropriate geographical area in that all major state and federal agencies within each river basin are represented in its deliberations. Furthermore, there is little doubt that the issues addressed by each initiative have a high degree of salience to the citizens of the region. Increasing public input in each initiative, especially in key decisions, is one indication that affected individuals recognize that agreements made by their respective initiatives have a significant, tangible effect on their lives—whether in drought mitigation, flood protection, fish species restoration, power generation, or water quality improvement.

Overcoming Mutual Suspicion

Are protagonists who represent different points of view, interests, or organizational or institutional affiliations naturally suspicious of others who hold opposite opinions or who work in organizations with different mandates? If so, then of the five river basin initiatives we examined, CALFED might be the best example of an effort that has made significant progress in overcoming mutual suspicion among stakeholders. To a greater degree than those representing the other initiatives, CALFED respondents tended to emphasize the divergent stakeholder interests and the history of conflict over regional water resources as the major obstacles to the establishment and success of the initiative. The CALFED respondents were also the group most likely to point to the open, stakeholder-driven negotiation process as the key to overcoming this obstacle. CALFED respondents were also unified in their assessment of what factor most contributed to the success of the initiative: willingness to compromise.

When asked about the initiative's opponents and proponents, CALFED respondents identified a broader range of stakeholders than other groups, stating that virtually all of the stakeholders support the overall initiative and its goals, although every interest group had reservations about some aspects of the agreements and decisions being made by the initiative. In this regard, it is noteworthy that CALFED appears to be the most thorough of the initiatives studied in using all available means of soliciting and incorporating public input.

It is clear that overcoming mutual suspicion has been a major challenge in each case. Concern over loss of sovereignty was a strong theme in the four interstate initiatives and was frequently cited as a major impediment to success. However, the critical nature of river basin problems and the strong commitment and leadership on the part of high-level officials appears to have helped overcome distrust. It is as if the opponents realized that they were all in the same (sinking) boat and that their only hope was to pull together in the same direction.

Building Consensus: CALFED as a Model?

CALFED seems to have been especially successful so far in building a broad base of support among some traditional enemies. Although CALFED has not had the particular type of interjurisdictional issues that are associated with interstate compacts, its challenges have been more like those experienced by the other initiatives than unlike. In fact, we speculate that conflicts among user groups might be more intense than conflicts between states with regard to river management goals. NGOs in California are widely perceived as being more vociferous than in other states, so consensus-building would seem to be an even greater challenge there.

We suggest two possible explanations for CALFED's success in getting traditional adversaries as environmentalists and agribusiness to compromise. First, there might be a greater balance of power between environmental interests and development interests in California than elsewhere. In the absence of an obvious advantage over one's opponent, compromise appears to be the only way of achieving some of one's objectives. As William Wade observed during a 1998 water policy conference in Chattanooga, Tennessee, water wars work only so long as one's political opposition is weak: this has not been the case in California for the past 20 years.

The history and culture of California might be a second factor that distinguishes CALFED from the other initiatives we have studied. Water has always been relatively scarcer in central and southern California than in the eastern United States. The densely populated areas in the southern and western portions of the state have been diverting water from the wetter northern and eastern areas since at least 1913. The three elements of early water policy in California—lawyers, engineers, and politicians—were unable to match water solutions to needs (Wade 1998). The magnitude and immediacy of crises related to water shortages in the Bay-Delta region is perhaps greater or more obvious than in the other river basins we have studied.

In contrast, the southeast has been considered water rich, and that has affected the region's culture in terms of attitudes toward water use and availability. Enjoying higher mean annual precipitation than most other regions of the country, it is difficult for most people in the southeast to think in terms of water shortages or the need for conservation. While the ACF negotiators continue to debate how much water they will have and the timing of its delivery at various points in the basin, the Californians seem to understand that their water needs must be approached from the standpoint of consumption rather than availability. Coming to terms with how to use whatever water is available is likely to be more effective than trying to guess how much will be available and how to apportion it in terms of absolute volume.

Cultural Context and Political Acceptability

While we did not explicitly address the cultural context of various initiatives in our questionnaire, we were able to glean some sense of how each initiative has enmeshed its activities within the cultural context of the region. For example, the DRBC's 1997 annual report describes the Delaware River and Lehigh Valley Sojourns, which are organized educational and recreational expeditions of up to eight days in length. Sojourners may raft or paddle the entire length of a river, viewing the landscape from a vantage seldom seen and long neglected. Interspersed with on-the-water activities are lectures and demonstrations about the history, geology, and ecology of the region. Engaging the public through this kind of event, which highlights the recreational and cultural values of the river, undoubtedly builds stronger local and regional support for the commission's larger program of river management.

The nomination of the Delaware River main stem and three of its tributary rivers as American Heritage Rivers provides another example of the successful union of cultural and environmental values in raising awareness and building support for watershed protection. The nomination package even underscored the historical ties to the river.[21]

Cultural issues have also clearly been major considerations in the restoration of the Columbia River system. As stated by the NPPC respondent, the influence of Native American groups in that initiative has increased over time. The recognition of the importance of salmon as a symbol and a way of life for Pacific Northwest tribes as well as the contemporary value of salmon in recreational fishing, commercial fishing, tourism, and the regional economy have been powerful motivations for changing the way the Columbia system is managed.

The importance of cultural issues and their integration into environmental concerns have also been important in the Susquehanna. One of the foremost proponents of strengthening this connection has been a nonprofit corporation, the Chesapeake Bay Foundation, founded by supporters of the SRBC. Excursions for public school students, the promotion of independent research and monitoring, and public outreach efforts (an estimated 35,000 people a year partake of the foundation's programs) are all components of the foundation's program to keep public awareness of the basin's environmental challenges at the forefront of public policy (Stranahan 1993: 279, 292). Interestingly, this innovation is a striking example of the kinds of public-private partnerships that have often sprung out where initiatives have developed.

As for the ACF compact, it is too early to determine the degree to which the activities of the initiative will be enmeshed in the cultural context of the region. However, it would seem that there are ample opportunities for using the shared cultural attributes of Georgia, Florida, and Alabama to create a sense of unity and shared purpose that would facilitate collaborative river basin management. As we shall see in chapter 5, this emphasis on cultural ties is also important to efforts to improve water quality—an issue whose dependence on adequate water quantity and flow is now widely recognized.

CHAPTER 4

Water Quality and Quantity
The Critical Interface

There's a lot of stories and a lot of things to be shared when you reflect back to the good use of the river. There is the flow . . . the real Indian aspect of being able to paddle on a river downstream. In addition . . . there was always good fishing . . . no matter where you stopped.

> —*Willie M., Cree nation member, on the changes brought about by Quebec's James Bay Hydroelectric Project*

"Fish need water everyday."

> —*Melinda Kassen*

This chapter examines the relationship among water quality, water supply, and sustainable development. Two issues are central: the difficulty in maintaining water supplies that are safe for people and other life and the challenge of ensuring adequate surface water flow in lakes, rivers, and streams to provide a sufficient water to sustain fish, wildlife, and human uses.

Thus far, we have focused on disputes that revolve around the development and use of water resources within large river basins. However, water quality issues—whether revolving around pollution or instream flow—arise in numerous geographical contexts large and small. Many of our nation's most polluted streams are actually small stream segments contained within a single community or small watersheds only a few dozen square miles in size. Likewise, issues of low flow often arise in tiny trout streams or other rivers that are no bigger than a creek. Yet these streams exhibit significant amounts of bio-diversity.

As we have seen, in large river basins instream flow and water pollution issues are embedded in management disputes. However, they sometimes become relegated to secondary stature due to the priority traditionally accorded questions related to allocating water for power generation, irrigation, and public supply or related to providing sufficient reservoir storage to abate floods and mitigate the effects of drought. Even when concern for protecting ecological resources and human health is high and demands to balance instream flow and pollution control against economic development are articulated (as in the Delaware, Susquehanna, and CALFED experiences and the Murray and La Plata basins), efforts at adaptive management (for instance, reallocation of water releases for fisheries) tend to be animated by issues of quantity, not quality.

This reality is reinforced by the fact that most river basin compacts have been established primarily to address water allocation, flood control, navigation, and hydropower. They are water quantity institutions—not water quality ones—as we have seen in the Colorado, Tennessee, Delaware, Sacramento, Chattahoochee-Apalachicola, and Columbia basins. Moreover, in the evolution of U.S. water policy, quality and quantity concerns have been managed through distinct sets of laws and management regimes. In effect, they have not been managed in an integrated manner—a precondition for adaptive management. In this chapter, we focus on how water quality is protected, and how quality and quantity concerns can be better integrated.

Integrated Water Resources Management: Quality, Quantity, and Adaptive Management

Water quality and quantity must be managed as a coherent whole for sustainable development to be achieved. In those places where decision-makers have attempted to fuse them with some success—in the areas of nonpoint pollution abatement, point source control, and instream flow protection—they have utilized adaptive management principles. The lessons they have learned apply to other communities seeking to balance economic development, environmental protection, and social justice concerns in water management (EPA 2002b).

To make this case, we examine two separate but related programs. The first is the effort by the EPA and states to protect water quality, principally through the Total Maximum Daily Load (TMDL) program. The second is the recent effort by the federal government, states, and stakeholder groups to protect instream flow by setting standards and instituting other measures.

Instream flow is defined as the flow, volume, and quality of surface water supply in lakes, streams, and rivers. Threats to natural flow include actions that impede—as well as those that detrimentally increase—natural surface water levels and volumes. In effect, instream flow is a quantity issue because it directly affects the amount of water in a given water body at any given time. It is also a quality issue because the ability to dilute contaminants (and waste heat from power plants or factories) remains an important method of water quality protection worldwide.

Both programs are directly related to water supply. Instream flow is related because it refers to the actual volumes of water necessary to support life viably. TMDLs are related because that portion of water supply used as a public drinking water source is, in effect, regulated by the EPA, and the volumetric flow of a stream affects its ability to "carry" pollutants. Despite this relationship, the ways in which water quality and instream flow are managed are very different. To illustrate why integrated water management is challenging, we must first understand how water law embraces two regimes—one for quality, the other for quantity.

Historically, U.S. water law has been fragmented, with authority divided between state and federal levels and quality and quantity concerns embraced in different sets of regulations. In both cases, but especially in regard to water supply, the "common law" tradition has prevailed. Most policies have been nonstatutory and based on precedent, tradition, and custom—occasionally amended by specific legislation. The particular version of common law adopted in the United States was the English system of riparian water law, adopted by most of the thirteen colonies when most of the land was privately owned. As lands passed out of federal ownership and into private settlers, particularly in the Northwest Territories and other frontier areas, law courts modified riparianism to meet "the needs of an American society" (Beck 1997: 217). Water law in the west evolved in a somewhat different direction, with the emergence of the so-called law of prior appropriation becoming ascendant by the mid–nineteenth century, as we shall see.

Initially, since the states west of the Mississippi River were carved out of the public domain—that is, from lands acquired by the federal government through treaties with France, the U.K., Spain, and even Native Americans—pressures on water supply tended to be driven by activities that benefited from the public lands disposition policies of the federal government. As land grants were made to railroads, states, and individuals through preemption and home-steading laws, water demands tended to arise more spontaneously—miners, ranchers and others took whatever they needed. As conflicts arose, western state courts began applying the principle of "first in time, first in right" among trespassers—and legislatures later codified the practices into law. Thus was born the prior appropriation doctrine (Beck 1997: 217).

Under both riparian and prior appropriation doctrine, conditions and strategies for protecting water quality have been somewhat vague. In eastern states governed by the riparian common law, it was assumed that reasonable use implied desisting from taking action on surface waters that could injure downstream users. In a dispute, judgment is to be based on whether or not an allegedly "harmful" use impedes the satisfaction of widely agreed-upon economic and social values in society—in other words, the preference of American common law for economic development (Wright 1998: 12–13). Under prior appropriation, how to protect water quality is vaguer still. As we shall see, in the absence of specific statutory authority to the contrary, a purely appropriative regime provides little protection against taking as much water from a stream as is needed by the first-in-time rights holder. Reasonable use, in fact, is defined as beneficial off-stream use—and it has only been in recent years that western states have explicitly moved to ensure adequate instream flow and protection against harmful discharges into streams (Laitos and Tomain 1992: 364).

As we shall see, major changes in water quality laws began in the 1960s when regulations requiring permits and employing command and control techniques to achieve specific quantitative goals were instituted. These changes represented a shift in policy strategy by explicitly forbidding actions—or requiring that certain conditions be met—before discharges into water bodies would be permitted. This was a major change from the common law tradition of simply acting despite a condition preventing action—and, then, only desisting from an action when problems warrant.[1] We provide a more extended discussion of riparian rights later in this chapter. Meanwhile, we turn now to a discussion of TMDLs—one of the most complex command and control aspects of water pollution policy in the United States.

TOTAL MAXIMUM DAILY LOADS: DILUTION IS ONLY
PART OF A SOLUTION

Section 303(d) of the federal Clean Water Act requires states to establish, for any lake, river, stream or other water body that fails to meet federal water quality standards, a "Total Maximum Daily Load" for those pollutants responsible for failure to meet these standards. Simply stated, TMDLs are the amount of pollutants a given water body can sustain without violating prescribed water quality limits (FWPCA of 1972/Clean Water Act, sections 303(c, d)). Such water quality limits exist in large part to protect human health and the drinking water supply.

The value at which TMDLs are set theoretically ensures that water quality standards can be maintained. To help assure this, every TMDL contains several parts including a margin of safety.[2] If a state fails to develop adequate TMDLs, the EPA is required to make its own and set priorities for meeting them (Copeland 2001). A TMDL may be seen as both a planning process for attaining water quality standards and a quantitative assessment of the problems, pollution sources, and pollutant reductions needed to restore a river, stream, lake, or other water body.

Numerous studies have been done on the challenges entailed by the EPA's TMDL program for improving water bodies in the United States (see, for example, Davenport and Kirschner 2002; Bosch et al. 2002; Edwards 2002). The accuracy of the states' lists of impaired streams has also been examined by many analysts (see Mandrup-Poulsen 2002). However, there has been little investigation of how states are actually implementing TMDLs, what strategies they are adopting to reduce the inflow of pollutants causing impairment, and if these strategies are contributing to sustainable development.

In general, states face five major challenges in effectively developing and implementing TMDLs. The first is ensuring that adequate data exists for assessing water body quality and developing standards—or, if it does not, that it is being collected. The second is setting appropriate criteria for potential pollutants and establishing credible milestones for ensuring compliance with the limits imposed by these criteria. Third, involving stakeholders in TMDL decision-making has been difficult. Fourth, avoiding lawsuits by effluent dischargers and environmentalists has been a continuing issue in the implementation of programs to reduce discharges and to establish TMDL limits. Finally, encompassing unique hydrological challenges, such as seasonally variable precipitation and terrain, has been difficult—exemplifying the challenge in encompassing factors in water quality management that may constantly change—such as the amount of rain that falls or changes in land use.

Why TMDLS Are Controversial

TMDLs represent a significant shift from the way water quality has been historically regulated in the United States. Instead of the technology-based, end-of-pipe approach to "point" sources of pollution that have long characterized water pollution policy (for example, releases from known discharge sources), the TMDL program utilizes an ambient approach to monitoring and standard-setting. The approach focuses upon *in situ* (on site) quality and embraces "non-point" (that is, diffuse or runoff sources) as well as point sources of discharge (Tarlock, Corbridge, and Getches 1993; Boyd 2000). This has radically changed the politics and administration of water quality regulation because ambient monitoring has determined that a large number of the nation's water bodies are impaired in large part by nonpoint discharges, such as pesticide runoff and sediments from farms and lawns and petroleum products from streets and parking lots.

The enormous challenges faced by states and the EPA in managing this impairment, developing TMDLs in response to it, and continually modifying the process of rule-making to accommodate the demands of policymaking, implementation, and new scientific knowledge and understanding has made the TMDL program one of the most controversial, vexing, and litigious environmental policies of our time. In general, the literature is rife with three sets of criticisms:

(1) Environmental groups charge that TMDLs are inadequately enforced, incorporate public comments and other citizen input poorly, and are being developed and implemented too hesitantly to be effective (Ward 2002; Franz 2002; Samuelsohn 2002).

(2) Economic interests regulated by TMDLs assert that they impose high mitigation costs on industry and agriculture, list streams as impaired without adequate up-to-date supporting data or adequately tested computer models, and permit few appeals from bureaucratically imposed pollution limits ("Eighth Circuit" 2002; Ward 2002).

(3) Independent assessments by scientists conclude that many water bodies placed on impairment lists have been improperly analyzed. They

also suggest that the states' approaches to identifying impaired waters are inconsistent (leading to criticisms that EPA's database on national water quality is of questionable reliability) and advocate more innovative and economical development of TMDLs (NAS 2001; Copeland 2001; Franz 2002; GAO 2002).

Exacerbating these criticisms is their ambiguous nature: any assessment of the TMDL process—and its successes, failures, and still uncertain outcomes—must take aim at an elusive, moving target. As this is written, for example, Congress is considering proposals to revise the TMDL program,[3] and some view the current high-level congressional and administration debate over the effectiveness of TMDLs as, in effect, a move to put the entire program on hold. That view has become popular despite the uninterrupted imposition of court-ordered TMDL projects nationwide (for example, "TMDLs Finalized" 2002). Understanding the challenges facing TMDLs and the need for reform requires placing the program in historical context.

A BRIEF HISTORY OF U.S. WATER QUALITY POLICY

Today's Clean Water Act (CWA) has been shaped by over 100 years of legislation designed to protect the nation's water resources. As we have seen, the need for legislation was partly spurred by the failure of common law practice (for instance, riparian doctrine) to accommodate itself easily to water quality protection needs. In 1899, the River and Harbors Act—the nation's first water pollution law—was enacted to protect the nation's waters and to promote commerce by banning discharge of pollutants into navigable waters (Switzer 2001). This initial legislative effort was little more than a nuisance ordinance designed to discourage the dumping of solid wastes into rivers where they could pose a navigation hazard.

The Federal Water Pollution Control Act of 1948 (P.L. 80–845) was the first modern attempt at creating a genuinely all-inclusive statement of federal interest in clean water (Copeland 1999; Switzer 2001). The act offered federal technical assistance for research and regulation as well as state grants for building sewage treatment plants (Bruninga 2002). Until the act's passage, water pollution in the United States was viewed primarily as a state and local problem, as would be expected given the common law basis of U.S. water law. Thus, there were no federally required goals, objectives, regulatory standards or limits, or even procedures to achieve water quality.

Uniform federal water quality standards arrived with passage of the 1965 Water Quality Act, which charged states with setting standards, but only for navigable interstate waters. By the late 1960s, it was becoming apparent that the existing enforcement measures provided by these laws were too lax and that the water quality standard-setting approach was unsound because of difficulties in linking violations of stream quality standards to any specific discharger (Copeland 1999). Additionally, there was increasing frustration over the slow pace of pollution cleanup efforts and concern that control technologies were being developed but not aggressively applied.

In 1969, the growing environmental movement found ready examples of gross pollution of America's waters. In Cleveland, Ohio, the Cuyahoga River burst into flames, destroying several bridges, because of high concentrations of chemicals and industrial wastes—in effect, the river became so highly concentrated with flammable substances that it caught fire. That same year, waste from a food processing plant killed 26 million fish in Florida's Lake Thonotosassa. In addition, an oil spill off of scenic Santa Barbara, California, proved an especially telegenic disaster, with oil-soaked seals and pelicans and miles of fouled beaches (Loeb 1998). These and other incidents alarmed many Americans and brought appeals for reform.

Congress responded, overriding President Richard Nixon's veto to pass the 1972 Federal Water Pollution Control Act (FWPCA) to "restore and maintain the chemical, physical, and biological integrity of the nation's waters." The FWPCA strengthened water quality standards and established a regulatory structure for controlling discharges of pollution into waters of the United States. It made it illegal to discharge any toxic or nontoxic pollutant without a permit and encouraged the use of "best available technology" for pollution control.

Because of this legislation, practically every U.S. city was required to build and operate wastewater treatment plants, with the newly formed Environmental Protection Agency providing most of the funding and technical assistance for their construction. Until this act, most cities discharged their untreated waste directly into the nation's waterways. The FWPCA also directed states to set water quality standards for waters other than those designated as interstate navigable waters, to design plans for limiting industrial and municipal discharges, and to implement wetland protection programs. It also strongly discouraged the practice of discharging pollutants into waterways and set as a nationwide goal widespread "fishable and swimmable" water (by 1983) and zero pollutant discharge (by 1985). These were to be met by prohibiting the discharge of pollutants in toxic amounts (Findley and Farber 1992). In effect, the act imposed a "use" standard (that is, how would the waterway be used—as a habitat for fish, a recreational resource, or a navigational channel, for instance) and a "criterion" standard (a numerical limit on discharges regardless of the uses a stream would be assigned).

As amended in 1977, section 402 of the FWPCA created a permit system, the National Pollutant Discharge Elimination System, under which discharge permits could be granted by the EPA or states with EPA-approved programs. This program involves the application of technology to ensure that industry decreases its water pollution emissions. Section 402 declared unlawful any discharges by point sources, except in compliance with the limitations imposed in a permit (Findley and Farber 1992). Permits must incorporate applicable effluent limitations (as established under sections 301, 302, 306 and 307), including enforceable schedules of compliance. Under section 505 of the act, citizens could file a suit to enforce effluent limitations in state or EPA permits and orders. Citizens also could take legal action against the EPA for failure to perform nondiscretionary regulatory duties.

A 1977 amendment to the FWPCA, the Clean Water Act, emphasized control of toxic pollutants and established a program to shift responsibility of clean water programs to the states. Under CWA, pollutants include dredged materials, solid waste, incinerator residue, sewage and sewage sludge, garbage, munitions, chemical wastes, biological materials, radioactive materials, heat, wrecked or discarded equipment, rock, sand, cellar dirt, and industrial, municipal, and agricultural waste discharged to water. Toxic pollutants are those pollutants or combinations of pollutants, which after discharge and on exposure, ingestion, inhalation, or assimilation by an organism, cause harm to public health or even death. The 1977 amendments also authorized EPA to grant case-by-case extensions to the 1972 deadline for industrial dischargers—at least those who attempted, in good faith, to comply. Full compliance was required by 1979.

Several additional amendments to the CWA have had the cumulative effect of imposing progressively stricter standards on dischargers. For example, the Clean Water Act of 1987 imposed tighter regulations on toxic chemicals from industry, acid rain, and "nonpoint source" pollution discharges such as agricultural and urban storm water runoff. The term "point" source is defined as "any discernible, confined, and discrete conveyance" including but not limited to any pipe, ditch, channel, tunnel, conduit, well, discrete fissure, container, rolling stock, concentrated animal feeding operation, or vessel or other floating craft from which pollutants are or may be discharged. This term does not include agricultural stormwater discharges or return flow from irrigated agriculture (CWA 33 U.S.C § 1362). Pollutants coming from any other source are classified as nonpoint sources; the 1987 act also added section 319 to address them. The 1987 amendment prevents regulatory backsliding: with few exceptions, new permits cannot be less stringent than existing ones for the same facility (Findley and Farber 1992).

Under the CWA, states can impose rules to protect water quality and aquatic habitats that are stricter than those imposed by EPA. They can also require that minimum stream flows be maintained, even on federal navigable streams. A later amendment to the Clean Water Act—in the 1987 amendments—led to establishment of the Total Maximum Daily Load Program.

Addressing Nonpoint Water Pollution: The Clean Water Act of 1987

The TMDL concept is traceable to the amended Clean Water Act of 1987— Section 303(d) of the act requires states to establish, for all streams that fail to meet water quality standards, the "total maximum daily load" for those pollutants responsible for the failure to meet the prescribed standards. As noted, the goal of the act was to shift the nation's water pollution control policy from a strictly point-source emphasis through the imposition of permits on dischargers to an emphasis on nonpoint threats, especially to surface water (O'Toole 1998: 314–315).

Following the passage of the 1987 act, TMDLs remained a largely ignored component (Boyd 2000). States did practically nothing that was called for under section 303(d) during the 1980s and early 1990s. Likewise, the EPA did very little until a series of citizen suits during the mid-1980s forced it into a hasty rereading of section 303(d) and the scramble through the 1990s to comply with the TMDL process as a result of the outcomes of these lawsuits. These suits constituted the principal driver for the new focus on section 303(d) by challenging the EPA's oversight of states' responsibilities (Houck 1997; Boyd 2000). Environmental and citizen groups sought the listing of waters and TMDL development—the real motive for these suits. Most states had not submitted their assessment of polluted waters and thus had failed to prioritize waters for cleanup—as required by law. Nor had states developed and disseminated TMDLs or implemented associated discharge controls, as called for under section 303(d).

HOW STATES ARE DEVELOPING TMDLS:
A STEP-BY-STEP APPROACH

Section 303(d) of the Clean Water Act and subsequent regulation prescribe a five-step process for TMDL development: (1) identifying stream segments that are water quality–limited—that is, unable to support additional development because they are already out of compliance; (2) prioritizing water quality–limited waters/stream segments; (3) developing TMDL plans for these waters (that is, determining the maximum amount of each pollutant allowable in the form of a pollutant load); (4) implementing water quality–improvement actions; and (5) assessing improvement actions. The process must be repeated for all polluted water bodies, and no load can impair any water body's designated use. We now examine the first three steps and the challenges they raise. Later sections will deal with implementation issues. While examples are cited from throughout the entire United States, we concentrate on examples from the Southeast.

Identify Water Quality–Limited Waters

All states and U.S. territories are required to establish lists of impaired streams and other waters and develop specific plans for their recovery. The EPA has determined that the greatest sources of continuing impairment (encompassing some 300,000 miles of streams and shoreline and 5 million acres of lakes) are sedimentation, nutrients, and harmful microorganisms (EPA 1999). "Impairment" of waters refers not only to human uses but also to maintenance of fish populations and aquatic ecosystems in general.[4]

States use technologies, including computer models, to establish the TMDLs. These models have built-in assumptions that create a degree of uncertainty—symbolized by the safety margins. Once established, TMDLs and state inventories must pass EPA scrutiny. If the EPA finds that the lists or TMDL calculations are inadequate, they will create their own list and calculate their own TMDLs, which states must then incorporate into their pollution reduction plans (Houck 1997). While experts agree that there is no panacea for managing nonpoint pollutants, there is growing consensus that only a comprehensive, decentralized approach focused on *watersheds* will achieve lasting solutions. Such an approach is envisioned as embracing land use, forestry, agricultural activities, water uses, and discharges to water from all sources.

While in principle identifying water quality–limited stream segments or other water bodies appear to be straightforward, in practice it is anything but. The collection of water quality data and the assessment of stream segments and other water bodies have proven to be Herculean tasks that are both capital- and labor-intensive—requiring resources states are already hard-pressed to provide due to other environmental priorities. Moreover, a 2000 National Academy of Sciences (NAS) study chaired by Kenneth Reckhow of Duke University found that, nationwide, many waters originally placed on the 303(d) list by states and the EPA may have been improperly analyzed. "Our view," Reckhow wrote, "is that the state assessments were not very rigorously done." One example cited is Mississippi, where TMDLs were initially produced through what is termed a "windshield survey," a term meant to be taken literally—observations conducted while driving around watersheds—a well-established educational tool but not a particularly rigorous scientific method (Franz 2002).

An example of state assessments being subject to resource constraints is offered by West Virginia, which for some time failed to write any TMDLs following the settlement of a 1995 lawsuit brought by a group of environmentalists. The reason for the state's failure to prepare TMDLs was said to be a lack of funding to undertake the supporting studies (Ward 2002). Meanwhile, as late as 2002 Kentucky was reported to have 949 severely polluted waterways— four times the number reported in 1998 when a list of impaired streams was last reported. The state had only one person working on the TMDL program at the time. The reason for the increase in reported streams, it was argued, was the development of a more stringent state-monitoring program ("More Monitoring" 2002). In effect, improved information-gathering increased the capacity of the state to manage one aspect of its water quality program adaptively.

One controversy surrounding stream assessment is offered by Florida's Department of Environmental Protection (DEP), which promulgated an "Impaired Waters Rule" (IWR) in 2002. Major features of the rule include the establishment of minimum sample sizes, minimum confidence levels for impairment decisions, data age and data quality requirements, and temporal and spatial conditions on data ("State Agency News" 2002: 6–7). This method raises the number of exceedances required to classify a water body as impaired and excludes the use of data collected "under certain circumstances"—that is, it excludes data collected through methods that do not fully conform to the tests prescribed by the state, which some environmentalists believe are not protective enough. According to environmental activists who oppose the rule, it "establishes minimum sample size requirements to demonstrate that a water body is impaired [and] thus changes water quality standards" ("Activists to Sue EPA" 2002: 33).

State officials reply that they are reinterpreting existing rules, not creating a new set of standards, and that the new rule is intended to "interpret water quality standards," not rewrite them (33). Florida environmentalists planned to sue the EPA for failing to decide if the state's actions weaken federal water quality standards. After employing this method to prepare its 2002 update of the state's 303(d) list of impaired waters, the net change in the total number of water segment listings was minor—with new listings nearly equaling the newly eliminated listings ("State Agency News" 2002: 6). This raises the question as to whether it may be necessary to establish a nationally consistent method for stream sampling—and whether adaptive management is possible without such an agreed-upon method for determining impairment.

Prioritize Water Quality–Limited Waters

Following identification of impaired streams, the TMDL process requires states to prioritize waters that fail to meet water quality standards. This, too, has proven to be a particularly contentious problem, principally because there is no consensus on how priorities should be established. Some contend that recent reforms in the TMDL process by the EPA (Franz 2002) will allow states to focus more on waters of the state that have the highest pollutant levels and, thus, to concentrate on ways to improve those streams found to be most impaired ("water quality–limited" according to TMDL criteria). Proposed EPA reforms may give states greater flexibility in developing water quality monitoring plans, assessing water quality, and designing implementation plans to improve water quality. This is because the EPA has delegated to states the authority to approve individual point source dischargers' plans (Franz 2002). This is currently done for some discharges from wastewater treatment plants as well as industrial and commercial facilities and concentrated animal feeding operations that discharge wastewater.

Flexibility in assessment will not solve all such problems. A special challenge in prioritizing impaired waters is that water quality is affected by unique terrain and hydrology (see chapter 2). These "natural" factors can be exacerbated by land use and development patterns. Georgia, for example, uses one-third less water per capita than neighboring Alabama (which has only a third of Georgia's population) but relies more heavily on agriculture as an economic base. However, rain falling on Georgia generally produces higher rates of runoff—creating acute nonpoint pollution problems (Georgia Public Policy Foundation 1999: 1). Moreover, the 10-county metro Atlanta area has experienced a 20% loss of trees and other vegetation in recent years. This loss has led to a increase in runoff of 4.4 billion cubic feet ("Loss of Trees" 1997).

Clean Water Act regulations acknowledge considerable uncertainty in the relationship between effluent limits and water quality due to these hydrological factors. Unfortunately, such factors have led states to employ different methods for setting priorities—raising questions about the ability to develop a national approach for TMDL implementation, and about their ability to manage adaptively water quality in a way that embraces societal needs and hydrological constraints. For example, Section 303(d) prescribes that "in accordance with the priority ranking, a TMDL [be established] at a level necessary to implement the applicable water quality standards with seasonal variations and a margin of safety which takes into account any lack of knowledge concerning the relationship between effluent limitations and water quality."

Tennessee uses general water quality criteria, continuous record station flow data, instream water quality–monitoring data, a "calibrated dynamic water quality model" (among other models being considered), and "an appropriate margin of safety" to establish allowable loadings of contaminants (Bass, Berry, and Sims 2002; TDEC 2002). Other states employ different models for embracing these uncertainties and have found it difficult to adduce the causes of stream impairment. West Virginia's Department of Environmental Protection recently found that several streams in the southern portion of that state do not meet water quality standards because of acid mine drainage. While the particular cause of the pollution of these streams is generally known, a number of other streams in McDowell County were determined to be impaired by "unknown, undetermined" causes ("Several West Virginia Streams" 2002). Figure 4.1 depicts impaired streams in 16 southern states and illustrates the range of the problem.

Florida's recent IWR incorporates a new procedure relevant to this debate over prioritizing impaired waters. It has established a two-step listing process for TMDLs. Waters are first identified as potentially impaired and placed on a planning list, which means that they will be targeted for additional monitoring. If monitoring results in a "verified listing," then they are submitted to the EPA. The process is integrated into the DEP's "Watershed Management Approach," which rotates through all the state's river basins over a five-year period by basin "group" ("State Agency News" 2002: 7). The purpose of this effort—and of Florida's IWR rule, as previously noted—is to reduce the need for

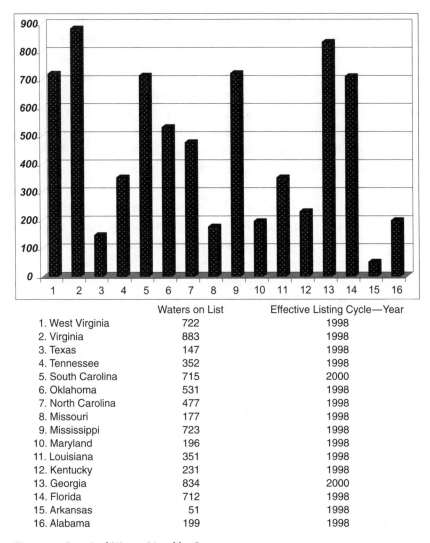

	Waters on List	Effective Listing Cycle—Year
1. West Virginia	722	1998
2. Virginia	883	1998
3. Texas	147	1998
4. Tennessee	352	1998
5. South Carolina	715	2000
6. Oklahoma	531	1998
7. North Carolina	477	1998
8. Missouri	177	1998
9. Mississippi	723	1998
10. Maryland	196	1998
11. Louisiana	351	1998
12. Kentucky	231	1998
13. Georgia	834	2000
14. Florida	712	1998
15. Arkansas	51	1998
16. Alabama	199	1998

Figure 4.1. Impaired Waters Listed by State

frequent updates on the condition of Florida's impaired waters by more systematically identifying stream impairments caused by pollutants.

Develop a TMDL Plan

For each pollutant in each water body, states must develop specific plans for their reduction and management. These plans describe to what degree pollutants must be reduced and impose a strategy for restoring water body health while monitoring progress toward its achievement. According to the Clean Water Act, each of these steps requires high levels of public involvement in articulating water quality objectives. Beyond this, the act acknowledges that water quality and supply issues cannot be managed in isolation from one another, since stream quality at any given point in time is a function not just of point and nonpoint discharges but of seasonally variable precipitation and stream flow, stream morphology, and even naturally occurring pollutants (see Haskins 1999). These factors all contribute to the difficulty of developing a TMDL plan (Boyd 2000; USDA 2000).

The three main challenges in developing TMDL plans that have often been cited are the lack of state authority for nonpoint sources such as logging, mining and agriculture (see Leclair 1997), court challenges to state timetables for developing TMDLs. and the difficulty of developing sound stakeholder representation processes. Examples of these three problems abound. In 1998 Alabama reached a settlement establishing a five-year time frame for the completion of its TMDLs. The plan charges the Alabama Department of Environmental Management with setting pollutant levels while the EPA prepares "watershed restoration plans" for the state's 303(d)-listed streams. The EPA also requires that new or additional point source discharges or problem pollutants be barred from entering impaired streams until TMDLs are prepared and "water quality recovered." The U.S. Fish and Wildlife Service and the National Marine Fisheries Service must be consulted regarding the implications of listing and TMDL development on endangered species, and the EPA has agreed to prepare special restoration plans for some water bodies (Parrish 1998).

Georgia's TMDL program operates under a 1996 court ruling that mandates that all TMDLs be established by 2001—since revised by the EPA to 2005. It has been estimated that 70% of the state's impaired waters are the result of nonpoint sources. The state relies heavily on stakeholder involvement to help "facilitate solutions" to identifying and regulating sources of pollution ("TMDL Status in Southeast" 2000: 3). Tennessee employs a "watershed perspective," and the current implementation strategy is for the state to develop agreements among storm water management officials, the Tennessee Department of Agriculture, and local governments—and to assess point source impacts on a seasonal basis rather than by producing yearly averages. The state believes that violations can be attributed to different point and nonpoint sources depending on flow, rainfall, and growing season ("TMDL Status in Southeast" 2000: 3).

Tennessee also employs an "ecoregion approach" in an effort to counteract the naturally high phosphorous content of some soils. By assigning different areas to different ecoregions, appropriate reference streams can be used for setting criteria baselines. South Carolina plans to complete its TMDLs by 2013. It is estimated that 80% of water body listings are due to fecal coliform contamination from nonpoint sources. The sheer volume of water quality data and the "lack of information on developing TMDLs" are viewed as the greatest challenges facing the state's water pollution program ("TMDL Status in Southeast" 2000: 3).

North Carolina's Department of Environmental Health and Department of Environment and Natural Resources (DENR) jointly committed to developing TMDLs for problem pollutants by 2008 and for all others by 2013. In 1998, state legislation gave the DENR authority to develop restoration strategies for waters impacted by point and nonpoint sources. The Neuse River currently has in place nonpoint source controls, but DENR officials believe that voluntary measures are adequate and obviate the need for intrusive, financially burdensome regulations ("TMDL Status in Southeast" 2000: 16). North Carolina's efforts, which we will describe in detail, represent an important innovation with adaptive management implications.

West Virginia's Department of Environmental Protection has made concerted efforts to determine which streams belong on the state's impaired stream list and to establish a firm schedule for TMDL development ("Several West Virginia Streams" 2002). In a well-publicized case, the state supreme court demanded that a TMDL for the upper Blackwater River be "updated and revised" due to "strong evidence" of a flawed initial TMDL (Ward 2002).

Nationwide, a number of states have begun allowing dischargers to monitor and set their own pollution limits for impaired water bodies. The goal is to encourage dischargers within a watershed to negotiate and develop more flexible remediation plans. In California and Texas—two states leading this effort—dischargers are using the process to allocate loads in such a way as to allow water treatment plants and other large dischargers "room to grow." Some states view the benefit of this approach to be reducing TMDL development costs ("States Increasingly Allow" 2002). Texas has one negotiated TMDL under development: an effort by Houston-area industries to determine whether a TMDL is necessary for a local water body. In all of these cases, it is noteworthy that solutions have been based on some effort to consult with industries, state legislators, interest groups, and others in an effort to develop TMDL approaches that are acceptable.

What can we make of this flurry of activity? From the aspect of adaptive management, we must first consider its implications for policy change—in other words, does this activity lead to real reform in the process by which we make decisions over how to protect water quality? Moreover, is that quality improving?

TMDL IMPLEMENTATION: TAKING ACTION
TO IMPROVE WATER QUALITY

Thus far, one might be forgiven for concluding from this discussion that the TMDL process is largely a technical exercise plagued by technical and administrative problems, which is slowly prodding states to change the way in which they make decisions regarding water quality. However, actions to improve water quality under the prescribed TMDL process are supposed to encourage local stakeholders living in the vicinity of impaired water bodies to form "watershed partnerships" or "initiatives" in order to craft broad-based, consensus-based solutions to water quality problems. Thus, the process involves questions of public engagement and decision-making fairness—important political attributes of adaptive management.

Watershed partnerships are envisioned as agreements between public agencies and private sector groups that encourage grassroots land use and water management strategies. Generally, these partnerships pursue novel approaches to abating nonpoint runoff from farms, feedlots, urban areas, and roadways through, for example, "off-set" formulae for new discharge sources, watershed modeling, stream bank restoration and anti-erosion programs, storm water retention ponds, and other techniques to address runoff sources of pollution. These approaches can improve the quality of instream flow by reducing turbidity and sedimentation, decreasing discharges and pollutant loadings, and reducing impermeable land surfaces (see Boyd 2000). Some of the most innovative efforts are discussed at the end of this chapter.

North Carolina is widely regarded as having made significant progress in developing credible implementation plans—perhaps because of the severe nonpoint water quality challenges caused by the state's poultry and other concentrated animal feeding operations (CAFO) industries. A recent initiative in the Coastal Plain watershed (Herrings Marsh) exemplifies how such innovative policy implementation may be achieved. This watershed, 5000 acres in size, has over 50,000 hogs, 48,000 turkeys, and 250,000 chickens and is characterized by shallow wells, small farms, and sandy soils. Since the 1990s, the widespread adoption of voluntary, incentive-based "best management practices" (BMPs) has resulted in reduced nitrate levels (from 4 PPM in 1990 to 0.5 by 1997) and an upgraded biological rating from "fair/poor" to "good/fair" (Werblow 1999).

Observers attribute success to the focus on a small area (a segment of the Neuse River basin), methodical water quality testing, adoption of nutrient management plans, voluntary adoption of BMPs, and a well-funded public education effort through the state's land-grant college (N.C. State). Moreover, growers have been eager to learn new approaches to production and conservation based on good science—overapplication of livestock manure was the major water quality nonpoint source problem. Hence they have managed to reduce nitrogen levels by 20 to 40 pounds/acre, to adopt conservation tillage practices on 1900 acres, and cover 70% of the watershed by individual conservation plans. Constant water quality monitoring has also helped achieve success (Werblow 1999: 8).

The Challenge of Litigation: A Costly Implementation Problem

According to the EPA, much of the progress made in TMDL reform and modification has been "driven by . . . litigation" (18 Federal Register, 66 FR 53043, October 18, 2001). To date, environmental groups have filed legal actions in 38 states. More than 20 of these have resulted in court orders or consent decrees under which the EPA is required to establish TMDLs if the state fails to do so, pursuant to specific schedules. The pace of TMDL establishment has increased greatly over the last few years, with almost twice as many TMDLs approved or established by EPA in 2001 as in 2000 (Zahodiakin 2001)—a clear demonstration of at least one measure of the power of litigation to spur change in this area. Currently, the EPA is under court order in many states to establish TMDLs if the appropriate state agencies fail to do so. In other states, litigation has been filed seeking to compel EPA establishment of TMDLs (Boyd 2000). Table 4.1 depicts current litigation by state according to the EPA Office of Water website on TMDLs. Litigation involving TMDLs has become so extensive that EPA's Office of Water features a website devoted to current lawsuits. It can be found at www.epa.gov/OWOW/tmdl/lawsuit1.html. As of late 2006, there were no fewer than 22 states with pending suits.

Court decisions in Georgia, Idaho, and West Virginia require states and the EPA to set TMDLs on aquatic systems. This is especially difficult because states lack authority over nonpoint sources such as logging, mining, and agri-

TABLE 4.1
Status of Current Litigation on TMDL Compliance

A. Twenty-two States in which EPA is under court order or agreed in consent decree to
establish TMDLs if States do not establish TMDLs

Alabama (1998; 5-yr schedule)	Kansas (1998; 10-yr schedule)
Alaska (1992; no schedule)	Louisiana (2002; 10-yr schedule)
Arkansas (2000; 10-yr schedule)	Mississippi (1998; 10-yr schedule)
California—LA (1999; 13-yr schedule)	Missouri (2001; 10-yr schedule)
California—North Coast (1997; 11-yr schedule)	Montana (2000; 7-yr schedule)
California—Newport Bay (1997; 4-yr schedule)	New Mexico (1997; 20-yr schedule)
Delaware (1997; 10-yr schedule)	Oregon (2000; 10-yr schedule)
District of Columbia (2000; 7-yr schedule)	Pennsylvania (1997; 12-yr schedule)
Florida (1999; 13-yr schedule)	Tennessee (2001; 10-yr schedule)
Georgia (1997; 7½-yr schedule)	Virginia (1999; 12-yr schedule)
Hawaii (partial cd; 2001; 1-yr schedule)	Washington (1998; 15-yr schedule)
Iowa (2001; 9-yr schedule)	West Virginia (1997; 10-yr schedule)

B. Five States in which plaintiffs have filed litigation seeking to compel
EPA to establish TMDLs

California (2000 appeal)	Ohio (2001 complaint)
Idaho (2000 complaint)	Wyoming (1996 complaint)
Nevada (2001 complaint)	

C. One State in which notice of intent to sue has been filed seeking court orders
for EPA to establish TMDLs

Arizona (1999 notice)

D. Fourteen States (11 Actions) dismissed without orders that EPA establish TMDLs
(some cases resolved with settlement agreements)

Arizona	EPA completed all consent decree obligations; decree terminated July 17, 2000
Colorado	Joint Motion for Administrative Closure filed August 24, 1999; parties signed settlement agreement in which EPA agreed to establish TMDLs if state did not
Idaho	EPA Motion to Dismiss granted 1997
Lake Michigan (WI, IL, IN, MI)	Scott case—final order 1984; related NWF case challenging EPA actions in response to Scott order—case dismissed 1991
Minnesota	Dismissed 1993
Maryland	Dismissed 2001
New Jersey	Dismissed 2002
New York	EPA Motion to Dismiss granted on all but one claim May 2, 2000
North Carolina	Joint Stipulation of Dismissal filed June 1998; EPA agreed by letter to ensure development of a TMDL for the Neuse River by date certain
Oklahoma	Tenth Circuit upheld dismissal of case August 29, 2001
South Dakota	Dismissed without prejudice August 27, 1999

culture (see Leclair 1997). Litigation remains a significant challenge for TMDL implementation. West Virginia is an especially noteworthy case because its problems exemplify those generally characterizing the TMDL process. Recently, the state supreme court held that the Department of Environmental Protection "properly processed and enforced . . . new water pollution limits" (Ward 2002). This decision came about through litigation first brought against the DEP in 1995 by the Ohio Valley Environmental Coalition. After a U.S. district court ruled that the EPA must write over 500 TMDLs for West Virginia unless the state did so, the latter failed to write TMDLs due to lack of money for adequate studies.

EVALUATION OF TMDLS

Has the Clean Water Act of 1972 (CWA) decreased water pollution? How do we know? Regulated polluters with easily defined discharges such as steel plants, municipalities, and industrial and wastewater treatment plants would likely answer in the affirmative because of reductions in "point source" discharges (Birkeland 2001). However, the answer is more complex than this. We must answer these questions on two levels—procedurally (Is a process in place that may lead to improvement?) and substantively (Is the process leading to qualitative improvement?).

The Significance of Process Changes

Point sources, as we have seen, were the first targets of regulation because it was believed that they were the primary sources of pollution. Furthermore, pollution originating from a single point is more easily eliminated. While important, this effort addressed only part of the problem. A 1996 National Water Quality Inventory study showed that the amount of water pollution in surface water bodies remained relatively constant due to nonpoint source pollution emanating primarily from "un-discernable, unconfined" sources (Anderson 1999). The remedy for this problem lay in better implementation of section 303(d) of the CWA, which focuses on "water quality standards" as a measurement tool for water body health (CWA, 33. U.S.C. §1313(d)).

In contrast to technology-based controls, water quality standards involve a determination of the maximum amount of each pollutant that can be present without impairing a water body's designated use (Anderson 1999). After determining pollution maximums for each pollutant, the EPA translates them into standards. An early version of the Federal Water Pollution Control Act had water quality standards as their focus. However, states did not actively enforce them, leading Congress to conclude that they were useless. In fact, their uselessness was at the heart of Senate debates prior to enactment of the 1972 amendments.

Section 303 is the only section of the 1972 Clean Water Act to preserve reference to water quality standards (Houck 1997). It provides an antidote when section 301 NPDES permits fail to prevent pollution adequately. Initial requirements of section 303 relied on state water quality standards—the same standards that had proven ineffective in the past. However, the inclusion of section 303(d), which added a recommendation for using water quality standards to upgrade waters that remained polluted after the application of technology-based requirements, represented a clear improvement in policy (Houck 1997). Congress intended for this new application of water quality standards to supersede the older version. But while it articulated the idea of using water quality standards as a vehicle for managing pollution, it did not go far enough.

Refining the Process of TMDL Development

In an effort to speed the nation's progress toward achieving water quality standards and improving the TMDL program, the EPA began, in 1996, an all-inclusive evaluation of the EPA and the states with respect to their section 303(d) responsibilities. The EPA also convened a committee under the Federal Advisory Committee Act (FACA), composed of 20 individuals with diverse backgrounds, including agriculture, forestry, environmental advocacy, industry, and state, local, and tribal government (EPA 2002b). The committee issued its recommendations in 1998 and, as a result, the EPA sought to commence a new rulemaking process intended to initiate discussion on "what, if any, changes were needed in the national water quality standards program to restore the quality of the Nation's waters" (Water Quality Standards Regulation, 1998).

This rulemaking process underscored the EPA's recognition that TMDL implementation was substandard and in need of revision. In 1999, the EPA published a proposed rule that "revises, clarifies, and strengthens" its regulatory requirements for establishing TMDLs. Its intent was to provide states, territories, and authorized tribes with the necessary information to identify impaired water and to establish TMDLs to restore water quality.

Prior to issuance of the final rule, a federal court decision gave further support to control of nonpoint source pollution under section 303(d). In *Prosolino v. Marcus,* issued just three and a half months before the EPA's issuance of the final update of the old TMDL rule, the court determined that the EPA and the states have the authority to identify waters impaired by nonpoint sources of pollution. It also found that the EPA can develop TMDLs for such waters under section 303(d) of the Clean Water Act. With this ruling in hand, the EPA incorporated nonpoint source pollution into their new rule, which was published on July 13, 2000 (Birkeland 2001).

These recommendations were used to guide the development of the additional proposed changes to the TMDL regulations discussed in the previous section. However, Congress added a rider to an appropriations bill that prohibited the EPA from spending FY2000 or FY2001 money to implement this new rule (EPA 2002b). The proposed modifications to the EPA's TMDL rules provided more specificity and organization to the operation of the program. The rules laid out a basic set of requirements for states, including initiating public review of the procedures by which it arrives at an impaired waters list, an excellent means to ensure robust public participation in the process (Boyd 2000); ranking waters by degree of impairment—with those streams designated as drinking water supply sources as the highest priority; and establishing implementation plans containing specific measures for compliance, monitoring, and allocation of load reductions to point and nonpoint sources (Boyd 2000). While the Clinton administration approved these changes, in December 2002 the Bush administration decided to drop these proposed revisions, leaving the program developed in 2000 in effect instead (see "Proposed Rule to Withdraw the July 2000 TMDL Rule," 2002).

The FY2001 appropriations act did have one legacy, however—it mandated studies by the National Academy of Sciences (NAS) on the scientific basis of the entire TMDL program and TMDL approach. The NAS report concluded that scientific knowledge exists to move forward with the TMDL program and recommended that the EPA and the states use adaptive implementation for TMDL development. In many cases, the report said, water quality problems and solutions are evident and should proceed without complex analysis. In other cases, solutions are more intricately designed. These may require a different level of understanding as well as phased implementation (NAS 2001). In short, the NAS concluded that states should welcome the TMDL process—despite its problems—as an opportunity to practice an adaptive management approach to solving the nation's water pollution problems.

While proposed changes would have left much enforcement power in the hands of states, it would also have created more power to enforce TMDL standards with respect to nonpoint sources (Pope 2000). For these reasons, implementation of the proposed TMDL rules met with significant obstacles. States were left scrambling to come up with their own plans to improve water quality. Given no standard guidelines, each state has applied different methods, as we have seen, and no two states have identical implementation plans. As we shall see, some believe that there needs to be some sort of prototype for all states to adopt—this may be the most important lesson of this issue. Such a prototype could draw from the vast experiences of TMDL plans that have actually succeeded—an issue we discuss at the end of the chapter.

EVOLUTION OF WATER QUALITY POLICY: BACK TO THE FUTURE?

Overall, it has become apparent that the laws and regulations created in the 1970s are not entirely sufficient to address the current problems facing the nation's water quality. Following the September 11, 2001, terrorist attacks on the World Trade Center and the Pentagon, congressional attention has focused on security, preparedness, and emergency response issues. Among the many topics of interest is protection of the nation's water infrastructure (Copeland and Cody 2002; Copeland 2002). Partly in response to this issue, in spring 2002 the EPA developed new guidelines requiring water managers and states to use watershed plans to guide the existing TMDL program. These rules were finalized in August 2002.

The watershed rule is a new aspect of the TMDL program initiated by the EPA. A new version of this rule was published in July 2000. When Congress objected to the rule and halted its implementation, in a flurry the EPA announced that it was drafting new guidelines for the TMDL program to give states greater leeway in deciding which waterways would be cleaned up. The EPA would not have the power to approve or reject state plans for cleaning them but would "trust the states" ("Clean Water: EPA Outlines" 2002). States could remove waterways from the program where there is not enough data on a particular water body. This decision would effectively have reversed a July 2000 Clinton administration rule requiring the EPA to sign off on more than 20,000 state plans to clean up polluted rivers, lakes, and estuaries—plans opposed by farm groups, timber companies, and municipalities.

The agency has reconsidered certain elements of the rule, however—thus the new watershed regulation. The EPA's goals have been to improve state monitoring and assessment programs; to strengthen existing federal, state, and local watershed planning processes to foster TMDL implementation and harmonize programs dealing with watersheds; to increase program flexibility to enhance stakeholder participation; and to foster opportunities for innovation, including emissions trading ("EPA Developing" 2002). The EPA would have the discretion to veto continued NPDES state permits and intends to move forward with an overhaul of the TMDL program in order to "allow polluted water bodies to be cleaned up more thoroughly and quickly" (Franz 2002). In 2003, the EPA withdrew the July 2000 rule, it reported, due to Congress prohibiting the agency from using funds "to make a determination or to implement" it, and because no fewer than ten legal challenges to the rule were filed by states, agricultural groups, industries, and environmental organizations (EPA 2003b). As of 2006, no new rule or guidance has been introduced in an effort to achieve the goals listed above more expeditiously.

Currently, the EPA and portions of the agriculture industry are at loggerheads over another issue—current policy that requires the agency, rather than states, to approve nonpoint source discharges for impaired waters. Agricultural interests prefer that the states undertake this task and argue that the EPA is overstepping its authority by, in effect, approving individual wasteload allocations for given streams rather than merely approving final TMDLs as states establish them ("EPA Stalemate" 2002). A possible prognosis for this dispute is that the EPA may drop its watershed rule rather than accede to agriculture's demands. In any event, there is no clear prognosis any time soon of an end to the contentiousness over the TMDL program—or over the TMDL approach.

THE PROBLEM OF INSTREAM FLOW: A LEGAL OVERVIEW

Instream flow presents a unique and important challenge to sustainable development in water policy. This is because the effort to ensure *adequate* flow (much less to define it) requires the integration of water quantity and quality considerations. While adequate instream flow is ordinarily defined as the volume of water in a given water body needed to sustain aquatic life—as well as other purposes for which that water body has been legally designated (in effect, a definition similar to what constitutes an appropriate TMDL)—adequacy is inherently a *qualitative* issue. In effect, what makes flow adequate at any given time is that it is sufficient to dilute contaminants, including waste heat from power plants and factories.

As was the case with water pollution policy, water law doctrines have been the basic source of instream flow protection policies. They serve as the point of departure for later statutory modifications and litigation, and they have constrained negotiated agreements to allocate off-stream uses—a principal driver of instream flow (another is precipitation). Instream flow policy also offers an excellent example of the role of institutions in adaptive management. Many laws and regulations have been used to protect instream flow, with varying records of success.

Riparian Approaches to Instream Flow Protection: Debate and Discord

Under riparian law, the prevailing legal system in the eastern United States, a landowner has the right to reasonable use of the water flowing past his or her property, subject to the equal rights of other riparian landowners. Water used but not consumed must be returned to the watercourse without impaired quality. Generally, diverting water from the drainage area of a stream without return flow, a practice harmful to instream flow, is deemed unreasonable and, if a downstream riparian complains, is forbidden (Butler, 1990; Laitos and Tomain 1992; Ballweber 1995).

Not only does the reasonableness test involve balancing the uses of one riparian against those of another claiming injury, but claims of harm traditionally do not include adverse impacts to fish and wildlife—only to human uses and property rights and, by implication, to natural resources considered private property. In addition, when controversies have arisen between riparian landowners, they have generally been settled differently in different places, depending on the size of the stream and the adverse effects suffered. In many states, those who supply water for general public use have been granted the right to condemn certain lands for the purpose of claiming water rights. Because these public water providers are granted greater rights to flow than ordinary riparians, riparian doctrine alone has been insufficient to prevent diminished instream flow by, for example, a water utility or municipal provider (Feldman 2000).

How effectively riparian doctrine protects instream flow is the subject of considerable scholarly debate. The vagueness of the "reasonableness" test, for example, is viewed by some scholars as an advantage rather than a drawback in using riparian law as a means to ensure adequate flow. As Tarlock notes, "Viewed from an environmental perspective, many . . . supposed defects in the common law of riparian rights are virtues, starting with the extreme inde-terminacy of the common law." Nonetheless, Tarlock concedes that a major water resource problem in the eastern United States is protection of instream uses and that "the East has an opportunity to develop a set of legal institutions suited to the nature of the resource rather than to simply copy western in-stitutions" (Tarlock 1990: 250, 252). He urges the adoption of innovative planning-based approaches to protecting water, such as more accurate water withdrawal information, permits for inter-basin diversion, and general legal reforms acknowledging that water is a "commons" issue that should be man-aged by a combination of private and public rights as opposed to sweeping comprehensive water use permit systems (Tarlock 1990).

Others are less equivocal in their criticisms of riparianism and the bureau-cratic remedies it has produced. Abrams (1990) attacks the practice of estab-lishing comprehensive water withdrawal permit systems—the typical state response to weaknesses in riparian doctrine—as cumbersome, inefficient, applied by legislatures in a piecemeal fashion, and ineffective in setting pri-orities. However, he is more adamant than Tarlock in charging that riparian-ism traditionally fails to provide any consistent basis on which to decide user conflicts, to set water use priorities, or to preempt disputes from arising in the first place. He concludes that legal reforms based on adding "concreteness and predictability" to permit-holders' rights and on meeting the public's expecta-tions for fair water allocation are needed (Abrams 1990: 285).

Sherk has argued that water quality requirements for "human and wildlife needs cannot be guaranteed under riparian law (even though the) cumulative impacts of a large number of reasonable uses can" reduce stream flow (Sherk 1990: 290). Noting that many eastern states have supplanted riparianism with eminent domain rights systems, impoundments, and stream flow require-ments to protect water quality *and* quantity, he suggests that the greatest prob-lem facing efforts at ensuring sustainable water management under the com-mon law is the lack of incentive for users to conserve and to forego use of a commonly shared resource. Avoiding a "tragedy of the commons" is the key challenge facing legislatures bent on state water law reform with an eye to pro-tecting instream flow (Sherk 1990: 321).

Butler (1990) offers a sophisticated critique of the ability of common law to protect instream flow. Under prior appropriation as well as riparian doctrine, protection of off-stream uses has always prevailed. Moreover, U.S. environ-mental law generally does a poor job of recognizing and protecting noncon-sumptive water uses even though, in theory, riparian doctrine could afford a high level of protection in at least three ways. First, the natural flow doctrine, which generally entitles each riparian to the use of an adjacent watercourse in its "natural condition" without interference by others, should ensure adequate stream flow. In practice, however, the aforementioned practice of reasonable use prevails: greater credence is given to property rights than to instream uses. Second, while reasonable use in theory protects against some threats to instream flow (recreation and sport fishing, for example), protection is not absolute and, in practice, is only realized when instream uses coincide with private rights (Butler 1990: 328–329).

Finally, the public trust doctrine provides a "potentially broad basis for protecting instream uses" by giving states considerable leeway in interpreting public rights regarding health, safety, and welfare. In practice, however, courts have often narrowly targeted public use rights to protect navigation, forcing responsibility for instream flow protection on legislatures and only ensuring public instream rights protection when these rights are in accord with commercial or recreational navigation (Butler 1990: 336–340). Butler's far-reaching remedy hinges on reforms that provide a system for resolving conflict and an array of public property rights. Such rights are identifiable, she contends, in situations where private uses might usurp an inherent public interest (navigation) or where the public actually contributes to establishing a resource's value (improvements to water quality). What we are left with from this assessment are four conclusions regarding riparian rights, instream flow, and adaptive management. First, riparianism is too vague and imprecise to afford inherent protections to instream flow. To the extent that riparianism affords an organizational design for recognizing previous mistakes in managing instream flow—the ability to correct mistakes being a characteristic of adaptive regimes—that design relies too heavily upon informal precedent and case-by-case judgment (a reliance on "reasonableness") and lacks systematic accountability. Most often, the protection of aquatic and other ecological considerations is an incidental benefit of efforts to protect property rights through adequate stream flow. Second, recognizing this organizational deficiency, states with riparian systems have generally adopted complex but bureaucratically rigid and inconsistent permitting systems in an effort to monitor environmental effects and to limit changes in flow regimes that might cause irreversible damage to the environment. Unfortunately, these permitting systems are not always credible, efficient, or effective. Third, dedicated reforms to balance instream flow needs and off-stream demands for water must confront the basic failure of the common law to protect instream flow for the sake of natural, non-economic, and intangible social ends like species preservation or fish wildlife habitat protection. In effect, so long as utilitarian views of water use prevail, efforts to balance natural needs and human uses will have little incentive behind them. Finally, in the absence of large-scale public rights to water, the best guarantee of protection is when the federal government is itself a principal landowner and riparian on an affected stream or other water body. This is sometimes the case in headwaters streams originating within national parks. Short of this, however, when the federal government is just another downstream riparian, its ability to ensure adequate instream flow under riparianism is highly limited. As we shall see, other instream flow protection tools have sought to address this limitation with varying success.

Prior Appropriation and Instream Flow Protection: Can "Beneficial Use" Be Adaptable?

Appropriation law is the predominant water rights doctrine in 19 western and southwestern states lying west of the 100th meridian. As we have seen, because water has been a scarce commodity in the region, miners, ranchers, and other early settlers sought to develop a system for acquiring water rights that did not tie the use of water to the land from which it was drawn. In this way, users could be assured of a specific volume of water for their benefit.

Unlike riparianism, appropriation law quantifies and prioritizes water rights according to the "first in time, first in right" principle: the first person to put water to a beneficial and reasonable use acquires a right superior to later appropriators. That user and his or her successors have the right to use a specified amount of water for a stated beneficial use each year, subject only to the rights of other prior appropriators (Pearson 2000). Evolving through a combination of Hispanic-American and even Mormon custom, codification of the "first in time and in right" principle emerged throughout the American west by 1851 (Gillilan and Brown 1997).

Land ownership is not the basis for the appropriation right—one can have a right to water from a watercourse or aquifer without owning land bordering or, in the case of aquifers, overlying the source. Regardless of *how* the right is acquired, however—whether by purchase or other means—water rights exist only when the water is actually appropriated (that is, diverted and used) for a beneficial purpose. In practice, most prior appropriation states define beneficial uses in statute, and preferred uses tend to be explicitly defined so that certain water uses considered beneficial are clearly elucidated (Laitos and Tomain 1992; Tarlock, Corbridge, and Getches 1993).

The concept of beneficial use under the appropriation doctrine has profoundly influenced instream flow and has numerous implications for the sustainable management of water. Traditionally, off-stream uses such as irrigation have generally been considered beneficial uses, although overflow or natural flood irrigation have been held to be inefficient and thus prohibited. Moreover, during periods of shortage or drought, there is no duty to abate use so as to share the amount available with other appropriators. Indeed appropriators whose rights are senior may take their full water rights even if this results in insufficient water remaining for junior appropriators' needs. This approach not only tends to ignore instream flow as a beneficial use but also, as occurred during the California Gold Rush in the 1840s, may result in streams being literally pumped dry (Gillilan and Brown 1997), which occurred, in some places, by the midde of the nineteenth century.

There is another aspect of "beneficial use" that affects instream flow. Under historical appropriation law, "instream uses are considered inherently wasteful since they require water to remain in place" (Butler 1990: 329). In effect, the result of this legal interpretation has been to bias the concept of "beneficial" to mean off-stream and consumptive uses. Moreover, instream uses have also been disfavored because of the prior appropriation doctrine's insistence on physical diversion of water from the stream "in order to perfect an appropriation" (Butler 1990: 328). This radical conception of beneficial use has undergone change only in the past few decades, with courts more recently deeming fishing and recreation to be beneficial uses.

In theory, water transfers are allowed in almost all western states for any beneficial use. In practice, however, most western states now treat instream flow differently from other uses. Whereas appropriated waters formerly could be used virtually anywhere—indeed, users were encouraged to divert—regardless of distance from a stream or aquifer (Laitos and Tomain 1992), this practice has gradually changed through legal reform on a state-by-state basis (NRLC 1997: 7). Concern with environmental damage has forced some appropriation states to require minimum flows to be maintained in watercourses, especially for protection of certain public lands, even if this impairs senior appropriators' rights (Kenney et al. 2000; Landry 2000).

Before these changes were made, traditional appropriation doctrine held little regard for the larger public interest in instream flow. From the standpoint of adaptive management, as we shall see later in this chapter, the reforms adopted by appropriation rights states to ensure that minimum flows remain in streams have in many cases been markedly innovative. They have tried to move the water-use culture of the American West incrementally from an acquisitive and utilitarian set of practices toward water withdrawal and allocation to one that is flexible, decentralized, and self-correctable.

INSTREAM FLOW PROTECTION: THE CLEAN WATER ACT AND OTHER LAWS

While we discussed the CWA in the context of water pollution, the statute has important implications for instream flow. The heart of the CWA's enforcement provisions, section 401, provides that any applicant for a federal license or permit to conduct any activity that may result in any discharge into navigable waters obtain a certification from the state in which the discharge originates (CWA, Sect. 401 (a) (1)). More importantly, section 401 also gives states the power to veto a federal license or to impose requirements to protect water quality or aquatic habitats.

In support of this objective, the U.S. Supreme Court has held that states have the power under section 401 to require that *minimum stream flows be maintained* (16 U.S.C. 1530, 50 CFR 400ff; Public Utility District no. 1 of Jefferson County, 1994) and that minimum flow is an "appropriate requirement of state law." Thus, consistent with our discussion earlier regarding the Clean Water Act, a water quality standard can have both a use-based stricture (like protection of fish and wildlife habitat) and a criterion-based rule (like a numerical standard for prescribing an amount of emissions per quantity of water). Moreover, the court held that a state may require a permit applicant to comply with the use independent of any criterion. This distinction between "use" and "criterion" is an important aspect of the TMDL debate.

In addition, section 404 of the CWA regulates the discharge of dredged and fill material from rivers and streams into U.S. waters, including wetlands. This provision's intent is to protect instream flow by reducing sediment and turbidity and by ensuring that there be no flow restrictions. This wide-ranging authority extends to fills for development, water projects, highways, and airports; it also extends to the conversion of wetlands to farms and forests (CWA, Sect. 404). The Army Corps of Engineers shares responsibility for implementing and enforcing section 404 with the EPA, an issue that has led some critics to contend that this shared inter-agency authority is, in practice, perhaps not viable for water quality and instream flow protection. This contention arises from past criticisms of Corps activities in navigational improvements and the implications of those improvements for riverine habitat and related ecological issues.[5]

While the fundamental purpose of the Endangered Species Act (ESA) is to prevent actions that affect endangered or threatened species, several sections of the law have been used to protect instream flow on federal lands. Section 7 requires that actions of federal agencies not jeopardize endangered species or destroy, or seriously alter or impair their habitat, while section 9 makes it a crime to "take" or "harm" an endangered species of fish or wildlife.

The Fish and Wildlife Service, which has authority for ensuring compliance with the act, has defined "harm" to include "significant habitat modification or degradation." In practice, guidance for defining "significant harm" is vague, a fact that poses great difficulties in ESA implementation—especially with regard to instream flow. Nevertheless, it is clear that it can be used to protect instream flow if that flow is deemed essential for protecting endangered or threatened species (33 U.S.C. 403; 33 CFR part 322).

The ESA has been the focal point of many cases directly pertaining to instream flow protection. One of the most controversial of such cases arose in the eastern United States—the Tellico Dam case involving the snail darter (*TVA v. Hill* 437 U.S. 153, 1978). This case involved an attempt to enjoin the agency from closing the nearly completed Tellico Dam, a water project on the Little Tennessee River, which was being constructed by the Tennessee Valley Authority. In the mid-1970s, several environmental organizations and the Fish and Wildlife Service contended that the completion of this dam would threaten the habitat and survival of the snail darter, a fish that had been placed on the endangered species list in late 1975.

The U.S. Supreme Court ruled six to three against project completion on the grounds that "operation of the Tellico Dam will either eradicate the known population of snail darters or destroy their critical habitat." However, Congress attached an amendment to an Energy and Water Appropriations Bill (H.R. 43888) in 1978 allowing the TVA to complete the dam despite its possible impact on the ESA and on the darter. After President Jimmy Carter vetoed the bill, Congress overrode the veto. The project's floodgates were closed, and, to the surprise of many, the snail darter survived (Wheeler and McDonald 1983; Coggins, Wilkinson, and Leshy 1993: 793). One lesson for sustainability from this case is that the power of a federal statute to protect instream flow *perma-*

nently and unambiguously in a given instance is subject to the will of Congress and the president not only to embrace it but to support litigation on its behalf.

A different case arose in 1992 when Klamath River basin ranchers in Oregon filed suit against the U.S. Fish and Wildlife Service (FWS) for curtailing irrigation water deliveries in order to preserve two endangered fish—the Lost River and short-nosed suckers (Switzer and Bryner 1998: 254). FWS biologists monitoring the species established minimum water levels in two nearby reservoirs to permit fish to migrate and thus spawn, but in doing so, they admitted they were uncertain that these measures would restore the species. In their suit, the ranchers argued that they were seriously harmed by these measures (losses estimated at $75 million) and that they were unnecessary and contrary to ESA provisions requiring regulators to consider the economic effects on a region when declaring it a "critical habitat."

In a unanimous 1997 decision, the U.S. Supreme Court agreed with the ranchers, ruling that they had the right to sue under the ESA. While the ruling applied only to these two species, it may over time become a precedent that could be used against other species protection plans involving instream flow management (Switzer and Bryner 1998: 254). In 2001, the Bureau of Reclamation acting under court order terminated two-thirds of the deliveries of water to area farmers and ranchers, diverting it to water bodies harboring endangered salmon and mullet. It is unclear whether this measure will become a permanent remedy or not (Satchell 2003: 38).

This case has produced one development that may lead to a firmer toehold for adaptive management remedies on water policy in the region. Water 2025, a series of meetings among states and communities in the West, was conceived following the Supreme Court's decision in an effort to encourage dialogue that could lead to longer-term planning and local solutions to water supply conflicts between rural and urban areas. Many of the remedies thus far discussed are old and familiar: greater use of water banking and marketing, increased conservation, better cooperation between agencies and stakeholders, among others (see Meiners and Kosnik 2003).

There is also a dedicated effort to identify watersheds in the region facing the greatest threats to supply in order to identify cooperative approaches that, in the words of Interior Department Secretary Gale Norton, "have the best chance of success" ("Interior Secretary Kicks Off Dialogue" 2003: 1345). Of special significance for the prospects of adaptive management, a 2002 report by the NAS prepared at the request of the Department of the Interior concluded that there is "no sound scientific basis for cutting off water to farmers . . . in order to help the habitat of endangered fish" (Meiners and Kosnick 2003: 3). That more and better information is needed to render credible decisions seems without question; that consensus over the validity of that information can soon be reached is doubtful.

The Wild and Scenic Rivers Act (82 Stat. 906, 16 U.S.C. Sects. 1271–1287 (1976)) grants the federal government the authority to designate certain rivers as "national, wild, scenic, or recreational" and provides mechanisms for limiting certain types of development and their protection as pristine resources. As with national parks, designation of a river as a wild, scenic, or recreational river explicitly reserves sufficient unappropriated water to fulfill the act's purpose—but not unambiguously (U.S. Department of the Interior 1979: 607).

The act states that the designation of any stream or portion thereof as a national wild and scenic river "shall not be construed as a reservation of the waters of such streams for purposes other than those specified [in this act] or in quantities greater than necessary to accomplish their purpose" (Section 13 (c), Wild and Scenic Rivers Act, 1976). Nevertheless, the legislative history of the act suggests that Congress intended that the law would have sufficient power to obtain unappropriated waters necessary for protecting aesthetic, recreational, scientific, biotic, and historic features (U.S. Department of the Interior 1979: 608).

A frequently debated issue pertinent to instream flow management on wild and scenic rivers is: what limitations are appropriate for riparian owners whose lands abut rivers that have been included in the system? An exemplary case is that of the 26.5-mile segment of the New River in North Carolina that, after a decade-long struggle to prevent construction of a pump-storage hydropower project, was included in the system through act of Congress in September 1976 (Schoenbaum 1979; Feldman 1995).

While scenic-river advocates and environmental groups on the one hand and local landowners on the other opposed the damming of this stretch of white water and thus supported the creation of a scenic river—albeit for different reasons—they initially disagreed over what this designation might mean. In part, their debate reflects continuing debates over instream flow management and protection on scenic rivers today. Many residents, unsure what a "scenic river" and national park would mean, feared federal intrusion and strong land and water use controls. Their fears were allayed when environmental groups supporting scenic river designation agreed to the establishment of a scenic river with few changes in land use, floodplain zoning, or restrictions on public access (Schoenbaum 1979: 160). Such compromises, common in scenic river negotiations, protect instream flow by building local political support through allowing traditional riparian custom to prevail. The assumption is that only through political compromise can the scenic river alternative be made palatable.

NEPA as an Instream Flow Tool

If a federal project or a federal permit for a privately funded project (for instance, a dam licensed to an investor-owned utility) entails "a major federal action significantly affecting the quality of the human environment," then an environmental impact statement (EIS) must be prepared. This EIS must set out what the proposed action will do to the environment and identify plausible alternatives to the action. Theoretically, identification of "significant impacts" invests the National Environmental Policy Act (NEPA) with considerable authority for protecting instream flow. In practice, however, National Environmental Policy Act (NEPA) is largely procedural. It does not mandate a particular outcome but merely requires proof that environmental effects have been adequately considered by an agency or federal licensee before a project goes forward (33 U.S.C. sects. 401–426; 40 CFR. Part 130). The Tellico Dam controversy is a good example.

Even though NEPA is primarily a "procedural" statute, the impact of public outrage, opposition, and negative publicity from the findings of an EIS—particularly if significant adverse impacts are shown to be likely—should not be underestimated. Agencies may, and frequently do, abandon plans for water projects that may adversely affect instream flow if the NEPA process demonstrates such likelihood. The abandonment of plans to construct a dam on Clear Creek, a tributary of the Obed River in Tennessee, is a case in point.

This proposed project was intended to provide additional water supply to communities on the Cumberland Plateau, but it was found that the dam would have withdrawn considerable amounts of water from Clear Creek, impairing summer stream flows and threatening the Obed Wild and Scenic River. It also would have resulted in the construction of a 120-acre reservoir (Pringle 2000: 977). Clearly, NEPA can have major effects on inter-agency decision-making by providing a sort of "whistle-blowing" role to prevent adverse decisions from being made. While hardly a long-term approach to adaptive management, NEPA does instill a "look before you leap" attitude into decisions regarding instream flow and other water quality issues. As a result, it introduces sustainability and the need to avoid irreversible harm into policy discussions.

The National Park Service

The National Park Service Organic Act (16 U.S.C. Sec. 1 (1916)) and its implementing regulations require that all water resources in the National Park System be afforded a level of protection comparable to that afforded other natural resources under National Park Service (NPS) jurisdiction. Specifically, the NPS is obliged to "conserve the scenery and the natural and historic objects of the wildlife therein and to provide for the enjoyment of the same in such manner . . . as will leave them unimpaired for the enjoyment of future generations" (NPSOA, U.S.C. 16, sec. 1, 1916). According to an Interior Department solicitor's opinion, scenic, natural, and historic conservation uses; wildlife conservation uses; sustained public enjoyment uses; and NPS personnel uses are under the park service's jurisdiction (U.S. Department of the Interior 1979: 596). As one observer notes, this mandate creates "an inevitable tension" between what may be incompatible goals: preserving the parks' resources and providing recreational experiences for many people in them (Lowry 1994: 3).

Implementing regulations of the NPS specifically provides for the protection of surface and ground waters as "integral components of park's aquatic and terrestrial ecosystems." The same regulations also provide that "water for the preservation and management of the national park system will be obtained and used in accordance with legal authorities." While management policies do not distinguish between western and eastern parks, they do provide that the NPS will consider all available authorities in order to protect water-related resources in parks.

Most NPS experience in protecting water resources in units of the park system has been in the west. The NPS water rights program monitors and enforces water rights and participates in state administrative proceedings that might affect water-dependent resources in its parks. One of the NPS's major tools is the federal reserved water right. Application of this right, however, has not been established for most national parks and no parks or federal public lands in the east.

In theory, as a riparian landowner the NPS has the right to all reasonable quantities of water, so long as such use does not interfere with the reasonable uses of other landowners. This is, therefore, an uncertain right since it depends on the actions of other riparian users (NPCA 1993). Theoretically, the NPS not only has control over water resources within the boundary of a park unit but also on actions outside the park boundary that could affect water flows within the boundary.

Generally, the NPS tries to balance its claims to needed instream flow against the reasonable desire of states to protect appropriative rights (in the case of western states) and, presumably, riparian landowner rights in the east. The general criterion for meeting this balance is described by the NPS as asserting rights "for quantities determined to be the minimum amounts needed to protect the primary purposes" of a given park (Gillilan and Brown 1997). As accommodating as the NPS tries to be, however, in the opinion of the Interior Department's solicitor, "appropriation for authorized federal purposes cannot be strictly limited by what state water law says is a 'diversion' of water or a 'beneficial use' or which water can be appropriated" (U.S. Department of the Interior 1979: 575).

In 1947, Congress required the NPS to allow the Bureau of Reclamation to construct a water diversion project through a portion of Rocky Mountain National Park (the Colorado–Big Thompson Project). The project's purpose was to transfer water from the uppermost reaches of the Colorado River, which rises on the state's western slope, to the Platte River, which flows east of the Rockies. With a water storage capacity exceeding 710,000 acre-feet and the ability to irrigate over 600,000 acres, this project's potential impact on instream flow is considerable (U.S. Bureau of Reclamation 1957). A series of storage reservoirs was constructed on the western slope, in part to ensure adequate instream flow on the Colorado and in part to enable dependable supply through the Alva B. Adams tunnel, which transfers water to the eastern slope.

But the NPS is also responsible for managing a variety of "national recreation areas" such as in Lake Mead and Glen Canyon. These areas came into existence as the result of the construction of massive impoundments, which, among other things, generated numerous opportunities for flatwater recreation and the operations of which have, until recently, been managed for the exclusive benefit of power generation and irrigation—not instream flow protection (Coggins, Wilkinson, and Leshy 1993: 140; Fradkin 1996).

As discussed in chapter 2, beginning in 1989 efforts were made to protect the Colorado River below Glen Canyon Dam through the partial restoration of the historical instream flow regime in the Grand Canyon National Park prior to the building of Glen Canyon Dam. The Grand Canyon Trust, along with other environmental NGOs and the NPS, played a critical role in the passage of the Grand Canyon Protection Act in 1992, which helped to redirect the Bureau of Reclamation's instream flow policies on the Colorado River. The act helped implement a highly successful controlled flood to rebuild beaches and to restore habitat as well as instream flows (Moody 1997).

If the snail darter case illustrates how federal laws can be exempted in ways potentially injurious to instream flow protection on public lands, the Grand Canyon Protection Act illustrates something far more heartening—that federal agency mandates toward instream flow policies for public lands can be changed if sufficient public pressure is applied and if historical conditions are right. While the NPS's need to share power with other agencies in managing instream flow has sometimes relegated instream flow considerations to a lower status than off-stream demands in the past (as with the Colorado-Big Thompson Canyon Project), this is less true today.

The Federal Reserved Water Rights Doctrine
and Instream Flow Protection

An important but controversial basis for federal authority to protect instream flow is the reserved water rights doctrine, developed in the early twentieth century. The doctrine posits that when the federal government removes lands from the public domain and "reserves" them for a federal purpose like establishing national forests, parks, or Indian reservations, it also reserves a portion of the water "then unappropriated . . . to fulfill the purpose of the reservation" (*Winters v. U.S.,* 207 U.S. 564, 1908; Coggins, Wilkinson, and Leshy 1993: 369). The Winters Case—where the doctrine originated—revolved around federal claims for reserving as yet unclaimed water rights on streams flowing through the Fort Belknap Indian Reservation in Montana, which was established to settle members of the Assiniboine and Gros Ventre tribes (Gillilan and Brown 1997). Prior to development of this doctrine, common law riparian rules of natural flow applied to public lands (U.S. Department of the Interior 1979: 565). The doctrine has become a basis for federal government instream flow rights, particularly in the West, where most public lands have been acquired though removal from the public domain.

As restated by the U.S. Supreme Court in *Arizona v. California* (1963), *Cappaert v. U.S.* (1976), and most recently *U.S. v. New Mexico* (1978), reserved rights apply to all federal lands reserved for particular purposes, not just tribal reservations (Burton 1991: 38–41). Moreover, these rights have the status, under the appropriation doctrine, of the most "senior rights" relative to other uses. The Supreme Court has also affirmed in *U.S. v. New Mexico* (438 U.S. 696, 1978) that in national parks, these reserved water rights reside in a variety of "consumptive and non-consumptive" purposes necessary to conserve scenic, natural, historic, and biotic elements." Such purposes may include scenic, natural and historic conservation; wildlife conservation; sustained public enjoyment; and NPS personnel uses to provide these above uses.

Explicit actions to "maintain minimum stream flows and lake levels" are cited as necessary to carry out these activities (Coggins, Wilkinson, and Leshy 1993: 387). In addition, as stated in *Cappaert,* congressional intent to reserve water should be inferred whenever water is required to achieve the purposes of a federally established reservation (Gillilan and Brown 1997). An example of this decision's intent is the NPS Organic Act of 1916, whose statement of fundamental purpose encompassed a variety of consumptive and nonconsumptive reserved water rights necessary for conserving scenic, natural, historic, and biotic elements (U.S. Department of the Interior 1979: 596). This mandate is also consistent with the premise that states may not exercise authority over federal property unless Congress grants that authority to them when creating a federal reservation, as in the case of a national park.

While in theory reserved rights engender a broad authority to protect instream flow for a federal purpose, in practice the amount of water reserved is generally limited to the minimum amount of previously unappropriated water necessary to accomplish the acquired land's federal purpose. Determining what constitutes an "acceptable" minimum is the subject of considerable contention. In *U.S. v. New Mexico,* for example, the court distinguished between "primary" and "secondary" purposes of federal lands as a way to determine the extent to which reserved water rights might take precedence over other uses and users. Reserved rights exist only for primary uses, as in the case of explicit mandates under law for a given federal agency (Gillilan and Brown 1997). This suggests that federal water rights are really minimal rights and limited to the volumetric amount that is absolutely necessary to carry out an explicitly defined function. A series of federal court decisions, as well as federal agency position papers defending their use of "reserved rights," would appear to lend confirmation to this narrowly construed notion of water rights and instream flow protection (see U.S. Department of Agriculture Forest Service 2000; Lazaroff 2000).

Other cases, legal opinions, and congressional actions would seem to confirm the legitimacy of this view. In *California v. U.S.* (438 U.S. 645, 648–668, 1978), for example, the Supreme Court ruled that congressional deference to state water law is a critical factor in establishing the extent of implied federal reserved rights (Memorandum for Carol E. Dinkins 1982). In addition, Congress has often explicitly limited reserved water rights when establishing federal reservations. Under the Wild and Scenic Rivers Act, for example, Congress confirmed a desire to acquire and preserve certain outstanding rivers in free-flowing condition and to protect these rivers and their immediate environments. However, the act, in its description of reserved water rights, asserts its powers negatively: "designation of any stream or portion thereof as a national wild, scenic or recreational river area shall *not* be construed as a reservation of the waters of such streams for purposes other than those specified, or in quantities greater than necessary to accomplish these purposes." Designation of a Wild and Scenic River does not imply, in other words, automatic reserved rights for the entire unappropriated flow of the river (16 U.S.C. sect. 1284(c), 1970; U.S. Department of the Interior 1979: 609).

Given the NPS's mandate, exercising the reserve water rights doctrine is problematic for adaptively managing the nation's rivers for three reasons. First, in the absence of specific congressional intent to preempt state water laws, the presumption is that federal agencies can only acquire water rights in accordance with state law, and federal authority must be clearly and specifically exercised by express legal foundation—that is, to serve and protect a congressionally mandated function (Memorandum to Carol E. Dinkins 1982: 5, 79). Mere assignment of land management functions to a federal agency does not provide assured reserved rights. This is one reason it is unclear whether early reserved rights proclamations also reserve water rights for "unstated" elements of certain federal parks and historic monuments, such as biological resources (U.S. Department of the Interior 1979: 600). The executive branch has construed federal reserved water rights for protection of wilderness areas narrowly: "Reserved water rights (on refuges) attach only to the extent necessary to fulfill the purposes or objectives named in the individual executive orders establishing the reservations" (U.S. Department of the Interior 1979: 602). Such narrowness does not engender administrative flexibility.

Second, it is uncertain whether reserved rights can be asserted in those instances where public lands are acquired by public donation or purchase rather than by removal from the public domain—the former two methods have been particularly popular in the eastern and southeastern United States (Great Smoky Mountains, Shenandoah). It is also unclear whether the doctrine applies in states operating under a riparian law regime (Coggins, Wilkinson, and Leshy 1993). One solicitor has opined that such reserved rights simply do not exist for entire categories of federal lands, such as those managed by the Bureau of Land Management: "Because most BLM-managed lands are by definition non-reserved public domain, the reserved water rights doctrine is, therefore, not applicable" (U.S. Department of the Interior 1979: 588).

Finally, there are serious ambiguities in the reserved rights doctrine that raise the question as to whether the federal government can assert rights to "unappropriated waters" without regard to state law. During the Reagan administration, for example, the Department of Justice asserted that this theory "does not provide an appropriate legal basis for assertion of water rights by federal agencies in the western states." Their argument stated that this was so because it was not intended by Congress, is unsupported by Supreme Court precedent, and is not usually based in specific congressional directives (Memorandum to Carol E. Dinkins 1982: 1).

Thus, while the reserved rights doctrine is an important tool for instream flow protection, its authority is subject to varied interpretation, application, and contention. Three constraints appear to hold true. First, while theoretically providing a high level of protection for instream flow, federal reserved water rights are limited by the demonstrated need of a federal agency to use unappropriated waters to protect the particular values that led to the establishment of the federal reservation in question. Second, assured reserved rights must be founded upon clear congressional intent and explicitly authorized. Finally, federal reserved water rights are vague. Simply stated, "the basic legal framework or assertion of such rights is in some cases clearly established and in other cases not" (U.S. Department of the Interior 1979: 617). Oftentimes, congressional intent must be "reconstructed" to discern what was initially intended. Increasingly, protracted negotiations involving federal agencies, states, and local water users may be required to establish—on a case-by-case basis—reserved rights for federal lands, as happened in a recent agreement between the U.S. Forest Service and other groups in the Rio Grande and Gunnison National Forests in Colorado (Lazaroff 2000).

The Federal Power Act and Hydropower Project Licensing

The authority of the federal government to license nonfederal hydropower projects on rivers and streams under the Federal Power Act of 1920 (16 U.S.C. 791–828c and 18 CFR Parts 4 and 16) is important in managing instream flow—and in establishing the viability of adaptive management as an approach to water resources management. Nearly 600,000 river miles of the nation's streams (approximately one-fifth) are impounded by dams, and the Federal Energy Regulatory Commission (FERC) is empowered to license those impoundments built and operated by nonfederal entities for periods ranging from 30 to 50 years ("Studies Show" 2001).

Currently, over 1000 hydropower project licenses are overseen by FERC. Since 1993, 160 licenses affecting 237 dams on 105 rivers expired—representing over 10% of FERC-licensed projects. Licenses for an estimated 650 more dams will expire in the next 15 years. These projects represent more than half of FERC's licensed hydropower capacity and provide an opportunity to reflect upon previous and current effects of these projects on instream flow.

The construction and operation of impoundments for power generation constitutes one of the most significant forms of hydrological alteration societies can undertake. Such impoundments affect river flow, aquatic habitat, fisheries, species survival and extinction, and ecosystem services. They also impose considerable social and economic costs (Rosenberg, McCully, and Pringle 2000: 749). Recognizing this impact, Congress amended the Federal Power Act in 1986 by requiring FERC to grant "equal consideration" in decisions regarding licenses, energy conservation, protection of fish and wildlife and recreation, and preservation of general environmental quality alongside the power generation potential of a riverine site. This "more balanced approach to dam relicensing" ("Studies Show" 2001) entails a 14-step relicensing process that embraces, among other things, broad-based public and resource-agency consultation and participation in license application review and comments as well as preparation of environmental assessment documentation in compliance with NEPA.

FERC consultation with federal and state resource agencies is required during the relicensing process (although federal agency recommendations may, in many cases, be ignored), and legal "standing" to participate in relicensing proceedings and to bring suit against FERC is relatively easy—one need only demonstrate that the license seeker has used, now use, or will use the riverine resources in the project's vicinity and that the hydropower project affects these resources. Moreover, section 401 of the Clean Water Act directly places states into the relicensing process by forbidding FERC from relicensing a project until the relevant, affected state certifies that the proposed relicensing effort will comply with applicable water quality standards. This may require conditions to be applied to a license or even license rejection (CWA, 33 U.S.C. Section 1341 (a)).

The FERC hydropower relicensing process is significant for adaptive management for three major reasons. First, aside from the sheer number of licenses anticipated for renewal in the next several years—and the relative ease with which citizens may become involved in the relicensing decision-making process—is the ecological significance of many of these projects. Many small-

or medium-scale (less than 100 MW) projects located on headwaters streams in the Pacific Northwest, California, New England, and the Southern Appalachians have already become the locus of fierce debates over whether the nominal amounts of power they generate outweigh the ecological harm they impose ("Studies Show" 2001). Some of these projects have been denied licenses; in some instances dams, both related and unrelated to FERC license renewal, have been removed in an effort to restore historical stream flow conditions and fisheries. Other projects have seen evidence of successful restoration ("Decreasing Dams" 1999: 15; "Bringing Down the Dam" 1999: 7ff.).

Second, the FERC relicensing process has introduced into instream flow management a debate over the efficacy of dam removal. As one author notes, "It was not too long ago that the call to dismantle . . . dams . . . was considered radical, unrealistic, or downright un-American. Yet, today, the dam-removal movement has entered the mainstream of public opinion" (Booth 2000: A3). The FERC relicensing process is teaching a great deal about the efficacy of dam removal and its advantages and disadvantages relative to instream flow management goals.

While it might seem that dam removal, especially on smaller streams, would significantly restore the riverine and riparian environments of many rivers, the environmental and economic costs of their removal also could be significant in some cases. Demolishing even a medium-sized dam raises questions about silt and sediment removal and the effects of silt and sediment on downstream ecosystems (Booth 2000). Ultimately, the issue of keeping or removing dams must be based on a careful weighing of risks. Clearly, dams do real harm to river systems generally and, in many instances, deny coastal areas of needed, and naturally accumulating sediments and sand, as along the Ventura River in California due to the Matilija Dam (Booth 2000). However, removing a dam can lead to the rapid accumulation of silt and sediment downstream in too great an amount to restore the environment. Clearly, the FERC relicensing process reminds us that instream flow management involves a serious consideration of several factors so tradeoffs may be inevitable. One irony of dam removal is that it is an overt effort to reverse an ecological process that has long been thought to be irreversible—to restore a river's natural condition.

Finally, the FERC relicensing process embraces the possibility of a wide array of mitigating measures short of simple license denial—suggesting the possibility that incremental, reversible reforms can be introduced into the hydropower project operating process. For example, changes in project operation, including flow regime, turbine design, stream oxygenation, reduction of generating capacity, and various structural measures such as fish ladders—prescribed by the Secretaries of Interior and Commerce if a project affects the passage of any fish species present in the project area—can be required of a licensee of a hydropower project. As regards the latter, such ladders can even be required for a fish species that is not even present but whose later introduction into the region would be affected (16 U.S.C. Section 811).

CAN WATER QUALITY AND INSTREAM FLOW
BE MANAGED ADAPTIVELY?
Legal Reform and Instream Flow Protection

Numerous modifications have taken place in riparian and prior appropriation systems at the state level that have led to improvements in stream flow management in recent years. Moreover, the public trust doctrine, based on tradition and custom, dictating that the government has a responsibility toward certain natural resources, including water, has been used in recent years to bolster sustainable management of flow. Although an old concept, it has been given renewed attention as a tool for addressing environmental concerns. It embraces not just water but submerged and submersible lands preserved for public use in navigation, fishing, and recreation. Under the doctrine, the state, as "trustee" for its citizens, bears responsibility for preserving and protecting the right of the public to use waters for these purposes (Stevens 1995).

Efforts to reform, modify, and codify various aspects of riparian and prior appropriation laws have their genesis in several places. Among the most important of these are the difficulty of quantifying water rights, an inability (particularly under riparianism) to protect specific uses against encroachment, the lack of managerial control over water use during drought, and an inability to guarantee water quality requirements for "both human and wildlife needs" (Sherk 1990: 290). These issues have moved water law reform in three significant directions as regards instream flow protection. First, many western states like Kansas, Washington, and Wyoming regulate instream flow indirectly by imposing water quality requirements on water users and water bodies. Such states prescribe minimum stream flows often at the behest of state wildlife or environmental protection agencies (Gillilan and Brown 1997). A number of eastern states also use such approaches.

Second, several states use permit systems that restrict the volume of water that may be removed from streams and rivers or aquifers assumed to connect hydraulically to streams. In prior appropriation states, permit systems are generally managed by a state water conservation or water resources board that can grant instream water rights to various entities and authorize individuals to change the purpose of existing water rights to instream protection. States employing such policies include California, Colorado, Idaho (with approval by the legislature), Montana, Nebraska, Nevada, Oregon, Texas, and Utah (Gillilan and Brown 1997). Several eastern states also employ such approaches, with Iowa (1957) and Florida (1972) being pioneers in using comprehensive permit systems for nondomestic water uses, employing volumetric limits, and establishing special regulatory agencies to enforce them (Abrams 1990).

Third, recent legislative initiatives have tried to regulate inter-basin diversion or transfer of water. Any attempt to describe these diverse systems of permitting in general terms would fail to do justice to their unique characteristics. However, they share certain features in common, especially in the eastern United States. Generally, state water quality and water supply laws provide for minimum stream flow for waste-load allocation, fisheries, recreation, and water quality protection and require impact assessment, with severe penalties for the violation of rules. Moreover, many states' permitting processes require reporting and registration of large withdrawals by industries, landowners, and farmers; authorize the denial of water withdrawals if environmental resources are threatened; and provide a standardized appeals process for affected parties claiming harm—whether from water withdrawals or their prohibition. Some permitting systems also require prior notification of intended withdrawals (Beck 1997). In some states, permits are required to draw even a relatively modest amount of water. In others, permits are only required for large withdrawals—for example, de minimis use in New York requires a permit, while one must use at least anywhere from 10,000 to 2 million gpd for consumptive uses in Minnesota, North Carolina and Ohio before having to obtain a permit (see Beck 1997). The preferred threshold appears to be 100,000 gpd (Sherk 1990: 298).

Minnesota's law requires that high-volume users must "make whole" small-volume users (Abrams 1990). Such laws can be a significant source of instream flow protection, as Virginia's permit law demonstrates. The law of "Old Dominion" is worthy of special mention because it empowers a state water control board to establish water use priorities by regulation, gives domestic and existing uses the highest priority, and requires impact assessments on existing uses before new permits are granted in surface and groundwater management areas. Virginia's law also defines beneficial use as including both instream as well as offstream use—a major departure from riparian tradition (Sherk 1990: 302, 307).

In those instances where inter-basin diversion is regulated, it may be forbidden outright or strongly discouraged (Georgia, Mississippi) or tightly regulated through a process that mandates justifications for diversion and allows large-scale public input into decision- making (Kentucky, New York, North Carolina, Ohio, Tennessee, Virginia). Some permit systems are designed to regulate diversions only from surface water bodies, while others grant to states the ability to regulate diversions from any water source that might affect the flow of a surface water body, as with Tennessee's new Inter-basin Water Transfer Act (see Feldman 2001).

In Wisconsin, riparian users must obtain a permit before diverting water for irrigation (the amount that can be drawn is limited by the extent of tillable land), other agriculture, restoration of the level of a lake or stream, or any diversion of 2 million gallons per day (mgd) or more. Diversion permits can only be granted with the consent of "prior beneficial users" (Beck 1997). In North Carolina, diversions over 2 mgd must be permitted, but an impact assessment must be completed prior to permit issuance. In many eastern states, particularly around the Great Lakes and in the Southeast, concern over inter-basin diversion has become a growing issue (Sherk 1990: 309–311). While these legal requirements place potential roadblocks in the path of threats to instream flow, in practice the effectiveness of these instream flow protection statutes varies according to their degree of enforcement, public awareness that there is a problem, and natural flow conditions.

A few western states have introduced innovative reforms of prior appropriation law in an effort to provide more instream flow. While standards and practices vary dramatically from state to state (Western Water Policy Review Advisory Commission 1998: 5–11), reserve rights and water marketing predominate, albeit in different combinations in different places. Montana allows public entities to set aside unappropriated water for instream flows and permits water interests to lease existing rights. In 1995, the state legislature passed HB 472, which allows holders of water rights to make a "temporary" change of their appropriative rights to instream rights "for the benefit of the fishery resource." Appropriators may also lease their water rights "to another person for instream flows" for fish (Sterne 2000).

Washington is working with tribes and federal agencies to develop a water budget in order to benefit wild salmon by assuring the necessary amounts and periods of flow for both spawning migrations upstream and smolt returning to the ocean. The state has granted regulators wide authority to set rules and involve the public. The Washington Department of Ecology (WDOE) has "exclusive" authority to "establish minimum water flows and/or levels for streams, lakes or other public waters for the purposes of protecting fish, game, birds or other wildlife resources, or recreational or aesthetic values of said public waters whenever it appears to be in the public interest to establish the same." The WDOE also establishes new instream flows by making rules, with notice, comment, and hearings for interested parties. A 1993 state supreme court decision determined that the WDOE can set minimum flows at the optimum level necessary to support fish populations. Washington also allows for state acquisition of "trust water rights" through purchase, lease, or gift or by state or federal investments in conservation.

Oklahoma and Idaho use scenic river designations while Kansas uses basin-of-origin methods (Western Water Policy Review Advisory Commission 1998: 5–11) to protect instream flow. In Idaho, the Water Resources Board files an application with the Idaho Department of Water Resources to reserve the minimum flow of water in all rivers or streams. Reservations can be made only from previously unappropriated water. A hearing is held and a determination is made regarding whether the flow level requested is the minimum flow or lake level that is acceptable as opposed to the ideal, most desirable flow or, where applicable, the lake level necessary for the beneficial use (Sterne 2000). Such improvements in public input, accountability, and monitoring of change have also characterized efforts to improve water quality management.

Success Stories in Local Water Quality Management: TMDLs Again

By 2000, states nationwide had identified nearly 22,000 water bodies impaired by nearly 42,000 various causes (known as impairments). Over 36,000 of these impairments are caused by pollutants that must be addressed by TMDLs (Edwards 2002). Despite progress in identifying impaired waters, there is some question whether the nation is making progress in cleaning up these waters. As in the case of instream flow, there are local examples where progress is being made. Across the country, state environmental protection agencies are forging innovative partnerships with industries, agricultural groups, scientists, and community and environmental organizations in an effort to improve water quality generally and to comply with the TMDL process.

One motive for these efforts is practical—as we have seen, most state environmental protection agencies lack the effective authority to mitigate nonpoint water pollution and generally have "only a small arsenal of regulatory means with which to control nonpoint sources such as farms, small repair shops and neighborhoods" (Pelley 1998). To compel compliance with TMDLs, states must resort to nonregulatory methods. Over the long run, such methods may be not only more effective in achieving water quality goals but less politically contentious as well.

We define an "innovative" partnership as one having three characteristics. First, it must be voluntary—groups agreeing to work together must do so without duress or compulsion from a legal milestone or some other time-limiting factor. Second, the effort must proactively address water quality issues. It is not enough to form a partnership to reach a minimal level of compliance with water quality standards as defined by the current TMDL process—the goal must be the long-term protection of water quality. Finally, each party to an agreement must offer some unique resource or skill that makes the partnership as a whole more effective than the various parts acting alone. The following are examples of programs that appear to meet these criteria.

Citizen Monitoring

One promising approach to TMDL development is the use of citizen monitoring programs. The challenge is not in finding citizens willing to undertake monitoring. It is in granting official sanction and, thus, legitimacy to these efforts. In Missouri, for example, the goals of the Department of Natural Resources include obtaining stakeholder input into TMDL policies and gaining support for decisions (Cleland 2002). The state's Public Participation Plan has developed a variety of mechanisms for sharing information with constituents, and the program is a true grassroots effort.

A number of benefits have been found in giving citizen-based volunteer efforts legal legitimacy in support of water quality monitoring. For one, it has proven to be one of the most effective ways to educate Missouri's citizens about watersheds and aquatic ecosystems. It also provides access to a clearly identified group of stakeholders with a proven commitment to watershed protection—local residents are often willing to get involved with watershed partnerships and TMDL issues (Cleland 2002). This has been a tremendous asset, particularly when trying to convince state residents of the importance of participating in voluntary restoration efforts.

Pollutant Trading

Minnesota has adopted pollution trading as a creative way to address nonpoint sources of pollution. The lower twenty-five miles of the Minnesota River have a Biochemical Oxygen Demand (BOD) TMDL for low dissolved oxygen conditions. The pollutant load is fully allocated to the Metropolitan Council's wastewater treatment plants, which combine point and nonpoint source allocations. The TMDL requires a 40% reduction in BOD. In the mid-1990s, the Rahr Malting Company and the Southern Minnesota Sugar Beet Cooperative sought permits to add loadings to the river (Klang 2002). A point/nonpoint pollutant trading permit issued by the Minnesota Pollution Control Agency provided a way for managers and industry to achieve economic expansion and load reductions simultaneously.

Pollutant trading permits require offsets for new or expanded discharges in fully allocated reaches. Minnesota developed a policy for requirements that facilitate point/nonpoint trading in a manner that protects resources. At the same time, monitoring and analysis improved the understanding of the processes occurring in the river. The cornerstone of Minnesota's pollutant-trading scheme is a voluntary agreement between the Minnesota Pollution Control Agency and Rahr Malting. In exchange for the malting plant's agreement to fund special upstream projects to reduce nonpoint pollution loads on the Minnesota River, the plant acquired rights to discharge treated effluent downstream. Under the policy, Rahr Malting has fulfilled the trading requirements as outlined in the permit, offsetting the 150 pounds of BOD per day at a two-to-one trading ratio built into the crediting process.

To date, the company has exceeded the required offset by an additional 62 pounds per day (Klang 2002). The Southern Minnesota Sugar Beet Cooperative also fulfilled their obligation within the first two years of operation. Further enhancement of the process is underway. The economic incentive for Rahr Malting was the high cost of building a state-of-the-art effluent treatment system to comply with the TMDL for the Minnesota River. Prior to this decision, the plant had run its effluent through Shakopee's municipal system at its own cost—however, the effectiveness of this policy was diminishing over time. From Rahr Malting's perspective, trading for effluent discharge rights saves money and complies with the law. Thus far, Rahr has funded the planting of over 14,000 poplar trees on upstream floodplains, funded the replanting of 105 acres of highly erodable land in native prairie grasses, and contributed to a series of small stream bank restoration and stabilization projects and residue management programs. State and community stakeholders have agreed to a series of livestock exclusion zones and the introduction of wetland treatment systems for nutrient removal (Eilers 1998: 11).

Subsequent to Minnesota's policy, the EPA issued a new policy that defines the conditions under which industrial facilities, municipalities, and agricultural interests may earn water-quality credits and then sell them to other sources. According to the EPA, regulated parties can earn the credits by reducing their water discharges below the levels required by the most stringent water quality-based requirements (Final Water Quality Trading Policy 2003).

North Carolina has implemented a similar trading system to Minnesota's, targeting nutrient reductions. In recent years, low dissolved oxygen levels, sporadic fish kills, loss of submerged vegetation, and other water quality problems have plagued North Carolina's Tar-Pamlico basin. Studies have linked many of these problems to increased nitrogen and phosphorus loading to the system (NCDEM 1987). In 1989, the North Carolina Environmental Management Commission (EMC) designated the Tar-Pamlico basin as a "nutrient-sensitive water." The classification was based on years of detailed nutrient-loading studies and required implementation of a strategy to manage point and nonpoint sources to meet water quality goals.

The North Carolina Division of Environmental Management (NCDEM) responded by developing stricter nitrogen and phosphorus effluent standards for dischargers in the basin. However, dischargers were concerned about the high capital costs that might be required to achieve the nutrient-reduction goals. So a coalition of dischargers, working in cooperation with the Environmental Defense Fund, the Pamlico-Tar River Foundation, and NCDEM, proposed a nutrient-trading framework through which dischargers pay for the development and implementation of agricultural best management practices (BMPs) to achieve all or part of the total nutrient reduction goals (NCDEM 1992).

The EMC approved the program in December 1989, and the implementation phase is currently under way. As a condition of the EMC's approval, the discharger coalition agreed to fund the development of an estuarine model. The model will be used as a tool to evaluate specific nutrient-reduction strategies for the basin. This information will then be used to revise effluent nutrient standards for the second phase of the project. The nutrient-trading program is proving to be a popular solution, largely because it achieves the state's nutrient-reduction goals and addresses nonpoint loadings while also reducing the economic burden to municipal dischargers (NCDEM 1987, 1992; EPA 2003a).

Best Management Practices

Virginia's Department of Conservation and Recreation (VDCR) selected the Nomini Creek watershed as an area in which to evaluate and monitor the effectiveness of best management practices (BMPs) for the Chesapeake Bay Program. By identifying the critical phosphorus and sediment loading areas within the watershed where BMPs could be effectively sited, VDCR tested the feasibility of integrating VirGIS, a state-run geographic information system (GIS), with two simple pollutant yield models called SLOSS and PHOSPH (Shanholz et al. 1990). Because Virginia's database was sufficiently large, VirGIS was able to provide the data required to run the models.

The output from these models successfully identified critical areas of nonpoint source loading. BMPs were implemented in these areas, and an intensive water quality monitoring effort was put into place in the late 1980s to evaluate BMP effectiveness and to verify estimated pollutant loads (DCR-DSWC 1986). GIS technology has been used to prioritize and target water bodies with multiple water quality concerns and to target BMPs to critical nonpoint source loading areas to meet load allocations more effectively.

The South Fork of the Salmon River, located in the mountains of central Idaho, is a highly valued Chinook salmon and steelhead trout spawning area. At one time, the river supported Idaho's largest run of summer Chinook salmon, but in recent years the number of fish spawning there has declined. While some of the population decline is attributable to downstream hydroelectric dams and commercial and sport fishing, monitoring data collected since the 1960s show that the excessive amount of fine sediment entering the river has also played a role in this decline by adversely affecting spawning, and possibly rearing, habitats (Platts et al. 1989). The 1988 *Idaho Water Quality Status Report and Nonpoint Source Assessment* listed three segments of the South Fork Salmon River as water quality–limited due to fine sediments originating from forestry activities. Because of these problems and public interest in restoring use of the South Fork fishery, resource agencies recognized the need to manage activities in the basin better, and the state made the water body a priority for TMDL development.

At this time, the Forest Service was already developing management plans for the Boise and Payette National Forests, which make up approximately two-thirds of the basin. Coordinating with these Forest Service efforts, a consensus team of Forest Service, EPA, and state representatives set interim numeric goals to attain the existing narrative sediment criteria and recover beneficial uses. The criteria are (1) a five-year mean of 27% depth fines by weight, with no single year over 29%; (2) a five-year mean of 32% cobble embeddedness, with no single year over 37%; or (3) acceptable improving trends in other monitored water quality parameters directly related to salmonid spawning and cold water biota beneficial use support (Payette National Forest 1991).

To meet these goals, the consensus team established a TMDL to reduce sed-iment loading to the river from human activities by 25% and, consistent with the phased approach to TMDL development, described implementation plans for BMPs and a monitoring program to assess and revise, if necessary, the in-terim criteria by the year 2001. If monitoring indicates that Chinook and steel-head spawning capability did increase to acceptable limits by 2001, the level of effort expended to achieve the 25% reduction will be maintained (Payette National Forest 1991). If spawning capability does not increase, additional re-covery projects and an analysis of the level of beneficial use attainability will be required. As of 2003, the Idaho Department of Environmental Quality re-ported that the South Fork salmon river has not attained 1991 quality targets for sediment and metals, although fisheries have somewhat improved (Idaho Department of Environmental Quality 2003).

General Partnerships

Pennsylvania has adopted a kind of "good neighbor" policy by becoming the first state in the country to launch a public forum whose purpose is to dis-cuss different states' contributions to downstream pollutants causing water quality problems in Chesapeake Bay. The principal pathway for Pennsylva-nia's pollutants is the Susquehanna River, although other streams, originating in other states, like the Potomac River, are also contributing to the problem. The idea is to use a voluntary partnership—the Chesapeake Executive Coun-cil, comprised of representatives from Pennsylvania, Maryland, Virginia, the District of Columbia, and the EPA—to enter into a nonbinding agreement to reduce nutrient flows by 40%. It is intended that this body will prod further innovative partnerships. The partnership does not prescribe specific mitiga-tion measures, only the objective of percentage reductions in nutrient flows. It is up to each state, working with local stakeholders, to introduce specific mea-sures. For its part, Pennsylvania has worked with country extension agents, farmers, and environmental groups to introduce land management techniques in areas that are highly susceptible to runoff (Stranahan 1993; Houck 1997).

Washington's Lower Yakima River Basin partnership has been nationally cited for achieving TMDL goals for that water body. The Yakima basin, some-times called the "nation's fruitbowl," is one of the most intensively farmed re-gions in the entire country (Reinhart 2002). The basin is characterized by ex-tensive irrigation systems, mountainous terrain, and erosive soil. Because of these factors, the major pollutant causing impairment is contaminated sedi-ment from furrow-irrigated fields. Following development by the Washington

State Department of Ecology of a TMDL for sediment, nutrients, pesticides, and bacteria, a series of steps were taken to address the sources of impairment. Following adoption of a monitoring plan in 1994, two irrigation districts, the Roza and Sunnyside Valley Districts, created a Roza-Sunnyside Board of Joint Control (RSBOJC) whose purpose is to develop policies and guidelines to meet water quality goals and a voluntary enforcement program to ensure compliance. Another goal was to spur further proactive measures by other irrigation districts.

The major components of the RSBOJC's efforts are public education, technical assistance to farmers, and cost sharing for restoration and anti-erosion programs. The latter were funded principally by the Natural Resources Conservation Service's Environmental Quality Incentive Program as well as by the state's conservation commission and the EPA's watershed restoration (Section 319) program. One advantage in soliciting funds for these programs was that the EPA designated the Lower Yakima basin as a geographic priority area. Other conservation districts followed suit, with the South Yakima Conservation District focusing on technical assistance and water quality monitoring projects, the North Yakima Conservation District convincing every farmer in a 7500-acre area to convert from furrow to drip irrigation, and the Benton Conservation District using Global Positioning System technology to "help target education and cost-share efforts" (Reinhart 2002).

A number of practical improvements have been introduced in the basin, including conservation tillage systems, constructed sediment basins, zero discharge farming (pumping collected water in sediment basins back onto farmland), and changes in irrigation techniques. The basin's TMDL goal of reducing suspended solids has been met (suspended solids loading has been lowered by 80%), and 75% of primary irrigation drains now meet the state's turbidity standards by a wide margin. The keys to the success of this effort were threefold. First, local stakeholders have been involved in an advisory capacity in the RSBOJC's efforts. Second, the concerted effort of existing institutions in committing their leadership to meeting TMDL goals has been important. And third, efforts were highly proactive—the RSBOJC was actually formed two years before the Department of Ecology established specific goals for turbidity, fisheries support and pesticides—and two years before the EPA approved the state's subsequent TMDL for the Lower Yakima Basin. In effect, local leaders recognized the problem and its potential long-term costs and realized that early efforts could leverage fiscal resources to achieve change.

Are There TMDLs in Our Future?

Every state now has vast experience with TMDLs for point and nonpoint sources. However, no entity exists to bring these experiences together. For section 303(d) to be an effective policy for addressing the nation's water quality, more is needed, including guidelines that states can adapt to their needs. The EPA needs to assess what states have done thus far, both good and bad, and help them determine what works. Several states have introduced innovative ways to improve water quality *and* to enhance the TMDL process, as we have seen. Many more examples could probably be cited. The problem, however, is that many states are unaware of activities elsewhere that may mirror their own efforts. A national clearinghouse of such efforts is needed.

It is unclear what the future holds for TMDLs. It may take another succession of citizen lawsuits against the EPA before any action is taken to formulate needed changes of existing laws. It seems certain that the process of TMDL development and implementation will remain contentious. While by no means panaceas, many of the innovative ideas discussed in this chapter could be applied elsewhere. While additional fiscal resources may be needed, equally important are imagination, public involvement, and the willingness to try creative nonregulatory solutions, economic incentives, and community buy-in. Adaptive management is as much a way of thinking about the problem as it is a way of postulating solutions.

LINKING LAND USE, ECONOMICS, AND WATER QUALITY

In general, urbanization, sprawl, and extensive land use lead to changes in stream hydrology, morphology, water quality, and stream habitat and ecology. These impacts affect instream flow and water pollution—especially runoff pollution—and lead to conflicts among water users. While these effects are obviously site-specific and vary considerably from place to place, there are some generalizations we can make. Sprawl generates a number of "cascading" impacts that begin upstream, including reduced genetic flow, changes in nutrient cycling, "flashy" discharge regimes (due to increased impervious surface), outright "burial" or diversion and rechannelization of urban streams, and severe streambank erosion (Baer and Pringle 2000). These impacts have long been observed to have negative effects on stream water quality and quantity. Consequently, the use of land use ordinances and other planning-related policies by states to regulate urban "sprawl" or the location and density of the built environment in order to protect these water parameters is not new. The use of these measures may represent one of the most adaptive sets of approaches to the problem of water quality.

Many American cities (for example, New York) have purchased land around their water supply reservoirs to protect them from encroaching development, and a number of urban stream protection efforts have also been pursued through public-private partnerships that discourage impervious surfaces, reduce runoff, enhance filtration, and encourage sustainable land use development (Baer and Pringle 2000).[6] A few of these developments are worth highlighting.

Since the early 1980s, the states of Maryland, Pennsylvania, and Virginia as well as the District of Columbia, the Chesapeake Bay Commission, and the EPA have joined together to sponsor a combined government–private sector restoration effort to reverse water quality declines and to address threats to fish and wildlife in the Chesapeake Bay estuary (Williams 2000). Working through a multi-stakeholder partnership, a 1987 agreement commits the partners to a cooperative approach to protect the shared resources of the bay and to restore it to a more productive state. Specific strategies include reductions in point source pollutants and targeted cooperative, voluntary landowner involvement programs strategies to begin addressing nonpoint runoff. The success of this and similar programs is open to debate; as of this writing, nitrogen and phosphorous levels still remain high, and water quality in the bay, while improving, remains low. For example, dissolved oxygen levels in the bay remain low as a result of excess pollution, high rainfall amounts, and—since 2005— higher than average water temperatures. Dissolved oxygen is the amount of oxygen present in a given quantity of water. This amount must be high enough to sustain a healthy, diverse ecosystem (Chesapeake Bay Program 2006).

As regards public lands protection, while a number of initiatives are taking place to mitigate the adverse impacts of land use developments on instream flow, it is too early to assess their effectiveness with confidence. Three national park examples include Big South Fork National River and Recreation Area (Kentucky-Tennessee), Buffalo National River (Arkansas), and the Chattahoochee River National Recreation Area (Georgia).

In 1997, in an effort to provide for reasonable off-stream uses while protecting instream flow, a water resources management plan was designed to establish and maintain a water data management and analysis program; to classify stream types for the Big South Fork River and select tributaries; to delineate, characterize, and map groundwater resources; and—most of all—to determine water rights and instream flow needs for a variety of aquatic species, especially endangered mussel species. In order to achieve these objectives, NPS officials developed a three-part institutional plan to reconcile instream flow needs and off-stream water rights. The plan includes developing inter-agency data coordination between NPS and other local, state, and federal agencies; undertaking long-term hydrologic inventory and monitoring, including an expanded gauging system; and performing long-term external land-use monitoring. In 1998, communities adjacent to Big South Fork proposed to build a water intake just inside the reservation's boundary in order to alleviate local needs for additional water supply. This decision was made after the initial assessment of instream flow was completed.

NPS officials face a slightly different challenge in working with states and NGOs in the Buffalo National River. To preserve the free-flowing condition of the river, park managers requested an environmental assessment for the project proposed to dam Bear Creek—a Buffalo River tributary. The park began taking routine monthly and storm-event samples that will be analyzed at the end of three years to determine, at each site, discharge and variability of discharge, water quality constituent concentrations and values, nutrient and suspended sediment yields, base flow and surface runoff loads, stream sediment, and geomorphic and habitat data. This data will be used to assess constituent land uses affecting flow and quality.

Finally, in the Chattahoochee National Scenic River, NPS officials seek to protect instream flows at a level that will sustain the park's natural and recreational values. There are two main issues that affect the outcome: better coordination with the operators of Buford and Morgan Falls dams and involvement in negotiations for the ACF compact. The NPS is also seeking to identify the flow necessary to sustain park resources by working with the Army Corps of Engineers and the Georgia Power Company to guarantee minimum flow within park boundaries. This flow quantity, it is believed, must be identified to provide leverage in ACF negotiations. The park is currently working on a water management plan and conducting a visitor-use study to determine how different levels of flow affect visitors' recreational experiences.

Water Marketing as a Collaborative Approach

As we recall, water marketing, a method of buying, selling, and leasing water rights, has been used extensively in some parts of the American West. It has recently come into favor as a possible tool for furnishing additional instream flows, and, as we have seen, a variant of marketing, "tradable permits," are be-ing used to reduce water pollution. There are institutional barriers to the use of marketing approaches.

In the eastern United States, where riparian doctrine prevails, water mar-kets for the buying and selling of water rights are difficult to establish because such markets assume that one can guarantee a fixed quantity of water for a given use—whether instream or off-stream. Riparian doctrine, however, does not ensure the right to a given volume or quantity of water-only access to a source of water under or adjacent to lands owned by a riparian landowner. Fur-thermore, few eastern states have the physical infrastructure needed to trans-fer large volumes of water from place to place and are unlikely to develop such infrastructure in light of public and decision-maker concerns against inter-basin diversion.

In parts of the west, special markets negotiated by environmental groups have attempted, with some success, to reduce the volume of water diverted off-stream for irrigation in favor of maintaining stream flows to protect the health of fish and other environmental or recreational interests (Landry 2000: 14). Environmental organizations such as the Environmental Defense Fund, the Nature Conservancy, and the Oregon Water Trust are starting to "broker" such water deals. Moreover, resistance from the agricultural community is de-creasing due to the perception that this tool is an attractive alternative to reg-ulation. However, there are other potential barriers to their widespread use, including the need for a physical infrastructure for "moving" water from place to place and ambiguities in water law–permitting markets—especially under riparian systems.

The Oregon Water Trust, a nonprofit organization established in 1993 and modeled on the Nature Conservancy and the Trust for Public Lands, has been effective in acquiring consumptive water rights from existing users and con-verting them to instream flows. It has raised funds for this purpose primarily from foundation grants and "mitigation payments," and leases are renewed an-nually or rights are completely sold to the Oregon Water Trust. Within three years of its establishment, 25 water rights transactions in various stages of com-pletion had been obtained, and approximately 20 cubic feet per second (cfs) of water had been converted from irrigation use to instream flows, at least on a temporary basis. However, it has been difficult to find a price that properly aligns the value to the seller or lessor of water with the value held by the trust. It may also be difficult for the trust to know how long it will take for the bene-fits of relatively good instream flow to exceed the purchase price paid. As in any long-term investment, the underlying assumption is that, over time, it will yield a greater benefit (NRLC 1997). Texas has also created a Texas Water Trust to hold rights dedicated to environmental needs, but there has been little study of its results (Western Water Policy Review Advisory Commission 1998: 5–11).

In 1998, Washoe County and the cities of Reno and Sparks, Nevada, purchased water rights to augment flows in the Truckee River in order to improve water quality. This is one of the few examples of governmental entities purchasing water rights for instream flow—although Montana has undertaken a similar plan for appropriated water flows (Western Water Policy Review Advisory Commission 1998: 5–11). In Washington, the Department of Ecology, beginning in 1991, undertook a program to publicly acquire water rights through the "Trust Water Right Program" for protection of instream flows. Designed to acquire "water rights . . . on a voluntary basis, to provide water for presently unmet needs and emerging needs," the program thus far has led to water rights settlements between the Yakima Indian nation and a corporation with appropriation rights. Minimum flows are not subject to regulation and are based on a 1976 agreement (NRLC 1997).

While many other western states use some version of tradable or sellable rights to protect instream flow, there have been no such examples arising in the eastern United States. This is most likely due to the lack of fit between riparian doctrine (which guarantees access to water but guarantees no actual volumetric amount) and the requirement that one be able to ensure delivery of a specified amount of water for an agreed-upon purpose. Moreover, as we have seen in our discussion of riparian doctrine, a person can divert water from a stream if they can demonstrate that it will be put to a "reasonable use." However, this right can be superseded if a subsequent user can demonstrate that his or her proposed use is more reasonable (Samson and Bacchus 2000: 15). It should also be kept in mind that the establishment of water markets—even in the west—rarely occurs without some resistance. Residents of water-exporting areas are, understandably, more likely to oppose any transfer of water, for any purpose, unless reciprocal conditions that protect fairness, future needs, and environmental effects are addressed (Keenan, Krannich, and Walker 1999). Realistically, these constraints on water markets may never change.

Private Initiative, Public Benefit: Land Trusts

Many private land trusts operating in the United States have pursued purchases of lands adjoining critical upstream stretches of rivers and streams, partly in an effort to protect water quality and instream flow. The Nature Conservancy, an organization long known for the pursuit of this strategy, began its efforts in 1954 with the purchase of a tract of land adjoining a gorge in upstate New York with exactly these goals in mind (Marzec 2001: 74).

While land purchases for this purpose are widespread, little effort has been made to evaluate their success independently. Anecdotal evidence suggests that, in combination with other tools, land trusts may be important tools for instream flow protection. The keys to effective use appear to lie in three areas—partnership-building with community groups and government agencies in conjunction with the land purchases, dedicated public education and outreach, and collaboration with scientists (Taylor 2000; Solzenburg, 2000; Calhoun 1999).

From an adaptive management standpoint, based on Nature Conservancy experience in the Green River in Kentucky, the Sacramento River Basin in California, and the San Pedro Valley in Arizona and the Republic of Mexico, effective instream flow protection measures and strategies are most effectively developed when community groups and public agencies are brought into the process. Such groups can help map watersheds and undertake joint environmental assessments. In this way, the value of river protection is made more apparent to local communities. Also helpful are collaboration with agencies and scientists familiar with data management as well as conjoint purchases and critical land use controls preventing or restricting overdevelopment along shorelines. In short, no single approach will be a panacea for these issues.

Used in combination with other approaches, such tools can become locally tailored innovations. However, there are more than institutional and economic impediments to overcome—and opportunities to be sought. As we have seen, innovations, like the problems they are designed to solve, generate controversy and differences over values. Is there a "right" to pollute? Is water a form of property than can or should be "bought" or "sold"? What obligations do polluters and water users have to pay society for the harm or damage they cause by their actions? In short, there is an ethical dimension to sustainable water policy. This dimension must somehow be embraced within an adaptive management scheme. How this might be done is the subject of our next chapter.

CHAPTER 5

Toward Sound Ethical Alternatives for Water Resources Management

The fact is that as a culture, we regard control over nature, progress, and material goods as far more important than the ideal of living in harmony with nature. Thus, a significant factor contributing to our environmental crisis is our value system, and major changes must take place to reprioritize [it].

—*David A. Camacho, "Environmental Ethics as a Political Choice"*

Defining stewardship as the call [or duty] to "earthkeeping" or "caring" is a position that has also been popular in recent years. . . . One [implication] is that caring is a moral imperative—a duty and an obligation. Another is the intense, interactive love relationships. Caring takes stewardship another step . . . toward closeness of humankind and nature. The major component is love, and in this regard, love leads to caring, which is what God expects of us regarding creation.

—*Robert Booth Fowler,* The Greening of Protestant Thought

In this chapter we show that while it is essential that policymakers embrace the elements of sustainable development for water management we have been discussing, there should be more attention paid to the ethical basis of water resources administration in order to achieve adaptive management. In a previous book (Feldman 1995) I argued that sound ethics are important to water resources management to protect the welfare of future generations; to prevent gratuitous decisions based on short-term, imprudent, or acquisitive aspirations; to bound people and resources within a given region under a social contract; to encourage consideration of a broad range of alternatives; and to promote public participation and consideration of equity and fairness issues.

In this chapter, we add another set of justifications, based on the experience of river basin initiatives. As we have seen, river basin and watershed management initiatives based on sustainability aspirations, such as CALFED in California, the Murray-Darling River Basin initiative in Australia, the La Plata compact in South America, the Northwest Power Planning Commission in the Pacific Northwest, water pollution marketing experiments in Minnesota and North Carolina, and various Best Management Practices adopted in Washington state, Pennsylvania, and elsewhere, seek above all else to be transparent, fair, democratic, and open to change and flexibility. Behind their institutional adaptability, the use of scientific knowledge, the ability to collaborate and develop partnerships, and an openness to innovation imply a set of ethical values predicated on finding the means to balance environmental protection, development, and social justice and promoting democratic decision-making.

While there are numerous ethical approaches and paradigms from which one can choose to establish policy justifications, when it comes to natural resources three approaches have explicitly sought to achieve this balance: covenants, categorical imperatives, and stewardship approaches. Covenantal thinking is an approach which assumes that there are obligations to care for nature and responsibly look after the welfare of our fellow citizens and that these obligations are based on a sense of dominion granted to all of us who live in a region and benefit from its natural bounty. Categorical imperatives are based on the premises that there are intrinsic obligations to keep promises and other freely made commitments and that these obligations connect past, present, and future generations. Finally, stewardship ethics contend that we are obliged to care for nature and other people.

Before discussing these approaches and their relevance to sustainable water management, we first consider a seldom-acknowledged factor important to understanding the role of ethics in sustainable development generally—and water resources management in particular. Most current water management initiatives are already based on an ethical foundation: utilitarianism—providing the greatest material benefits to the greatest number of people.

This utilitarian foundation has been epitomized in the United States by a water resources policy that has traditionally embraced economic growth through river basin development *and* economic efficiency by federalizing a process of decision-making strategies, as we shall see in the next major section, that was intended to satisfy the "greatest good." In the first instance, public policy was geared toward ensuring adequate water for power, domestic use, agriculture, and other needs identified by regional interests (Kundell, DeMeo, and Myszewski 2001). In the second instance, water projects were provided at minimal direct cost to these constituencies, making them, in effect, a "gratuity." Thus, when we discuss ethical alternatives, we are really referring to alternatives to the idea that the only sound ethical foundation is promoting the greatest good for the greatest number.

Politics and Ethics: Squaring the Circle?

While there are sound ethical alternatives to utilitarianism for managing water resources that would help avoid the types of adverse environmental and social effects currently experienced in river basin management, implementing any of them will be difficult for three reasons. This chapter is about these reasons and our proposals to deal with them.

The first impediment to adopting any viable ethical alternative to utilitarianism in natural resources management is that democratic politics are to a large extent predicated on the belief that individuals as well as groups make policy decisions on the basis of rational self-interest. In the United States, we could even claim that there is a longstanding bias in American politics toward defending policy decisions on the basis of such self-interest. This bias inhibits public interest–based solutions to environmental and other policy problems because it assumes that individual economic gain is a sign of virtue and because it rejects civic republicanism—the conviction that citizens have an obligation to serve the needs of the larger community (Bellah 1996).

In many polities—particularly in developing societies—studies show that autocratic governments perform poorly in achieving economic development and social justice in part because their leaders' authority is based on pleasing the interests of a small group of elites. Democratic-reformist regimes succeed in changing such oppressive situations because they remove impediments to the articulation of interests by large, popular coalitions. Achievement-based values, decentralized market-based economic decisions, and diffusion of policy innovation are all important factors in promoting such reformist systems

and bringing about the possibility of open decision-making (Bueno de Mesquita and Root 2002). Moreover, restoration of openness and a public-regarding
approach to policy are necessary to overcome self-interested policy.

Second, each of the ethical alternatives we will discuss in this chapter has
significant practical and political shortcomings. These shortcomings are most
glaring when one tries to adopt any single ethical alternative. We can see that
this is true because all three have been utilized throughout history as justifications, at least in part, for environmental policy decisions and all have on
some level failed, at least in part, to meet the prevailing ecological or societal
challenges. Thus, one of our policy recommendations in this chapter is to try
to adopt ethical eclecticism—drawing from the strengths of many approaches
while managing their weaknesses and shortcomings. In short, to be effective,
these alternatives must be implemented in ways that embrace the needs of watersheds and the demands of democratic theory, or they will fail.

Finally, it is difficult to achieve clear and transparent policy objectives that
are ethical and practical through a political process. Ethical discourse is concerned with defining fundamental issues of right and wrong. Politics, on the
other hand, as a venerable study by the political scientist Harold D. Lasswell
reminds us, is the study of "who gets what, when, and how" (Lasswell 1958).
Figuring out how to use power to achieve one's goals is at the heart of politics.
Determining how to exercise power justly is a secondary concern—one often
ignored entirely. For this reason, there is no ethical panacea for achieving a
just environmental policy.

Democratic politics must be deliberately bowed to the demands of ethical
values in order to be just, and advocates of ethical ideals must find a way to
implement their ideals within a contentious, interest-driven context that
places a premium on consensus-building, conformity, and obedience to law
and order. The challenge, therefore, is to identify approaches to the implementation of ethical ideals that temper the struggle for justice with a proper
indignation toward self-interest, on the one hand, and due regard for the in-
evitability of the struggle for power—endemic in all polities—on the other
(Niebuhr 1932). We now turn to the defects of previous policy, and the features
of the three alternative ethical approaches to water management. These are:
covenants, categorical imperatives, and stewardship. We also consider how
they can be implemented.

CURRENT AND PAST WATER POLICY
AS DEFECTIVE PHILOSOPHY

As we saw in chapter 2 in our discussion of various river basin management schemes, a key challenge facing any ethical alternative to the prevailing management of water resource policy is to embrace simultaneously the demands of democratic practice and the needs of watersheds. To do both, any alternative must address three issues at the heart of this challenge:

- The value of *structural* (dams) v. *nonstructural* (conservation) measures;
- The advantages of *comprehensive, conjoint decision-making* by a single entity; and
- The appropriate role of *public participation* in decisions, as well as that of NGOs.

Ethics and Values in Historical Water Policy:
Focus on the United States

As discussed in chapter 2, giving federally funded water projects more than one purpose has been a longstanding concern. By the late nineteenth century, reform efforts gradually incorporated multiple objectives in water projects, and an effort was initiated to *harmonize* environmental and economic concerns while more effectively involving the public in decisions (Feldman 1995; Grigg 1996). These efforts accelerated in the 1920s with passage of the Federal Water Power Act, which established the Federal Power Commission, forerunner of the Federal Energy Regulatory Commission. The act established a uniform process for the licensing of private hydroelectric power projects, checked the authority of private interests, and instituted "the first comprehensive river basin development plans for the nation." Unfortunately, the River and Harbor Act of 1927, while continuing the effort to comprehensively manage river basins, would also encourage a rigid overreliance on benefit-cost assessment for new water projects. This approach endured well into the 1970s (NAS 1999: 11).[1]

The apex of efforts to encourage multi-objective planning was the U.S. Water Resources Council (WRC), which was formed in 1961. Empowered to engage in comprehensive water supply planning, its mission was to "encourage the conservation, development, and utilization of water and related land resources of the United States on a comprehensive and coordinated basis" and to "maintain a continuing study of the nation's water and related land resources and to prepare periodic assessments to determine the adequacy of these resources to meet present and future requirements" (WRC 1978). Unfortunately, as we have seen, despite efforts to incorporate meaningful stakeholder participation, unified water resources planning was opposed by the traditional beneficiaries of water projects, and public works bureaus continued to adhere to their own plans and to bypass instruments that would encourage public participation.

When the WRC introduced "Principles and Standards for Planning Water and Related Land Resources" in 1973, the overall effect, as we have noted, was to require agencies to consider nonstructural alternatives to water resource problems; to undertake rigorous, systematic benefit-cost assessments that considered all viable options for achieving the same resource management objectives; and to incorporate the views of states and the general public in plans and programs. Controversy came to a head during the presidency of Jimmy Carter, who actively sought to diminish Congress's tradition of pork barrel water projects, charging that they were wasteful of public expenditures, economically unjustifiable, and, in many cases, ecologically harmful. Criticism grew in Congress that the WRC was simply using budget cuts and impoundments to eliminate locally popular, necessary projects (see Fradkin 1996).

What the WRC represented from an ethical-political perspective was a rejection of traditional client-centered politics—what Theodore Lowi (1979) has termed "distributive politics"—that relied on decisions made by a tightly knit network of stakeholders animated by an understandable, if less than fully reasonable, desire to seek large, publicly funded projects and programs from government. What some viewed as subsidies to "special interests" beneficiaries saw as entitlements: compensation for enduring the hardships of migrating to a hostile environment and helping to sustain a prosperous way of life there. Many argue that distributive politics contributed to consumptive uses of water and wasteful public expenditures; on top of that, in an effort to maximize their political influence, resource agencies were increasingly in cahoots with regional interests (Conservation Foundation 1984; Wilkinson 1992; Mann 1993; Pitzer 1995; Harden 1997).

Regarding the three major issues at the heart of debate over how to manage water resources cited earlier, this traditional philosophy promoted three responses. First, it endorsed structural solutions, especially dams, levees, dikes, and irrigation systems. While the structural bias of this philosophy was predictable—the objective of regional economic development required expensive public works projects—what was less predictable was this philosophy's underlying hostility to comprehensive planning, its second principal response. Had such planning been adopted, it might have led to a better balancing of environmental and economic needs.

The logic of this resistance was compelling. Initially, water development agencies served not merely as policy coordinators but as evangelical, mission-driven advocates. Coordinated planning by a national or regional entity might have diminished this mission and the ability of these agencies to collaborate with the regional interests who supported it (Wilkinson 1992). The Bureau of Reclamation, for example, charged in 1902 with developing Western water supply projects, was given an ethical—not just a political—mandate to reclaim arid lands in order to guarantee a maximum sustained yield for present and future generations.[2] The hubris of this mandate is now apparent. Aridity was seen as "un-natural," and people living under God's will had a right to employ tools to "re-claim" what nature had removed from the domain of social utility.

William Ellsworth Smythe, the ardent Massachusetts-born champion of irrigation and publisher of the influential journal *The Irrigation Age,* transformed this mandate into a fervent secular religion. Smythe wove together economic development, technology, patriotism, and Jeffersonian idealism toward rural democracy into a philosophy that extolled irrigation as an incomparable instrument for unleashing democratic prosperity and egalitarian reform (Smythe 1900; Bokovoy 1999). Reclaiming the desert would not only produce useful products but would fulfill America's destiny toward "cooperative citizenship" (Bokovoy 1999). As Churchill said of the Israelis—and as Smythe exhorted Westerners—they should "make the desert bloom."[3]

Finally, this philosophy inhibited public participation and thus the development of a democratic ethos. Aided by water laws that promoted individual benefit through private water rights rather than through communal interests, broad-based groups were shut out of supply and allocation policies. Those without direct legal standing (that is, without appropriative water rights) were, in effect, excluded from decision-making. Western water law, especially the doctrine of "first in time, first in right," hastened the exploitation of limited, fragile supplies by those prudent enough to lay claim to them. Thus, there arose an *inverse* relationship between water scarcity and democracy. The higher the stakes in decisions over water use, the greater the tendency to limit participation to those having legal rights to it (Wilkinson 1992: 21–22).[4]

This traditional paradigm suffered from two major ethical problems. First, it failed to acknowledge that in a democracy, policies must be defended according to principles of popular consent. Second, it failed to appreciate that to assure this consent, methods must be provided to counterbalance the ascendancy of private interests. Without such a check, resources are viewed as purely private, economic commodities, and there are no moral incentives to treat them as common property needed by everyone. In essence, this is the normative implication of Garrett Hardin's classic formulation of the "tragedy of the commons"—that without widely agreed-upon methods of public management and prudent stewardship, natural resources will diminish in quality and eventually become depleted (Hardin 1968).

Regarding the first problem, the value of efficiency promoted by utilitarianism is an *instrumental* criterion and is by no means the only basis for defining a rational choice. As Charles Anderson (1979) notes, other principles are also important for assessing a policy's "rightness" or "wrongness" by reference to its conformity with reason. Procedurally, for example, a policy's amenability to setting priorities among conflicting choices and the possibility that a particular decision harbors uncertainty as well as risk are important considerations in deciding whether a decision is a rational one. Economically efficient water policies have often harbored adverse ecological and social risks: by now, this is obvious to us—even if it was not obvious to our predecessors. Thus, for water resources policy, it is now not too much to ask that policy choices embrace fairness, integrity, and an eclectic definition of individual welfare.

Considering the second issue, Caldwell (1947) points out that the federal government first became actively involved in river basin management in part to counter the power and influence of regional development interests. Many of these interests sought to control the management of river basins in order to develop hydropower for industrial developments directly benefiting themselves. The advent of the Missouri River Commission in 1879, for example, foreshadowed efforts to coordinate federal-state water supply planning within a single basin to protect the public interest and promote "multipurpose" development.

In our review of the evolution of U.S. water policy (chapter 2), we noted that one of Theodore Roosevelt's goals in establishing river basin management authorities at the turn of the century was to reduce the influence of private interests. He was partly driven by fear that these interests would exploit the development of water resources for their own gain and became "interested in securing state cooperation and assistance in his program" to manage the nation's rivers comprehensively. This idea, first introduced in the context of the debate over the Muscle Shoals portion of the Tennessee River in the early 1900s, became the centerpiece of the Tennessee Valley Authority's mandate in 1933 as articulated by Franklin Roosevelt. In fact, the idea of a broad public interest in river basin development arose earlier, as we saw, with the advent of the Federal Power Commission. It was explicitly based on the ethical notion that the pursuit of private interest was a barrier to the achievement of a public good.[5]

As to the need for an ethical alternative for water management, other examples abound from other historical periods. In 1958, the Fish and Wildlife Coordination Act explicitly recognized the importance of conservation principles in the development of water resources. While rarely enforced until the 1970s, the act required that the Fish and Wildlife Service "provide that wildlife conservation shall receive *equal consideration,* and be coordinated with, other features of water-resource development programs through the effectual and harmonious planning, development, maintenance, and coordination of wildlife conservation and rehabilitation" (16 USC 661 (1958) & PL 85–624; emphasis added). In short, even during the era when utilitarianism was the dominant philosophy of water management, legislative and programmatic exceptions predicated on balancing utility against other ethical concerns (fair allocation of water, or the protection of fish and wildlife) were introduced.

These alternative policy developments are also significant because they suggest that utilitarianism cannot serve the common good without allowance for how the benefits of natural resources management are allocated. Ralph Ellis lucidly summarizes this position in noting that "no matter how the principle of utility maximization is interpreted, dressed up, or socio-politically contextualized, there is no way to erase the fundamental conflict between the value of maximizing human well being on the one hand [however "well-being" is conceived], and on the other hand, the fairness or justice of the way this human well-being is distributed among the population, either in the form of desirable benefits and situations for people or in the form of opportunities to achieve" them (Ellis 1998: 84). Recognition of this distribution problem led policymakers to develop grand schemes for regional natural resources development such as the TVA. It is also the impulse that gave birth to a number of federal programs and projects to develop western water resources, justifying them not only as compensation for the hardship endured in western migration but as a means of developing resources whose benefits would extend to easterners as well.

How These Issues Play Out in Other Nations

One of the greatest impediments to both comprehensive decision-making for water and public participation in developing nations, as we have seen, is the existence of water "stress" (chapters 1 and 2). While the concept has been defined in various ways by international aid organizations, academics, and others, there is no serious doubt that these countries faced growing urbanization, population growth, pressures on food supplies, and increased freshwater demands—all of which make it difficult to balance supply against demand and to avoid reallocations of water without inflicting pain.

While more difficult to document, there is also anecdotal evidence that stress inhibits public participation in decisions—a precondition for an ethical approach to sustainable water management. The countries with the world's largest mega-cities are generally authoritarian states with weak democratic institutions, low per capita incomes, and high levels of distrust among institutions, groups, and even nations themselves (in the case of river basin compacts). The Plata and Zambezi River basin initiatives, for example, are characterized by top-down decision-making approaches that ignore both the public and many intervener groups.

Antiquated legal systems that encourage profligate water use persist in Mexico and other countries, as we have seen, and cultural perceptions about water-related activities like recreation or residential shoreline development play an important role in shaping conflicts and way they are managed in many of the initiatives we have examined. These differing perceptions are sometimes reflected in the continued existence of, for example, dual management structures based on different sets of values that hamper the comprehensive management of a river basin.

COVENANTS AND WATER RESOURCES MANAGEMENT

The concept of covenants as a means for defining our responsibilities for managing natural resources—and the benefits received in managing them well—began in ancient Israel about 4000 years ago. However, archeologists note that "covenantal" language was also used throughout the ancient Near East even earlier, having been employed by officials in ancient Assyria and Sumeria, for example (see Bright 2000). While often confused with contracts—a legal agreement among parties—covenants are based upon considerable more robust ethical strictures than mere reciprocity. Specifically, covenants are predicated upon three principles.

First, by agreeing to specific laws and responsibilities regarding the management of natural resources, people within a geographical region achieve a "dominion," or right to rule, over nature.[6] It is not enough for an individual to agree to these stipulations; an entire society and culture must submit to this framework. Second, covenants, unlike mere contracts, are deemed permanent, a fact to which we shall return shortly. Likewise, only a few individuals need to break the covenant for many to suffer the consequences of doing so—in effect serving to confirm the collective responsibility of a society for the protection of natural resources.

Third, covenants derive their authority from a deity—God. This places them on a higher moral plateau than mere contracts. Consequently, the dominion granted to mankind for covenantal enforcement explicitly embraces *all* forms of life. In effect, a covenant differs from a contract (the latter being a "tit for tat" reciprocal agreement among equals) in that obedience is predicated not on prudential, human-centered interest but on reverence and respect for a higher and more noble interest—God's desire that those created in his image care for and protect *all* of his creation—not just themselves.

It might seem archaic today to speak of covenants as providing lessons for the ethical management of water resources. In fact, however, covenantal language and concepts implicitly permeate current water resource management methods—as well as those of the past—and covenantal lessons remain relevant to contemporary considerations facing water policy advocates. A good—albeit imperfect (because of its practical shortcomings)—example of the covenantal principle is the concept of a river basin compact and the way this principle has been historically applied. Historian Joe Gelt (1997) has argued, for example, that the 1922 Colorado River Compact was much more than a contractual agreement among seven states. It was the keystone to the "Law of the River" whose advocates wanted to avoid, as much as possible, two things: federal intrusion in managing the region's scarce water and protracted litigation. These advocates agreed to apportion the waters of the river "in perpetuity" between upper and lower basins; the states would work out their percentage allocations later on. That the compact did not embrace environmental issues and Indian rights is, as Gelt notes, a function of the era in which it was consummated, not an inherent defect of compacts. At the time, ethics were less a concern in concluding an agreement than political expedience:

An environmental ethic arises as a force in contemporary life through a somewhat different historical process than, say, water marketing and to some extent Indian water rights. Espousing an environmental ethic involves a shift in thinking, a reorientation of values, away from the human-centered and toward acknowledging an obligation to the natural world. *Development,* however, was the overriding concern of the 1922 compact. Its intent was "to secure the expeditious agricultural and industrial development of the Colorado Basin, the storage of its waters, and the protection of life and property from floods." Establishing Colorado River rights was a prerequisite to building flood control and storage projects, to better manage the river to serve human needs. This boosted states' potential to grow and develop.

The Old Testament contains at least two illustrative examples of how a covenantal relationship functions—including its political consequences—which have a bearing on water resources management. In the Book of Genesis, for example, the story of Noah's Ark obviously had water as a central focus. As punishment for mankind's becoming "corrupt and full of violence," Yahweh brought about the Great Flood to cleanse the Earth of evil. What is often forgotten about this story, however, is that once punishment was meted out, a restored humanity—in particular, those elements deemed "righteous" and capable of exercising moral responsibility—was given the opportunity to submit to a new covenant. This covenant promised abundant prosperity and protection from future calamity in exchange for agreeing to obey God and to care for nature—benefits enumerated quite clearly in Genesis, at the foundation of the Hebrew nation and in Deuteronomy, when Moses read the law to the Israelites.[7]

In short, what is most important about this story for modern water resources management is that the covenant described in Genesis and Deuteronomy embraces *all* forms of life and is based on submission to everyone's mutual interest and to God. Clearly, for the operation of a river basin compact, this entails a broader conception of cooperation than that characterizing most legal agreements, as noted above.

A second example of the benefits of a covenantal relationship comes from the Book of Ezekiel where the prophet Ezekiel shares with the Hebrews living in captivity in Babylon his vision of a restored nation that one day will again find life in Canaan: "Swarms of living creatures will live wherever the river flows. There will be large numbers of fish, because the river flows there. . . . The fish will be of many kinds. . . . Fruit trees of all kinds will grow on both banks. Their leaves will not wither, nor will their fruit fail . . . because the water flows to them" (Ezekiel 47: 8–12). The significance of this story is the implicit recognition that biodiversity and a sustainable environment are characteristic of freely flowing, unfettered waters. Moreover, such an environment is a "gift" in perpetuity for nations who submit to God's authority. In modern times, covenantal approaches to managing natural resources have been characterized by great variability, ranging from Thomas Hobbes's notion of the social contract, which directly influenced the emergence of the liberal state and its emphasis upon protecting individual rights[8] to John Rawls's 1971 book *A Theory of Justice,* which, as I have discussed elsewhere (Feldman 1995), offers a viable basis for a covenantal approach to managing water resources. Rawls would endorse the principle of rational, moral individuals agreeing on the allocation of water and other natural resources by agreeing upon a set of formal principles for their regional management.

While the concept of covenant is not explicitly incorporated into the operation of river basin initiatives elsewhere, something approaching the covenantal principle of reciprocity is found in a number of initiatives. In France, for example, in response to the need for an adequate funding base, river basin agencies—as we have seen—charge user fees to assure adequate financing of project and programmatic needs. Moreover, this fee structure is based on the amount of water withdrawn and polluted.

All the principles for water use justified by covenants are guided by the premises that water is an essential good and that each person's use of it has some impact on the quantity and quality available for the next user. Pareto optimality is employed to assure that no change in use or allocation would be permitted unless the change makes others better off without making anyone worse off. Inequalities can be justified if they result in an increase in efficiency, making everyone better off. For example, a new irrigation or public water supply project could be defensible, even if the costs of building it are borne by everyone in a society (and not just the project's direct users) if it leads to the production of more food and fiber—which, presumably, would benefit all—and if there are no identifiable alternative means of promoting these same ends. Rawls's example provides an interesting benchmark for managing the Colorado River.

Finally, the Rawlsian approach is consistent with the premises of democratic theory because it obligates citizens to reject narrow self-interest in favor of actions that make us better citizens—just like the Hebrew conception of covenant. This view concedes we are all finite, fallible creatures and that, before we can make decisions over water management that promote a tangible, material end, we must first agree on procedures that define the "rightness" of an allocation system—the kind of system that would be just (Rawls 1971).

Before leaving this ethical principle, there is another important issue to weigh: in the New Testament, the foundation of a New Covenant between God and mankind was viewed by early Christian writers, as it was by the Hebrews, as embracing both nature and humanity. A major difference, to be discussed later, is the subtle—but important—movement away from dominion to "stewardship." The Apostle Paul, for example, viewed the freeing of man from the bondage of sin as part of a larger liberation of nature from exploitation and "decay."[9] The new covenant obliges us to care for the resources provided by the Lord lovingly, not dominate or exploit them.

In sum, covenants take no explicit position regarding the rightness of structural or nonstructural approaches to managing water. The correct basis for a decision depends on choosing a strategy that can provide the most "righteous" solution to a given policy problem. In the absence of clear, objective criteria on which every participant can agree, quandaries for democratic decision-making will arise. In addition, covenants implicitly endorse the notion of comprehensive planning insofar as they stress regional management under a single set of laws. Moreover, covenants appear to encourage at least some public participation in decision-making sufficient to allow individuals to become cognizant of their roles and responsibilities in the context of the needs of the larger community and to exercise their authority for the consequences of decisions.

Finally, while covenants focus on the mutuality of civic obligations and provide guidance useful for the structure of frameworks for managing river basin compacts, they have at least three drawbacks. First, evidence of actual historical covenants is difficult to identify. In fact, covenants are more logical than empirical artifacts. They illustrate how political and legal obligations should come about in the absence of authoritative institutions (Rawls 1971). Second, it may be difficult to change or redesign a covenant once it is consummated—even if changing conditions warrant such redesign—since it is rooted in eternal principles.

Modification may be warranted based on new knowledge about the actual distribution and availability of a resource (whether a greater abundance has been discovered, or a shortage discerned) or because of some demographic or social change. This may also be problematic for democratic theory and for watershed protection—as experience shows—insofar as much of what we now know about the behavior of watersheds, including the Colorado basin, has only been learned in the past three to four decades. One criticism of the Rawlsian formulation of the social contract relevant to this discussion is that Rawls himself claims that in attempting to achieve justice, the actual material or resource wealth of a nation is not an important factor in defining the potential for justice (see, for example, Caney 2001: 984, 986). Empirically, however, material wealth can be extremely important in determining whether or not parties to an agreement will be willing to continue working together.

A final problem with covenants is that our obligations to nature remain unclear, as we have seen. Are we to subjugate other forms of life within watersheds for our own ultimate benefit, or are we instructed to protect nature for its own sake? Recent investigations into this problem from a Judeo-Christian perspective suggest that the problem can be resolved if we understand that the dualistic division between humans and nature—a distinction derived from the hierarchical "order of creation" concept, in which humans are viewed as separate from the rest of creation (McFague 1993)—is incorrect. A preferred alternative, it has been argued, is the notion of the "integrity of creation": this means recognizing creation as a holistic unit, where the emphasis should be upon the communal relationship between God and creation (McFague 1993).

CATEGORIAL IMPERATIVES, ENVIRONMENTAL ETHICS, AND WATER RESOURCES MANAGEMENT

Immanuel Kant, the German philosopher identified with the development of the concept of the "categorical imperative," was interested mainly in moral philosophy and ethical relationships among people. Nevertheless, because Kant's ideas were partly a response to the dominant position held by utilitarian views, his ideas have important implications for our discussion of natural resources management. The *categorical imperative,* says Kant, is a "command . . . which present[s] an action as of itself objectively necessary, without regard to any other end. . . . It is [to] act only according to that maxim by which you can at the same time will that it should become a universal law" (Kant 1975: 31, 39). A moral decision should not aggrandize our own happiness, Kant believed, but must be generalizable to all who face a comparable choice within a similar situation. As proof that this core ideal is not radically divergent from a covenantal approach, we should remember that, in practical and rigorous terms, Kant was really asking us to "do unto others as we would have them do to us."[10]

How does this apply to natural resources management, and especially river

basin policy? In effect, while some view the ethical basis for managing resources as maximizing social utility, others view it "deontologically." That is,
what is good or right is determined by the intrinsic properties of an action.
Promises, commitments, and obligations are examples of intrinsic properties,
which should be embraced in public policies because they are usually freely
made.

I have argued elsewhere (Feldman 1995) that the Pick-Sloan Missouri Basin
project is a good example of a river basin program with ethical implications
related to the categorical imperative. In exchange for the taking of arable lands
from Western settlers in order to construct this project, the federal government
made an implicit promise to them that their children would be compensated
through the provision of irrigation water and electricity. Such an exchange was
implicit in government reports defending the economic benefits of the project.
It was more explicitly stated earlier by Congress in promises made to late
nineteenth-century "homesteaders" who were told that, in exchange for the
hazards they were enduring to establish settlements in the arid West, the
federal government would provide water projects.[11] Some aspects of Pick-
Sloan—in particular the Garrison Diversion Project, designed to irrigate the
farms of North Dakotans who were promised compensation for the loss of
lands to Pick-Sloan dams—also did not meet satisfactory benefit-cost criteria
to justify them in purely economic terms (Feldman 1995).

In recent years, it has become common in our society to justify educational,
environmental, and even employment policies (for instance, affirmative action
programs) as forms of "compensation" to certain groups or constituencies for
past injustices. These justifications often conflict with utilitarian defenses
based on the view that policies should primarily maximize social benefits in
some measurable way like efficiency. Such conflict is exemplified in the Colorado basin by periodic demands to increase, say, water supplies to urban areas through diversion of water from farms and ranches or to replenish the
instream flow needs of fisheries or wildlife at the expense of agricultural
interests. Students of prior appropriation law note that the "first in time, first
in right" principle in effect asserts a sort of preemptive principle: historical
commitments should take precedence over other demands. Thus, off-stream
uses that are deemed reasonable and beneficial take priority over instream
needs (Pearson 2000).

Historically, under appropriation law, "instream uses [were] considered inherently wasteful since they require[d] water to remain in place." The result
of this legal interpretation biased the concept of "beneficial" to mean off-

stream, consumptive uses that divert water from a stream "in order to perfect an appropriation" (Butler 1990: 328–329). This conception of beneficial use has undergone change only in the past few decades, with courts more recently deciding in favor of fishing and recreation as beneficial uses. It should be noted that Native American water rights similarly failed to derive advantage from the conception of beneficial use until recently. Although the U.S. Supreme Court acknowledged tribal use as a legitimate "reserve right," tribes lacked the political influence to demand reclamation projects or "actual beneficial use of their waters" (Burton 1991: 23).

Whereas appropriated waters formerly could be used virtually anywhere (with users encouraged to divert), regardless of distance from a stream or aquifer (Laitos and Tomain 1992), legal reform on a state-by-state basis, prompted by concerns with environmental damage, have forced appropriation states to require that minimum flows be maintained in watercourses for protecting public lands, even if doing so impairs senior appropriators' prior rights (Natural Resources Law Center 1997: 7; Landry 2000).

Significantly, this example reveals some of the problems, as well as the promises, of categorical imperatives. In short, what happens if the conditions in place when a freely made commitment or promise was initially made undergo change, as could occur through urbanization, climatic change, or even political revolution? And how does a promise made to one generation inhibit opportunities for future ones? For river basin management, this is far from an academic question. It is a practical issue that frequently arises, as we shall see, and it suggests that categorical imperatives can only work effectively if they are designed in such a way as to embrace the interests and needs of those who are unable to be represented in decision-making: in this case, persons who are not yet born. How and why should their interests be embraced in a categorical imperative approach? Philosophers offer three scenarios.

The first approach we might call the "restricted choice" argument. In effect, this argument contends that all of us, regardless of the generation into which we may be born, have—at birth—free will and the capacity for independent choice. Any environmental decision made by people in any society that precludes or denies this capacity for exercising free will is morally wrong because it denies to present generations the ability to select the benefits they feel are most important, and it denies future generations the opportunity to freely change decisions in ways that best fit their choices (see Beatley 1994).

Environmental examples of restricted choices include clearcutting old growth forests, filling in wetlands, and building a large dam on a river or stream. In effect, such actions place a severe restriction on freedom of choice, for two reasons: (1) they potentially deny a whole range of future benefits without the consent of those affected by such decisions (for example, receiving the flood mitigation benefits of a swamp, experiencing the beauty and tangible environmental benefits of an old-growth forest, and being able to fish for salmon in a free-flowing stream), and (2) they are actions that may be irreversible, or at least not easily reversible. As Holmes Rolston points out, it may be impossible to restore environmental damages once they occur—for example, tearing down a large dam might not automatically restore riparian conditions in a stream.

In effect, the reversibility of an action creates a sort of "ratcheted" obligation. The more reversible the action, the less risk we impose on the future—and thus, the less obliged we are to consider the long-term effects of our decisions. The less reversible an action, however, the greater the risk it poses to future generations. It is inherently wrong to deny to future generations the capacity to exercise a choice that we would have expected past generations to extend to ourselves (Rolston 1988). Perhaps the most severe example of this dilemma is the disposal of high-level radioactive waste. This is an issue that is certainly a concern to residents of the Colorado plateau region because of its implications both for water quality and for human and ecological health and welfare.

In ancient Rome, the head of the City of Rome's water supply system, appointed by emperor Nerva in 97 A.D., expressed concern for intergenerational justice and water management. Sextus Julius Frontinus wrote, "It is plain . . . how much more our forefathers cared for the general good rather than for private luxury, inasmuch as even the water which private parties conducted was made to serve the public interest." Sextus applauded the efforts of Rome's ancient leaders, who, he said, insulated the city from the effects of drought, improved the health of its residents, and enhanced the city's environment by building and maintaining an efficient water supply system and the policies to maintain it—all for the benefit of generations yet unborn as a result of an implicit promise to citizens past, present, and future.[12]

There is a second approach to the categorical imperative problem relevant to the welfare of future generations. We might term this approach the "labor value" argument. While similar to the first approach, it differs in emphasizing the manner in which environmental value is initially determined. Following the arguments of classical liberals such as John Locke, this approach contends that the value of land, water, and other natural resources is determined by the amount of effort we infuse into their development and management. When we fail to leave the land and water resources of our world in a condition where

they can at least be at the same level of productive benefit for future generations as for ourselves, we not only deny them the direct benefits of the resources, but we leave them less "well off" in other, indirect ways, like a reduced yield of farmland; a reduced yield of fish in a lake, stream or river; and
even a lower tax base and foundation for economic development (Kavka 1978).

In essence, if we define "sustainable development" as the management of
renewable resources in such a way as to support the economic and environmental needs of future as well as present generations, then the implications of
this argument include the need for each generation to make certain assumptions about the "needs" of subsequent generations—including how much food
they would require as well as how much land and water, and in what kind of
condition, is required to sustain them (Beatley 1994).

Clearly, while categorical imperatives have the advantage of articulating intrinsic principles to guide behavior, they also impose on us the further obligation to amend or modify how these principles are applied as science and
other sources of knowledge modify our understanding of the environment.
Four sources of modification are changes in river operation, climate change,
population growth, and the rights of native peoples.

An example depicting the first source was agreement to modify the operation of the Glen Canyon Dam so as not only to meet the "promises and commitments" made to farmers, ranchers, and power consumers through the Colorado River Compact but also to ensure that other intrinsic principles are
embraced—in particular, the needs of future generations (see chapter 2). When
Congress passed the Grand Canyon Protection Act of 1992, a law that redi-
rected the Bureau of Reclamation's instream flow policies on the Colorado
River, the intent was—in the light of new knowledge and understanding of the
river—to modify the flow regime of the river's impoundments in such a way
as to help rebuild beaches and restore habitat (Moody 1997).

A bigger challenge in using categorical imperatives for managing water is
afforded by the case of climate change. As we saw in chapter 1, this is a more
contentious scientific issue than merely modifying river operations or impoundments—and it plays out in unique ways in the Colorado basin. The balance of evidence suggests not only that climate change has occurred but also
that previous changes in the region have dramatically altered the flow of the
Colorado River and, thus, the amount of water available for off-stream use
(Merideth 2001). This exacerbates the uncertainty of adhering to a categorical
imperative for two reasons. First, when the Colorado River compact was consummated in the early 1920s, allocation of flow to the upper and lower basins

was based on an assumed annual flow that we now realize was atypical of the mean annual flow of the river—precipitation and flow were higher during the period in which flows were measured just prior to the allocation agreement.

The problem is that the categorical imperative of "promising" to accept one's allocation is based on a faulty premise—states are committed to using more water than is actually generally available, as we now know. The second problem is that changes in the economy of the region exacerbate the difficulty in providing a prearranged allocation of water given the likelihood of diminished future supplies due to climate change (Merideth 2001: 13).

This raises a final point—perhaps the biggest reason a categorical imperative has been difficult to implement in the Colorado River Compact is California's rapid population growth this past century. By the early 1920s, southern California was one of the prime movers and shakers insisting on larger allocations from the Colorado River for its particular needs, even at the expense of other states. This insistence is one of many reasons Arizona resisted ratifying the Colorado River Compact for many years. In effect, Arizona declared that California was a "water hustler" and could not be trusted to obey any agreement allocating the river.[13]

For their part, tribal nations in the Colorado basin are increasingly asserting "both their economic independence and political sovereignty" (Merideth 2001: 13). This is important for a categorical imperative approach to water management because promises for water made to these nations are of course quite old and are written in treaties ratified decades ago. Moreover, the traditional beneficial use doctrine of the law of prior appropriation (e.g., Burton 1991: 23) does acknowledge the rights of tribal nations to "reserve" a portion of instream flow for their benefit and grants special rights to "senior appropriators" such as tribes that can claim longtime access to water.[14] The problem is not the durability of the promise—it is, instead, the conscious decision by courts and other policymaking bodies to enforce it today. This political character of promises and commitments is endemic to all ethical approaches to water resources management.

As we saw in chapter 3, one challenge facing CALFED has been finding ways to protect endangered and threatened species while at the same time accommodating the needs and desires of farmers and others who have depended on water deliveries to produce food for several generations. Recent proposals to amend the Colorado River compact by requiring California to cut back its use of water from the basin have precipitated severe conflicts between the previous commitments and contemporary needs.

Summing up the relevance of categorical imperatives to water resources management, the debate over the virtues of structural vs. nonstructural measures depends on the extent to which one measure or the other best achieves the fulfillment of past promises or commitments to some group. In general, when categorical imperatives have been used as ethical criteria in water policy debates (as in the case of the Pick-Sloan Missouri basin project), the result has generally been to promote civil works projects designed to ensure that the promised benefits are delivered. Generally, too, comprehensive planning is viewed as a vehicle to ensure the fulfillment of intrinsically desirable obligations. Such planning provides a means to ensure that commitments remain enforceable across generations. Finally, categorical imperatives imply the need for a high level of active participation by protagonists—otherwise there is no way to guarantee that promises and commitments are freely made and *explicitly* articulated.

While categorical imperatives generally encourage water management approaches to be modified in the face of new knowledge about the environmental and societal effects of water projects—irreversible effects in particular—they do have one major potential drawback. In short, it is unclear how adequately these imperatives embrace nonrenewable or endangered resources. Indeed, it is not clear how categorical imperatives could be used to protect future generations from harm since a nonrenewable resource and its use, presumably, do not really affect the availability of that energy resource for future generations (although decisions by previous generations about how to develop or exploit it could affect their well-being). By definition, since the resource is not renewable, it would not be available in any event. Such challenges make categorical imperatives problematic when trying to determine whether, and when, to decide that a promise or commitment outweighs more traditional utilitarian arguments in public policy discourse—that is, do the benefits of a water project exceed its economic or environmental costs? This issue is particularly problematic for a democratic society in which public policies must, in part, be defended on practical grounds of policy feasibility.

ENVIRONMENTAL STEWARDSHIP AND ENVIRONMENTAL ETHICS: RULING LIKE A SERVANT

Perhaps the simplest definition of stewardship is the aphorism "We have not inherited the environment from our grandparents, we are only borrowing it from our grandchildren." Not unlike the two previous approaches, stew-

ardship ethics are based on the premise that we are obliged to care for creation and to concern ourselves with what anyone—regardless of generation—
must do in order to ensure that creation is sustained. This obligation, ultimately, is rooted in a "humble anthropocentrism," which, instead of putting
man at the center of the world, asserts that all species have inherent value and
that all individuals have moral standing. Because humans are made in God's
image, humankind is both within and above the broader ecosystem. Thus, to
rule nature is to *serve* it. As Grizzle and Barrett (1996) make the case, humans
must act humbly: "Only such holistic environmental perspectives, where societal needs are more directly coupled with environmental protection, are capable of successfully addressing the complex issues we face today" (Grizzle
and Barrett 1996).

While the exact meaning of stewardship is subject to wide debate, at its center is the notion that humans, as servants of God, have been given responsibility to care for the natural environment—that is, creation. Not only is nature
special and unique, but life is also sacred (Fowler 1995). In the Judeo-
Christian tradition, stewardship has become linked to the role of sin—which
is operationally defined as the foundation of failed stewardship or the failure
to treat creation as a holistic unit by violating its integrity. The practical man-
ifestation of this is the relationship between rampant environmental degradation and spiritual decline in the contemporary world (Fowler 1995). Other
philosophers like Calvin DeWitt suggest that this spiritual decline is manifested even in our partial and incomplete understanding of rulership. For example, traditional interpretations of Genesis 1:28 ("Be fruitful and multiply,
and fill the earth and subdue it; and have dominion . . . over every living
thing") have been used to justify the exploitation of land and water resources.
To DeWitt, true stewardship requires us to "till and keep" the earth, just as God
"keeps" humans. "To keep" in this context means "keep with full integrity and
wholeness"—thus protecting the soil, air, and plant and animal communities
as part of the "whole of dynamic stewardship" (DeWitt 2002).[15]

Stewardship ethics owe their greatest debt to two separate traditions—the
Judeo-Christian tradition, which, we have noted, is "set in distinct . . . perspectives, justified by the Bible and Christian theology, intertwined with images of Christ and creation, of the . . . Reformation, and of God's calling to
stewardship, images that reflect the Protestant worldview" (Fowler 1995: 158).
The second tradition consists of pragmatically derived ecological views that
emerged in the late nineteenth and early twentieth centuries—most notably
through the writings of Gifford Pinchot, the first director of the U.S. Forest Ser-

vice; J. Wesley Powell, the first director of what became the U.S. Geological Survey; and, later, the naturalist and forester Aldo Leopold.[16]

All of these advocates of the "progressive conservationist" tradition saw humanity's obligation to care for nature as rooted in a combination of the unique stature held by people as creatures of reason who hold a unique capacity to serve as a caretaker and guardian of natural resources. Leopold (1949) would add another stricture—in caring for natural resources, we care for our own welfare and are cognizant of nature's limits. As he stated, "A thing is right when it tends to preserve the integrity, stability, and beauty of the biosphere" (Leopold 1949).

Before discussing an example of a stewardship approach to river basin management, we need to consider two issues. First, as previously noted, stewardship approaches do not obviate or supplant the other two approaches we have discussed. One should—perhaps must—adopt a type of covenantal understanding of one's obligations to nature in order to practice stewardship. Likewise, there is an intrinsic value—a categorical imperative, as it were—in the stewardship principle to "care for creation" unselfishly, as a servant-ruler. So, is there an example that manifests the peculiar essence of stewardship: the need to balance creation and human interests? One example might be the Northwest Power Planning Council (NPPC), established in 1980 by the Pacific Northwest Electric Power Planning and Conservation Act (16 U.S.C. § 839b(h)). This council's purpose is to elevate the concept of river basin management to a higher level—to cement a new set of relations among water users in the Pacific Northwest in an effort to restore salmon spawning runs on the Columbia and Snake Rivers. What makes the Planning and Conservation Act unique in this regard is that it makes the *salmon* a "coequal partner" with hydroelectric power in the operation of the Columbia Basin's more than 150 dams (Blumm 1998).

The NPPC itself, as we have seen, is a multi-state, multi-agency partnership comprised of the Bonneville Power Authority (BPA), the Pacific Northwest Electric Power and Conservation Council, and governor-appointed representatives from Washington, Oregon, Idaho, and Montana. The NPPC has encouraged cooperation among utility systems, energy conservation and efficient power use, greater involvement of state and local governments in regional planning, and oversight of electric power system planning and regional fish and wildlife recovery. It is developing a long-range plan to ensure low-cost power for the region while protecting and rebuilding fishery and wildlife populations depleted by hydropower development.

As we have also seen, the NPPC's record of achievement is mixed at best. It has succeeded in establishing a regional water budget designed to protect fisheries and provide for other services and has set aside thousands of river miles of prime fish and wildlife habitat from new hydropower development. It has also failed to prevent several species of Snake River salmon from being listed as endangered and salmon runs from declining by over two-thirds annually. At least one federal court, the Ninth Circuit Court of Appeals, rejected its initial "Salmon Strategy," criticizing the council's "sacrificing the Act's fish and wildlife goals" (Getches 1998c: 190).

Despite its mixed record, however, the NPPC has forced environmental issues onto the agenda of water and power agencies in the Pacific Northwest. As one observer has stated, ecological imperatives, aesthetics, and demands for equity "have given rise to a greater consciousness of the ethical implications of water use." Moreover, unlike previous federal efforts, the NPPC has encouraged extensive public involvement and planning for long-term threats by incorporating local community and tribal concerns (Volkman 1996).

Clearly, as we have seen, the NPPC is a major departure from previous federal water supply planning efforts in the United States and has much to teach us about stewardship as a practical strategy. The NPPC illustrates the practical ambiguities in stewardship approaches to river basin management—as well as the ethical convictions required to do so effectively. While these approaches suggest that care for the environment is a moral imperative, they also imply "intense, interactive love relationships" between humans and creation (Fowler 1995: 82). In practice, the NPPC has had greater success in "raising consciousness" than in generating results—a moral imperative.

Finally, stewardship—by rejecting the dominionism characteristic of earlier approaches to environmental ethics, including early covenantal approaches—forces us to eradicate the dualistic "split" between humans and nature, a distinction originally derived from the hierarchical "order of creation" concept in which humans are viewed as separate from the rest of creation (see, for example, McFague 1993). The preferred alternative to dualism is "integrity of creation." Stated simply, this means recognizing that creation as a holistic unit, where the emphasis is on the communal relationship between God and creation, a concept derived from ecological principles of complex ecosystems and the interrelatedness of their parts. Each part has a function, and the whole system is changed when any part of is changed.

Are Alternative Approaches Implementable?
The Social Learning Paradigm

In chapter 1, we asserted that to be effective, any alternative approach for managing water resources based on the principle of sustainable development must be implemented in ways that embrace the needs of watersheds *and* the demands of democratic theory. This is a difficult policy challenge to meet because ethical theories are not ordinarily developed with the specific purpose of being disseminated in the form of, say, laws or public policies. Another reason it is difficult is that none of the approaches we discussed provides clear responses to the three water policy debates we outlined at the beginning of this paper. Table 1 depicts each of these three ethical theories and how they would address the three issues we discussed earlier as well as their distinct advantages and disadvantages in terms, largely, of two issues: conformity with democratic theory and the ability to address the needs of watersheds.

Regardless of which approach is adopted—and for reasons about to be made clear, a combination of approaches is probably required—effective implementation that embraces both the needs of democracies and of watersheds requires that we be prepared to adhere to a novel approach to public policy different from that traditionally employed in natural resources management. Some social scientists call this approach a *social learning* paradigm, implying that, through trial and error, policymakers are afforded an opportunity to adapt public policies to new conditions and compelling evidence. Others prefer the label *adaptive management*—a moniker that better implies the needs of policies to "adapt" themselves to changing ecological and other contexts by "managing according to a plan by which decisions are made and modified as a function of what is known and learned about the system" (Ingram 2001).

I contend that both labels are acceptable, but while the former term refers to the *process* by which we generate adaptable decisions, the latter refers to the *outcome* we hope to bring about by employing the process. Moreover, both labels imply decision-making that is not merely flexible and adaptable but implicitly moral, by acknowledging that we humans are neither omniscient nor omnipotent but must bow to our ignorance and humbly acknowledge our capacity for error and need for correction.

The social learning/adaptive management paradigm requires that we adopt an approach to water resources decision-making that permits us to realize previous mistakes made in the management of resources, to monitor and measure

TABLE 5.1

Ethical Frameworks Adopted to River Basin Management: Comparing Criteria

Ethical approach	How do they address traditional controversies?	Advantages	Disadvantages
Covenant	1) Neutral regarding structural/nonstructural approaches—decide on basis of what is most "righteous" solution; 2) Favors comprehensive planning; 3) Encourages public awareness and participation in decision-making and public process of responsibility.	1) Focuses on mutuality of obligations; 2) Offers guidance for specific structure of political frameworks such as river basin compacts.	1) Evidence of actual historical covenants are difficult to identify—they are more of a logical than an empirical artifact; 2) May be difficult to change a covenant once it is consummated—thus may be problematic for democracy; 3) Historically, obligations to nature are unclear—is it subjugation of nature or protection of resources?
Categorical imperative	1) Structural/nonstructural debate boils down to impact on fulfilling promises, commitments, and other intrinsic moral properties; 2) Comprehensive planning important to ensure fulfillment of obligations—and to ensure that they can be enforced across generations; 3) Participation required to ensure that promises/obligations are freely and explicitly made.	1) Permits management approach to be modified in face of new knowledge and information; 2) Provides early warning of problems that inhibit fair/honest/judicious decisions (for example, irreversible impacts)	1) Does not adequately embrace nonrenewable nor endangered resources—problematic for watersheds; 2) Does not provide a clear means of determining whether or when an intrinsic promise or other commitment outweighs the merits of a teleological argument (for example, a more traditional "benefits" vs. "costs" approach)—for this reason problematic for democracy.
Stewardship	1) Weight of evidence supports nonstructural approaches to minimize adverse impacts and to be faithful to protection of creation; 2) Planning should be done in an organized, comprehensive way to protect creation; 3) Public participation must include broad range of issues/concerns including nature—not just people.	1) Tries to balance human and ecological needs—rejects the notion of human "dominion" over nature; 2) Does not supplant or replace other approaches—is really a supplement to them.	1) Reasons for caring for nature somewhat ambiguous—is it a "moral imperative" enforceable by public policy or an act of unselfish love that requires a change of attitude? 2) Requires a deep sense of humility toward nature.

change empirically, to adopt midcourse corrections to any policy chosen to manage water problems (implying that all decisions should be tentative and reversible—recall our discussion of categorical imperatives and future generations), and to allow us to apply what we have learned about effective management to larger, more complex challenges and geospatial contexts. Such a paradigm also conforms to the aspiration for sustainable development, especially the notion that reconciling the natural distribution of water with environmental needs *and* society's demands requires an understanding of the carrying capacity of one's local environment, a dedication to advancing policies that forge links between quality-of-life concerns *and* concerns for economic growth, and a commitment by decision-makers to seek participation, fairness, and environmental protection (Ascher 1999a).

So, how can this be achieved? And, what—if anything—does it say about the advantages of one ethical approach over others? Let us begin with learning from prior mistakes. As Ingram reminds us, the difficulty in managing many natural resource problems is that they are "poorly structured for the application of straightforward, disciplinary-based rational science" (Ingram 2001: 1). This is because many of these problems are difficult to define, may have unclear and even incompatible goals (like protecting endangered species while maximizing water supply for human use). While better science can be instructive about how to define and resolve such problems, reaching a political consensus over management goals and objectives themselves requires agreement on the *values* that stakeholders wish to pursue.

Learning from previous mistakes in water policy requires that we be willing to evaluate previous decisions in the light of our failure to define what we want and our failure to agree on basic goals. If we could do this, we could then actually learn from our errors and avoid them in the future. In too many instances, failures in water policy under the utilitarian paradigm occurred because policymakers sought to please every constituency without facing the incompatibility of policy goals or the narrow basis on which they were often predicated.

Learning from mistakes thus requires the adoption of a process of decision-making that permits the airing of the widest possible set of values and preferences, the acceptance of ground rules for what will be accepted as credible evidence to support these values, a willingness to make decisions tentatively (with allowance for their reversal if they are found faulty), modification (if changing conditions warrant doing so), and avoidance, under any circumstances, of severe impacts. Again, the case of the NPPC affords an excellent example—one amenable to application on the Colorado River as well. In 1994, after the Ninth Circuit Court of Appeals rejected the NPPC's initial "Salmon Strategy" by criticizing the council's "sacrificing the Act's fish and wildlife goals" (Getches 1998c: 190), the NPPC promulgated a new plan to provide for endangered salmon recovery as well as to ensure protection of other fish species. While it is arguable whether such adaptation measures could have been selected under several ethical approaches, it would seem to conform most closely to the sort of "humble anthropocentric" view of stewardship we previously mentioned in that it grants some moral standing to nature as well as to humans.

Monitoring and Measuring Change

Over and above good ethical conduct, effective water policy needs good information and data. But what, exactly, makes data "good"? For one thing, it is collected and analyzed dispassionately and without regard to "political" ends. It also avoids a predisposition for the selective promotion of certain claims that serve to advance the cause of one group at the expense of another—a practice that has taken over U.S. environmental policy (see, for example, Kantrowitz 1993). This "advocacy science," which has become a common feature of environmental decision-making generally and water policy in particular, inhibits adaptive management (Ingram 2001). How can change be measured and monitored in an ethical manner? The categorical imperative approach provides one avenue: in essence, adopting no policy outcome for water management that one would not accept if another party adopted it due to fear of the consequences upon oneself.

As Ingram notes, however, politically weak parties are often disadvantaged in the "game" of scientific research for solving environmental problems because they cannot take advantage of good research, have political difficulty confronting detractors, and find it difficult to resist the pressure to make rapid decisions rather than the sort of scientific experimentation required for ensuring more environmentally hospitable policies (Ingram 2001). Would powerful parties be willing to submit themselves to the same conditions for policies they favor? Again, the NPPC provides a good case study of how this problem has been managed. The NPPC has developed a regional "water budget" designed both to protect fisheries and provide for other services (over 4 million acre-feet for salmon, seasonally allocated on the Columbia and Snake Rivers), and to set aside 44,000 river miles of prime fish and wildlife habitat from new hydropower development. While this budget has not yet prevented several species of Snake River salmon from being threatened and reduced in numbers, it has promoted a process of decision-making that prevents alternations of the river system that would compromise this water budget—perhaps it will also lead to a restoration of salmon. Only time will tell.[17]

Making Midcourse Corrections

A good example of midcourse correction is the emerging consensus in water resources management (for example, Hartig et al. 1992; Landre and Knuth 1993; Cortner and Moote 1994), especially among natural, engineering, and social scientists, that the best approach to water management is one that permits stakeholders to evaluate structural as well as nonstructural alternatives systematically and make rational and fair policy choices. Such an aspiration is found in the executive summary of the Western Water Policy Review Advisory Commission's final report—a report that has not been as well received in the west as was initially hoped. Congress charged the commission with formulating recommendations on the federal government's role in managing the region's water. Its charge fits well with the prospect of making midcourse corrections to a faulty policy. As the preamble to the report states:

> Part of the impetus for our . . . formation was the Congress's finding that current federal water policy suffers from unclear and conflicting goals implemented by a maze of agencies and programs. . . . Lack of policy clarity and coordination resulting in gridlock . . . we have concluded . . . cannot be resolved piecemeal but, rather, must be addressed by fundamental changes in institutional structure and government process. . . . [the] geographic, hydrologic, ecologic, social and economic diversity of the West will require regionally and locally tailored solutions. (Western Water Policy Review Advisory Commission 1998: xiii)

Adapting to Larger and More Complex Contexts

Since the 1980s, a new paradigm for river basin management water management has evolved based on three values: (1) stakeholder participation in formulating and implementing policy alternatives; (2) environmentally sound, socially just water resources management; and (3) a comprehensive approach to planning that recognizes the centrality of drainage basins (Hartig et al. 1992; Landre and Knuth 1993; Cortner and Moote 1994). These values have the virtue, say their advocates, of promoting a decentralized management system accountable to *varied* interests. They are also amenable to "regionally and locally tailored solutions" to water problems and thus more democratic as well as protective of the environment (Western Water Policy Review Advisory Commission 1998). Finally, this new paradigm is practical, advocates claim, in light of eroding federal interest in water management, exemplified by Congress's 1997 zeroing out of funding for river basin commissions (McGinnis 1995; Miller, Rhodes, and MacDonnell 1996; Cody 1999a, b; Marino and Kemper 1999).

While these claims regarding the desirability of "integrated" management schemes based on watersheds make intuitive sense, political scientists and others who study water resources decisions recognize that they face a difficult challenge in implementing them, specifically in reconciling the roles of science and public values in decision-making. In practice, it is difficult to square the view that better watershed decisions result when policies and programs are mostly driven by science, with the view that decisions are more efficacious when they are influenced by public and stakeholder input. While these views need not necessarily be at odds with one another, reconciling them is by no means obvious. There seems to be an emerging consensus that reconciliation must begin from the premise that one goal of scientists—a comprehensive assessment of problems—can only be achieved through the help of an astute public that identifies the salient problems within a watershed that they want assessed (Landre and Knuth 1993; Cortner and Moote 1994; Western Water Policy Review Advisory Commission 1998).

Consensus, however, does not avoid the larger question of priority setting: Is it possible to adopt a framework that can help to order various aspirations in such a way as to rank some as more important than others? Or, short of this, is there a way to make a list of priorities? This is the subject of our conclusions.

MAKING SUSTAINABILITY WORK IN AN ETHICAL FRAME

In water resources policy, as we have shown, sustainability refers to a region's ability to provide enough clean water to maintain essential economic activities while protecting its natural environment and the human activities that depend upon that environment. A sustainable water management system is one that ensures a reasonable level of development (defined as a level that does not exceed a region's carrying capacity), protects and maintains ecological values (such as sufficient instream flow to protect flora and fauna, critical to preserving habitat and species), and ensures equity, defined as a fair apportionment of water and related resources to satisfy stakeholder needs. In short, a framework for sustainability is one that is flexible, amendable, participatory, and fair—not just efficient (Stoerker 1994).

Critics rightly contend that sustainability is a highly idealized objective that is difficult to define and frequently "bereft of meaning" (Sneddon et al. 2002: 669). Nevertheless, there are two reasons that a regional framework for resolving water resource conflicts might profit by employing the concept of sustainability as a guiding principle. First, the various criteria for sustainability cited above provide a framework for setting priorities among values that promote a multitude of uses of water, from uses that conserve the rewouce in order to protect the environment to uses that exploit water to promote economic benefits for people. In essence, they constitute a kind of crucible or test for determining if a decision regarding the management of water is likely to resolve conflicts by embracing solutions to several problems simultaneously or merely to exacerbate them by promoting one objective at the expense of others. Many policy makers have begun to draw attention to the need for priority setting due to growing competition over resources (Ostrom 1990; President's Council on Sustainable Development 1996).

Second, these criteria are benchmarks that may help identify deficiencies in current decision-making frameworks. In essence, they can be used to gauge whether a proposed decision is likely to benefit an entire region or only a part of it, to enhance or impede the ability to form partnerships for resolving water problems, or to produce durable decisions acceptable to stakeholders. If we agree that this is a desirable goal, then an effective ethical approach should:

- *Aim for inclusiveness and ethical "eclecticism."* No ethical approach to the management of water resources should be adopted that categorically rejects any constituency or alternative approach to management out of hand. This means that any approach should emphasize process as much as outcome—providing a means for the widest possible debate and deliberation over the broadest range of viable alternatives possible. Moreover, there is a consensus among scholars who have tried to apply ethical principles to the analysis of public policy that, regardless of the ethical approach one adopts, there are some general principles that should be adhered to as normative policy objectives. At a minimum, it is reasonable to demand of government that water and other public policies be *efficient* (use natural resources in a beneficial, unwasteful fashion), *equitable* (accessible to all who need them and fair with regard to its burdens and benefits), *sustainable* (aware of the interests of future generations), and *transparent* (simple and clear policy).

As a practical matter, we must consider a potential impediment to this solution—can ethical eclecticism be reconciled with the need to set priorities among differing goals? The simple answer would seem to be no—the best we can hope to achieve is a just process. This is too simple a solution, however. Social constructionist literature suggests another path. Natural phenomena such as water have different meanings to different groups. These meanings depend on culturally conditioned perspectives that are shaped by social status, a group's goals and aspirations, a society's history, and individual needs (Blatter and Ingram 2001).

We may not be able to reconcile these divergent perspectives, but we can at least aim to make different meanings transparent so that parties to a water dispute understand the basis for their disagreement. We can even negotiate the resolution of particular conflicts over water use through mediation of these conflicting perspectives and contemplate legal reform to permit the equitable representation of these perspectives (see the final bullet point for more about this). Finally, we can show how non-instrumental uses of water are viewed as legitimate and important to some groups (Blatter and Ingram 2001)—a fact illustrated by the number and type of water disputes in regions such as the Colorado basin, where conflicts over Native American religious traditions, western settler values, capitalistic interests driven by profit, and governmental bureaucracy animated by linear, instrumental forms of thinking about water problems have historically led to irreconcilable conflicts, which ultimately lead to a failure to gain lasting policy solutions that would benefit everyone, not just a few.

- *Be committed to democratic decision-making.* Diverse, even divergent ethical approaches to the environment can, if filtered through the appropriate political frameworks, serve as complementary and not mutually exclusive prisms for viewing nature, the world, and our obligations to both. To make this ethical pluralism possible—and to derive the benefits from the exchange of views that these different approaches provide—we must demand that decision-making institutions respond to deliberative processes of discussion and reflection and justify the policies they choose—and to be willing to justify these policies by reference to the broader needs of a society, not a single region. The public must be assured that water resource decisions are not—as they have too often been in the past—pre-decided (see Ankrah 1998). Moreover, ethical inclusiveness implies accepting responsibility for unanticipated effects by endorsing consultative mechanisms. Related to this is the need to acknowledge that scientific reasoning is often probabilistic in nature—this is significant because it means that people who are "motivated to deceive either themselves or others about an issue may use forms of reasoning . . . that contain hidden fallacies" (Ellis 1998: 179).

We can approximate a setting of priorities if we acknowledge these reasoning fallacies and, thus, the need for scientifically supported policy propositions based on the best available evidence. What would constitute such evidence? At a minimum, propositions would be predictive and statistically significant, contain well-defined terms based on observable information, and eliminate plausible alternative explanations for a water-resource problem (Ellis 1998: 179–180).

We saw in chapter 2 how the MDBC has created a partnership between Australian state governments and local communities through Community Advisory Councils (CACs) that represent the wider community. CACs work with farmers to improve adoption of so-called Best Management Practices (BMPs) to prevent pollution, nutrient runoff, and salinity problems. Securing and protecting the rights of indigenous peoples is also important. The chairs of CACs attend meetings of both the ministerial council and the Murray-Darling Basin Commission.

- *Make ethical assumptions clear and transparent.* No ethical approach will please everyone, or achieve universal acclaim. However, to the extent that we articulate our ethical claims publicly, in full view of others, and not in some secluded bureaucratic environment that breeds interpersonal and governmental distrust (see Warren 1999) and honestly try to get others to understand our assumptions—and try to understand theirs—then we stand a better chance of ensuring that whatever perspectives we adopt conform to a broader notion of justice (Rawls 1971). Such an approach is modest, cautious, and careful. It would advocate no major change in the status quo designed to make any group or region better off at the expense of making another region or group worse off.

- *Collaborate with those with whom you disagree.* While counterintuitive, pioneering works in collaborative resource management argue for the need for collaborative learning. The idea behind this is that genuine collaboration that puts aside self-interest and partiality requires the development of a collaborative stakeholder process that lets independent, role-bound "adults" engage in a safe, secure, nonthreatening, and open process of cooperation based upon mutual respect, integrity, and teamwork in the development of solutions to the management of resource problems (Program for Community Problem Solving 1996; Daniels and Walker 2001).

These are all difficult and dogged challenges for water policy, but they are hardly impossible challenges to meet. In the United States, federal water policies began as attempts to promote support for regional power, reclamation, or flood control projects or to thwart the influence of private interests who wanted to develop such projects. For most of their history, these efforts limited public involvement to a "consultative" role, failed to provide adequate interagency coordination, and sometimes fell short of being truly comprehensive. We now know from empirical research that effective planning requires the ability to overcome agency "turf wars" by pursuing objectives defined by regional stakeholders, to supplant authority vested in several agencies to manage comprehensively several policy needs simultaneously, and to encourage collaboration among stakeholders affected by water problems. Effective planning efforts are perceived as economical and efficient, so they are able to generate public support for projects and programs (ASCE 1984). Collaboration overcomes resistance to change, facilitates new opportunities for funding, and stimulates resilient policy ideas (Chrislip and Larson 1994).

There are still several unanswered questions this discussion raises—above all, how do we reconcile an ethically credible frame for policymaking with practical political constraints? In chapter 6, we argue that this reconciliation requires a sound base of knowledge to promote adaptive management and a willingness to confront several critical challenges that, until a few years ago, hardly anyone even worried about—such as climate change. There are also instances where some reforms should take place on a trans-spatial level across institutions that make policy (agencies, NGOs, and the like). We will also consider how to implement a social learning or adaptive management framework given what we have learned in our case studies. Finally, we will examine the potential effects of various problems on water management—including climate change, growing competition, and population growth.

As we begin a new millennium, we are faced with the challenge of determining what the state's role in water policy development and implementation should be—what should be left to markets to decide and what should be determined through command and control regulations? An essential avenue to answering these questions is ensuring that environmental ethics are better incorporated in policymaking. While the challenges are great, the benefits are greater still.

CHAPTER 6

Water Resources Management as an Adaptive Process

Indigenous knowledge can be a useful tool for environmental sustainability in rural areas. The state of Karnataka (India) is implementing the first stage of an ambitious program to rehabilitate, jointly with communities, traditional water harvesting structures, some of them centuries old.

—*World Bank*

There is a huge body of information and knowledge on water, but language problems, limited access to Information and Communication Technologies (ICT) facilities and limited finances deny many people, especially in lower income countries, access to such information . . . there is a marked lack of indigenous knowledge and expertise relevant to local problems. . . .

—*United Nations World Water Assessment Programme*

The purpose of this chapter is twofold. First, we want to draw together the key components of an adaptive management framework for water resources policy in a useful summary that focuses on the four policy needs advanced in the book's introduction. These are: encouraging social learning, drawing upon local or indigenous knowledge of water problems and independently validated scientific information, conforming the structure of a decisional framework to principles of place-based decision-making, and effectively resolving conflicts over water use. We will summarize lessons from the foregoing analysis that suggest how these objectives can be achieved—as well as what possible impediments we can expect to face in trying to achieve them. The one factor of the four that we have not yet discussed in detail is local or indigenous knowledge—even though many scholars believe that drawing upon such knowledge where it exists and cultivating it where it is not adequately developed are essential for successful place-based environmental decision-making (Goldstein 1999; Fischer 2000).

Second, we will discuss remaining critical challenges facing water resources management—ones that will continue to constitute barriers to sustainable development for some time to come. These include the potential effects of global climate change on water resources, and the growing competition over water as a result of population growth. One constructive tool is the prospect of using water more efficiently and carefully through education and the fostering of behavioral change.

COMPONENTS OF ADAPTIVE MANAGEMENT: KNOWLEDGE, INFORMATION, EDUCATION, AND WISE USE

Throughout this book, we have discussed the importance of a sound knowledge base for ensuring sustainable water resource management. We have chronicled impediments to achieving this knowledge base due to ideological, economic, political, and other conditions prevailing at various times and places. As we have seen, a deficient knowledge base for sustainable development has often characterized river basin planning, and other water resource decisions falter because of cultural or other barriers, the failure to monitor environmental change, or the lack of institutional capacity to measure and assess water demands and their effects.

In the United States, the historically dominant water resources management philosophy of promoting regional economic growth through river basin development tended to favor certain types of knowledge (engineering and economics) and paid far less attention to the environmental effects of that development and thus to other appropriate knowledge sources that were more responsive to societal and resource management needs (ecology, sociology, planning). As it became apparent that many water problems—including pollution, species extinction, and water supply reallocation—were not being optimally addressed through these techniques, it began to occur to decision-makers that new institutional arrangements—and new sources of knowledge— were required to manage water wisely (chapters 2 and 3). These arrangements ranged from interstate compacts (the Colorado River, Delaware River) and government corporations (Tennessee Valley Authority) to novel federal-state partnerships (CALFED, the NPPC).

Collective Choice and Water Knowledge:
History, Culture, Attitudes

The first real acknowledgement in the United States that social attitudes and, by implication, different sets of knowledge about water needed to be better adapted to environmental conditions arose under John Wesley Powell. Powell's Colorado River exploration missions, coupled with his later policy writings as director of the forerunner agency to the U.S. Geological Survey, helped encourage greater awareness of the limitations of economic development in the American West imposed by the challenges of aridity and climatic extremes. Powell's arguments focused on what might be termed the operational level of decision-making, that level of decision-making at which actors and resources directly interact under institutional rules within a given place or region (see Kenney and Lord 1999: 4)

This is significant because there arose an appreciable lag between awareness of the need for change at this operational level as opposed to awareness of the need for change at the level of *collective choice* processes. According to many political scientists, this level of decision-making embraces agency rule making, litigation, market exchanges, common law, and "bargaining and collaboration" (Kenney and Lord 1999: 4). It was at this latter level, as we saw, that the managerial considerations and strategies adopted by established federal water agencies, as well as the practices encouraged by traditional water law doctrines, inhibited adaptation of policies to changing environmental conditions. This failure to adapt took many forms: riparian and prior appropriation doctrines paid too little attention to the need to protect instream flow and to inhibit water pollution, much less how to do it. The Corps of Engineers and the Bureau of Reclamation mostly pursued major structural programs for harnessing rivers and allocating water—largely in response to the need to placate powerful interest groups and in response to pressing local and regional problems. Both agencies often pursued their programs without regard to either their adverse social and ecological effects or the existence of available nonstructural alternatives. Also, as we have discussed, laws about water supply, as opposed to water quality and antipollution, evolved through a largely independent and segmented path of development.

Even though this latter set of processes continues to lag behind the ideal required for an adaptive management approach to the sustainable development of water resources, some adaptation has occurred to varying degrees in various regions—in part through the introduction of policy strategies that encourage more real-time environmental monitoring, greater public involvement in decisions, explicit consideration of the interaction between economic development and environmental factors within watersheds, and—as we shall discuss next—more incorporation of local knowledge in decisions. The most important factor to bear in mind about this adaptive process is that in most cases it came about through the pressure of key actors who were faced with intractable disagreement, conflict, and impasse—sometimes resulting in litigious or, at the very least, bureaucratically slow and interminable delay.

For their part, various states within the United States experienced comparable problems in water management, generated in part by urban and rural competition for water supply, urban growth, point source pollution, and conflicts over water withdrawal and inter-basin diversion. Unlike the federal government, however, many of the states whose policies we explored have been more open to dramatic, innovative policy change. In addition, in many respects they have proven themselves to be far more adaptive in their management approaches. This seems to have been the case largely because policy debates have been confined to smaller geographical areas, and the negotiations have often been limited to fewer sets of stakeholders. However, these are not the only reasons for states' proclivity toward adaptive management.

As we have seen, in the area of water quality policy, states have been far more willing than the federal government to adopt innovative measures involving unconventional partnerships—particularly to reduce nonpoint water pollution and to manage instream flow. In many instances, this was because states suffered the most from the failure to resolve policy impasses in these problem areas. Also, many states have had far more to gain or lose from policy change or its absence. Gains accruing to states included the possibility of spurring continued agricultural and industrial growth if they could find ways to address their water problems creatively. They could also improve the quality of the environment and the economic activities that hinge on them (fishing, rafting, tourism) while better complying with national laws and policies over which they exercised little control. Losses revolved around continued policy impasses, economic uncertainty, and ostracism from environmental groups.

In other policy areas, adaptive management innovations were also much more willingly undertaken by states. This is an area we have not discussed in any detail. Some of the most significant efforts at enhancing water supply planning made a priority out of strengthening the scientific basis for decision-making. In Florida, Missouri, California, and Texas, to mention but a few examples, these efforts included bolstering the collection of social and economic information as well as natural and engineering science data through multiple sources. The purpose of this information collection effort is to improve decision-making for drought mitigation planning, instream flow management, water and energy use, and long-term assessment of water supply needs (for example, see Loh 1995; Knowles 1998; South Florida Water Management District 2000; Kundell, DeMeo, and Myszewski 2001; "California Energy Challenge" 2001; ACWA 2001; "Florida Water Plan 1995" 2001; Missouri DNR 2002, 2003; "Panel Says Florida Needs" 2003).

These innovations have also been pursued out of necessity and uncertainty. Without internal preparation for the challenges to water supply posed by population growth and drought, for example, states could be vulnerable to other states that covet their water supplies. This was certainly a lesson of the ACF dispute in chapter 3. Remaining information needs that we have identified include factors that affect long-term demand, the implications of combining local community efforts to enhance supply, and the effects of climate change on water supply.

In international efforts to manage river basins, ensuring that the knowledge base for adaptively managing water resources is strong and vibrant has also been a pressing concern. It has also been a factor in other large-scale place-based water management efforts. On the whole, and on the basis of what we have gleaned from the cases we investigated, the greatest challenge facing the establishment of an adequate knowledge base is the high degree of uncertainty associated with three issues: the consequences of global climate change, the social effects of population growth, and the effects of types of water use on water supply stress. Perhaps the highest degree of uncertainty surrounds the first of these issues—climate change—mainly due to the difficulty in predicting watershed-scale (much less, basin-scale) effects from the warming of global average annual temperatures (see, for instance, Clarkson and Smerdon 1989).

One of the strongest arguments in favor of adaptive management is precisely the difficulty in translating continent-scale changes in temperature, precipitation, cloud albedo, evapo-transpiration, and other variables into discernible and predictable changes in water supply and quality at a locally manageable level. When in doubt, in other words, water supply should be managed in such a way as to be able to serve everyone's needs—and to do so in a fair, equitable, and efficient manner—regardless of the amount of water available.

What we described as a "no regrets" strategy could be a viable alternative. By "no regrets" we mean a policy designed to reduce vulnerabilities to public water supply, agriculture, industry, power generation, and environmental quality that would be beneficial regardless of whether climate change actually occurs or not. Such a policy relies on conservation as a cornerstone of management and emphasizes enhanced end-use efficiency for water as well as effective drought management. While more will be said about this particular issue later on when we discuss impediments to (and opportunities for) conservation, at this juncture it is important to note that such a resilient policy requires knowledge of behavioral attributes of water use as well as information about the technical characteristics of conservation.

We also suggested that, given the broad implications of climate change and the fact that its effects are intertwined with changes in population growth and in-migration in those societies already undergoing water shortages or other stressors, increased resiliency in the face of the uncertain consequences of climate change is also likely to reduce stress on water supply. This is especially likely if that resiliency is based on encouraging behavioral change—whether through market-induced and voluntarily initiated changes in allocation, distribution, and management of demand on the one hand, or governmentally mandated alterations of behavior on the other. The most difficult challenge to overcome in bringing about these changes—regardless of the strategy pursued—is the ignorance of the general public and more than a few decision-makers. Such ignorance can only be overcome by a combination of education and information dissemination efforts that draw on indigenous, preexisting sources of water knowledge.

Our discussion of various river basin management efforts in chapters 2 and 3 demonstrated the importance of strong state capacity to manage the means to bring about change (institutional adaptation through compacts, commissions, more novel measures). It also emphsized the need for vibrant public participation and involvement to ensure a high degree of representativeness. Finally, it noted the importance of cooperation among provinces within nation-states as well as among nation-states to generate and maintain the base of knowledge essential for promoting sustainable water resources management. It should be recalled that an important element of the debate over the privatization of water supply infrastructure, both in developing and developed countries (and especially with regard to utility-scale issues of management) is the extent to which private ownership or control hinders citizen knowledge of water supply conditions that could make their participation in decisions more effective and influential. Where privatization has been readily accepted, as in parts of Western Europe, it is usually because of the presence of a "counter-weight" source of water knowledge—and political power—such as local knowledge, information possessed by government agencies trusted by the public, or available data and information possessed by nongovernmental organizations.

Finally, all the U.S. river basin initiatives we discussed in chapter 3 arose, in part, because of a widely perceived need to improve the knowledge base for water management. This need often manifested itself in various forms, such as better forecasting of water demand and supply; better assessment of the prospects for long-term drought; more efficacious balancing of instream requirements for protecting flora and fauna against off-stream demands for agriculture, municipal use, and power generation; more effective flood mitigation and floodplain management; and better management of the means to protect, preserve, and regenerate threatened aquatic species, such as shad and salmon. In all cases, this expanded knowledge base was promoted as a means to help participants identify problems, set priorities, and identify solutions.

That no initiative has yet found the means to achieve any of these ends optimally or perfectly only underscores the importance of an adaptively credible process for collecting, disseminating, and revising such knowledge. Underpinning the efforts of all of these initiatives is not only a dedicated process for developing valid, verifiable, and commonly agreed-upon methods for assessing hydrological, ecological, and societal conditions but one that can incorporate indigenous as well as expert knowledge of these conditions. Before we turn to this topic, we need to consider the process of knowledge dissemination for water.

A Note on Public Education: Perceptions of Water's Value and Use

Despite the growing importance of water supply as an issue of concern both internationally and in the United States, there are surprisingly few empirical studies of what the general public actually knows about water and what it thinks decision-makers should do to enhance its safety, security, and continued availability. For example, most scientifically sampled studies of public opinion in the United States have focused mostly on water quality. These studies share some striking similarities in their findings—a heartening fact insofar as it suggests that certain key issues and concerns are consistently important (see Hurd 1993; NCWQ 1997). On the other hand, while some issues have been found to be commonly resonant, the public's perception of its own role in causing or helping to resolve water supply and quality problems is poorly developed.

For example, these surveys suggest a remarkable consensus on issues related to the safety of local water supply by Americans. Approximately three-quarters of the public has concerns of one sort or another regarding their household water supply. Approximately a third believes that their water supply is "not as safe as it should be." And approximately 40% believe that standards for protecting drinking water quality should be "stricter." Where problems arise, however, is in trying to determine if the public's concerns are at all contributing to a heightened effort to acquire greater knowledge about the sources of these perceived problems. The verdict here is less than sanguine. For example, these same studies suggest that less than a third of the American pubic knows the major sources of water pollution in their communities—that is, most do not think that runoff from farms, parking lots, or even residences are a major cause of water pollution. Less than a third can distinguish the characteristics of aquatically healthy streams, and less than 40% of the American people can even define the term *watershed*.

Clearly, the general public appears to be deficient on the most basic information about water. This does not bode well for the future of adaptive management. On the other hand, studies suggest that the public wants to see water supply adequately protected (Public Agenda 2006; Rosenbaum 2005: 58, 171). If there is good news to be taken from these ambivalent conclusions, it would appear to be that the public is aware that its knowledge and understanding of water problems are deficient and thus need to be improved—a first step in accepting the need for change. Also, the public is generally inclined to learn more about water problems if the opportunity to do so is afforded them. In short, the value of safe, secure water supplies is definitely a high priority among the general public—even if knowledge about water is generally low.

The significance of all this is that any reliance on local or indigenous knowledge for improving sustainable water management must begin from a sober awareness of what people do not know—as well as what they do know. Water is no longer a free resource whose value is fixed only by engineering costs. Education is required to teach consumers what is involved in keeping clean water flowing from their taps. The costs of policy failure with regard to education may be incalculable. This is because the effects of our continued ignorance about water are likely to last for several generations. Only education can reverse such ignorance.

Indigenous or Local Knowledge: What It Is, How To Apply It

There is a growing consensus among ecologists, social scientists, and policy analysts across disciplines that the objective of sustainable development requires that local and indigenous knowledge of the communities residing within watersheds and river basins—whose residents are after all affected by decisions—be drawn upon to ensure sustainable decisions. There are many reasons for this growing consensus, but three are most relevant for our discussion.

First, there is a demonstrable need to conform or "attune" regional water management approaches to the institutional constraints of particular basins or watersheds. These institutional constraints are shaped as much by cultural values and traditions as they are by formal organizations (Burson 2000). Thus, only by understanding the epistemic basis for these values and traditions—in other words, how people perceive the natural environment and the impact of their actions upon it—can we understand the impediments to achieving sustainability. For example, the historical absence of water conflicts stemming from shortages of water supply has been a major cultural determinant of southerners' attitudes toward water—and a very real impediment toward encouraging greater water conservation in the Apalachicola-Chattahoochee-Flint case, as we have seen. Conversely, cultural expectations of periodic water shortage in much of the American West gave rise, in part, to the appropriation law system for water allocation characterizing water rights policy in that region. As we also saw, the cultural artifact of "first in time, first in right," characteristic of this appropriation rights doctrine sometimes resisted reform in light of later knowledge about the environmental effects of this doctrine on instream flow, the health of fisheries, and wildlife. Ironically, native groups (mainly American Indians) often had knowledge about the conditions that resulted from overfishing and water diversion but their subjugation also made the legitimacy of their knowledge appear insignificant.

Second, as we have also seen, building social capital within regional partnerships formed to improve water management is an important means of enhancing democratic decision-making and consensus building. In order to build social capital, however, one must first find the means to agree about how problems might be defined and then how they might be addressed. While evidence supporting this proposition is widespread throughout the cases we studied, especially those in which stakeholders began their deliberations to form basin-wide initiatives from policy positions that were initially polarized or at least highly divergent—CALFED, the NPPC, and the Apalachicola-Chattahoochee-Flint Compact—a number of other cases across the nation buttress this contention. For example, emerging cases of stakeholder collaboration on the small-watershed scale, such as those we examined in our discussion of TMDLs in chapter 4, reveal the importance of participants believing that their joining together in partnership actually make a difference in improving long-term water quality and in enhancing other environmental amenities like recreation or local economic development.

In part, such beliefs on the part of participants result from their perception that watershed health is improving as a result of measures they helped to adopt—a perception influenced by the confidence they have in the capacity of the partnership to achieve tangible change. Such beliefs also result from the conviction of participants that the partnerships formed to address these environmental problems can competently integrate and amalgamate scientific knowledge, societal beliefs, and community values into one comprehensive package of information. As we have seen, this type of conviction has been important to the success of many of the basin-scale partnerships we have studied, including the Murray River Basin Commission in Australia, the U.S.-Mexican Border Environment Cooperation Commission, and CALFED (Leach, Pelkey, and Sabatier 2002; Blood and Hook 2003).

Finally, while there is little question that expert knowledge based on the most rigorous scientifically agreed-upon standards and procedures available is essential for good decision-making, it is becoming clear that, in order to refine understanding of these conditions to facilitate policy change, the opinions and perspectives of the people most affected by these conditions must also be incorporated into decisions. Conversely, the absence of any effort to take into account such indigenous or local knowledge can be an important political impediment to consensus-building—as was the case in the Apalachicola-Chattahoochee-Flint Compact (state and local consensus over water allocation formulae), Northwest Power Planning Council (Native American cultural attitudes toward salmon and the need for its restoration), and, initially, in CALFED (public concerns over water uses and the inequities in allocating water).

Indigenous knowledge originates from many sources, including farmers and ranchers, local community residents, and tribal nations. A critical issue in making use of such knowledge is finding a means to synthesize expert and local sources of information, especially about environmental conditions. The emerging literature on this subject suggests that there are two important constraints to be overcome in using local and indigenous knowledge effectively. First, experts must do a better job of incorporating community perspectives and including local cultural practices, norms, and mores into their professional judgment about environmental conditions. They must also be prepared to translate their own knowledge into usable information for a region's local populace (Blood and Hook 2003).

Second, special care must be taken to develop methods for gathering local information and insight about environmental and social conditions affecting water use. The key to doing this lies in taking a "place-based" perspective toward local knowledge. In chapter 1, we suggested that one of the keys to building awareness of problems and to formulating cooperative plans for resolving them lies in finding a way to enmesh an initiative's activities within the cultural context of the region. The concept of indigenous or local knowledge is central to this "enmeshing" process and is predicated on the view that local communities within a watershed or basin are often in the best position to understand the critical ecological, social, and other conditions affecting their water resources. Some term this place-based perspective a "bioregional" approach toward environmental knowledge—one that views people and natural resources in a region as intrinsically connected to one another, even though the people reside within—and avow allegiance to—different political jurisdictions (Parenteau 1994; Morphet and Hams 1994; McGinnis 1995; McGinnis 1999a, b).

There are two major issues associated with this place-based perspective on local and indigenous knowledge that are relevant to efforts to enhance adaptive water management. First, people must be encouraged to develop an understanding of place and to chronicle and disseminate local knowledge about environmental conditions to decision-makers. This attitude is not something that simply develops automatically: it must be encouraged by decision-makers, and water management institutions must foster participatory mechanisms that make it possible to incorporate local perspectives in decisions formally and to solicit indigenous opinion (Goldstein 1999; see also EPA 1994).

The Murray River Basin Commission, for example, aimed to develop greater local input into its sustainability decisions by establishing a community advisory council. The main function of this council was to serve as a sort of extension-service instrument to learn from—and to teach—farmers techniques to abate soil salinization and to reduce runoff pollution. One key to understanding the council's efforts is its emphasis on monitoring community perceptions and values—important considerations in putting forward cooperative solutions whose benefits as well as costs will ultimately be shared by local communities and basin decision-makers alike. The incorporation of these values and perceptions is intended to empower communities and assure that they will be able to offer genuinely independent perspectives—not coopt them. While the verdict remains uncertain at this date regarding the council's success in incorporating public attitudes in sustainability decisions, it is clear, as we have seen, that the CAC's efforts are at least aiming in a constructive direction—and have yielded some success in protecting aboriginal water rights, for example.

Likewise, in the case of U.S.-Mexico interaction on sustainable water management initiatives within their borderlands, the policies of the Border Environment Cooperation Commission (BECC) for incorporating public opinion have influenced many decisional outcomes—particularly those regarding water project investment and the kinds of environmental procedures that should be used to review the efficacy and value of projects. In this instance, incorporation of local or indigenous knowledge has been aided by mechanisms that encourage project requests to originate within the border communities themselves. It is also assisted by formal voting procedures and the incorporation of public input along functional (NGO) as well as geographic (community jurisdiction) lines. Such functionality permits crosscutting sources of information and knowledge to be incorporated in decisions.

The CALFED Bay-Delta Program has also explicitly incorporated local and indigenous knowledge in an effort to promote adaptive management in the Sacramento–San Joaquin basins. It has done so by actively encouraging broad public input into the process of formulating programmatic goals through a multitude of mechanisms—ranging from advisory committees to public hearings, telephone hotlines, a website, and an "Ecosystem Roundtable" that, as we have seen, provides specific input on how to coordinate the various components of CALFED's ecosystem restoration program. As we have also seen, however, challenges to effective incorporation of local and indigenous knowledge are common within CALFED: conflicts, especially in southern California, over water allocation for agriculture, municipal use, and environmental protection continue to pit various stakeholder interests against one another—demonstrating that indigenous knowledge in itself is not a panacea.

For example, protection of the Salton Sea ecosystem depends on the commitment of local agricultural interests who have thus far been opposed to reallocating Colorado River water to cities. It is important to bear in mind that their opposition stems only partly from economic concerns, contrary to the often overly simplified characterization of their position. Resistance to giving up a portion of their water also stems from the perception of local farmers and ranchers that they are legally obligated to protect the endangered species within the Salton Sea. On the other hand, local knowledge in California's cities suggests a real need for this water—especially in light of growing demands and long-term drought. Aquatic species in the Salton Sea benefit from the continued runoff of salty water from farms and ranches in the Imperial Valley. This runoff sustains a variety of sea birds and other life. In short, local knowledge in this case suggests that it is prudent to consider the implications of any water reallocation decision. As this case shows, one irony in soliciting and trying to incorporate local knowledge is that one region's indigenous knowledge may lead to policy conclusions that conflict with those suggested by local knowledge generated in another.

The second major issue associated with developing and using indigenous or local knowledge for adaptive water resources management is that of *incentives*. Political scientists, economists, and other policy scholars often note that when deciding on whether to adopt a course of policy that will necessitate the expenditure of considerable resources—whether time, money, in-kind contribution, or a willingness to forego opportunities in order to address other, higher priority problems—actors often resist making a decision unless there is a high likelihood of some direct benefit accruing to them or, at least, a net avoidance of costs (see Olson 1965; Ostrom 1990). This issue is relevant for understanding the impediments to using local knowledge because communities within particular watersheds may have little or even no incentive to institute programs to collect, disseminate, and use indigenous knowledge about water resources in order to aid sustainable development. This is so for three reasons.

First, many local jurisdictions, especially in developing nations, are already hard-pressed by environmental and economic development problems and thus have limited resources to devote to knowledge-building processes. The types of resources that could build up this local capacity are often absent—

postsecondary science education, for example, is practically nonexistent in many developing countries, and there is a widespread belief in many societies that science has itself failed to address the most severe environmental and public health problems decision-makers currently face (UNWWAP 2003). These conditions and this widespread cynicism toward science education characterize many of the nations whose basin initiatives we have examined, including those in South America, Sub-Saharan Africa, and Southeast Asia.

Second, many of the most knowledge-intensive problems these countries face regarding water resource management—and this is also true of many developed nations—are ones that local levels of authority are often poorly equipped to address. For example, while the effects of global climate change on local water supply are likely, as we have seen, to become acute over time, especially in regions already undergoing severe water stress (because the threat of global warming remains highly uncertain), local governments, watershed authorities, river basin commissions and other non-national jurisdictions may have little incentive to react to this perceived threat conscientiously and systematically.

This is especially true if one considers that they are already called upon to perform a broad array of short-term management functions that are expensive, time-consuming, and often contentious (flood abatement, drought mitigation, water supply allocation). Ironically, even though these short-term management functions are directly affected by the possibility of global warming, there is little economic or political gain to be had by a single local entity contributing to fixing the problem unless all the other local entities within a nation-state that are affected by the problem are also willing to do so. In effect, the goal of many farsighted local jurisdictions is to avoid the classic "free rider" problem—spending resources on fixing a problem, therefore benefiting others—which doesn't make these other jurisdictions any more inclined to spend resources to fix (Olson 1965; also Nordhaus 1991; Devall and Parresol 1994).

The lesson here is that for local entities to acquire knowledge and use it, there must be national-level incentives to encourage all affected local entities to plan for future climate change and to develop an adequate base of local knowledge to address its consequences. All such local entities must become convinced that there are ancillary benefits to be gained in developing such a knowledge base—what we previously termed "no regrets" strategies. Such prudential decision-making is at the very heart of adaptive management, and it requires national decision-maker awareness and a willingness to support this activity financially.

Experience also suggests that asymmetrical knowledge and information, characteristic of relations between experts and lay people jointly responsible for environmental decisions, also comes into play when discussions of how to use indigenous or local knowledge arise. So-called principals (those at high levels of organizations such as government agencies) and agents (those empowered to implement the decisions formulated by principals) frequently hold divergent perceptions about the severity of environmental problems and what to do about them. Economists refer to this divergence as a "principal-agent" problem. This explanation is important in understanding the resistance of actors to take decisive action in the face of problems for which local or indigenous knowledge of water resources is essential.

For example, the indeterminacy of global climate change and its impact on water supply—especially at the local or watershed level—may serve to deter adoption of policies that will be costly in the short term (greater conservation, water reuse) even if prudent in the long run. Moreover, while principals may better know what sorts of national-level decisions need to be made to reduce the risks of global warming—reducing greenhouse gas emissions, or adapting to a warmer climate through rotating the types of crops grown in an agrarian region—agents may know far better than principals the true costs of adapting such measures as well as their political feasibility and acceptability.

As we saw in chapter 3 in our review of the reports issued by RAND and the Tellus Institute, both of which promoted an alternative energy vision for the future of the Columbia River basin and its surrounding region, while the economic and engineering assumptions used in these studies were generally clear and logical, neither study adequately considered the adaptation constraints imposed by either principal or agent opinions, roles, or previous commitments. One cannot alter behavior in a vacuum—the motives that drive principals and agents to commit themselves to one course of action or another are based on numerous behavioral drivers and perceptions. Without understanding public attitudes about accepting or rejecting an alternative energy future, one cannot confidently advance a policy strategy, as one might rub up against a strongly held set of local aesthetic or ethical values.

The bottom line is that knowledge and information are not merely independent variables that determine and shape opinion and policy—they are themselves products of social forces, which often bias decision-makers toward one course of action or another. They are dependent, in other words, on cultural and social as well as temporal constraints. When confronted with water resource problems that pose long-term and uncertain risks, for instance, previous experience indicates that both principals and agents are most likely to use science, technology, and other sources of knowledge and information to respond to what they perceive as readily fixable problems. Such fixable problems tend to include structural measures to mitigate sea-level rise or more frequent chances for flooding—for instance, building sea walls. It may also include building dams and impoundments to abate anticipated future water supply shortages (Meo 1991; Lee 1993; Deyle, Meo, and James 1994). In all cases, however, the last thing that decision-makers will choose to rely on are nonstructural innovations that might, or might not, be found acceptable. We shall revisit this nonstructural issue later.

CONFORMING STRUCTURE TO FUNCTION: MAKING PLACE-BASED DECISIONS WORK

We have said quite a lot in this book—especially in the case studies—about the challenges of conforming the structure of water management frameworks to the principles of place-based decision-making. We have considered how to do both of these things while addressing the underlying sources of water supply conflict. However, we have not yet considered how to synthesize these lessons in a coherent manner. Until such lessons are distilled systematically, we will not be able to achieve our underlying goal of prescribing how these lessons may be applied to enhancing sustainable, adaptive management of water resources. We now turn to the major place-based lessons of our analysis and consider how they can be implemented, as well as the impediments we can expect to face in trying to achieve them.

Managing River Basins as Social-Ecological Entities

Blatter and Ingram (2002) suggest that effective water management initiatives must seek to combine social and ecological principles in their operation. While watershed boundaries are critically important, so too is recognition that people living within a watershed share a common heritage and culture. The survey findings for the five U.S. river basin initiatives we discussed in chapter 3 generally confirm that water resource management initiatives that take sustainability principles seriously strive to conform to effective ecosystem management principles. One lesson, however, is that effective conformity is not solely a scientific issue—it is also a legal and political principle (see Cheng, Kruger, and Daniels 2003).

For example, of the early U.S. initiatives to establish a comprehensive, basin-wide entity for water and other natural resources management, only the Tennessee Valley Authority (TVA) was invested with the authority to legally supplant *existing* agencies in its region of operation. In other basins, inadequate provision for meaningful citizen participation coupled with strong linkages between established water agencies and powerful local elites allowed the traditional beneficiaries of water projects to maintain power and exclude consideration of a wider range of water resource planning and use concerns. In the 1970s, the lack of broad public support for the river basin commissions established under the Water Resources Planning Act of 1965 eventually led to the demise of the Title II river basin commissions. As we recall from our discussion in chapter 2, while their administrative organization may have made sense in light of "social-ecological" principles, they became embroiled in inter-agency (and intergovernmental) disputes between Congress and the executive branch that weakened their authority to oversee river basin planning objectives and to implement basin-wide reform.

For its part, the TVA experiment, which had the potential to achieve fully integrated river basin management, was never replicated in other regions, perhaps due to state concerns over loss of sovereignty. Moreover, as we also saw, changes in the TVA's operating philosophy—together with changes in the overlying region and its expectations—may have served to narrow even its aspirations, especially regarding the promotion of broad public values. The TVA is only now returning to this mandate, thanks to its required reservoir operations study. In short, while the mission is very important, so is the ability to involve the public formally in decisions to assure that the mission—whatever it is—will serve democratic ends.

Conformity with effective ecosystem management principles thus seems to depend upon achieving, or at least approximating, five objectives. The initiatives we have examined in this book have experienced differential success on each of these objectives.

- Be spatially relevant: have boundaries that encompass all issues and players.

The boundaries of an initiative must be broad enough to encompass all regional issues and stakeholders. Boundaries include political jurisdictions and economically bounded areas sharing trade and other interactions. All relevant stakeholders within a basin must be identified and incorporated into the initiative from the start. Recognition of mutually beneficial goals, including economic vitality and stability, is critical to resolving complex problems, and sound technical information is also needed. Three major lessons derive from our cases.

First, each initiative we studied employed watershed boundaries to delineate the geographic scope of its management area consistent with the concept of an ecosystem as a relatively enclosed physical system in which "flows of matter and energy" are greater within the system than between the system and its surroundings. This delineation is perhaps the easiest means of conforming to an integrated social-ecological principle. For practical reasons, however, each has also had to make compromises, in its own way, with more straightforward political considerations. Political membership is generally restricted to officials representing state governments and federal agencies who have recognized authority for various water resource management functions. The three river basin compacts we discussed seek to represent states and federal agencies fairly—while the two more recent innovative partnerships, CALFED and NPPC, seek to do the same thing, but they also embrace, as do some of the more traditional initiatives, a variety of nongovernmental groups from throughout basin political jurisdictions by means of advisory councils and other instruments.

Second, each initiative we examined has endeavored to provide policies and programs designed to address each of the components of the watershed, in effect treating the whole system as greater than the sum of its parts. This is shown by efforts to incorporate stakeholder groups representing a variety of water user groups as well as formal resource management agencies. The use of special-interest seminars as well as public hearings also exemplifies this effort. We also found that each of the initiatives had several motivations, ranging from practical concerns such as economic growth and avoidance of litigation to more esoteric goals like the peaceable allocation of water.

These multiple goals challenged efforts to establish an integrated, holistic approach to sustainable management at the very same time that they encouraged the incorporation of nontraditional interests. Nevertheless, each initiative coincided with the drainage area of the major rivers embraced by their charters, and they all endeavored to consider the pertinent economic and political boundaries. Each also used a wide variety of tools to solicit public input, which the participants we surveyed stated was used in every aspect of water resources decision-making.

Third, each initiative has also tried to encompass the integrity of the system as being a higher concern than the condition of any single component.

Here, however, the effectiveness of the initiatives in achieving this goal varied considerably. Some observers credit the NPPC, despite its failure to restore salmon or to reaching full consensus among key stakeholders on fundamental water management issues, with at least acknowledging the need to embrace a broad range of aesthetic, preservationist, equity, and conservation-oriented values. CALFED's champions also claim success in bridging the chasm between agricultural and environmental interests by agreeing on participation mechanisms that seek to maximize watershed restoration efforts as a priority and that frame allocation decisions in accordance with their likelihood of promoting—rather than retarding—this prospect.

We are less sanguine, however, about the prospects for seeing the adoption of such a holistic approach within the context of the ACF dispute. In this case study, the long-term demands on the basin's surface water resources are not only hotly contested but, in large part, also incompatible. Moreover, existing riparian rights systems on which protagonists base their arguments for equity tend to favor individual states and users as opposed to embracing ways of reconciling relationships between up- and downstream users as part of an integrated, interdependent management entity. For their part, both the DRBC and the SRBC have made considerable strides in viewing their respective river systems—the Delaware and the Susquehanna—as integrated entities whose service functions should be managed holistically. Shad restoration efforts in the SRBC, as well as policies designed to deter inter-basin transfers in this initiative, have their origins in reactive policies, rather than proactive ones. They are engineered responses to problems that were already well along the path to becoming serious and possibly irreversible. In fairness, however, had there not been a Susquehanna basin commission with the authority to formulate a comprehensive response across the basin's states to water management problems, any concerted and effective response might have been impossible to develop.

The DRBC has been effective in serving as a sounding board for member states' efforts to formulate coordinated drought-mitigation policies and watershed-scale restoration and pollution prevention efforts. Even if problems are addressed in a somewhat piecemeal fashion in response to pressing issues, at least they are being addressed in a coordinated, conjoint manner and the commission is finding a means of persuading member states to harmonize their actions.

- Integrate quality and quantity concerns: embrace up- and downstream issues

An effective water resources management initiative that sets out to promote sustainable development must seek to address water pollution as well as water supply problems. All five of the initiatives discussed in chapter 3 have done so. As we saw in chapter 4, unless both of these parameters are addressed, we cannot call an initiative an effective instrument for promoting sustainable development. While this should now be obvious, there is an aspect of this integration of these two issues—quality and quantity—that has yet to be explicitly addressed: two of the initiatives we have discussed are faced with an unusual hydrological challenge—estuary management. These initiatives are the Susquehanna River Basin Commission and CALFED.

The Susquehanna drains to Chesapeake Bay, and it is the largest single source of nonpoint pollutants that contribute to the degradation of the bay's water quality, oyster and crab harvests, and other quality measures. For its part, CALFED feeds into San Francisco Bay, and its health has a dramatic impact on sea life. A less explicit but no less important example is offered by the Apalachicola-Chattahoochee-Flint (ACF) dispute. Florida's primary concern, and the reason for its initial involvement in what has become a three state dispute over water allocation, has been the impact of water pollution and water withdrawals on the health of gulf oyster fisheries, especially from metropolitan Atlanta.

Our cases suggest that a formidable challenge in managing estuary-freshwater disputes is the often intractable differences in the objectives between freshwater and estuarine interests. While no panacea exists to satisfy both sets of interests simultaneously, it does seem that whatever measures are introduced must be reciprocal: if additional water supply is to be allocated to preserve estuarine resources, some compensation to upstream users must be provided to permit negotiations to succeed in finalizing agreements that can be consummated. Likewise, upstream measures that have proven to be most effective are nonstructural BMPs (as in the upstream portions of the Susquehanna basin) or even trading schemes that have been introduced on an experimental basis (as in the Neuse in North Carolina; see chapter 4).

Finally, each initiative recognizes the importance of achieving "health" among the economic, social, and political components of the system, as well as the biological and physical components, to ensure optimal functioning of the entire system. This should be obvious from the vast range of activities they are involved in, including allocation, quality, environmental and habitat restoration, water conservation and drought mitigation. Perhaps most significantly, the sheer existence of these initiatives provided a framework for the gradual embrace of different activities as political demands arose to undertake them. This is perhaps one of the strongest endorsements of their capacity for adaptive management—in the case of the SRBC and the DRBC, especially; these initiatives now undertake efforts that they had not originally established to implement.

That their decision-making institutions, participation mechanisms, and science infrastructure were able to embrace these concerns in a cross-jurisdictional fashion may be a key to understanding one aspect of uniting structure and function—it simply takes time. Moreover, it is difficult for an initiative designed to address one set of problems suddenly to be expected to shift focus and address others. That other initiatives (Colorado river compact, Delaware and Susquehanna River Basin Commissions) have made this transition at all is testimony to their openness to new problems, flexibility in decision-making, and, perhaps most of all, the efficacy of their decision-maker interactions—appointed staffs with expertise in a number of functional areas are viewed as nonpolitical officials and have developed the ability to work well together in ironing out differences, depoliticizing potentially contentious issues, and finding common ground for negotiation and bargaining (see Weston 1995).

- Balance and identify roles of federal/national and state/regional governments

One of the more surprising findings of our cases is that while federal commitment and financial support are obviously desirable in making possible an effective water management initiative, this commitment and support are neither necessary nor sufficient conditions for effective and sustainable management. What is needed is federal agency cooperation to help set instream flow standards and guarantee minimum flows (if necessary), operate federal water projects in accordance with the wishes and needs of stakeholders, and assess ecological impacts.

The three river basin commissions we discussed (DRBC, SRBC, ACF) no longer receive direct federal support, as we have seen. Nevertheless, federal agency cooperation with states (DRBC, CALFED) remains absolutely critical in meeting their needs. Why? Simply stated, all the cases in this chapter depend on elaborate collaborative arrangements between federal agencies responsible for certain management functions—in particular the setting of water quality standards—for which no state has authority. In short, without the cooperation of these agencies, these initiatives would not be possible—regardless of how much local and state interest there is—because only federal agencies can establish credible, generalizable methods for setting coherent interstate instream flow standards and mandate minimum flows for navigable streams.

Federal partners, as we have seen, can range from the Army Corps of Engineers, responsible for reservoir management in all of these systems (in the case of the NPPC, this authority is shared with the Bureau of Reclamation) to the EPA, responsible for water quality regulation, and the Fish and Wildlife Service, responsible for fisheries regulation and the protection of endangered and threatened species. Problematically, as we have seen (chapter 4), when federal agencies cannot put into place credible, acceptable standards for data collection and validation, assessment of water body conditions, and determination of acceptable levels of pollution—when that happens, federal-state partnerships become difficult to operate. A climate of litigation, distrust, state-federal antipathy, and local stakeholder frustration becomes widespread, as with the TMDL issue in the United States.

Cooperation and role "blending" among federal and state government partners—when it successfully occurs—is also probably due, in no small measure, to public input. Various stakeholder groups with an interest in water supply and quality issues have, in effect, forced agencies and jurisdictions to come together—sometimes in spite of themselves. Moreover, regardless of the divergent stakeholder interests represented by various public interest and environmental organizations, initiative missions that have grown faster than available resources, and continued institutional resistance to change, it would appear that two factors have been paramount in contributing to initiative success thus far: the inclusiveness of stakeholder involvement and the growing sophistication on the part of the public with regard to water management crises. When the public is involved, and wants to be involved because they recognize the severity of problems, success in designing an initiative capable of blending the talents and abilities of federal and state agencies is made more likely.

If federal efforts are best seen as supplementary to those initiated at lower levels, then the commitment of state level officials is obviously an important factor for several reasons: to hasten negotiation, bargaining, and conjoint management; to heighten public awareness; and to encourage a hands-on approach to management. State officials, as we have seen, also have the authority to institute a number of innovations that federal officials may not be able to initiate as easily, including anti-diversion laws that strengthen a state's bargaining position relative to others with whom it is in conflict. Methods of verification and compliance are also important. Such dispute resolution tools, together with methods of verification and compliance, hasten the development and cultivation of an adaptively managed organization that is able to respond constructively to change.

It should be obvious by now that the willingness of state-level officials to become committed—if they were not already so committed when a dispute begins—is absolutely essential to the success of a water management initiative. To a great extent, the Susquehanna River Basin Commission, the Delaware River Bain Commission, and CALFED all exemplify this truism. Conversely, the lack of success on the part of the ACF initiative is at least partly due to the inability of some state officials to commit to the process of reaching a collaborative settlement. It is noteworthy that the involvement and commitment of these officials is considerably more important than that of federal officials. It is also important that in the former cases, officials are willing to take a hands-on approach to management and policy. Again, the DRBC and the SRBC demonstrate this observation, and it has been a key reason for their endurance as platforms for dispute settlement and discussion.

High-level leadership is also a relative concept. As shown in chapter 3, for example, local officials representing powerful stakeholder groups or holding elected or appointed political positions in local or state government have been critical components of many watershed restoration initiatives, which have reduced runoff pollution and improved water quality.

Finally, when we talk about educating officials, we must recognize that these officials not only require better education and information themselves, they also have an important role to play in educating citizens. Their efforts can help in providing an overall assessment of the status of water education efforts in the region; identifying key educational audiences and developing specific learning approaches appropriate for each; and promoting the establishment of educational clearinghouses in partnership with businesses, community groups, and religious organizations to hasten a more watershed-based approach to water supply and quality awareness.

- Employ effective dispute resolution mechanisms

One of the most striking, if underappreciated, characteristics of dispute resolution efforts in water policy is that successful resolution of interstate disputes depends, to a large degree, on intra-state policy reform. In short, cooperation among different states is best facilitated by the adoption of internal re-forms—such as drought protection acts (Georgia); water conservation and end-use programs (California, Washington); and water withdrawal, water registra-tion, and anti-diversion laws (Florida, Georgia, Tennessee). These policies not only put a state in the position of being better able to protect its water resources through internal regulation of water allocation, they also strengthen its bar-gaining position relative to others with whom it is likely to come into conflict.

Without reforms, bargaining from a position of strength—especially in the event of litigation—is virtually impossible because a state cannot really dem-onstrate that it has a need for the amount of water it is currently using and that it is equipped to manage its water well. As with other water disputes around the world, if a party lacks the resources, power, or legal tools to resolve dis-putes, it will be at a disadvantage in negotiations. This has been the predom-inant pattern, for example, in the Mekong River basin (chapter 2).

Regardless of how and why a river basin initiative is formed—and inde-pendent of the motives for initiating a common set of solutions to a basin's wa-ter supply or quality problems—there are six important summary lessons. First, finding a means to negotiate a consensus among diverse interests and agencies not only over conflicts but also over the processes for avoiding and mitigating future conflicts is essential. Second, overcoming mutual suspicion and distrust is absolutely necessary—bargaining cannot take place except where transparency and the possibility of verifying both compliance and vio-lation of an agreement are likely. Third, finding an adequate funding base to achieve the practical objectives of ecological restoration and natural resource management is a constant challenge for any initiative. Fourth, identifying and sustaining sources of expertise that can be drawn upon to address new chal-lenges and problems is a precondition for long-term success. Fifth, a good base of fundamental data and information about environmental conditions and how these conditions are affected by changes in economic and other condi-tions is important. Finally, the experiences of the initiatives reviewed in chap-ter 4 reveal the importance of meaningful citizen participation in embracing sustainability objectives and empowering stakeholders with a sense of policy ownership. While all these measures can go a long way toward meeting the challenges water initiatives face, it should not be assumed that the challenges themselves won't remain formidable. We now turn to some of those challenges we deem most important—today and for the foreseeable future.

CONTINUING CHALLENGES: CLIMATE CHANGE, DEMAND-SIDE MANAGEMENT, AND CONSERVATION

In its analysis of the future of global water management, the Organization for Economic Cooperation and Development concluded that significant changes in the pricing, allocation, and management of water supplies will be important in order to achieve more efficient and ecologically sustainable water consumption patterns (OECD 1997). Its examination of water policy options yielded the following conclusions that remain relevant today. First, integrated water management must consider both production and demand-side pressures. Second, the optimal allocation of water resources requires a full recognition of the environment as a "user" and the ability to identify the minimum water requirements to support ecological systems. Third, developing more appropriate institutional structures and strengthening the information base on available resources, environmental pressures, and present and future demand are critical needs. Finally, explicit mechanisms to promote user "ownership" of water issues and involvement and responsibility in water policy planning and implementation are needed.

Worldwide, as we have seen, the management of water supply is approaching a crossroads. The demand for freshwater for human consumption has increased fourfold in the last 50 years, during which time the world's population has approximately doubled. At the same time, supplies are decreasing due to point and nonpoint source pollution. The combined effect of a 100 percent increase in population size, a 100 percent increase in per capita water consumption, and a steady decline in supplies of sufficient quality for human use has created more potential than ever before for intense competition for finite water resources. Some projections estimate that 13 to 20% of the world's population will be living in water-scarce countries by 2050. Most of these will be in the Middle East and Africa, but four continents will be affected (OECD 1997).

Water demands are increasing in part due to population growth. The southeast United States—a region that, as we saw in chapter 3, is just beginning to experience the types of water supply challenges and disputes that have long been characteristic of the western United States—is projected to grow by 50% by 2040. Moreover, three of the nation's fastest-growing states (Florida, Georgia, and North Carolina) are located in this region—and all have begun to ex-

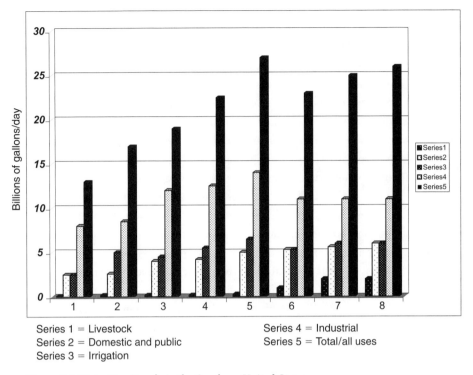

Series 1 = Livestock
Series 2 = Domestic and public
Series 3 = Irrigation

Series 4 = Industrial
Series 5 = Total/all uses

Figure 6.1. Water Use Trends in the Southern United States
Sources: Solley, Pierce, and Perlman (1998); Solley (1998)
Key: 1 = 1960; 2 = 1965; 3 = 1970; 4 = 1975; 5 = 1980; 6 = 1985; 7 = 1990; 8 = 1995

perience serious internal and external water supply conflicts, as we have seen. In addition, however, demand patterns are changing (see figure 6.1).

Although water use by industry has, over time, actually declined as a result of the Clean Water Act—which encourages manufacturers to recycle, reuse, and conserve—water-domestic and agricultural needs have been increasing in this region of the United States (see, for example, Arrandale 1999; Feldman 2000). Moreover, until recently, instream flow benefits, including protection of fish and wildlife habitat and endangered species, pollutant dilution, and recreation have been ignored by national policymakers. Finally, consumptive water uses that remove and do not immediately return water from a basin continue to grow, in part due to irrigation.

A legitimate question one can raise is: to what extent are the pressing water supply problems that are embroiling certain parts of the nation in political conflict a microcosm of things to come? Do these trends portend a true crisis, or are they temporary setbacks due to periodic drought, sudden population growth, or other issues? Overall, one would have to conclude that these trends do portend a major—if gradual—change in water problems. Despite this prognosis, there are actually some reasons for optimism.

Attempts during the late 1990s to identify concerns of key stakeholder groups within the region stemming from efforts to bring together state and local government water, environmental, and economic development officials as well as representatives from environmental and community groups and even federal officials suggests that there is widespread and growing consensus that water supply problems are now a permanent part of the region's policy agenda.[1] There appears to be broad agreement on four priorities: (1) improving acquisition and dissemination of reliable and consistent regional water data; (2) increasing state and regional water conservation and end-use efficiency efforts; (3) better education of the public and decision-makers on water supply issues; and (4) improving regional water management planning and capacity to resolve conflict. Because decision-makers are increasingly willing to support these measures, it is clear that these priorities have a national importance transcending any particular region.

Climate Change . . . Again

Competition for water resources—in every region—is likely to be exacerbated by global climate change. Human activities, especially those related to the burning of fossil fuels, have increased carbon dioxide (CO_2) levels in the atmosphere. This increase in CO_2 has the potential to warm the earth's climate by the so-called greenhouse effect, in which CO_2 absorbs infrared radiation and re-radiates it back toward the earth's surface. Other gases generated by human activities also act as greenhouse gases and may warm the climate even more (Mahlman 1997).[2]

Although there is considerable uncertainty about the precise effects of such climate change, there is a growing consensus among scientists that weather patterns and soil moisture levels over large regions will change. Some models predict that most of the interior of North America will become drier, particularly during the summer. This would be the result of a northward movement of the mid-latitude rain belt, earlier onset of winter snowmelt and spring runoff, and increased evaporation during the summer months. Only the Pacific and Gulf Coasts are predicted to be spared this drying trend. Even the higher precipitation predicted for the deep South is expected to contribute little to groundwater recharge, because the increase in precipitation is likely to be in the form of tropical storms (Clarkson and Smerdon 1989).

If precipitation patterns change, efforts to alleviate inland shortages by the inter-basin transfer of water from coastal areas may intensify. Increases of absolute precipitation in the Gulf and Pacific coastal areas might create the impression that those areas have abundant water supplies that can be shared with other regions. However, those precipitation increases are expected to be in the form of intense tropical storms that contribute little to groundwater supply. Furthermore, reservoir management for flood control during and immediately following such storms would require maintaining low reservoir levels. Since tropical storms occur most often during the summer, the greatest need for floodwater storage capacity will coincide with the period of highest demand for water supply. Thus, it is unlikely that coastal areas will have any more surplus water than at present and might even have less.

What will these changes mean to water supplies? According to Clarkson and Smerdon (1989), increases in temperature are likely to be accompanied by an increase in demand for water at the same time that surface water supplies are adversely affected. Less precipitation will result in a reduction in stream base flows, and increased evaporation from the surface of reservoirs will significantly reduce the amount of available stored water. A two-degree rise in mean annual temperature with an associated 10% decrease in total precipitation could result in a 40 to 60% reduction in annual surface water supplies.

Planning for water development projects is greatly complicated by the high sensitivity of water availability to climate change. Planning and managing reservoirs for the dual purposes of water storage and flood control is especially problematic. The specter of prolonged drought calls for maximizing water storage, whereas the probability that storms will be more intense implies a strategy of maintaining low reservoir levels. Moreover, other water resource challenges are likely to arise. It will become uneconomical to grow many of the crops that are currently sustained by irrigation, increased salinity of estuaries will damage fisheries and wildlife, and sea level rise and salt-water intrusion into coastal freshwater aquifers will reduce the availability of groundwater suitable for human uses (Clarkson and Smerdon 1989; see also Riebsame 1992).

The need for more efficient and equitable management of water supplies is already evident under current conditions. Even with the uncertainties regarding the precise effects of global climate change, it is very likely that more frequent and prolonged periods of adverse conditions can be expected over at least the next century. Most of the desirable reservoir sites have already been used. These observations underscore the immediate, urgent need for greater water conservation as well as a system for effective, regional collaboration in planning for surface water resources that sustain all life.

These challenges are proving difficult to resolve, in part because traditional management approaches alone will not solve them. Those approaches seek to build more storage reservoirs and divert water from one drainage basin to another. In many regions of the world, building more dams is unlikely to be an option of more than limited value because surface water supplies and suitable dam sites are nearly fully developed everywhere. Moreover, there are few prospects for building new dams without significant public opposition in virtually every country—China's success in building the Three Gorges Dam notwithstanding. In fact, international as well as domestic opposition to that project may end up producing the kind of delayed policy reaction so often seen elsewhere: it will hasten opposition to other new water projects elsewhere by providing a model for what happens when public participation fails. Elsewhere, global opposition to renewed inter-basin diversion raises prospects for conflict between water-importing and -exporting regions over losses of water rights and economic impacts. In short, innovative approaches are needed that encourage collaboration among stakeholders.

Demand-Side Management: The Future of Water Conservation

Water resource professionals, public officials, and water scientists have long been intrigued with the prospect of improving the efficiency of water use by using less water and using it more efficiently in given applications and uses ranging from agricultural and industrial consumption to cooling and diluting pollution (Gleick and Adams 2000). In water-scarce regions especially, there has developed a considerable body of research that has examined ways to conserve water in order to use available supplies better; to minimize the social dislocations, economic costs, and environmental impacts of developing additional sources; and to forestall the need to undertake new investments in water supply infrastructure. Moreover, there is widespread agreement that conservation is not merely a "feel-good" endeavor based on some idealistic notion of using less water as a measure of personal virtue or civic pride (Platt and DelForge 2001) but a useful and valuable means of augmenting water supply.

For adaptive management, conservation poses two challenges. The first is the need for decision-makers to be absolutely clear and realistic about the objectives they seek to achieve (ITPF 2000). The second is *how to achieve* it. While there is wide consensus over the value of conservation, how to induce people to conserve water is a topic laden with controversy—mainly because there is not much agreement over the efficacy and applicability of various methods intended to get people to use less (AWWA Government Affairs 1995).

There are many technical and operational methods available to water utilities and other water suppliers to achieve reductions in water use, including improvements in plumbing, public education, industrial and commercial water reuse and changes in agricultural irrigation—among many others (Gleick and Adams 2000: 117–118). Moreover, in the United States, the Energy Policy and Conservation Act of 1992 requires the adoption of numerous conservation-related technologies like low-flow plumbing fixtures and toilets. Ultimately, however, achieving conservation, social scientists realize, is quite difficult to encourage. The reasons for this are not so much technical as economic, educational/pedagogical, and political.

Among the reasons conservation is difficult to encourage is that the general public is unsure whence it derives its water and thus often fails to realize its role in water demand and its potential role in water savings (Kenney 2000). This is an educational issue, which requires greater information about water use and the public's effect on it. Moreover, it has long been known that water use is relatively "inelastic" to changes in price (Nauges and Thomas 2000). Doubling the cost of water in metropolitan areas achieves, on average, only about a 20% reduction in demand. From an economic perspective, this means that encouraging conservation is a far more complicated issue that one might initially presume. Efforts to use price as a conservation tool must be sustained over long periods of time and cannot assume linear responses to marginal increases in price. A related issue is that the public is probably equally uncertain as to how it uses its water, especially in residential applications (see figure 6.2). Again, this is an issue requiring greater dissemination of information to the public.

Figure 6.2 makes clear that outdoor water uses in the United States account for well over half of most residential needs. Moreover, these outdoor uses are far more discretionary than indoor ones. We know, for example, that people exercise greater choice in reducing lawn irrigation or washing cars than they do in showering or flushing toilets—and outdoor uses decline more rapidly when prices rise (ITPF 2000). One recent study in California claims that the use of "cost-effective, well-tested, and readily available technologies and practices" can dramatically reduce outdoor water uses (Haasz 2002). In short, there

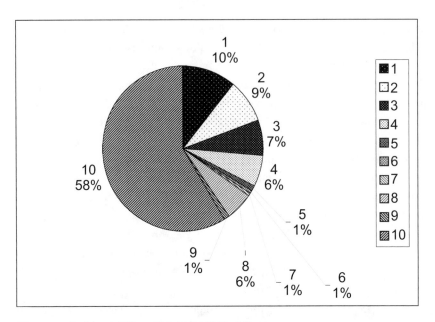

Figure 6.2. Residential Water Use in the United States
Source: ITPF (2000)
Key: 1, toilet; 2, clothes washer; 3, shower; 4, faucet; 5, other domestic; 6, bath;
7, dishwasher; 8, leak; 9, unknown; 10, outdoor.

are many factors—environmental, economic, and cultural—that influence conservation. Here are a few that gave been discovered by researchers in recent years:

- Homes with in-ground sprinkler systems use 35% more water outdoors than those without in-ground systems.
- Households that maintain gardens use 30% more water outdoors than those without.
- Because outdoor water use is more discretionary than indoor use, the former declines more rapidly when prices rise (ITPF 2000: 10).
- Contrary to widespread conception, consumer water demand *does not* increase with income. In fact, water use and income share an "inverse-U" relationship. While low-income citizens use less water per capita, so do higher-than-average income people—the intensity of freshwater use may actually decline with income growth, probably due to greater efficiencies in water use (Rock 2000).
- While individual consumer choices toward water use and lifestyle can

have a dramatic, cumulative effect on conservation, the importance of large water-intensive sectors (for example, electric power generation) on conservation efforts should not be ignored (see "California Energy Challenge" 2001; Association of California Water Agencies 2001; Carns 2001).

- At the beginning of this section, we stated that decision-makers must be clear about conservation objectives: Conservation is not only about reducing water use but also about vigilantly managing supply. In the United States, up to 10% of all homes is responsible for 58% of leaks found. Households with pools have 55% greater overage leakage than other households.

So what do we know about effective conservation programs, and how do these lessons apply to adaptive management for sustainable development? Three lessons are paramount. First, conservation programs are most effective when introduced in phases. The usual first step is to change public attitudes gradually by education in public schools and the media. This builds consensus around the principle of conservation and helps involve the public in suggesting the most feasible ways to achieve the objective of conservation (Nero 1995). Second, after educational strategies have been introduced, price incentives, rebates for conserving, and other economic alternatives can be introduced (see, for example, Noble-Goodman 2001). Requiring conservation through law or regulation and achieving a change in public behavior toward water use are generally found to be most effective after these introductory steps have been introduced.

Third, the most widely cited successful conservation programs operate in Western states such as Arizona, California, and Washington and tend to run the gamut from "mandatory" to "voluntary." The choice of emphasis in strategy seems to depend upon the context in which it is applied—in some places and under certain conditions, mandatory measures may be publicly acceptable; in others, it probably will not be. In all cases, the mix of strategies depends upon the community or other entity in which the strategy is introduced. Most successful conservation programs appear to draw on features that are part voluntary and part mandatory. For the purposes of illustration, Tucson, Arizona, and Southern California—areas of the country that face comparable water supply constraints—have embarked on two different conservation approaches.

Tucson's Water Waste Ordinance of 1983 imposes fines and penalties for sprinkling sidewalks and driveways, inappropriate use of water on one's own property, and other infractions. The city offers free training and auditing of home irrigation systems as well as mandatory "conservation seminars" for repeat violators in an effort to encourage conservation ("Tucson Saves Water" 2000). Its water waste deterrence program is combined with an aggressive program of effluent reuse and groundwater recharge (Natural Resources Law Center 1997: 46).

California's "Urban Water Conservation Council and Memorandum of Understanding" or MOU of 1991, represents a different strategy toward conservation. The MOU embraces 150 agencies and 13 million people throughout Southern California. Each agency and its jurisdiction agrees to adopt a series of 16 "best management practices" (BMPs) to reduce water use, and various "self-auditing" procedures have been adopted for use by large water users and even some smaller ones (California Urban Water Conservation Council 2001). Proponents of the MOU argue that by 2010, the plan will save at least one million acre-feet of water that would have otherwise been used. On the other hand, some charge that because the MOU is voluntary, some communities are not aggressively implementing the BMPs (Natural Resources Law Center 1997).

If the above cases represent somewhat polar opposites, then Seattle's water conservation efforts represent a "middle way" between these extremes, one that depends strongly on an adaptive approach. Through a combination of public education programs that stress the importance of conservation to protect salmon during critical spawning periods to utility company rebates for customer purchases of water-saving appliances and the availability of "self-tracking" point systems for marking their own water use, Seattle-area users have reduced per capita water use by 20% (Noble-Goodman 2001).

In effect, there is no dearth of possible water conservation models available that can be adopted by states and communities in the United States and other nations. The real challenge lies in identifying the particular needs states and communities face and the best means to satisfy them. Three policy challenges are suggested by the available information on conservation programs. First, demand-side management programs do not simply come about out of good will or progressive thinking. They are encouraged by growing competition for limited supplies, increasing costs in providing supply, delays in capacity expansion, and growing public awareness of—and support for—the need to conserve to support other policy objectives, as in Seattle (AWWA Government Affairs 1995). Public awareness and public education programs have a nearly incalculable value in promoting conservation. Such programs not only raise public consciousness but also may provide the public with specific options and approaches to reduce their own water use and create "water efficient homes" (see Dickinson 2001).

Second, the advantages of conservation are clearly well documented, and experts have long been familiar with a number of technical fixes (reducing UAW, retrofitting of older plumbing systems in major metropolitan communities, and so on). What is needed are not more examples but rather a better understanding of what would best fit the particular needs of different communities whose culture, economies, history of water use, and experience with water problems differ from the experiences of those that successfully initiated conservation programs.

Finally, given the efforts made on the domestic/household use side, greater effort could be expended on encouraging large water users (power generators, even water utilities—water treatment being an energy intensive enterprise) to undertake efforts beyond those attempted or contemplated to reduce water use. There is an emerging body of research pointing to the connection between energy and water conservation ("California Energy Challenge" 2001; Association of California Water Agencies 2001; Carns 2001).

A recent campaign begun in California, in part as a result of that state's recent energy problems, is designed to encourage electric utilities, water utilities, communities, and public agencies to understand the relationship between energy and water demand as well as to foster practical methods to reduce both sets of demands. Centered on a series of educational efforts, the program is designed to convey to citizens and organizations the link between energy and water saving devices like high efficiency washing machines, high-efficiency agricultural irrigation devices and techniques as well as an increased awareness of the impact that large users have on energy and water use.

California's water supply problems are unique in part because the state's water supply plan is mostly designed to move water around the state—especially from north to south. What we did not note earlier is that this large-scale movement of water accounts for nearly 40% of the state's total energy supply. Thus, reducing water demand at the end-user level also reduces the need to pump water from lakes, reservoirs, and groundwater basins—thus saving energy *and* water. Conversely, reducing agency needs for pumping and treating water also helps customers save water. For example, local or other ordinances that mandate irrigation of farms and yards during off-peak energy demand periods need not conserve only electricity, but water too—since such periods of off-peak demand tend to correlate with low evapo-transpiration periods (see, for example, "California Energy Challenge" 2001: 11).

There are at least two lessons here for other states as well. First, large institutional reductions in water use, as for energy use, still boil down—in the final analysis—to inducing changes in consumer demand. If end users reduce their electricity consumption, they relieve energy providers from having to generate electricity and, thus, using large volumes of water. Second, it is necessary to find ways to communicate the need for large as well as small end users to reduce water consumption due to the relative *impact* such users have on the problem of water conservation itself. Not only electric utilities but also water utilities can introduce a number of techniques to reduce water and energy use simultaneously.

In some regions, energy use has been shown to account for 30 to 50% of total operating costs for certain water-providing facilities, like pumping plants in California. At wastewater treatment facilities, energy accounts for 25 to 40% of operating costs. Large users can reduce demand by load shifting, adopting high-efficiency motors and drives, implementing better process optimization, and modifying equipment (Carns 2001).

While there are no panaceas for either small or large users, the ultimate lesson for both is that energy *and* water conservation efforts must be encouraged by better information-sharing and demonstration efforts and through greater awareness of the precious character of *both* resources. As in so many other areas of water use, necessity appears to be the parent of innovation and adaptation. As in other areas of state water policy reviewed earlier in this chapter, the willingness to pursue conservation appears to be the type of offspring that is born both of necessity and the intellectual need to acknowledge risk.

In conclusion, there are many technical and managerial innovations available to promote conservation. Three innovations include developing rate structures and using other economic incentives to promote wiser use of water; providing an array of user-friendly, reliable, economical water-saving devices; retaining water via wetlands, storm water retention systems, and water harvesting; disseminating information better regarding the benefits and costs of conservation and improved end-use efficiencies; and providing product evaluations of water-conserving devices and methods to consumers. The problem is not the availability of innovation—it is the willingness to be innovative when necessity dictates doing so. As we discuss in the next section, however, one should not equate a lack of innovation with an unwillingness to adapt. "Old-fashioned" methods of water management can still be consistent with adaptive management *if* they are used in beneficial, thoughtful, balanced, and appropriate ways.

What do we know about effective conservation programs and what do they teach us about adaptive management for sustainable development? Three lessons are paramount. First, conservation programs appear to be most effective when they are introduced in phases. The usual first step is to change public attitudes gradually through education in public schools and the media. This step seeks to build consensus around the principle of conservation and helps involve the public in suggesting ways to achieve the objective of conservation (Nero 1995). Second, after educational strategies have been introduced, other methods such as price incentives, rebates for conserving, and other economic alternatives can be introduced (see Noble-Goodman 2001). Finally, requiring conservation through law or regulation—and achieving a change in public behavior toward water use—is generally found to be most effective after these introductory steps have been introduced. One measure that may hasten such behavioral change is Integrated Resources Planning, or IRP.

IRP is becoming widely used as a means of "balancing water supply and demand management considerations by identifying feasible planning alternatives that meet the test of least cost without sacrificing other policy goals" (Beecher 1995). Promoted by the Army Corps of Engineers as well as by various communities across the nation confronted with rising water supply costs and prices, demand growth, resource constraints, environmental demands, and political opposition to expanding capacity through building new impoundments or diverting supplies from adjacent regions, IRP has been used as a means of addressing long-term water demands. In places as varied as California, Kansas, southern Nevada, Pennsylvania, and New Mexico, IRP has led to numerous reforms, including aquifer recharge (Wichita, Kansas), dedicated conservation (southern California), adoption of growth management strategies (Clark County/Las Vegas region), and application of least-cost planning principles to large investor-owned water utilities (Pennsylvania/New Mexico) (Warren et al. 1995; Fiske and Dong 1995).

There are a number of practical hurdles that must be surmounted to permit effective adaptation of IRP principles. First, water supply utilities must adopt new roles and responsibilities, including integration of environmental engineering, public health, financial, ratemaking, and social and economic considerations in the planning process. Second, the ability to plan effectively is constrained—to some degree—by water utility size; while large investor-owned utilities may well afford to conduct sophisticated needs analyses entailing the screening of feasible alternatives, development of scenarios for demand, and strategy evaluation, smaller utility districts might not be as able to undertake such analyses on their own.

Finally, experience shows that IRP requires a combination of self-regulation or incentive-based economic advantages as well as regulatory inducement. In short, IRP offers an "evolving" approach to water supply planning, allowing policymakers to weigh in a systematic way nonstructural means for augmenting water supply and managing demand (Beecher 1995).

Flood Abatement: Myths and Realities

At first glance, floods and flooding might not appear to be water supply issues. However, there are at least three reasons why they are. First, flooding is a natural *and* a technological hazard whose resolution and management—if done poorly—can adversely affect other water supply issues like runoff pollution or risks to municipal water quality (Kartez 1994; White 1994). Second, poor floodplain management can increase the risk of flooding, with adverse implications for other aspects of water resources management. For example, activities such as dredging, channelizing/stream straightening, and riparian development—all of which are measures traditionally taken to reduce or alleviate flooding—can also adversely affect riparian habitat and aquatic resources (see EPA 2000). For its part, riparian development also can increase the speed and force of precipitation's impacts. Third, intensive use of floodplains can expose more property to flood damage, and many protective measures taken to alleviate flooding may lead to an "illusion of safety," thus exacerbating all these problems (Faber 1996).

Fortunately, we have learned a great deal about appropriate floodplain management that can be applied to adaptive water management. Moreover, these lessons reveal the compatibility of well-reasoned structural measures with adaptive management principles. For starters, we now know that both flood damage and the costs borne by the public in repairing damage caused by flooding can be reduced through the adoption of several structural and nonstructural management measures adopted in combination. Such measures include limiting development in and around floodplains and, in some instances, relocating at-risk development; adopting early warning systems to permit those at risk to seek expedient measures to avoid damage or life-threatening situations; and flood proofing some homes and businesses (UMRBA 1993).

Perhaps surprising to some, there is a continuing place for structural measures for flood abatement out of simple necessity. This is one of the most profound lessons of Hurricane Katrina, as we discuss below. One of the prepon-
derant myths in floodplain management is that structural solutions are of little
or no value. According to one study, the 1993 Mississippi River floods would
probably have caused an additional $19 billion in damage without the exist-
ing system of federal dams, levees, and other river control structures in place
as a result of the efforts of the Army Corps of Engineers and other organizations and agencies (Wetland Initiative 1994). Rather than regard this finding
as polarizing, we should welcome such confirmation of the wisdom of *both*
projects: reducing flood risk by relocating people away from flood hazards and
ensuring that existing structural measures continue to be maintained and improved.

The lessons of Hurricane Katrina, a natural disaster that in property damage, loss of life, and arduous recovery rivals the great disasters of the previous
century (the Galveston hurricane of 1900, the San Francisco earthquake of
1906), are still being assessed. However, there is an emerging consensus on
two issues that relate to the foregoing discussion about the relative value of
structural versus nonstructural measures to abate flooding and the damages it
can cause. First, the flood damage Katrina caused to New Orleans and the Mississippi and Louisiana coasts, while not entirely preventable, could have been
reduced had long-recommended policies been properly implemented and enforced. Second, Katrina reminds us that once societies make decisions (however unwise) to settle in low-lying areas prone to floods and hurricanes, resettlement policies alone cannot avert disaster. A combination of structural and
nonstructural measures are required to make communities currently vulnerable to flood damage, storm surges, and other hurricane-induced water problems
more disaster-resilient (Subcommittee on Disaster Reduction 2005; Leatherman and White 2005; Waugh 2005).

As for the first lesson, the weaknesses of the levee system protecting New
Orleans and adjoining parishes had been known for decades. However, Congress cut funding for Corps of Engineers levee maintenance and repair due to
priorities perceived to be more urgent. And while the vulnerability of new development to flooding had been documented years before the disaster struck,
the political will to regulate such development did not exist (Leatherman and
White 2005). In effect, the disaster was caused, in part, by hubris. As one observer states: "There were few hazards in the U.S. more studied by scientists

and engineers and there was ample warning that a strong storm could cause the city of New Orleans to flood" (Waugh, 2005: 7).

The second lesson is shown by the futility of calls for "outright retreat" from the gulf coastline. In the United States, "rapidly increasing beachfront development combined with soaring real estate values make the option of retreat and abandonment politically unpalatable and popularly unacceptable" (Leatherman and White 2005: 6). While nonstructural measures such as land use plans and zoning laws that recognize hurricane risks are needed, technological fixes are also required for existing settlements. Such fixes include disaster resistant design and materials for homes and businesses, better erosion control and coastal barrier protection, more effective maintenance of wetlands, and greater hardening of infrastructure—including water supply, communications, power, and sewage (Subcommittee on Disaster Reduction 2005). In short, Katrina was a "man-made, nature-assisted disaster" (Waugh 2005: 8) prompted by inadequate—and poorly funded—implementation of policies designed to make U.S. coastal areas more resilient to hurricanes.

In the southern United States, structural measures adopted shortly after the Tennessee Valley Authority (TVA) came into existence and implemented on the Tennessee River system confirm that structural measures can be made to work well. Since the 1930s, TVA dams and other flood control measures have prevented approximately $5 billion in damages along the Tennessee and lower Ohio and Mississippi River systems—an average of $173 million annually. Of course, in some years the damages prevented will be higher than average. In the Chattanooga area, about $450 million in damages were averted from the April 1998 floods due to TVA dams. Urban areas are not the only beneficiaries of these measures. In April 1999, 2,500 acres of prime farmland around Savannah, Tennessee, saw their flood damages reduced by TVA measures (TVA 1999). In effect, the best floodplain management policies from the standpoint of effectiveness and efficiency are those that combine structural and nonstructural measures in ways that optimize their respective advantages.

There have been comparable findings in other regions and nations, but *only* when structural and nonstructural measures are systematically embraced within a comprehensive framework for river basin management. This has been shown in the SRBC and DRBC initiatives and in several of the international cases we reviewed. When structural measures have come under attack, as in the Colorado River or the Plata basin (chapter 2), the reasons are twofold. First, population dislocations caused by the construction of massive water projects have often been ignored by governments, alleviated through only half-hearted efforts, or have failed to take into account the ethical inequity of project impacts on certain populations. Second, governments have often failed to consider with the requisite seriousness alternative means of providing the benefits against flooding the projects were constructed to prevent in the first place. At times, they have produced worse problems.

Research on water projects indicates that, at times, structural mitigation measures to prevent or alleviate floods have been adopted for political reasons—that is, many federal flood control projects would not have been undertaken by local beneficiaries at their own expense. Moreover, the low percentage paid by local beneficiaries for such projects has "distorted" land use decisions "in favor of occupation of risky terrain" (see, for instance, Faber 1996). If there is one piece of good news that can be taken from this research, however, it is that these findings are now fairly widely known—so water planners and others are actually learning from prior mistakes. The adoption of many nonstructural flood abatement measures, for example, has been undertaken worldwide in part as a response to criticism that large dams are really "subsidies" to certain regions and that they encourage foolish settlement patterns in floodplains.

What must also be kept in mind, however, is that nonstructural methods are not immune to comparable criticisms. For example, how public funds should be used to "buy out misplaced occupation" is a recurring policy question following major flood events like the Mississippi River floods of 1993 or Hurricane Katrina in 2005 (see Faber 1996). The United States must seriously consider a national policy for shoreline and floodplain management. In some cases, policies to discourage settlement outright should be pursued; in other cases, where resettlement is impractical, structural measures must be pursued. In the case of New Orleans and the post-Katrina recovery, one of the things we are learning is the need to adopt coherent, consistent measures rather than project-by-project approaches to managing flood plain areas along coasts and rivers. This means adopting and enforcing region-wide zoning ordinances for development, construction standards that are consistent across communities, and structural protection measures that protect some populations while leaving others exposed (Waugh 2005). In short, whether one contemplates adopting structural, nonstructural, or both sets of measures together, the principles of adaptive management—coupled with what has been learned in the cases we have reviewed, and elsewhere—suggest that the solution adopted should be chosen after consideration of its multiple impacts. The worst mistake is to set out with the intention of instituting a structural or nonstructural solution without first being clear about the problems one is trying to resolve. Finding a balance is a worthwhile objective for adaptive water supply policymaking.

LONG-TERM POLICY RECOMMENDATIONS

Good water management starts with understanding that water is a limited resource, which requires sound information about how it is used and collaboration among those who use it. That we have generally avoided many of the worst water resource problems faced by developing nations here in the United States shows that, historically, many of our water management policies have worked pretty well. So, what reforms should be undertaken?

Any policy change should start with three major objectives designed to enhance the resiliency of the water supply of the nation, to become a policy template for international organizations and agencies to apply and adapt elsewhere, and to offer a framework for adaptive, sustainable water resources management. Policymakers should:

- Encourage states and communities to develop, with federal assistance, comprehensive water management plans that embrace many objectives and communities within drainage basins. Objectives should include flood control, domestic supply, environmental protection, navigation, energy, and agricultural/industrial needs, among others. Plans should embrace ethical, economic, cultural, and ecological concerns.
- Require that these comprehensive plans assess the benefits of water conservation and better end-use efficiency. Such an assessment can help satisfy water demand *and* reduce the need for new, large, costly water storage, distribution, and treatment projects. Such projects can generate adverse environmental or social impacts, which must later be remediated—often at federal cost. By assessing the merits of conservation, resiliency is better assured, and adaptive management is better facilitated.
- Undertake a new, broad-based national water assessment, taking as its point of departure U.S. WRC studies that are now over thirty years old. This assessment should evaluate emerging and established trends affecting water quality and supply, including possible climate change, population growth, new demands, drought impacts, and in stream flow needs.

To institute these policy objectives, we propose a domestic water supply agenda consisting of three general anchors. First, we must recognize that multi-program federal water agency budgets have shrunk in recent years, as has funding for interstate river basin commissions. In this modest budget climate, it is incumbent on states and communities to be more proactive in working together to identify water supply needs and problems *early on* so that federal agencies can optimally target their resources in ways that benefit as many water needs as possible. States and communities should be encouraged to undertake comprehensive water supply and watershed management plans that address multiple policy objectives from the start.

These objectives should include flood control, public supply, environmental protection, navigation, power, and industrial needs. These regional assessments should assess future needs, supply options, and quality/quantity relationships as conditions for receiving assistance from federal agencies to support specific water supply projects. Credit toward local or state-level cost-share obligations could be given to communities that engage in broad-scale watershed planning—rather than to efforts limited to only one or a few communities. This would provide added incentive to engage in comprehensive planning.

Second, the federal government should establish national criteria to promote better management of water supply—in the same way it provides overall standards for water pollutants and drinking water standards, for example. Two areas where water-supply standards may be needed are in stream flow and water conservation. Once standards are developed, it should be the task of states to meet them through locally tailored solutions. We now know that many threats to water supply, including nonpoint runoff, diminished stream flow, and disputes over allocation are partly attributable to unplanned growth in water demands, growing consumptive uses, and practices that encourage wasteful water use such as artificially low water prices and land-use policies that subsidize urban sprawl. These practices are most directly affected by state and local—not federal—decisions over land use and water management.

Enabling legislation should require multi-community—and, within larger communities, multi-watershed—assessments to include studies of the appropriate role of conservation and improved end-use efficiency as means of augmenting supply. This would help reduce costs for new water supply infrastructure—such as storage, distribution, and treatment facilities—as well as their adverse impacts. In short, proposals for new dams and inter-basin transfers would be linked to the adoption of demand-side management programs. These multi-community assessments should also consider the effects of urban sprawl and other land use practices on water supply.

Third, there is a need for detailed, consistent, reliable baseline data for anticipating conflict between off-stream demands on the one hand and instream needs on the other. This issue is at the heart of the ACF/ACT controversy as well as other recent water disputes. The Corps of Engineers, the U.S. Geological Survey, and other agencies could help initiate and lead an updated *national* water assessment—comparable to those undertaken by the U.S. Water Resources Council in the 1960s and early 1970s.

Enabling legislation should require a national assessment to generate consistent, reliable data for planning and to evaluate the effects of potential climate changes on available water supply and quality; population growth and changing water use patterns on water demand; and instream flow needs for fish and wildlife. This assessment should *not* aim for a "one-time" evaluation of water needs but should be the first step in a permanent state-federal data sharing, regional assessment network. This network should serve as a permanent clearinghouse to gather, compile, and update water data; to assure and certify data quality; and to encourage information dissemination to water users and public officials.

Effective change must be accompanied by efforts of citizen groups, nongovernmental organizations, and local, state, and federal officials working together to identify and resolve underlying impediments to agreement. Such efforts, originating outside of government, can encourage interests to explore problems creatively before they become contentious. Moreover, they can strengthen government efforts by establishing a sound basis for trust, especially among elected officials who have had little experience managing competing water uses during drought; undertaking inter-basin water transfer; and balancing in- and off-stream demands. While the challenges are formidable, the basis for innovative solutions has never been stronger.

As a pioneer in solutions to water resource management problems and as a nation founded upon the blessings of both abundant water and the innovative insight to find ways to prosper on those rare occasions when that abundance not there, the United States can help develop a framework for adaptive water management that can also be applied to other countries. It can also adapt within its own borders those innovations that have been introduced elsewhere. In the short term, efforts to improve the management of our own water problems will have a potentially beneficial impact on other countries such as Mexico by allowing greater diffusion of innovation (through NAFTA, for example, as we discussed in chapter 2) and by using our own supply better.

Over the longer term, having greater knowledge and insight into the conditions promoting adaptive management can help leverage the resources and talents of international aid organizations who look to the United States for leadership. Despite recent criticisms to the contrary, the United States has been the world's leader in the progressive management of natural resources for generations with regard to national parklands, forests, rangelands, antipollution policies, and environmental impact assessments. The challenges to that leadership have perhaps never been greater—but the need for such leadership has also never been higher, especially in the management of our water. The future of the planet, and of future generations, depends on it. Both deserve nothing less than the best we can accomplish.

Instructions: The following questions pertain to your involvement in, and perception of, the *Delaware River Basin Commission.* Please feel free to write on the back of this questionnaire or provide attachments if you need additional space to answer the questions or to provide information you feel is pertinent about your river basin initiative (RBI) that is not addressed in this questionnaire. *Thank you for your support in assisting us in our research! Your identity and all information provided in this survey will be kept confidential.*

1. Please indicate which of the following motivated establishing the RBI and which are current reasons for continuing it today. (Check all that apply and/or supply your own responses.) *initial current*
   a. avoiding litigation _____
   b. ensuring peaceable allocation of water supply _____
   c. meeting a regulatory compliance requirement _____
   d. enabling continued economic growth by reducing future uncertainty _____
   e. established programs failed to address an environmental problem _____
   f. crisis arose with regard to water resource or other problems _____
   g. a desire to achieve more local or regional decision-making flexibility _____
   h. a desire to be proactive in addressing a potential, future river basin problem _____
   i. other (please describe) _____

2. Which of the above was the *single most important* motivator for establishing the RBI, and which is the *single most important* motivator for maintaining it today? (Please mark appropriate letter from question #1 above.)
   _____ initial _____ current

3. Describe the processes that are currently used to negotiate decisions and develop consensus in your RBI (e.g., facilitators, mediators, public referenda, etc.).

4. What methods are, or will be, used to inform the public about the RBI and to solicit public input in its decisions? (Please check all that apply.)
    __ a. public meetings
    __ b. newsletter or other mail publication
    __ c. interactive workshops
    __ d. presentations to schools and/or other organizations
    __ e. television/radio advertising
    __ f. other

5. On average, how much public input has been received with regard to your RBI's current decisions/initiatives?
    __ a. a great deal
    __ b. some
    __ c. very little

6. Has there been a noticeable change in the degree or nature of public input in your RBI's decision making process over time?
    __ a. slight increase
    __ b. significant increase
    __ c. slight decrease
    __ d. significant decrease
    __ e. no change

7. If there has been a change in the degree of public input, to what do you attribute the change?

8. How is public input incorporated into the decisions and actions taken by the RBI?

9. How has scientific information been used in your RBI? (Check all that apply.)
    __ a. not at all
    __ b. to identify problems
    __ c. to set priorities

__ d. to formally model the dynamics (working operation) of the river
   system
__ e. to identify solutions or management options
__ f. other (describe)

10. What individuals or groups have championed the RBI?

11. What individuals or groups have opposed the RBI?

12. In whatever agreements have been reached so far, rank the following in-
    terest groups with regard to their level of influence on those decisions
    (1 = least influence, 11 = most influence).
    __ a. electric power production
    __ b. manufacturing
    __ c. economic development
    __ d. municipal government
    __ e. navigation/barging
    __ f. recreation (other than fishing)
    __ g. recreational fishing
    __ h. commercial fishing
    __ i. environmental/ecological
    __ j. Native American
    __ k. other

13. Has the influence of any of the interest groups listed in Question #12
    changed over time?   __ yes   __ no
    If yes, which ones and how?

14. Does your RBI have adequate sources of funding, staffing, and other
    resources to carry out its mission?

15. Has the adequacy of these resources changed over time?

16. If there has been a change in the adequacy of resources over time, what
    caused it? (For example, has funding been cut, or has the mission of the
    RBI been expanded with no concurrent increase in funding?)

17. What is your source of funding?

18. What was, or is, the most significant obstacle to establishing the RBI?

19. How was this obstacle overcome, or how do you think it can be overcome?

20. What was/is the most significant obstacle to the RBI achieving its goals?

21. How was this obstacle overcome (or, how will it likely be overcome)?

22. How successful has the RBI been in meeting its goals?
    __ a. very successful
    __ b. somewhat successful
    __ c. somewhat unsuccessful
    __ d. completely unsuccessful
    __ e. too soon to judge

23. Have formal means been developed to assess RBI effectiveness?
    __ yes __ no
    If yes, what are they?

24. What factors have most contributed, or will likely most contribute, to the success or failure of the RBI?

25. Has your RBI created (or will it create) a new permitting, certification, or other formal mechanism for approval of projects that affect water quality or supply? __ yes __ no
    If yes, please describe.

26. Would you like a copy of our final project report? __ yes __ no

Thank you for taking the time to participate in our survey.

Notes

Epigraph: Scully (2000).

1. According to the PAGE analysis from which the World Resources Institute and the World Bank draw their definition of stress, as of 1995 some 2.3 billion people (41% of the world's population) live in river basins under stress, that is, with per capita water supply below 1,700 m³/year. Of these, some 1.7 billion people reside in highly stressed basins where water supply falls below 1,000 m³/year. The PAGE analysis projects that, if current consumption patterns continue, by 2025 at least 3.5 billion people (48% of the world's population) will live in water-stressed basins. Of these, 2.4 billion will live under high-stress conditions.

2. The cities and their estimated 2000 populations (in millions) are Dhaka, Bangladesh (11.5); Lagos, Nigeria (13.5); New Delhi, India (11.7); Cairo, Egypt (10.8); Calcutta, India (12.7); Seoul, South Korea (12.9); and Bombay/Mumbai, India (18.1). See WRI 1995: 400.

3. The U.S. Geological Survey continues to monitor the effects of land use on water quality and has reported on various efforts to reduce inflows of suspended solids, heavy metals, and nutrients through detention ponds, stream buffers, and other tools. Studies indicate that, in areas experiencing rapid population growth, dramatic impacts to aquatic life and stream water quality result from intensive land use development. However, these impacts can be mitigated by "best management practices" (USGS 2002).

4. The EPA has also produced a series of reports on the possible effects of climate change in states (EPA 1999b). Aspects of water resources evaluated in these reports include the effects of climate change on precipitation and runoff; degraded water quality due to higher water temperatures (and greater effects on cold-water fisheries); lower dissolved oxygen levels, which makes pollution-dilution problematic; increased flooding; and disruptions of navigation. While uncertainty also characterizes the findings of the EPA's reports, their underlying policy recommendations are similar to those made by the GCRP in stressing adaptive management: in effect, they claim, states would be in a far better position to manage the possible effects of global climate change on water resources if they pursued efforts to reduce supply vulnerabilities now.

5. "Another 29 basins will descend further into scarcity by 2025, including the Jubba, Godavari, Indus, Tapti, Syr Darya, Orange, Limpopo, Huang He, Seine, Balsas, and Rio Grande" (WRI 2000).

6. William Finnegan has suggested that in countries such as Bolivia, corporate strategic planners should view freshwater shortages as an opportunity for privatization, citing an official from the European Bank for Reconstruction and Development: "Water is the last infrastructure frontier for private investors" (Finnegan 2002: 43–53).

CHAPTER 2: U.S. AND INTERNATIONAL WATER RESOURCE
MANAGEMENT EFFORTS

Epigraph: Speech at the 2001 Stockholm Water Symposium.

1. Some (Cairo 1997) argue that the classic interstate water compact and the interstate water resources commission—a newer device—are similar in that they both derive their authority from the compact clause of the U.S. Constitution (Article I, Sect. 10, clause 3). This clause mandates congressional consent when states enter into binding agreements with one another. Nonetheless, because of their unique history and evolution, we discuss them separately.

2. The term *basin* has a somewhat different connotation in other geographic contexts (for example, the Great Basin in Nevada and Utah). In such contexts it signifies a depression that has no outlet to the sea.

3. Recent research has uncovered a technical monograph prepared in 1939 for the Norris Dam—the TVA's first project on the Clinch River. It suggests that opportunities for river development may have earlier antecedents than first thought by stating that water control in the Tennessee Valley was an issue as far back as 1824 when Secretary of War John C. Calhoun recommended improvements "as apart of a broad waterway development plan" (Wilson 2003: A1).

4. For those who insist that the major water quality problems within reservoirs stem from the existence of dams, at least as far as the TVA system goes, this does not appear to be the case. According to one fisheries biologist with the TVA, the aquatic life of Norris Lake—the agency's oldest reservoir—and the tail waters below Norris Dam are "as diverse as any place on the planet." What remains a problem, however, is pollution caused by shoreline development and lake user activities. This pollution includes human and animal wastes, trash, and debris (Wilson 2003).

5. It was named for the original canyon it was to be built in—Boulder Canyon. The actual dam site was Black Canyon, further downstream of Boulder Canyon.

6. While it was initially formed in 1961 by executive order and called the President's Water Resources Council, its powers of comprehensive planning had to wait until congressional authorization four years later.

7. There are a number of analyses of Carter's decision to generate a "hit list" of water projects, to strengthen the Water Resources Council, to confront Congress over water policy, and to attempt to create a new national water policy (see, for instance, Fradkin 1996). Few analyses, however, have actually drawn from the former president's own reflections. In 2001, Carter discussed his rejection, as governor of Georgia, of the Sprewell Bluff Dam, a proposed Corps of Engineers Flint River flood control project: "If anybody had wanted to go back and look at [their] analysis of benefits that would accrue in tourism, they would find that those benefits are just a complete passel of lies and ex-

aggerations to justify a project the Corps wanted to construct, and that a member of congress wanted to have constructed. . . . When I became President . . . the Sprewell Bluff Dam even was a very important memory for me, an experience that was instructive" (Carter 2001: 15).

8. In 1983, the "Principles and Standards" were repealed by the WRC, now a vestige of its former self. They were replaced by a set of guidelines called the "Economic and Environmental Principles and Guidelines for Water and Related Land Resources Implementation Studies." The significance of this change was more than semantic—they were removed from the rules section of the Federal Register and placed in the notice section— thus becoming, according to a National Research Council study, "guidelines rather than rules for agency planning" (National Academy of Sciences 1999: 16; see also Eisel, Seinwill, and Wheeler 1982).

9. The six river basin agencies are the Loire, the Seine, the Somme, the Rhine, the Rhone, and the Garonne.

10. These national prices, used for relative comparison, are for 2001.

11. Hungary claims that water quality has markedly improved in its portion of the Danube and that monitoring of quality at inflow and outflow points indicate that water quality is virtually indistinguishable (Institute of Hydrology 1994: 50–51).

12. The purpose of this plan was to strengthen consultation procedures among countries in the basin to facilitate the exchange of information and discussion among countries to ensure that input into national plans and actions is received at all levels and that "the people who will affect, and be affected by, [their] implementation" will support them (Beach et al. 2000: 86–87).

13. This "old" water management regime was also, Mumme suggests, territorially defensive (sought to secure the dominion of each country over resources on its respective side-and to assure water rights), exclusive (limited to a narrow range of participants); and distributive (interested in providing substantive benefits to members of the user community) (Mumme 1995: 828–829). In short, it sought to maximize economic benefits and minimize broad participation. It did not adhere to what now think of as sustainable values—a conscientious attempt to balance economic development with environmental protection needs—or promote social justice.

14. Russia is a good example, since the importance of civil society as a basis for environmental reform has arisen frequently since the fall of the USSR. According to economist Leonid Polishchuk, the Russian term for "civil society," *grzhdanskoe obshchestvo,* means a society based "on the rule of law with limited government and sovereign citizens enjoying a comprehensive set of civil rights" (1997: 4). Clearly, these are the preconditions needed by any institutions charged with representing public views on natural resource protection and economic development.

CHAPTER 3: FIVE U.S. RIVER BASIN INITIATIVES

Epigraph: DRBC document available at www.state.nj.us/drbc/vision.htm.

1. Questionnaires were mailed with a cover letter explaining the purpose of the survey. Pre-addressed, stamped envelopes were enclosed for use in returning the completed

questionnaires. The cover letter also invited respondents to request an electronic copy of the survey if they wished to respond by e-mail. Reminder letters were mailed approximately one month after the initial mailing, and a duplicate copy of the questionnaire was sent to each of the NPPC and ACF key participants due to the especially low rate of response from those initiatives.

2. Heritage Foundation's recommendation to eliminate federally chartered river basin commissions such as the DRBC and the SRBC actually took as its point of departure prior efforts, by the Department of the Interior, to eliminate the so-called Level II river basin commissions established under the Water Resources Planning Act of 1965. This move, under the Reagan administration, was predicated on the conclusion that "commissions do not perform any function or provide any service that states are not able to accomplish themselves." While the General Accounting Office remained sanguine about recommending restoration of RBCs under this act, it did state that the commissions made "meaningful contributions to water resources planning" through providing a "forum for communication" and by "coordinating studies." The GAO recommends that, if retained, they be empowered to incorporate the participation of state and regional input in a meaningful way (U.S. GAO 1981).

3. However, it is not the very first controversy in the region. A serious dispute arose in the 1970s between North Carolina and Virginia over plans for diverting about 10 million gallons per day (mgd) from the Roanoke River along the North Carolina-Virginia border to satisfy the growing demands of Virginia Beach, Virginia, and other surrounding coastal communities. In part, as with the ACF controversy, the dispute between North Carolina and Virginia led, at first, to litigation and protracted controversy over allocation issues. After a series of failed court challenges and attempts at encouraging federal agency intervention against the project, Virginia unilaterally went ahead with a pipeline, which went into operation in 1998. What the controversy did not result in, however, was a compact between the three states—nor to a cooperative and durable solution to future water allocation problems (see Leahy 1998). For background on regional disputes in the Southeast, see Arrandale (1999: 30–34).

4. The largest consumptive user of water in the region is Mississippi, which consumes fully half the water it withdraws—while the lowest is Tennessee, with 3% consumption.

5. For a discussion of the Shared Vision Modeling approach and its application in the ACF, see: Palmer (1998a, b).

6. See the Clean Water Act of 1972, Section 101(a)(2).

7. The Fish and Wildlife Service, the EPA, and other federal agencies, as well as affected states and stakeholder groups, have attempted to arrive at a means to protect instream flow—in support of the ACF negotiations—by developing credible guidelines for allocation. Aside from efforts to ensure a minimum flow that would adequately protect "the present structure and function of the riverine environment" (EPA 1999b; see also EPA 2002), protagonists have also tried to promote a cooperative effort by the federal government and the three ACF states to improving monitoring of streams to measure ecological responses to flow changes, to collect basic data on flow alteration impacts, to assess the effects of water management options, and—most of all—to ensure an adap-

tive management system for water allocation. And, despite the negotiating impasse among the three states, Georgia has sought to develop a Comprehensive Water Plan that, among other things, would address the problem of protecting minimum flows. Early on, a controversy erupted in Georgia over whether stream flow was a statewide issue or one confined to some parts of the state—a debate that underscores the political and economic sensitivity of the issue (see Georgia BNR 2001; see also Krueger 2001).

8. In *Kansas v. Colorado* (1907), the Supreme Court stated: "One cardinal rule, underlying all the relations of the states to each other, is that of equality of right. Each state stands on the same level with all the rest. It can impose its own legislation on no one of the others, and is bound to yield its own views to none" (206 U.S., 97, quoted in Grant 1998). Because of this, the Court applies federal common law to make an apportionment. It is also generally reluctant to take on interstate disputes over water allocation. In crafting an apportionment, however, the general principle is that the court will avoid appointing a federal master to administer a river or otherwise entangle itself in river management. When willing to make adjustments, it desires to avoid lengthy entanglements and thus allocates a set amount of water to a state while disregarding actual flow in a river (Grant 1998).

9. According to Getches (1998c), these included coho, sockeye, chinook, chum, and humpback species.

10. Over time, it may turn out that the costs of restoration of the Everglades ecosystem exceed this figure by a considerable margin.

11. The agreement of December 15, 1994, provided that spring export limits would be expressed as a percentage of delta inflow; the "salinity gradient" in the estuary would be regulated so that salt concentrations of two parts per thousand would be maintained (a number deemed beneficial to aquatic life); spring flows on the lower San Joaquin would be geared to the protection of Chinook salmon; and the Delta Cross Channel gates would be closed intermittently to reduce entrainment of fish into the Delta. See CALFED Bay Delta Program (1999).

12. Funding for CALFED remains a contentious issue, and a number of cutbacks have been made in new reservoir work and other programs. Also, the program remains subject to the viccisitudes of congressional budgetary processes (see, for instance, Doyle 1994).

13. California is legally entitled to 4.4 million acre-feet/year but had been using 5.2 million.

14. As regards underground storage, California recently rejected one option that proved to be controversial on at least two grounds—its anticipated negative environmental impacts—and its ownership and control. The so-called Cadiz Project, owned by the Brackpool Corporation—a British-owned company—would have employed a novel means of storing water underground. Cadiz, a depleted aquifer under the Mojave Desert, would have been used to store surplus water from the Colorado River pumped in by the Metropolitan water district of Southern California. In dry years, Cadiz would "sell" water through a 35-mile pipeline; in wet ones, it would replenish its own aquifer. Aside from fears that the project would have adverse effects on neighboring aquifers and aggravate groundwater recharge issues in the region, a bigger fear was that a private en-

trepreneur might not be as vigilant as a public authority in either monitoring or mitigating such problems. The project was rejected by California under pressure from Senator Dianne Feinstein and numerous environmental groups (see Booth 2002: 29).

15. Specifically, increases in salinity levels in the Salton Sea, some believe, could threaten the protection of four species—desert pupfish, brown pelican, black rail, and Yuma clapper rail. U.S. Bureau of Reclamation staff researchers have developed a Salton Sea Accounting Model to help govern and regulate the level of salt in the lake and thereby protect threatened or endangered species. While what constitutes a "safe" salinity level remains an issue of contention (see Siciliano 2002), a California Fish and Game Department finding released in late 2002 declared that proposed water transfers would have a negligible effect on total salinity levels, and therefore, on salinity-dependent species (Siciliano 2002).

16. In early 2003, the Department of the Interior confirmed the magnitude of cuts in water deliveries to the Metropolitan Water District of Southern California and the Coachella Valley Water District. Due to the failure to work out a reduction in the state's use of the Colorado River, the former will be cut about 20% while the latter will be reduced by 30% (see Siciliano 2003: 1009). In 2004, the Bush administration was threatening to impose unilateral cutbacks on California, Arizona, and Nevada unless all three states can come up with a plan to manage the Colorado River in the face of five years of continuing drought (see: Leavenworth 2004: A1–12). As of 2006, a series of countermeasures by these three states to conserve water better, including plans by the Metropolitan Water District of Southern California to leave water in the Colorado River and then receive credit for it, has allayed cutoff threats. In essence, Metropolitan has agreed to use water conserved through various land management and crop rotation measures and "bank" this surplus (50,000–200,000 acre-feet per year) in Lake Mead. In future years, if water shortages make it necessary, Metropolitan will be able to "recover" (that is, use) the water that was banked for its customers (Metropolitan Water District of Southern California 2006).

17. The Nature Conservancy's interest in adaptive management and water resources is both longstanding and national in scope. The "Rivers of Life: Critical Watersheds for Protecting Freshwater Biodiversity" project has established the goal of identifying the top 15% of the 2,100 small watershed areas in the United States that can conserve populations of all freshwater fish and mussel species that are at risk (see Nature Conservancy 1999). Battle Creek fits these criteria. The theory behind this approach is that, while at-risk freshwater species can be assessed at larger levels (like states or large watersheds/ river basins), these smaller hydrological units "reflect a scale appropriate for planning and carrying out conservation actions." The goal of the project is to help local communities use this information to develop actions to preserve the health of these watersheds. One unique feature of the effort—in California and elsewhere—is that both the data-gathering/analysis component of the initiative and the political action component are matched to the same small-watershed scale.

18. Leading many of these efforts is the Pacific Institute, a research organization based in Oakland, California, and led by Peter Gleick, a hydrologist and longtime advocate of policy reform in water resources management (see Gomez 1997).

19. Despite an initial mailing of seven questionnaires preceded by a telephone contact and followed by reminder letters, a second telephone contact, and a second mailing of questionnaires, only two responses were received from ACF participants.

20. Ten NPPC questionnaires were mailed following initial telephone contacts, and reminder letters were followed with a second questionnaire mailing, yet only one completed questionnaire was returned. After the second questionnaire mailing, a representative of the NPPC replied to the effect that no additional completed questionnaires would be returned and that it had been this individual's desire to prepare a single, unified response that represented the collective viewpoint of the commission. After one NPPC committee member completed and returned the questionnaire, it appears that there was a decision made to not send other responses that might create an appearance of a lack of solidarity within the NPPC.

21. Such ties include the signing of the Declaration of Independence in Philadelphia, five blocks from the Delaware's banks; the first public reading of this historic document in the Centre Square of Easton, Pennsylvania, three blocks from the river; the drafting of the United States Constitution in Philadelphia; General George Washington's icy trip across the Delaware with his Continental Army on Christmas Night of 1776, and his defeat of British and Hessian troops stationed in Trenton, New Jersey, a pivotal turning point in the American Revolution.

CHAPTER 4: WATER QUALITY AND QUANTITY

Epigraph: Ettenger (1998): 54; Kassen quoted by Taylor Hawes, NRLC 2000.

1. Under riparian law, water is legally and historically a public resource. Although private property rights can be "perfected" in the use of water—meaning access can be ensured—it remains essentially public; private rights are always incomplete and subject to the public's common needs. In the event of a conflict between these rights, conflicts are supposed to be resolved through the reasonable use rule that entitles each riparian proprietor to take reasonable uses of the adjoining watercourse for the benefit of his or her riparian land. A riparian's rights are not absolute: other riparians along the same watercourse also have an "equal" right to make a reasonable use of water (Butler 1990). In short, riparians "have a right to make reasonable use of a watercourse so long as such use does not interfere with reasonable uses of the water by other riparians. . . . [E]ach riparian has a right equal to the rights of other riparians along the watercourse. [The] rule requires harm to other riparians before a use can be alleged unreasonable" (Laitos and Tomain 1992: 359).

2. This margin of safety accounts for uncertainty in the loading calculation for TMDLs and may not be the same for different water bodies due to differences in the availability and strength of data used in calculations (for example, see TDEC 2002). The component parts of the TMDL equation may be depicted in the form of an equation, as follows: TMDL = Sum of Nonpoint Sources + Sum of Point Sources + Margin of Safety.

3. Current discussion centers on the so-called (but little used) "continuous planning process" (section 303(e) of the Clean Water Act) in an effort to encourage states to develop mechanisms to control all pollution sources on a watershed basis (Bruninga 2002).

4. While there are several workable definitions of an "impaired" water body used by state and federal officials, one of the clearest is that employed by California—it is both legally accurate, yet accessible to the layperson: "Informally, an impaired water body is any water that is not meeting the water quality standards that have been established for that water. Formally, an Impaired water body is one that is not attaining water quality standards after technology based discharge limits on point sources are implemented. Section 303(d) of the federal Clean Water Act requires each state to maintain a list of impaired water bodies and revise the list from time to time" (see SWRCB 2000).

5. An organization called the Corps Reform Coalition, made up of several environmental groups with an interest in water policy, has charged that the Corps "consistently abuses its authority to issue permits for wetlands destruction." The coalition has recommended that the CWA be amended to give the EPA sole regulatory authority for determining 404 compliance in projects that affect sizeable wetlands or aquatic habitat areas (Corps Reform Coalition n.d.: 10, 27). For an exposé that discusses how Corps efforts to straighten, widen, and deepen major rivers has transformed them from free-flowing streams to highly controlled waterways that often result in reductions in nutrient flow, eradication of habitat, and species decline, see Grunwald (2000a, b).

6. New York's water supply comes from five major reservoirs in the Catskills. As water quality in these reservoirs began serious deterioration in the 1960s due to sewage and agricultural runoff, the city weighed several options for restoring the quality of water in the reservoirs. It was long known that hardwood, evergreen forests have the effect of filtering pollutants and retarding erosion and that land clearance in the Catskills watersheds supplying the city with water was contributing to the problem. A series of economic analyses concluded that costs for an artificial filtration plant (NYC has no water treatment plants) could run from 6 to 8 billion dollars with an annual operating cost of $300 million. By contrast, restoring forests and preserving riparian lands around the watersheds would cost between 1 and 1.5 billion dollars through issuing bonds to raise money to purchase lands and to compensate property owners for acquiring easement rights. The issue remains controversial, however, in part due to occasional waterborne disease outbreaks.

CHAPTER 5: TOWARD SOUND ETHICAL ALTERNATIVES
FOR WATER RESOURCES MANAGEMENT

Epigraphs: Camacho (1998) and Fowler (1995).

An early version of this chapter was presented as a keynote address entitled "Covenants, Categorical Imperatives, and Stewardship Ethics: Are There Sound Alternatives to Utilitarianism for River Basin Management?" at Moving Waters: The Colorado River and the West, Northern Arizona University, Flagstaff, Arizona, September 2002. The event was sponsored by the Arizona Humanities Foundation and the National Endowment for the Humanities.

1. For a history of planning efforts—and a critique of the rigid reliance on benefit-cost analysis—see Feldman (1995). As previously noted, the Rivers and Harbors Act of 1927 requested that the Corps and the Federal Power Commission investigate the feasi-

bility and cost of developing hydroelectric projects—in combination with other functions (for instance, navigation, flood control, irrigation)—on all of the country's navigable rivers (National Academy of Sciences 1999: 11). Later, the TVA Act provided statutory authority to the Tennessee Valley Authority to manage the entire multi-state basin for flood control, power, and navigation on an economically sound basis. The agency is charged with guiding "the extent, sequence, and nature of development that may be equitably and economically advanced through the expenditure of public funds" and generally ensuring the protection of the environment and promoting regional economic development (16 U.S.C. 831; especially sect. 22).

2. It should be noted that the Bureau of Reclamation's mission and vision have undergone considerable revision. Today, it describes its goals as managing, developing, and protecting "water and related resources in an environmentally and economically sound manner in the interest of the American public." Moreover, its vision is to "seek to protect local economies and preserve natural resources and ecosystems through the effective use of water" (U.S. Bureau of Reclamation 2005).

3. Churchill and Smythe actually did use the same words. In the western United States, such a theologically metaphorical view of natural resource development generally, and of water resources policy in particular, is often identified with the Mormon tradition. In fact, however, such views on reclamation, while associated with Utah, are strongly espoused by Westerners who are not Mormons and who live in other states (see Farmer 2000).

4. Donald Worster is even more critical of the results of previous policies on governance in the West, describing the region as a "hydraulic society" characterized by "a coercive, monolithic, and hierarchical system" of control (Worster 1985: 7). The pattern described above also arose in the eastern United States in such areas as navigation, hydropower, and domestic supply (see, for example, Stine 1993). Despite continued efforts at reform, this pattern continues to dominate water supply policy, as evidenced by the difficulty in developing popularly based "watershed management initiatives" that reconcile the interests of private users, overcome jurisdictional rivalries, and include all relevant stakeholders (see Landre and Knuth 1993; Foster and Rogers 1988).

5. There is another figure whose prominence in this debate must be acknowledged: Senator George Norris, (R., Nebraska), a champion of electrification of rural America and of a public river basin authority in the Tennessee Valley. After World War I, Norris visited Wilson Dam near Muscle Shoals, Alabama—a federal project built in part to provide power for a munitions plant. Two events combined to make Norris a strong proponent of federal power and the plan that would eventually create a Tennessee Valley Authority. First, according to Nebraska State Senator David Landis, Norris's visit to Wilson Dam coincided with plans by Henry Ford to purchase the dam and munitions plant for $5 million to produce nitrogen fertilizer for farmers in the region and to sell the power to private companies. According to Landis, an authority on Norris, the latter opposed the plan because he "realized that the Ford plan would do nothing to bring power to rural farmers in the area because the power Ford sold would go to the cities 'where the money was.'" The second event influencing Norris was a set of plans forged by five private power and industrial companies between 1923 and 1926 to build a dam on the

Clinch River to provide power to cities in the region. Eventually, the project was recommended by the Corps of Engineers in 1930 and authorized but never funded—eventually Senator Norris introduced a previously vetoed plan with a provision that Tennessee receive 5% of the power generation revenues of any project. While this plan too
was vetoed, it set the stage for the full-blown policy debate over what eventually became
the TVA (see Wilson 2003: A-1, A-16).

6. See, for example, Deuteronomy 4:5–6: "See, I have taught you decrees and laws
as the LORD my God commanded me, so that you may follow them in the land you are
entering to take possession of it. Observe them carefully, for this will show your wisdom
and understanding to the nations, who will hear about all these decrees and say, 'Surely
this great nation is a wise and understanding people.'"

7. In Genesis 9, God blesses Noah and his descendants, stating: "I now establish my
covenant with you and with your descendants after you and with every living creature
that was with you-the birds, the livestock and all the wild animals, all those that came
out of the ark with you-every living creature on earth. . . . Never again will the waters of
a flood cut off all life; never again will there be a flood to destroy the earth. And God
said, This is the sign of the covenant I am making between me and you and every living
creature with you, a covenant for all generations to come: I have set my rainbow in the
clouds, and it will be the sign of the covenant between me and the earth. Whenever I
bring clouds over the earth and the rainbow appears in the clouds, I will remember my
covenant between me and you and all living creatures of every kind. Never again will
the waters become a flood to destroy all life. Whenever the rainbow appears in the
clouds, I will see it and remember the everlasting covenant between God and all living
creatures of every kind on the earth."

Moses' act was a reinvocation of a perpetual covenant. In Deuteronomy 7: 11–15,
Moses says: "Therefore, take care to follow the commands, decrees and laws I give you
today. If you pay attention to these laws and are careful to follow them, then the LORD
your God will keep his covenant of love with you, as he swore to your forefathers. He
will love you and bless you and increase your numbers. He will bless the fruit of your
womb, the crops of your land-your grain, new wine and oil-the calves of your herds and
the lambs of your flocks in the land that he swore to your forefathers to give you. You
will be blessed more than any other people; none of your men or women will be child-
less, nor any of your livestock without young. The LORD will keep you free from every
disease. He will not inflict on you the horrible diseases you knew in Egypt, but he will
inflict them on all who hate you."

8. Hobbes's distinction between a covenant—an agreement based on trust between
parties for performance of an act "at some indeterminate time"—and a contract, which
he viewed as a "mutual transference of right," is also instructive. Clearly, he appreciated
his readers' familiarity with biblical language and deliberated upon this distinction as
a logical departure from his views on religion—which saw the emergence of God as "created by human fear" (Hobbes 1958: 94, 112).

9. See, for example, Romans 8:19–21: "The creation waits in eager expectation for
the sons of God to be revealed. For the creation was subjected to frustration, not by its
own choice, but by the will of the one who subjected it, in hope that the creation itself

will be liberated from its bondage to decay and brought into the glorious freedom of the children of God." Note, also, that water baptism—a symbol of liberation from the oppression of sin that separates us from God—is a water-centered ritual. It has its origins in the symbolism of the Israelites being led by Moses out of slavery in Egypt through the Red Sea and from the baptism of Jesus by John the Baptist in the Jordan. After Jesus' resurrection he commanded his disciples to baptize "in the name of the Father, Son, and Holy Spirit" (Matthew 28:19–20).

10. Or, in New Covenant terms, "So in everything, do to others what you would have them do to you, for this sums up the Law and the Prophets" (Matthew 7:12).

11. See, for example, J. E. Johnson et al. (1962: 3).

12. Sextus argued that Rome's water system had been in decline due to (1) neglect—a lack of maintenance was common, as were water losses, and politicians refused to invest in improvements; (2) political favoritism—outright "theft" of water was not only common but was not punished if the thieves had friends in high places, and the distribution of water often favored the interests of a privileged few who lived in prosperous parts of the city (20% of the water went to the emperor's friends); and (3) declining quality—efforts to deal with pollution were often half-hearted, even though laws on the books called for stiff fines and other punishments. See Frontinus (1997).

13. As Sheridan (1998: 171) notes, when Los Angeles announced they wanted 1500 cubic feet/second of Colorado water for domestic supply, the wrath of several Arizona officials, including former Senator Carl Hayden, led to their legislature's refusal to ratify the compact and to seek to block the Boulder Canyon Project that led to construction of Hoover Dam in Congress.

14. The federal "reserved rights" doctrine posits that when the federal government removes lands from the public domain and "reserves" them for a federal purpose (for instance, Indian reservations), it reserves a portion of the water "then unappropriated . . . to fulfill the purpose of the reservation" (*Winters v. U.S.*, 207 U.S. 564, 1908; Coggins, Wilkinson, and Leshy 1993: 369). *Winters* case involved reserving unclaimed water rights on streams flowing through the Fort Belknap Indian Reservation in Montana, which was established to settle members of the Assiniboine and Gros Ventre tribes (Gillilan and Brown 1997). As restated by the U.S. Supreme Court in 1978 (*U.S. v. New Mexico*), the doctrine applies to all federal lands reserved for particular purposes, not just tribal reservations (for example, see Burton 1991: 38–41).

15. See Genesis 2:15.

16. Recent scholarship has suggested that Powell's environmental views of "progressive conservation" owed at least as much to his Methodist upbringing as to his belief in utilitarian ethics. As Donald Worster notes, for example, he was named for his parents' hero, John Wesley, and "he would grow up, they prayed, to become a spiritual leader for America." Furthermore, he was taught to "put the love of God above the things of the earth and subdue his naturally selfish will" (Worster 2001: 5). For another view of Powell and his values, see Pyne (1999).

17. See chapter 3. Recall that salmon runs have declined from an estimated 10 to 16 million to fewer than 3 million, despite over $100 million in expenditures on environmental improvements at dams and decreased hydropower production.

CHAPTER 6: WATER RESOURCES MANAGEMENT
AS AN ADAPTIVE PROCESS

Epigraphs: World Bank (2003): 57; UNWWAP (2003): 29.

1. One such effort included the Southeastern Water Policy Initiative, which involved the author of this book. Organizers included the Appalachian Regional Commission, the EPA, the Oak Ridge National Laboratory, the Southern States Energy Board, the Tennessee Valley Authority, the U.S. Geological Survey, the University of Tennessee, and local and regional environmental groups from the Southeast. Two meetings involving over 300 people were held in 1998 and 1999.

2. The increase in greenhouse gases is expected to continue for many years. A doubling of CO_2 concentrations in the atmosphere over the next 100 years due to the burning of fossil fuels and deforestation is anticipated. Computer modeling has been used to estimate the magnitude of climate change that is likely to result from such an increase in greenhouse gases. The GISS model of global climate change developed by NASA predicts that, 100 years from now, average annual temperatures will be 2° to 5°C higher than present. The GFDL model developed by the National Oceanographic and Atmospheric Administration (NOAA) predicts an increase of 6.5°C in average annual temperatures within the next 100 years. This means that the earth will not only be hotter than it has been in one million years, but the change will be more rapid than any on record (Davis and Zabinski 1991). Furthermore, the temperature increase is not expected to be uniformly experienced by all regions. Relatively little effect will be evident at the equator, whereas increases of between 7° and 14°C are predicted for polar regions (see Clarkson and Smerdon 1989).

Bibliography

Abrams, Robert H. 1990. "Water Allocation by Comprehensive Permit Systems in the East: Considering a Move Away from Orthodoxy." *Virginia Environmental Law Journal* 9 (2) Spring: 255–286.

Abu-Zeid, Mahmoud A., and Asit K. Biswas. 1996. *River Basin Planning and Management.* Calcutta, India: Oxford University Press.

"Activists to Sue EPA over Strict Florida TMDL Assessment Method." 2002. *Risk Policy Report* 9 (15) October 15: 33.

American Society of Civil Engineers [ASCE]. 1984. *Environmental Objectives in Water Resources Planning and Management.* Water Resources Planning and Management Division. New York: ASCE.

Anderson, Charles W. 1979. "The Place of Principles in Policy Analysis." *American Political Science Review* 73 (September): 711–723.

Anderson, Frederick, et al. 1999. *Environmental Protection: Law and Policy.* New York: Aspen Law and Business.

Anderson, Terry L., and Donald R. Leal. 1988. "Going with the Flow: Expanding the Water Markets." *Policy Analysis: A Cato Institute Publication* 104 (April 26).

Ankrah, Rodges. 1998. "Successful State and Local Partnerships." *Synergy: Green Mountain Institute for Environmental Democracy,* Spring: 3.

Annan, Kofi A. 2002. "Toward a Sustainable Future." *Environment* 44 (7) September: 0–15.

Arrandale, T. 1999. "The Eastern Water Wars." *Governing* (August): 30–34.

Ascher, William. 1999a. "Resolving the Hidden Differences among Perspectives on Sustainable Development." *Policy Sciences* 32: 351–377.

Ascher, William. 1999b. *Why Governments Waste Natural Resources: Policy Failures in Developing Countries.* Baltimore: Johns Hopkins University Press.

Associated Press. 2002a. "More Monitoring Shows More Pollution."

Associated Press. 2002b. "Several West Virginia Streams Fail to Meet Quality Standards."

Association of California Water Agencies [ACWA]. 2001. *Facing California's Energy Challenge: A Guide for Water and Wastewater Utilities.* Sacramento, California.

Atlanta Journal and Constitution. 1993. News brief. February 2.

Atlanta Journal and Constitution. 1998. "Deadline on Water Extended." December 19.

Atlanta Journal and Constitution. 1999. "The Water War: A Drought of Compromise." February 15: E5.

Atlanta Regional Commission [ARC]. 1997. "Atlanta Regional Water Supply Plan Update." Unpublished report. December 3.

AWWA Government Affairs. 1995. *Water Conservation and Water Utility Programs.* Approved for publication in *AWWA Mainstream,* June 28. Available at www.awwa.org/govtaff/watcopap.htm.

Babbie, Earl. 1989. *The Practice of Social Research.* 5th ed. Belmont, CA: Wadsworth.

Baer, K. E. and C. M. Pringle. 2000. "Special Problems of Urban River Conservation: The Encroaching Megalopolis." In *Global Perspectives on River Conservation: Science, Policy and Practice,* ed. P. J. Boon, B. R. Davies, and G. E. Potts, 385–402. New York: John Wiley and Sons.

Ballweber, J. A. 1995. "Prospects for Comprehensive, Integrated Watershed Management under Existing Law." *Water Resources Update* 100 (Summer): 19–27.

Barbosa, Luiz C. 2000. *The Brazilian Amazon Rain Forest: Global Ecopolitics, Development and Democracy.* Washington, D.C.: University Press of America.

Barlow, Maude, and Tony Clarke. 2002. *Blue Gold: The Fight to Stop the Corporate Theft of the World's Water.* New York: New Press.

Barry, John M. 1998. *A Rising Tide: The Great Mississippi Flood of 1927 and How It Changed America.* New York: Touchstone Books.

Bass, Berry, and Sims. 2002. "WPC Proposes TMDLs." *Tennessee Environmental Law Letter* 14 (4) May.

Beach, Heather L, Jesse Hamner, J. Joseph Hewitt, Edy Kaufman, Anja Kurki, Joe A. Oppenheimer, and Aaron T. Wolf. 2000. *Transboundary Freshwater Dispute Resolution: Theory, Practice, and Annotated References.* Tokyo: United Nations University.

Beatley, Timothy. 1994. *Ethical Land Use: Principles of Policy and Planning.* Baltimore: Johns Hopkins University Press.

Beck, Robert. E., ed. 1997. *Water and Water Rights.* Charlottesville, VA: Michie.

Beecher, J. A. 1995. "Integrated Resource Planning Fundamentals." *Journal AWWA* 87 (6) June: 34–48.

Bellah, Robert N., ed. 1996. *Habits of the Heart: Individualism and Commitment in American Life.* Berkeley: University of California Press.

Bennett, Lynne Lewis, and Charles W. Howe. 1998. "The Interstate River Compact: Incentives for Noncompliance." *Water Resources Research* 34 (3): 488–495.

Biniek, Joseph P. 1985. "Benefit-Cost Analysis; An Evaluation." In *Controversies in Environmental Policy,* ed. Sheldon P. Kaminiecki, 136–152. Albany: State University of New York Press.

Birkeland, Sarah. 2001. "EPA's TMDL Program." *Ecology Law Quarterly* 297, 301.

Blatter, Joachim, and Ingram, Helen. 2001. *Reflections on Water: New Approaches to Transboundary Conflicts and Cooperation.* Cambridge, MA: MIT Press.

Blood, Elizabeth R., and James Hook. 2003. "Science, Culture, and the Need for Local Knowledge in Understanding Process and Implementation." *Proceedings of the Ecological Society of America, 88th Annual Meeting: Uplands to Lowlands-Coastal Processes in a Time of Change,* August 3–8: 36.

Blumm, Michael. 1998. "Columbia River Basin." In *Waters and Water Rights,* vol. 6, ed. Robert E. Beck. Charlottesville, Virginia: Michie Publishing.

Bokovoy, Matthew F. 1999. "Inventing Agriculture in Southern California." *Journal of San Diego History* 45 (2) Spring, www.sandiegohistory.org/journal/99spring/agriculture.htm.

Booth, William. 2000. "Restoring Rivers—at a High Price: Ecosystems May Pay if Dams Are Demolished." *Washington Post,* December 10: A3.

Booth, William. 2002. "California's Simmering Water Wars." *Washington Post National Weekly Edition,* August 19–25: 29.

Bosch, D., et. al. 2002. "Dissolved Oxygen and Stream Flow Rates: Implications for TMDLs." In *Total Maximum Daily Load Environmental Regulations,* 92. Proceedings of the March 2002 Conference. St Joseph, Michigan: ASAE.

Boyd, James. 2000. "The New Faces of the Clean Water Act: A Critical Review of the EPA's Proposed TMDL Rules." *Resources* 139 (March).

Brahana, J. V., W. S. Parks, and M. W. Gaydos. 1987. *Quality of Water from Freshwater Aquifers and Principal Well Fields in the Memphis Area, Tennessee.* Prepared in Co-operation with the City of Memphis, Memphis Light, Gas and Water Division. Water Resources Investigations Report 87–405. Nashville, TN: U.S. Geological Survey.

Bright, John. 2000. *A History of Israel.* Westminster, England: John Knox Press.

"Bringing Down the Dam: Edwards Dam Removal." 1999. *American Rivers* (Summer) 26 (2): 6–9.

British Broadcasting Corporation [BBC]. 2003. "Water War Leaves Palestinians Thirsty." June 16, news.bbc.co.uk/1/hi/world/middleeast/2982730.stm.

Browder, Greg, and Leonard Ortolano. 2000. "The Evolution of an International Water Resources Management Regime in the Mekong River Basin." *Natural Resources Journal* 40 (3): 499–532.

Brown, Christopher. 1997. "The Watershed Approach." *River Voices* 7 (4) Winter: 1, 4–7.

Bruninga, Susan. 2002. "On 30th Anniversary of Water Act Passage, Successes Touted, But More Challenges Seen." *Special Report-Environment Reporter* 33 (41) October 18: 2279–2282.

Bueno de Mesquita, Bruce, and Hilton S. Root. 2002. *Governing for Prosperity.* New Haven: Yale University Press.

Buller, H. 1996. "Towards Sustainable Water Management: Catchment Planning in France and Britain," *Land Use Policy* 13 (4): 289–302.

Burson, James M. 2000. "Middle Rio Grande Regional Water Resource Planning: The Pitfalls and the Promises." *Natural Resources Journal* 40 (3) Summer: 533–569.

Burton, Lloyd. 1991. *American Indian Water Rights and the Limits of Law.* Lawrence: University Press of Kansas.

Butler, Lynda L. 1990. "Environmental Water Rights: An Evolving Concept of Public Property." *Virginia Environmental Law Journal* 9 (2) Spring: 323–379.

Cairo, Richard A. 1997. "Dealing With Interstate Water Issues: The Federal Interstate Compact Experience." In *Conflict and Cooperation on Trans-Boundary Water Resources,* ed. Richard E. Just and Sinaia Netanyahu. Boston: Kluwer.

Caldwell, Lynton K. 1947. "Interstate Cooperation in River Basin Development." *Iowa Law Review* 32: 232–243.

CALFED Bay-Delta Program. 1999a. *Overview.* Sacramento, California: CALFED Bay-Delta Program. Available at calfed.ca.gov/general/overview.html.

CALFED Bay-Delta Program. 1999b. *Working Together for a Solution.* Sacramento: CALFED Bay-Delta Program.

CALFED Bay-Delta Program. 2005. "Battle Creek Salmon and Steelhead Restoration Project. Agency Response to Initial Recommendation from California Bay-Delta Authority Ecosystem Restoration Program Selection Panel." CALFED Ecosystem restoration program. Sacramento, California: June 20.

Calhoun, Fryar. 1999. "Run, River, Run: Dams to Come Down on a California Stream." *Nature Conservancy* 49 (6) November/December: 6.

"California Energy Challenge." 2001. *Water Conservation News* (July): 9, 11.

California State Water Resources Control Board [SWRCB]. 2002. "Total Maximum Daily Loads (TMDL) Questions and Answers." Available at www.swrcb.ca.gov/tmdl/docs/tmdl_factsheet.pdf.

California Urban Water Conservation Council. 2001. *Partners for a Water-Efficient California.* Available at www.cuwcc.org.

Camacho, David E. 1998. "Environmental Ethics as a Political Choice." In *Environmental Injustices, Political Struggles: Race, Class, and the Environment,* ed. David Camacho, 210–224. Durham, NC: Duke University Press.

"Canada Implements Regulations to Prohibit Bulk Water Exports From Boundary Waters." 2002. *Environment Reporter* 33 (49): 2698.

Caney, Simon. 2001. "Review Article: International Distributive Justice." *Political Studies* 49 (5) December: 974–997.

Carns, Keith. 2001. *Operational Issues Related to Energy Use by Water and Wastewater Utilities: Presentation to California Regional Workshops.* May.

Carter, Jimmy. 2001. "Preface: Preserving a Georgia Treasure." In *The Flint River: A Recreational Guidebook to the Flint River and Environs,* ed. Fred Brown and Sherri Smith, 13–15. Atlanta: CI Publishing.

Chang, L. H., C. T. Hunsaker, and J. D. Draves. 1992. "Recent Research on Effects of Climate Change on Water Resources." *Water Resources Bulletin* 28 (2) April: 1–14.

Charlier, T. 1999. "Memphis Taps into DeSoto County Well Levels." *Commercial Appeal* (Memphis, Tennessee), May 23: A1–9.

Chattanooga Times Free Press. 2006. "Alabama: Three States Working Out Details to Share Water." June 28.

Cheng, Anthony S., Linda S. Kruger, and Steven E. Daniels. 2003. "'Place' as an Integrating Concept in Natural Resource Politics: Propositions for a Social Science Research Agenda." *Society and Natural Resources* 16 (2): 87–104.

Chesapeake Bay Program. 2006. Annapolis, Maryland. Available at www.chesapeakebay.net/index.cfm.

Chrislip, David D., and Carl E. Larson. 1994. *Collaborative Leadership: How Citizens and Civic Leaders Can Make a Difference.* San Francisco, CA: Jossey-Bass.

Clark, S. D. 1982. "The River Murray Waters Agreement: Down the Drain or Up the Creek?" *Civil Engineering Transactions* 24: 201–208.

Clarke, Jeanne Nienaber, and Daniel McCool. 1985. *Staking Out the Terrain: Power Dif-*

ferentials among Natural Resource Management Agencies. Albany: State University of New York Press.

Clarkson, Judith M., and Ernest T. Smerdon. 1989. "Effects of Climate Change on Water Resources." *Phi Kappa Phi Journal* (Winter): 29–31.

"Clean Water: EPA Outlines Plan to Give States Control Over TMDL." 2002. *Greenwire: Environment and Energy Publishing* 10 (9) August: 8.

Cleland, Bruce. 2002. "TMDL Talk." *American Clean Water Foundation.* Available at www.tmdls.net/tipstools/docs/feature/TMDL05-02.pdf.

Cody, Betsy A. 1999a. *IB10019: Western Water Resource Issues.* CRS Issue Brief for Congress. Washington, D.C.: Congressional Research Service, April 30, www.chie.org/nle/h20-31.html.

Cody, B. A. 1999b. "Western Water Resource Issues." Washington, D.C.: Congressional Research Service, March 18.

Cody, Betsy A. 2000. "IB10019: Western Water Resource Issues." *CRS Issue Brief for Congress.* Washington, D.C.: Congressional Research Service, October 17.

Cody, Betsy A., and H. Steven Hughes. 2000. "RS20569: Water Resource Issues in the 106th Congress." *Congressional Research Service Report for Congress,* October 20.

Cody, Betsy A., and H. Steven Hughes. 1999. *Congressional Research Service Report for Congress—98–985: Water Resource Issues in the 106th Congress.* May 4. Washington, D.C.: Congressional Research Service, www.cnie.org/nle/h20-28.html.

Coggins, George Cameron, C. F. Wilkinson, and J. D. Leshy. 1993. "Endangered Species Protection." In *Federal Public Land and Resources Law,* 3d ed., 790–838. University Casebook Series. Westbury, NY: Foundation Press.

Columbia River Basin Institute. 1994. "Water Conservation for Instream Re-capture on the Bureau of Reclamation's Columbia Basin Project: Opportunities and Obstacles." Submitted to the Subcommittee on Oversight and Investigation of the House Committee on Natural Resources. Washington, D.C.: July 19.

Conkin, Paul K. 1986. "Intellectual and Political Roots." In *TVA: Fifty Years of Grass-roots Bureaucracy,* ed. Erwin Hargrove and Paul K. Conkin, 3–34. Urbana: University of Illinois Press.

Conservation Foundation. 1984. *State of the Environment: An Assessment at Mid-decade.* Washington, D.C.: Conservation Foundation.

Copeland, Claudia. 1999. "Clean Water Act: A Summary of the Law." *Congressional Research Service Report for Congress,* January 20.

Copeland, Claudia. 2001. "Clean Water Act and Total Maximum Daily Loads (TMDLs) of Pollutants." *Congressional Research Service Report for Congress,* October 30.

Copeland, Claudia. 2002. "Clean Water Act Issues in the 107th Congress." *Congressional Research Service Report for Congress,* August 28.

Copeland, Claudia and Betsy Cody. 2002. "Terrorist and Security Issues Facing the Water Infrastructure Sector." *Congressional Research Service Report for Congress,* February 7.

Corps Reform Coalition. n.d. *Reforming the U.S. Army Corps of Engineers: New Approaches to Water Resources Development.*

Cortner, Hanna A., and M. A. Moote. 1994. "Setting the Political Agenda: Paradigmatic

Shifts in Land and Water Policy." In *Environmental Policy and Biodiversity,* ed. R. E. Grumbine, 365–377. Washington, D.C.: Island Press.

Coulomb, Rene. 2001. "Speech Presented by the Vice President of the World Water Council at the Closing Session of the 11th Stockholm Water Symposium." World Water Council-3rd World Water Forum-Stockholm Water Symposium, August 16, www.worldwatercouncil.org.

Cowie, Gail, et al. 2002. *Reservoirs in Georgia: Meeting Water Supply Needs while Minimizing Impacts.* Athens, GA: River Basin Science and Policy Center, University of Georgia, May.

Crow, Ben, and Farhana Sultana. 2002. "Gender, Class, and Access to Water: Three Cases in a Poor and Crowded Delta." *Society and Natural Resources* 15 (8): 709–724.

Cruise, James F., A. S. Limaye, and N. Al-Abed. 1999. "Assessment of Impacts of Climate Change on Water Quality in the Southeastern U.S." *Journal of the American Water Resources Association* 35 (6) December: 1539–1550.

Curlin, James W. 1972. "The Interstate Water Pollution Compact: Paper Tiger or Effective Regulatory Device?" *Ecology Law Quarterly* 2: 333–356.

Daniels, Steven E., and Gregg B. Walker. 2001. *Working through Environmental Conflict: The Collaborative Learning Approach.* Westport, CT: Praeger.

Davenport, T. E., and L. Kirschner. 2002. "Landscape Approach to TMDL Implementation Planning." In *Total Maximum Daily Load Environmental Regulations,* 26–32. Proceedings of the March 2002 Conference. St Joseph, MI: American Society of Agricultural Engineers.

Davis, M. B., and C. Zabinski. 1991. "Changes in the Geographical Range Resulting from Greenhouse Warming-Effects of Biodiversity in Forests." In *Consequences of Greenhouse Warming to Biodiversity,* ed. R. L. Peters and T. Lovejoy. New Haven: Yale University Press.

Day, J. C. 1977. "The Plate River Basin." In *Environmental Effects of Complex River Development,* ed. Gilbert White, 123–145. Boulder, CO: Westview Press.

DCR-DSWC. 1986. *Nomini Creek Watershed Plan Westmoreland County, Virginia.* Virginia Department of Conservation and Recreation, Division of Soil and Water Recreation. Revised June 6, 1986.

"Decreasing Dams, Increasing Salmon." 1999. *American Rivers* 26 (1): Spring 15.

Delaware River Basin Commission [DRBC]. 1998. *Annual Report 1997.* W. Trenton, NJ: DRBC.

Delaware River Basin Compact Commission. 2001. "No. 2001-32–A: Resolution pursuant to Articles 3.3 and 10.4 of the Delaware River Basin Compact to preserve and protect water supplies in the Delaware River Basin." Issued by John P. Carroll and Pamela M. Bush. West Trenton, NJ: December 18.

Delfino, Joseph. 2001. "Stockholm Water Symposium." Report by Comtech regional vice president for North America. Available at www.wfeo-comtech.org/WorldWaterVision/DelfinoReportStockholmWaterSymposium.

Derman, Bill. 1998. "Balancing the Waters: Development and Hydropolitics in Contemporary Zimbabwe." In *Water, Culture, and Power: Local Struggles in a Global Con-*

text, ed. John M. Donahue and Barbara Rose Johnston, 73–94. Washington, D.C.: Island Press.

Derthick, Martha, 1974. *Between State and Nation: Regional Organizations of the United States.* Washington, D.C.: Brookings Institution.

Devall, M. S., and Parresol, B.R. 1994. "Global Climate Change and Biodiversity in Forests in the Southern U.S." *World Resource Review* 6: 376–394.

DeWitt, Calvin. 2002. "Remarks on Stewardship, Ecology, Theology and Judeo-Christian Environmental Ethics: A Conference at the University of Notre Dame." South Bend, Indiana, February 21–24.

Deyle, R. E., M. Meo, and T. E. James. 1994. "State Policy Innovation and Climate Change: A Coastal Erosion Analogy." In *Global Climate Change and Public Policy,* ed. D. Feldman, 39–66. Chicago: Nelson-Hall.

Dickinson, Mary Ann. 2001. "California Urban Water Conservation Council." *Water Conservation News* (July): 11.

Dimitrov, Radoslav S. 2002. "Water, Conflict, and Security: A Conceptual Minefield." *Society and Natural Resources* 15 (8): 677–691.

Downing, Paul B. 1984. *Environmental Economics and Policy.* Boston: Little, Brown.

Dryukker, V. V. 2001. "Interaction of Nongovernmental Organizations and Regional Authorities in Solving Problems of the Lake Baikal Region." In *The Role of Environmental NGOs-Russian Challenges, American Lessons,* 169–178. Washington, D.C.: National Academy of Sciences.

Dunphy, R. T. 1997. *Moving Beyond Gridlock.* Washington, D.C.: Urban Land Institute.

Durlin, R. R., and W.P. Schaffstall. 1997. *Water Resources Data for Pennsylvania, Water Year 1997.* Vol. 1. Delaware River Basin: U.S. Geological Survey Water-Data Report PA–97–1.

Eastburn, D. 1990. *The River Murray History at a Glance.* Canberra, Australia: Murray-Darling Basin Commission.

Economic Commission for Africa. 2000. *Regional and Sub-regional Cooperation through Integrated Development of Trans-boundary Water Resources.* Addis Ababa, Ethiopia: United Nations Economic Commission for Africa. Available at www.uneca.org/eca _programmes/regional_integration.

Edwards, Todd. 2002. "Water Permitting Fees and TMDL Development in Southern States." *Regional Resource* (April).

"Eighth Circuit: Nonprofit Agency's Claim for Lack of Pollution Documentation Not Ripe for Review." 2002. *Real Estate/Environmental Liability News* 13 (15) May 24.

Eilers, Denny. 1998. "Minnesota River Gets New Lease on Life." *Partners: Conservation Technology Information Center* 16 (2) February/March: 10–11.

Eisel, L. M., G. D. Seinwill, and R. M. Wheeler Jr. 1982. "Improved Principles, Standards, and Procedures for Evaluating Federal Water Projects." *Water Resources Research* 18 (April): 203–210.

Ellis, Ralph D. 1998. *Just Results: Ethical Foundations for Policy Analysis.* Washington, D.C.: Georgetown University Press.

Elmusa, Sharif S. 1995. "Dividing Common Water Resources According To International

Water Law: The Case of The Palestinian Israeli Waters." *Natural Resources Journal* 223 (Spring): 35.

Environmental Protection Agency [EPA]. 1994. *Toward a Place-Driven Approach: The Edgewater Consensus on an EPA Strategy for Ecosystem Protection.* Washington, D.C., March.

Environmental Protection Agency [EPA]. 1999. *Climate Change and Tennessee.* EPA 236–F–99–002. Washington, D.C.: Office of Policy, EPA, May.

Environmental Protection Agency [EPA]. 2000. "Droughts, Floods, and Sprawl: They're All Connected." *EPA Watershed Events.* EPA 840–N–00–001. Washington, D.C.: Office of Water, Summer.

Environmental Protection Agency [EPA]. 2002a. "Total Maximum Daily Load Program." www.epa.gov/owow/tmdl.html.

Environmental Protection Agency [EPA]. 2002b. *Water Quantity and Quality in the Clean Water Act.* Washington, D.C.: U.S. EPA, February 25.

Environmental Protection Agency [EPA]. 2003a. *Case #10: TMDL Case Study: Tar-Pamlico Basin, North Carolina.* Available at www.epa.gov/owow/watershed/trading/cs10.htm.

Environmental Protection Agency [EPA]. 2003b. "Withdrawal of Revisions to the Water Quality Planning and Management Regulation and Revisions to the National Pollutant Discharge Elimination System Program." *Federal Register* 68 (53) March 19. Available at www.epa.gov/EPA-WATER/2003/March/Day-19/.

"EPA Developing Watershed Rule to Move TMDL Program Forward." 2002. *Clean Water Report* 40 (June).

"EPA Stalemate with Agriculture Industry May Jeopardize TMDL Rule." 2002. *Inside EPA's Environmental Policy Alert* 19 (24) November 27: 22.

Ettenger, Kreg. 1998. "A River that Once Was Strong and Deep." In *Water, Culture, and Power: Local Struggles in a Global Context,* ed. John M. Donahue and Barbara Rose Johnston, 47–72. Washington, D.C.: Island Press.

Ezcurra, Exequiel, and Marisa Mazari-Hiriart. 1996. "Are Megacities Viable? A Cautionary Tale from Mexico City." *Environment* 38 (1) January/February; 6–15, 26–35.

Faber, Scott. 1996. *On Borrowed Land: Public Policies for Floodplains.* Cambridge, MA: Lincoln Institute of Land Policy.

Farmer, Jared. 2000. *Glen Canyon Dammed: Inventing Lake Powell and the Canyon Country.* Tucson: University of Arizona Press.

Faruqee, R. and Y. A. Choudhry. 1996. *Improving Water Resource Management in Bangladesh.* Washington, D.C.: Agricultural and Natural Resources Division, World Bank, January.

Feitelson, E., and M. Haddad. 1998. *Identification of Joint Management Structures for Shared Aquifers: A Cooperative Palestinian-Israeli Effort.* World Bank Technical Paper no. 415. Washington, D.C.: World Bank, August 1.

Feldman, David L. 1995. *Water Resources Management: In Search of an Environmental Ethic.* Baltimore: Johns Hopkins University Press.

Feldman, David L., ed. 1996. *The Energy Crisis: Unresolved Issues and Enduring Legacies.* Baltimore: Johns Hopkins University Press.

Feldman, David L. 2000. "Southeastern Water Conflicts: Can a Stakeholder Forum Enhance Long-Term Planning?" *Rivers: Studies in the Science, Environmental Policy
and Law of Instream Flow* 7 (3): 191–204.

Feldman, David L. 2001. "Tennessee's Inter-basin Water Transfer Act: A Changing Water Policy Agenda." *Water Policy* 3 (1): 1–12.

Final Water Quality Trading Policy. 2003. Washington, D.C.: U.S. EPA, January 13,
www.epa.gov/owow/watershed/trading/finalpolicy2003.html.

Findley, Roger, and Daniel Farber. 1992. *Environmental Law: In a Nutshell.* St. Paul, MN:
West Publishing.

Finnegan, William. 2002. "Leasing the Rain." *New Yorker,* April 8: 43–53.

Fischer, Frank. 1995. "Situational Validation." In *Evaluating Public Policy,* ed. Frank
Fischer. Chicago: Nelson-Hall.

Fischer, Frank. 2000. *Citizens, Experts, and the Environment: The Politics of Local
Knowledge.* Durham, NC: Duke University Press.

Fischer, Jeff. 2002. *National Water-Quality Assessment (NAWQA) Program.*

Fiske, Gary, and Anh Dong. 1995. "IRP: A Case Study From Nevada." *Journal of the
American Water Works Association* 87 (6) June: 72–83.

Fleming, William M., and G. Emlen Hall. 2000. "Water Conservation Incentives for New
Mexico: Policy and Legal Alternatives." *Natural Resources Journal* 40 (1) Winter: 69–
92.

Florida Water Plan. 2006. *State of Florida Home Page.* Tallahassee, Florida. Available at
www.dep.state.fl.us/water/waterpolicy/fwp.htm.

Foster, C. H., and P. Rogers. 1988. *Federal Water Policy: Toward an Agenda for Action.*
Cambridge, MA: Energy and Environmental Policy Center, JFK School of Government, Harvard University, August.

Fowler, Robert Booth. 1995. *The Greening of Protestant Thought.* Chapel Hill: University of North Carolina Press.

Fradkin, Philip L. 1996. *A River No More: The Colorado River and the West.* Berkeley:
University of California Press.

Franz, Damon. 2002. "EPA Will Proceed with TMDL Rule Change, Officials Say." *Land
Letter-Environment and Energy Publishing, LLC* 10 (9) August: 15.

Frederick, Kenneth D. 1998. "Marketing Water: The Obstacles and the Impetus." *Resources* 132 Summer: 7–10.

Frederick, Kenneth D., and Gregory E. Schwarz. 1999. "Socioeconomic Impacts of Climate Change on U.S. Water Supplies." *Journal of the American Water Resources Association* 35 (6) December: 1563–1583.

Frick, Elizabeth A., et al. 1998. *Water Quality in the Apalachicola-Chattahoochee-Flint
River Basin, Georgia, Alabama, and Florida, 1992–95.* U.S. Geological Survey Circular 1164, National Water Quality Assessment (NAWQA) Program. Denver, Colorado: USGS.

Frontinus, Sextus Julius. 1997. *Frontinus: The Stratagems and the Aqueducts of Rome.*
English translation by C. E. Bennett. Cambridge, MA: Loeb Classical Library, Harvard
University Press.

Gelt, Joe. 1997. "Sharing Colorado River Water: History, Public Policy and the Colorado River Compact." *Arroyo* (10) August: 1.

Georgia Board of Natural Resources [BNR]. 2001. *Water Issues White Paper.* Atlanta, Georgia, BNR, May 23.

Georgia Environmental Protection Division [EPD]. 2002a. *Progress on Interstate Water Compact.* Department of Natural Resources. Atlanta: Georgia DNR, January 16.

Georgia Environmental Protection Division [EPD]. 2002b. *Severe Drought Declaration May Be Issued for Flint River Basin.* Department of Natural Resources. Atlanta, Georgia DNR, February 7.

Georgia Public Policy Foundation. 1999. *The Georgia 1999 Index of Leading Environmental Indicators.* Atlanta.

Getches, David H. 1998a. *Report to the Northwest Power Planning Council from the Workshop on Fish and Wildlife Governance.* Boulder: University of Colorado. Available at www.newsdat.com/enernet/fishletter.

Getches, David H. 1998b. "Some Irreverent Questions About Watershed-Based Efforts." *Chronicle of Community,* Northern Lights Institute.

Getches, David H. 1998c. "Water in the Columbia River Basin: From a Source of Permanence to an Instrument for Economic Growth." In *Traditional and Modern Approaches to the Environment on the Pacific Rim: Tensions and Values,* ed. Harold Coward, 177–193. Albany: State University of New York Press.

Gillilan, David M., and Thomas C. Brown. 1997. *Instream Flow Protection: Seeking a Balance in Western Water Use.* Washington, D.C.: Island Press.

Glaser, Barney, and Anselm Strauss. 1967. *The Discovery of Grounded Theory.* Chicago: Aldine.

Gleick, Peter H. 1993. "Water and Conflict: Freshwater Resources and International Security." *International Security* 18 (1): 79–112.

Gleick, Peter H. 1998. "Water in Crisis: Paths to Sustainable Water Use." *Ecological Applications* 8: 571–579.

Gleick, Peter H. 2000. "The Changing Water Paradigm: A Look at Twenty-First Century Development." *Water International* 25 (1) March: 127–138.

Gleick, Peter H., and D. Briane Adams. 2000. *Water: The Potential Consequences of Climate Variability and Change for the Water Resources of the United States.* The Report of the Water Sector Assessment Team of the National Assessment of the Potential Consequences of Climate Change, for the U.S. Global Change Research Program. Oakland, CA: Prepared by the Pacific Institute for Studies in Development, Environment, and Security, September.

Goffman, Erving. 1974. *Frame Analysis.* Cambridge, MA: Harvard University Press.

Goldstein, Bruce Evan. 1999. "Combining Science and Place-Based Knowledge: Pragmatic and Visionary Approaches to Bioregional Understanding." In *Bioregionalism,* ed. Michael V. McGinnis, 157–170. London: Routledge.

Gomes, Laurentino. 1997. "Creating a River, Destroying a Swamp: Birds or Barges?" *World Press Review* (August): 10–11.

Gomez, Santos. 1997. "California Water: The Need for Greater Community Participation." *Pacific Institute Report: Studies in Development, Environment and Security* (Fall): 1, 7.

Goslin, Ival V. 1978. "Colorado River Development." In *Values and Choices in the Development of the Colorado River Basin,* ed. D. F. Peterson and A. B. Crawford. Tucson: University of Arizona Press.

Graham, Keith. 1998. "ACT and ACF River Basins: Water Resources Activities of Alabama, Florida and Georgia." Summarized in David L. Feldman and Ruth Anne Hanahan, *Southeast Water Resources: Management and Supply.* Report on a symposium held in Chattanooga, Tennessee, August 24–26, 1998. Energy, Environment and Resources Center and Water Resources Research Center, University of Tennessee, May.

Grant, Douglas L. 1998. "Introduction to Interstate Allocation Problems." In *Waters and Water Rights,* ed. Robert E. Beck. Replacement volumes and Supplemental Pocket Parts. Charlottesville, VA: Michie, 1997.

Grigg, Neil S. 1996. *Water Resources Management: Principles, Regulations, and Cases.* New York: McGraw Hill.

Grizzle, Raymond E., and Christopher B. Barrett. 1996. *The One Body of Christian Environmentalism.* UAES Journal Paper, Pew Charitable Trust Report, August. Available at cesc.montreat.edu/GSI/GSI-Conf/Mini-Grants/Taylor-OneBody.html.

Ground Water Institute. 1995. *A Ground Water Flow Analysis of the Memphis Sand Aquifer in the Memphis, Tennessee Area.* Technical Brief No. 7. Memphis, TN: University of Memphis, February.

Grubb, M., A. Koch, F. Munson, K. Sullivan. 1993. *The Earth Summit Agreements: A Guide and Assessment: An Analysis of the Rio '92 UN Conference on Environment and Development.* London, England: Energy and Environmental Programme, Royal Institute of International Affairs, Earthscan Publications.

Grunwald, Michael. 2000a. "Corps' Balancing Act in Crosscurrents, Engineers Explore 'Greener' Projects," *Washington Post,* January 10: A1, A12–17.

Grunwald, Michael. 2000b. "A River in the Red: Channel was Tamed for Barges that Never Came." *Washington Post,* January 9: A1, A16–21.

Haas, Peter. 1988. "Ozone Alone, No CFCs: Epistemic Communities and the Protection of Stratospheric Ozone." American Political Science Association annual meeting, Washington, D.C., September.

Haas, Peter. 1990. *Saving the Mediterranean: The Politics of International Environmental Cooperation.* New York: Columbia University Press.

Haasz, Dana. 2002. "Water Efficiency: More Savings to Give." *Pacific Institute Report* (Spring): 5–6.

Haliy, I. A. 2001. "History of the Development of Ecological Non-Governmental Organizations in Russia." In *The Role of Environmental NGOs-Russian Challenges, American Lessons.* Workshop proceedings. Washington, D.C.: National Academy of Sciences.

Hamburg, Steven P., et al. 2000. *Common Questions about Climate Change.* Nairobi, Kenya: United Nations Environment Programme/World Meteorological Organization.

Harden, Blaine, 1997. *A River Lost: The Life and Death of the Columbia*. New York: W.W. Norton.

Hardin, Garrett. 1968. "The Tragedy of the Commons." *Science* 162: 1243–1248. Available at www.sciencemag.org/sciext/sotp/commons/dtl#essay.

Hart, Henry. 1957. *The Dark Missouri*. Madison: University of Wisconsin Press.

Hartig, J. H., D. P. Dodge, L. Lovett-Doust, K. Fuller. 1992. "Identifying the Critical Path and Building Coalitions for Restoring Degraded Areas of the Great Lakes." In *Water Resources Planning and Management: Saving a Threatened Resource*, 823–830. New York: Conference on Water Resources Planning and Management, ASCE.

Haskins, Lisa. 1999. "TMDL Status in the Southeast." *Georgia and Southeast Environmental News*. September/October.

Hassoun, Rosina. 1998. "Water between Arabs and Israelis: Reaching Twice-Promised Resources." In *Water, Culture, and Power: Local Struggles in a Global Context*, ed. John M. Donahue and Barbara Rose Johnston, 313–338. Washington, D.C.: Island Press.

Hatch, Upton, S. Jagtap, J. Jones, M. Lamb. 1999. "Potential Effects of Climate Change on Agricultural Water Use in the Southeast U.S." *Journal of the American Water Resources Association* 35 (6) December: 1551–1561.

Hirji, Rafik. 2002. "An Environmentally Sustainable Approach to Water in Southern Africa." *Environment Matters: Annual Review at the World Bank*, July 2001–June 2002: 20–23.

Hobbes, Thomas. 1958. *Leviathan*. Parts I and II. Edited by Herbert W. Schneider. Indianapolis: Bobbs-Merrill.

Hoberg, George. 2001. "Globalization and Policy Convergence: Symposium Overview." *Journal of Comparative Policy Analysis* 3: 127–132.

Holliday, Pamela P. 2002. "Fighting over the Flint: Balancing Human Demands with Ecosystem Needs." *Sherpa Guides: The Natural Georgia Series* online guide. Available at www.sherpaguides.com/Georgia/flint-river/water_resources/index.html.

Holmes, Beatrice Hort. 1979. *A History of Federal Water Resources Programs and Policies, 1961–1970*. Washington, D.C.: Economics, Statistics, and Cooperatives Service, U.S. Department of Agriculture.

Homer-Dixon, Thomas. 1999. *Environment, Society, and Violence*. Princeton, NJ: Princeton University Press.

Houck, Oliver A. 1997. "TMDLs, Are We There Yet? The Long Road Toward Water Quality-Based Regulation under the Clean Water Act." *Environmental Law Review* 27 (August): 10401.

Hull, Jonathan Watts. 2000. "The War Over Water." *Regional Resource*. Atlanta, GA: Council of State Governments, October.

Hurd, Robert E. 1993. "Consumer Attitude Survey on Water Quality Issues." *American Water Works Association Research Foundation*. Available at www.awwarf.com/exsums/.

Idaho Department of Environmental Quality. 2006. *Surface Water: South Fork Salmon River Sub-Basin Assessment*. July. Available at www.deq.state.id.us/water/data_reports/surface_water/tmdls/salmon_river_sf.

Ingram, Helen. 2001. *Falling on Deaf Ears? Science and Natural Resources Policy.* Working paper, University of California at Irvine.

Institute of Hydrology—Hungary. 1994. *Assessment of the State of Water Resources of Hungary.* Budapest, Hungary: Water Resources Research Centre.

"Interior Secretary Kicks Off Dialogue on Preventing Conflicts Over Western Water." 2003. *Environment Reporter* 34 (24) June 13: 1345.

International Commission for the Protection of the Rhine [ICPR]. 2002. Available at iksr.firmen-netz.de/icpr.

International Consortium of Investigative Journalists [ICIJ]. 2003a. "Defending the Internal Water Empire." February 5. Available at www.enn.com/news/2003-02-05.

International Consortium of Investigative Journalists [ICIJ]. 2003b. "Water and Power: The French Connection." February 5. Available at www.enn.com/news/2003/02-05.

International Joint Commission. 2000. *Protection of the Waters of the Great Lakes: Final Report to the Governments of Canada and the United States.* IJC.

International Turf Producers Foundation [ITPF]. 2000. *Water Right: Conserving Our Water, Preserving Our Environment.* Rolling Meadows, IL: ITPF.

Jacobs, Katherine L., Samuel N. Luoma, and Kim A. Taylor. 2003. "CALFED: An Experiment in Science and Decisionmaking." *Environment* 45 (1) January/February: 30–41.

Jehl, Douglas. 2003. "A New Frontier in Water Wars Emerges in East." *New York Times,* March 3.

Jenkins-Smith, Hank. 1982. "Professional Roles for Policy Analysts: A Critical Assessment." *Journal of Policy Analysis and Management* 2 (1): 88–100.

Jenner, C. B., and H. F. Lins. 1991. *Climatic Atlas of the Delaware River Basin.* U.S. Geological Survey Professional Paper no. 1392.

Johnson, J. E., et al. 1962. *Negative Impacts of Garrison and Oahe Reservoirs on the North Dakota Economy.* Fargo: North Dakota State University Extension Service Monograph, 3.

Kant, Immanuel. 1975. *Foundations of the Metaphysics of Morals.* Translated with an introduction by Lewis Beck. Indianapolis, IN: Bobbs-Merrill.

Kantrowitz, Arthur. 1993. "Elitism vs. Checks and Balances in Communicating Risk Information to the Public." *Risk, Health, Safety and the Environment* 4: 101.

Karasov, Corliss. 2000. "On a Different Scale: Putting China's Environmental Crisis in Perspective." *Environmental Health Perspectives* 108 (10) October: A453–A459.

Kartez, Jack D. 1994. "Collaboration and Responsibility: Intergovernmental Relationships in Flood Hazard Management." Background paper prepared for Lincoln Institute of Land Policy, Community Land Policy and River Flooding Conference.

Kasindorf, Martin. 2002. "War over Water Splits California Cities, Farms." *USA Today,* October 2: 11–12A.

Kavka, Greg. 1978. "The Futurity Problem." In *Obligations to Future Generations,* ed. R. I. Sikora and Brian Berry. Philadelphia: Temple University Press.

Keenan, Sean P., Richard S. Krannich, and Michael S. Walker. 1999. "Public Perceptions of Water Transfers and Markets: Describing Differences in Water Use Communities." *Society and Natural Resources* 12: 279–292.

Kelley, Misty Smith. 2000. "Current Statutory and Regulatory Provisions that Protect

Tennessee's Water Resources." Unpublished manuscript. Chattanooga, TN: Baker, Donelson, Bearman, and Caldwell, March 7.

Kenney, Douglas S. 2000. *Summary Report: Arguing about Consensus: Examining the Case against Western Watershed Initiatives and Other Collaborative Groups Active in Natural Resources Management.* Boulder: Natural Resources Law Center, University of Colorado.

Kenney, Douglas S., and William B. Lord. 1994. *Coordination Mechanisms for the Control of Interstate Water Resources: A Synthesis and Review of the Literature.* Report for the ACF-ACT Comprehensive Study. U.S. Army Corps of Engineers, Mobile District, July.

Kenney, Douglas S., and William B. Lord. 1999. *Analysis of Institutional Innovation in the Natural Resources and Environmental Realm: The Emergence of Alternative Problem-Solving Strategies in the American West—Executive Summary.* Natural Resources Law Center Newsletter, University of Colorado School of Law, Summer: 3–5, 10.

Kenney, Douglas S., S. T. McAllister, W. H. Caile, and J. S. Peckham. 2000. *The New Watershed Sourcebook: A Directory of Initiatives in the Western U.S.* Boulder, CO: Natural Resources Law Center, University of Colorado School of Law.

Kilgour, D.M., and A. Dinar. 1995. *Are Stable Agreements for Sharing International River Waters Now Possible?* Washington, D.C.: Agricultural Policies Division, World Bank, June.

Kiy, Richard, and John D. Wirth. 1998. *Environmental Management on North America's Borders.* College Station: Texas A&M University Press.

Klang, James. 2002. "Point Nonpoint Trading in Minnesota." Minnesota Pollution Control Agency. Available at www.epa.gov/opei/symposium/docs/trk4-sess2.pdf.

Knowles, Tommy. 1998. "Case Study: Implementation Issues Associated with Water Policy Reform in Texas." In *Southeast Water Resources: Management and Supply Issues—A Report on a Symposium held in Chattanooga, Tennessee, August 24–26, 1998,* ed. David L. Feldman and Ruth Anne Hanahan. University of Tennessee, May.

Krueger, Gail. 2001. "Water Issues Swamp Committees with Conflicts." *Savannah Morning News on the Web,* July 19, www.savannahnow.com.stories/071901/LOCwater.shtml.

Kundell, James E., Terry A. DeMeo, and Margaret Myszewski. 2001. *Developing a Comprehensive State Water Management Plan: A Framework for Managing Georgia's Water Resources.* Atlanta: Research Atlanta, Inc., and Georgia State University, Andrew Young School of Policy Studies.

Kundell, J. E., and D. Tetens. 1998. *Whose Water Is It? Major Water Allocation Issues Facing Georgia.* Public Policy Research Series. Richard W. Campbell, Series Editor. Athens: Carl Vinson Institute of Government, University of Georgia.

Laitos, Jan G., and Joseph P. Tomain. 1992. *Energy and Natural Resources Law in a Nutshell.* St. Paul, MN: West Publishing.

Landre, B. K., and B. A. Knuth. 1993. "Success of Citizen Advisory Committees in Consensus Based Water Resources Planning in the Great Lakes Basin." *Society and Natural Resources* 6 (3) July-September: 229.

Landry, Clay J. 2000. "Agriculture and Water Markets in the New Millennium." *Water Resources Impact* 2 (3) May: 13–15.

Lasswell, Harold D. 1958. *Politics: Who Gets What, When, and How?* New York: Peter Smith Publishers.

Lavelle, Marianne, and Joshua Kurlantzick. 2002. "The Coming Water Crisis." *U.S. News and World Report,* August 12: 23–30.

Lazaroff, Cat. 2000. "U.S. Asserts Water Rights in National Forests." *Environment News Service,* March 16, ens.lycos.com/ens/mar2000/2000L-03–16–06.html.

Lazarus, Michael, David von Hippel, and Stephen Bernow. 2002. *Clean Electricity Options for the Pacific Northwest: An Assessment of Efficiency and Renewable Potentials through the Year 2020.* Report to the Northwest Energy Coalition. Seattle: Tellus Institute, October, www.nwenergy.org/Outreach/Tellus_Report.html.

Leach, William D., Neil W. Pelkey, and Paul A. Sabatier. 2002. "Stakeholder Partnerships as Collaborative Policymaking: Evaluation Criteria Applied to Watershed Management in California and Washington." *Journal of Policy Analysis and Management* 21 (4): 645–670.

Leahy, Stephen. 2001. "Our Most Valuable Resource." *Conservation Voices* 3 (6) December/January: 13–15.

Leahy, Thomas. 1998. "Lake Gaston Project Resolves Water Supply Shortage." *Public Works: Engineering, Construction, and Maintenance* 129 (7) June: 44–48.

Leatherman, Stephen P., and Gilbert White. 2005. "Living on the Edge: The Coastal Collision Course." *Natural Hazards Observer* 30 (2) November: 5–6.

Leavenworth, Stuart. 2004. "U.S. May Cut Water to State: Southwest Drought Slashes Colorado River Flows." *Sacramento Bee,* April 27: A1–12.

Leclair, Vincent. 1997. "Courts Push States, EPA to Create TMDL Water Programs." *Environmental Science and Technology* 31 (4) April: 178A.

Lee, Kai N. 1993. *Compass and Gyroscope: Integrating Science and Politics for the Environment.* Washington, D.C.: Island Press.

Leopold, Aldo. 1949. *A Sand County Almanac: With Essays on Conservation from Round River.* New York: Oxford University Press.

Leslie, Jacques. 2000. "Running Dry: What Happens When the World No Longer Has Enough Fresh Water." *Harper's Magazine,* July.

Lipford, Jody W. 2004. "Averting Water Disputes: A Southeastern Case Study." *PERC Policy Series* PS-30, February 2004. Available at www.perc.org/pdf/ps30.pdf.

Liverman, D. M., M. E. Hansen, B. J. Brown, and R. W. Meredith. 1988. "Global Sustainability: Toward Measurement." *Environmental Management* 12: 133–143.

Loeb, Penny. 1998. "Very Troubled Waters." *U.S. News and World Report,* September 28: 39, 41–42.

Loh, Penn. 1995. "Planning for the Sustainability of California's Water." *Pacific Institute Report* (Spring): 3.

Loker, William M. 1998. "Water, Rights, and the El Cajon Dam, Honduras." In *Water, Culture, and Power: Local Struggles in a Global Context,* ed. John M. Donahue and Barbara Rose Johnston, 95–122. Washington, D.C.: Island Press.

Long, B. D. 1993. "Water Resources Development at a Crossroads," In *Water Resources*

Administration in the United States: Policy, Practice, and Emerging Issues, ed. M. Reuss, 258–263. East Lansing: Michigan State University Press.

Lowi, Theodore. 1979. *The End of Liberalism: The Second Republic of the United States.* 2d ed. New York: W.W. Norton.

Lowry, William R. 1994. *The Capacity for Wonder: Preserving National Parks.* Washington, D.C.: Brookings Institution.

Luterbacher, Urs, John Schnellenhuber, and Ellen Wiegandt. 1998. "Water Resource Conflicts: The Use of Formal Approaches." Graduate Institute of International Studies and Potsdam Institute for Climate Impact Research. Paper presented at the annual meeting of the American Political Science Association, Boston, Massachusetts, August.

Mahlman, J. D., 1997. "Uncertainties in Projections of Human-caused Climate Warming." *Science* 78: 1416–1417.

Majumdar, Shyamal K., E. Willard Miller, and Louis E. Sage, eds. 1988. *Ecology and Restoration of the Delaware River Basin.* Easton: Pennsylvania Academy of Science.

Mandrup-Poulsen, J. 2002. "Findings of the National Research Council's Committee on Assessing the TMDL Approach to Water Quality Management." In *Total Maximum Daily Load Environmental Regulations,* 307–311. Proceedings of the March 2002 Conference. St Joseph, MI: American Society of Agricultural Engineers.

Mann, Dean E. 1993. "Political Science: The Past and Future of Water Resources Policy and Management." In *Water Resources Administration in the United States: Policy, Practice, and Emerging Issues,* ed. M. Reuss, 55–65. East Lansing: Michigan State University Press.

Mansbridge, Jane. 1996. "Public Spirit in Political Systems." In *Values and Public Policy,* ed. Henry J. Aaron, Thomas E. Mann, and Timothy Taylor, 146–172. Washington, D.C.: Brookings Institution.

Marino, M., and K. E. Kemper, eds. 1999. *Institutional Frameworks in Successful Water Markets: Brazil, Spain, and Colorado, USA.* World Bank Technical Paper 247. Washington, D.C.: World Bank.

Marzec, Colleen. 2001. "Mianus Gorge, New York." *Nature Conservancy* 51 (1) January/February: 74.

May, Peter J., Raymond J. Burby, Neil J. Ericksen, John W. Handmer, Jennifer E. Dixon, Sarah Michael, and D. Ingle Smith. 1996. *Environmental Management and Governance: Intergovernmental Approaches to Hazards and Sustainability.* New York: Routledge.

McCormick, Zachary L. 1994. "Interstate Water Allocation Compacts in the Western United States: Some Suggestions." *Water Resources Bulletin* 30 (3): 385–395.

McFague, Sally. 1993. *The Body of God: An Ecological Theology.* Minneapolis, MN: Fortress Press.

McGinnis, Michael V. 1995. "On the Verge of Collapse: The Columbia River System, Wild Salmon, and the Northwest Power Planning Council." *Natural Resources Journal* 35: 63–92.

McGinnis, Michael V., ed. 1999a. *Bioregionalism.* London: Routledge.

McGinnis, Michael V. 1999b. "Making the Watershed Connection." *Policy Studies Journal* 27 (3): 497–501.

McNamee, Greg. 1994. *Gila: The Life and Death of an American River.* Albuquerque: University of New Mexico Press.

McNeely, Jeffrey A., and David Pitt. 1985. "Culture: A Missing Element in Conservation and Development." In *Culture and Conservation: The Human Dimension in Environmental Planning,* ed. J. McNeely and D. Pitt, 1–10. International Union for Conservation of Nature. Dover, DE: Croom Helm.

Mederly, Peter, Pavel Novacek, and Jan Torpercer. 2002. "How To Measure Progress towards Sustainability: The Sustainable Development Index." *Futures Research Quarterly* 18 (2) Summer: 5–24.

Meiners, Roger E., and Lea-Rachel Kosnik. 2003. *Restoring Harmony in the Klamath Basin.* Issue No. PS–27. Bozeman, MO: PERC.

Meltsner, A. J. 1976. *Policy Analysts in the Bureaucracy.* Berkeley: University of California Press.

Meo, Mark. 1991. "Sea Level Rise and Policy Change: Land use Management in the Sacramento-San Jaoquin and Mississippi Rivers." *Policy Studies Journal* 19 (2): 83–92.

Merideth, Robert. 2001. *A Primer on Climatic Variability and Change in the Southwest.* Udall Center for Studies in Public Policy and the Institute for the Study of Planet Earth, University of Arizona, Tucson, Arizona, March.

Merritt, Raymond H. 1979. *Creativity, Conflict, and Controversy: A History of the St. Paul District, U.S. Army Corps of Engineers.* Washington, D.C.: Government Printing Office.

Metropolitan Water District of Southern California. 2006. "Reclamation MWD Sign Agreement for 'Intentionally Created Surplus' Water Demonstration Program at Lake Mead." Los Angeles, California. June 1. Available at www.mwdh2o.com/mwdh2o/pages/news/press_releases/reclamation_and_met.htm.

Milich, Lenard, and Robert G. Varady, 1998. "Managing Transboundary Resources: Lessons from River-Basin Accords." *Environment* 40, 10–15.

Miller, K., S. L. Rhodes, and L. J. MacDonnell. 1996. "Global Change in Microcosm: The Case of U.S. Water Institutions." *Policy Sciences* 29: 271–272.

Ministère de l'Aménagement du Territoire et de l'Environnement [MATE]. 1999. *The Water Resources Department, Dialogue at the Local Level, and State-Supervised and Jointly-Supervised Agencies.* Government of France. Available at www.environnement.gouv.fr/ENGLISH/agencies.htm.

Mischenko, V. L. 2001. "Public Participation in Environmentally-sound Decision-making: Legal Aspects." In *The Role of Environmental NGOs-Russian Challenges, American Lessons,* 179–190. Workshop proceedings. Washington, D.C.: National Academy of Sciences.

Missouri Department of Natural Resources [DNR]. 2003. *Geological Survey and Resource Assessment Division, Water Resources Program-State Water Plan: Phase II.* Jefferson City, Missouri. Available at www.dnr.missouri.gov/geologu/wrp/statewater planPhase2.htm.

Missouri Department of Natural Resources [DNR]. 2002. *Missouri Drought Plan.* Geological Survey and Resource Assessment Division, revised by Water Resources Program, Rolla, Missouri.

Moody, Tom. 1997. "Glen Canyon Dam: Coming to an Informed Decision." Colorado River Advocate-Grand Canyon Trust, www.glencanyon.org/Articles97.htm.

Moreau, David H. 1996. "Principles of Planning and Financing for Water Resources in the United States." In *Water Resources Handbook,* ed. L. W. Mays (New York: McGraw-Hill), 4.1–4.41.

Morphet, J., and T. Hams. 1994. "Responding to Rio: A Local Authority Approach." *Journal of Environmental Planning and Management* 38 (2): 149–166.

Morris, Mary E. 1992. *Poisoned Wells: The Politics of Water in the Middle East.* Reprinted from *Middle East* magazine, RAND/RP–139. Santa Monica, CA: RAND Corporation.

Morris, Mary E. 1993. *Dividing the Waters: Reaching Equitable Water Solutions in the Middle East.* RAND/P–7840. Santa Monica, CA: RAND Corporation.

Muckleston, Keith W. 1990. "Salmon vs. Hydropower: Striking a Balance in the Pacific Northwest." *Environment* 32 (1).

Mumme, Stephen P. 1995. "The New Regime for Managing U.S.-Mexican Water Resources." *Environmental Management* 19 (6): 827–835.

Mumme, Stephen P. 2003. "Strengthening Binational Drought Management." *Utton Center Report: University of New Mexico School of Law* 2 (1) Winter: 3–7.

Murphy, Dean E. 2002. "California Vote Threatens Deal on Colorado River." *New York Times* Internet edition, December 10.

Murray-Darling River Basin [MDBC]. 2002. "About the Initiative." Available at www.mdbc.gov.au/about/governance/agreement_history.htm.

Nagel, John. 2002. "NADBank developments." *Environment Reporter* 33 (49) December 13: 2698. Washington, D.C.: Bureau of National Affairs.

National Academy of Sciences [NAS]. 1999. *New Directions in Water Resources Planning for the U.S. Army Corps of Engineers.* Washington, D.C.: National Academy Press.

National Academy of Sciences [NAS]. 2001. "Assessing the TMDL Approach to Water Quality Management." Washington D.C.: National Academy Press, June.

National Consumer Water Quality [NCWQ]. 1997. "Survey Shows Americans Are Concerned about Household Water Quality, More are Seeking Solutions." Reproduced on the *U.S. Water News* website, June. Available at www.uswaternews.com/archives/arcquality/7sursho6.html.

National Parks Conservation Association [NPCA]. 1993. *Park Waters in Peril.* Washington, D.C.: NPCA.

National Oceanic and Atmospheric Administration [NOAA]. 2002. CALFED Forum. Office of Global Programs. January 8.

National Water Commission. 1974. *Final Report: Water Policies for the Future.* Port Washington, NY: Water Resource Information Center.

Natural Resources Law Center [NRLC]. 1997. *Restoring the Waters.* Boulder: University of Colorado School of Law.

Natural Resources Law Center [NRLC]. 2000. "Water and Growth in the West: NRLC Conference Explores Problems and Solutions." *Resource Law Notes.* University of Colorado, Boulder.

Nature Conservancy. 1999. *Rivers of Life: Critical Watersheds for Protecting Freshwater Biodiversity.* Arlington, VA: Nature Conservancy.

Nauges, Celine, and Alban Thomas. 2000. "Privately Operated Water Utilities, Municipal Price Negotiation, and Estimation of Residential Water Demand: The Case of France." *Land Economics* 76 (1) February: 68–85.

Nemeth, Miklos. 1994. *Characteristic Processes in the Transition of Water Management into Market Economy.* Working paper, Assistant Secretary of State for Water Management of Hungary. Budapest.

Nero, Wendy. 1995. "Seven Steps to Successful Water Savings." *Opflow: American Water Works Association* 21 (3) March: 8–10.

Newson, Malcolm. 1997. *Land, Water, and Development: Sustainable Management of River Basin Systems.* 2nd ed. New York: Routledge.

Niebuhr, Reinhold. 1960. *Moral Man and Immoral Society: A Study of Ethics and Politics.* Rev. ed. New York: Simon and Schuster.

Noble-Goodman, Katherine. 2001. "Cutting-edge Water Conservation Efforts Yield Additional Supplies." *U.S. Water News* 18 (1): 16.

Nordhaus, William D. 1991. "To Slow or Not to Slow: The Economics of the Greenhouse Effect." *Economic Journal* 101: 920–937.

North Carolina Division of Environmental Management [NCDEM]. 1987. *Surface Water Quality Concerns in the Tar-Pamlico River Basin.* Report No. 87-04. Raleigh: NCDEM.

North Carolina Division of Environmental Management [NCDEM]. 1992. *Tar-Pamlico NSW Implementation Strategy.* Raleigh: NCDEM.

Ohlsson, L. 1999. *Environment, Scarcity, and Conflict: A Study of Malthusian Concerns.* Goteburg, Sweden: Department of Peace and Development Research, Goteburg University.

Olivera, Marcela, and Jorge Viana. 2003. "Winning the Water War." *Human Rights Dialogue* (Spring): 10–11.

Olson, Mancur. 1965. *The Logic of Collective Action.* Cambridge, MA: Harvard University Press.

Organization for Economic Cooperation and Development [OECD]. 1997. *Sustainable Consumption and Production.* Paris: OECD.

Ortolano, Leonard, and Katherine Kao Cushing. 2002. "Grand Coulee Dam 70 Years Later: What Can We Learn?" *International Journal of Water Resources Development* 18 (3) September: 373–390.

Ostrom, Elinor. 1990. *Governing the Commons: The Evolution of Institutions for Collective Action.* Cambridge, England: Cambridge University Press.

Otchet, Amy. 2001. "Sabre-rattling among Thirsty Nations." *UNESCO Courier* 54 (10): 18–19.

"Other River Basin Accords." 1998. *Environment* 40 (8).

O'Toole, Laurence J., Jr. 1998. "Control Capacity: The United States." In *Drinking Water Supply and Agricultural Pollution: Preventive Action by the Water Supply Sector in the European Union and the United States,* ed. Geerten J. I. Schrama, 341–364. Dordrecht, the Netherlands: Kluwer Academic Publishers.

Palmer, Richard N. 1998a. "A History of Shared Vision Modeling in the ACT-ACF Comprehensive Study: A Modeler's Perspective." Working paper. Department of Civil Engineering, University of Washington, Seattle. Available at www.taj.washington.edu/publications/papers/Palmer.1998.ASCE-CONF-PROC.0-7844-0378-4.pdf.

Palmer, Richard N. 1998b. *Task Committee Proposal-Use of Shared Vision Modeling in Water Resource Planning.* Water Resource System Committee, Water Resource Planning Committee, American Society of Civil Engineers. Available at maximus.ce. washington.edu/~palmer/taskcom.html.

"Panel Says Florida Needs Water Commission." 2003. *U.S. Water News Online.* September. Available at www.uswaternews.com/archives/arcpolicy/3pansay9.html.

Parenteau, R. 1994. "Local Action Plans for Sustainable Communities." *Environment and Urbanization* 6 (2) October: 183–200.

Parker, G. G., A. G. Hely, F. H. Keighton, F. H. Olmsted, and others. 1964. *Water Resources of the Delaware River Basin.* U.S. Geological Survey Professional Paper No. 381.

Parks, W., and J. K. Carmichael. 1990a. *Altitude of Potentiometric Surface, Fall, 1985, and Historic Water-level Changes in the Memphis Aquifer in Western Tennessee.* Water-Resources Investigations Report 88–4180. Memphis, TN: U.S. Geological Survey.

Parks, W., and J. K. Carmichael. 1990b. *Geology and Ground-Water Resources of the Memphis Sand in Western Tennessee.* Water Resources Investigations Report 88–4182. Memphis, TN: U.S. Geological Survey.

Parmelee, Mary A. 2001. "Impact of Climate Changes on Water Resources Serious." *American Water Works Association Journal* 93 (3) March: 46.

Parrish, Rick. 1998. "Clean Water Lawsuit Settled." *Alabama Rivers Alliance—River Ties* 2 (3) Winter: 1.

Paulsens, Charles M., and Kris Wernstedt. 1995. "Cost-Effectiveness Analysis for Complex Managed Hydrosystems: An Application to the Columbia River Basin." *Journal of Environmental Economics and Management* 28: 388–400.

Payette National Forest. 1991. *FY 1991 Payette National Forest Soil, Water, Air and Fisheries Monitoring Results.* Payette, ID: U.S. Department of Agriculture, Forest Service.

Pearson, Rita P. 2000. "Managing Water Scarcity-Southwestern Style." *Troubled Waters: Managing a Vital Resources: Global Issues Electronic Journal,* March. Available at www.usinfo.state.gov/journals/itgic/.

Pelley, Janet. 1998. "The Challenge of Watershed Cleanup: States are Finding Innovative Ways to Implement the Clean Water Act's TMDL Program." *Environmental Science and Technology* 32 (15) August 1: 346A.

Pennsylvania Fish and Boat Commission. 1997. *Fish Restoration and Passage on the Susquehanna River.* Harrisburg, PA: Alliance for the Chesapeake Bay, Chesapeake Bay Foundation, Pennsylvania DER and Fish and Boat Commission, Susquehanna River Basin Commission, and U.S. Fish and Wildlife Service.

Pernin, Christopher G., Mark A. Bernstein, Andrea Mejia, Howard Shih, Fred Reuter, and Wilbur Steger. 2002. *Generating Electric Power in the Pacific Northwest: Impli-*

cations of Alternative Technologies. Santa Monica, CA: RAND Corporation. Available at www.rand.org/publications/MR/MR1604/.

Pitzer, Paul A. 1995. *Grand Coulee: Harnessing a Dream.* Pullman: Washington State University Press.

Platt, Jennifer L., and Marie Cefalo DelForge. 2001. "The Cost-Effectiveness of Water Conservation." *Journal of the American Water Works Association* 93 (3) March: 73–83.

Platts, W. S., R. J. Torquemada, M. McHenry, and C. K. Graham. 1989. "Changes in Salmon Spawning and Rearing Habitat from Increased Delivery of Fine Sediment to the South Fork Salmon River, Idaho." *Transactions of the American Fisheries Society* 118: 274–283.

Polishchuk, Leonid. 1997. *Russian Civil Society.* Working Paper No. 202. College Park: Center for Institutional Reform and the Informal Sector, University of Maryland.

Pope, Charles. 2002. "Clean Water: The Next Wave." *CQ Weekly,* March 18.

Poppe, Wayne, R. Hurst, and B. Burks. 1997. "Bringing in Partners and Dollars: TVA's River Action Teams Share Their Strategies." *Water Environment and Technology* 9 (9): 67–72.

Postel, Sandra. 1997. "Dividing the Waters." *Technology Review* (April): 54–62.

Postel, Sandra. 1999. *Pillar of Sand: Can the Irrigation Miracle Last?* New York: W.W. Norton.

Postel, Sandra. 2000. "Entering an Era of Water Scarcity: The Challenges Ahead." *Ecological Applications* 10 (4): 941–948.

Powell, J. M. 1993. *The Emergence of Bioregionalism in the Murray-Darling Basin.* Canberra, Australia: Murray-Darling Basin Commission.

Powell, John Wesley. 1879. *Lands of the Arid Region of the United States.* Washington, D.C.: Government Printing Office.

President's Council on Sustainable Development. 1996. *Sustainable America: A New Consensus for Prosperity, Opportunity, and a Healthy Environment for the Future.* Washington, D.C.: Government Printing Office, February.

Pringle, Catherine M. 2000. "Threats to U.S. Public Lands From Cumulative Hydrologic Alterations Outside of their Boundaries." *Ecological Applications* 10 (4) August: 971–989.

Program for Community Problem Solving. 1996. *Negotiated Approaches to Environmental Decision Making in Communities, An Exploration of Lessons Learned.* Washington, D.C.: PCPS, National Civic League, May.

Public Agenda. 2006. "Environment: People's Chief Concerns." Available at publicagenda .org/issues/pcc_detail2.cfm?issue_type=environment&concern_graphic=pccenviro worryRF.jpg.

Pyne, Stephen J. 1999. *How the Canyon Became Grand: A Short History.* New York: Penguin.

Raskin, J., Peter Gleick, Paul Kirshen, Robert G. Pontius Jr., and Kenneth Strzepek. 1997. "Water Futures: Assessment of Long-Range Patterns and Problems." *Comprehensive Assessment of the Freshwater Resources of the World.* Stockholm: Stockholm Environment Institute.

Rawls, John. 1971. *A Theory of Justice.* Cambridge, MA: Belknap Books/Harvard University Press.

Reinhart, Jill. 2002. "Conservation Proves Successful: Washington Partnership Meets TMDL Goals." *Conservation Technology Information Center Partners* 20 (6) November/December: 10–11.

Reuss, M. 1991. *Reshaping National Water Politics: The Emergence of the Water Resources Development Act of 1986.* IWR Policy Study 91–PS–1. Washington, D.C.: Government Printing Office.

Riebsame, William E. 1992. "Social Constraints on Adjusting Water Resources Management to Anthropogenic Climate Change." In *Climatic Fluctuations and Water Management,* ed. M.A. Abu-Zeid and A.K. Biswas, 210–226. Oxford: Butterworth-Heinemann.

Robie, Ronald B. 1980. "The Impact of Federal Policy on State Planning: A Cautionary Example." *American Water Works Association Journal* 72 (February): 70–73.

Rock, Michael T. 2000. "The Dewatering of Economic Growth: What Accounts for the Declining Water-Use Intensity of Income?" *Journal of Industrial Ecology* 4 (1): 57.

Rolston, Holmes. 1988. *Environmental Ethics: Duties to and Values in the Natural World.* Philadelphia: Temple University Press.

Rosenbaum, Mort. 2002. "Water Crisis Looms in Mexico's Future." *Knoxville News-Sentinel,* August 18: A5.

Rosenbaum, Walter A. 2005. Environmental Politics and Policy. 6th ed. Washington, D.C.: Congressional Quarterly Press.

Rosenberg, David M., Patrick McCully, and Catherine M. Pringle. 2000. "Global-Scale Environmental Effects of Hydrological Alterations: Introduction." *BioScience* 50 (9) September: 746–751.

Rowe, Peter G., John Mixon, Barton A. Smith, James B. Blackburn Jr., Gelanda L. Callaway, and Joel L. Gevirtz. 1978. *Principles for Local Environmental Management.* Cambridge, MA: Ballinger.

Samson, S. Ansley, and Sidney Bacchus. 2000. "Point-Water Marketing: The Other Side of the Coin." *Water Resources Report* 2 (6) November: 15–16.

Samuelsohn, Darren. 2002. "Louisiana Court Orders EPA to Set State's Water Pollution Limits." *Environment and Energy Publishing-Greenwire* 10 (9) April 8.

Satchell, Michael. 2003. "Troubled Waters." *National Wildlife* 41 (2) February/March: 35–41.

Schaake, J. M., and T. Tisdale. 1997. "Climate Impacts: Major Findings and Recommendations, Section G: Water Resources." Summary Report of the Workshop on Climate Variability and Water Resource Management in the Southeastern United States, Vanderbilt University, June 25–27, 1997. Sponsored by USGS, NASA, and NOAA, August.

Schoenbaum, Thomas J. 1979. *The New River Controversy.* Winston-Salem, NC: John F. Blair.

Scully, Malcolm. 2000. "The Politics of Running Out of Water." *Chronicle of Higher Education* 47 (12) November 17.

Seabrook, Charles. 1998. "The Water Wars." *Atlanta Journal and Constitution,* October 5: E-5.

Seabrook, Charles. 1999. "Tri-State Water War Rages Again." *Atlanta Journal and Constitution,* May 24: 2/8.

Seabrook, Charles. 2002. "Water Talks End in Failure." *Atlanta Journal and Constitution,* March 19: A1–8.

Selznick, Philip W. 1966. *TVA and the Grassroots: A Study in the Sociology of Formal Organization.* New York: Harper Torchbooks/Harper and Row.

Senate Standing Committee on Science and the Environment [SSCSE]. 1979. *Continuing Scrutiny of Pollution: The River Murray.* Parliamentary Paper 117/79. Canberra, Australia: Government Printer, Canberra.

Serageldin, I. 1995. *Toward Sustainable Management of Water Resources.* Directions in Development Series. Washington, D.C.: World Bank, November 1.

Shabman, L. 1994. "Bargaining, Markets, and Watershed Restoration: Some Elements of a New National Water Policy." In *Water Resources Administration in the United States: Policy, Practice, and Emerging Issues,* ed. M. Reuss, 94–104. East Lansing: Michigan State University Press.

Shanholz, V. O., C. J. Desai, N. Zhang, J. W. Kleene, and C. D. Metz. 1990. *Hydrologic/Water Quality Modeling in a GIS Environment.* Paper No. 90–3033. Written for presentation at the 1990 International Summer Meeting sponsored by the American Society of Agricultural Engineers, Columbus, Ohio, June 24–27, 1990.

Sheridan, Thomas. 1998. "The Big Canal: The Political Ecology of the Central Arizona Project." In *Water, Culture, and Power: Local Struggles in a Global Context,* ed. John M. Donahue and Barbara Rose Johnston, 163–186. Washington, D.C.: Island Press.

Sherk, George William. 1990. "Eastern Water Law: Trends in State Legislation." *Virginia Environmental Law Journal* 9 (2) Spring: 287–322.

Sherk, George William. 1994. "Resolving Interstate Water Conflicts in the Eastern United States: The Re-emergence of the Federal-Interstate Compact." *Water Resources Bulletin* 30 (3): 397–408.

Shiva, Vandana. 2002. *Water Wars: Privatization, Pollution, and Profit.* London: Pluto Press.

Siciliano, Stephen. 2002. "Agency Says Water Transfers Would Have little Effect on Salton Salinity, Reclamation." *Environment Reporter* 33 (49). Washington, D.C.: Bureau of National Affairs, December 13: 2714–2715.

Siciliano, Stephen. 2003. "Imperial Valley's Water Order Restored; Urban, Desert Districts Suffer Reductions." *Environment Reporter* 34 (18). Washington, D.C.: Bureau of National Affairs, May 2: 1009.

Smith, Sherri. 2001. "Introduction: A Recreational Guidebook," In *The Flint River: A Recreational Guidebook to the Flint River and Environs,* ed. Fred Brown and Sherri Smith, 17–31. Atlanta: CI Publishing.

Smythe, William Ellsworth. 1900. *The Conquest of Arid America.* New York: Harper and Brothers.

Sneddon, Chris, L. Harris, R. Dimitrov, and U. Ozesmi. 2002. "Contested Waters: Conflict, Scale and Sustainability in Aquatic Socioecological Systems." *Society and Natural Resources* 15 (8) September: 663–675.

Solley, Wayne B. 1998. "Status and Trends of Water Use in the Southeast." In *Southeast Water Resources: Management and Supply: Report on a Symposium Held in Chattanooga, Tennessee, August 24–26, 1998,* ed. David L. Feldman and Ruth Anne Hanahan. Energy, Environment, and Resources Center and Water Resources Research Center, University of Tennessee, May.

Solley, Wayne B., Robert R. Pierce, and Howard A. Perlman. 1998. *Estimated Use of Water in the United States in 1995.* U.S. Geological Survey. Circular No. 1200. Denver: U.S. Geological Survey.

South Florida Water Management District [SFWMD]. 2000. "Draft-Minimum Flows and Levels for the Caloosahatchee River and Estuary." West Palm Beach, FL: SFWMD.

Starling, Grover. 1989. "The Case Study Method in the Study of Public Policy." In *The Politics and Economics of Public Policy: An Introductory Analysis with Cases.* Homewood, IL: Dorsey.

Starling, Grover. 1979. *Strategies for Policy Making.* Chicago: Dorsey.

"State Agency News." 2002. *Southeast Watershed Forum* 5 (2) Fall/Winter: 6–8.

"States Increasingly Allow Dischargers to Develop TMDLs." 2002. *Environmental Policy Alert* 19 (23) November 13: 24.

Sterne, Jack. 2000. "Instream Rights and Invisible Hands: Prospects for Private Instream Rights in the Northwest." Unpublished manuscript.

Stevens, Jan S. 1995. "Current Developments in the Public Trust Doctrine and Other Instream Protection Measures." In *Water Law: Trends, Policies, and Practice,* ed. Kathleen Marion Carr and James D. Crammond. Chicago: American Bar Association, Section of Natural Resources, Energy and Environmental Law.

Stevens, Joseph. 1988. *Hoover Dam: An American Adventure.* Norman: University of Oklahoma Press.

Stine, Jeffrey K. 1993. *Mixing the Waters: Environment, Politics, and the Building of the Tennessee-Tombigbee Waterway.* Akron, OH: University of Akron Press.

Stoerker, H. A. 1994. "The State Perspective." In *Water Resources Administration in the United States: Policy, Practice, and Emerging Issues,* ed. M. Reuss, 274–282. East Lansing: Michigan State University Press.

Stolzenburg, William. 2000. "Southwest Passage: Sustaining the Waters of the San Pedro River." *Nature Conservancy* 50 (1) January/February: 12–17.

Stone, Deborah K. 1988. *Policy Paradox and Political Reason.* Glenview, IL: Scott, Foresman.

Stranahan, Susan. 1993. *Susquehanna: River of Dreams.* Baltimore: Johns Hopkins University Press.

"Studies Show New Energy Sources may Help Save Salmon." 2003. *American Rivers* 31 (1) Winter: 12.

Susquehanna River Basin Commission [SRBC]. 1998. *Policy regarding Diversions of Water from the Susquehanna River Basin and Susquehanna River Basin Commission Out-of-basin Diversion Protocol.* Policy No. 98–01. Harrisburg, PA: SRBC, March 12.

Subcommittee on Disaster Reduction. 2005. "Grand Challenges for Disaster Reduction." *Natural Hazards Observer* 30 (2) November: 1–3.

Switzer, Jacqueline. 2001. *Environmental Politics: Domestic and Global Dimensions.* Boston: Bedford/St. Martin's.

Switzer, Jacqueline, and Gary Bryner. 1998. *Environmental Politics: Domestic and Global Dimensions.* 2nd ed. New York: St. Martin's.

Tarlock, A. Dan. 1990. "Discovering the Virtues of Riparianism." *Virginia Environmental Law Journal* 9 (2) Spring: 249–254.

Tarlock, Dan, James Corbridge Jr., and Getches, David. 1993. *Water Resource Management: A Casebook in Law and Public Policy.* 4th ed. Westbury, NY: Foundation Press.

Taylor, Richard. 2000. "Green to the Corps: Engineer Works to Build Aquatic Balance." *Nature Conservancy* 50 (5) September/October: 12–13.

Tennessee Department of Environmental Conservation [TDEC]. 2002. "Total Maximum Daily Loads." Available at www.state.tn.us/environment/wpc/tmdl/.

Teerink, J. R. and Nakashima, M. 1993. *Water Allocation, Rights, and Pricing: Examples From Japan and the U.S.* World Bank Discussion Paper 198. Washington, D.C.: World Bank, February 1.

Tisdell, J. G., and J. R. Ward. 2003. "Attitudes toward Water Markets: An Australian Case Study." *Society and Natural Resources* 16 (1): 61–76.

"TMDL Concerns for Agriculture." 2002. *Partners: Conservation Technology Information Center* 20 (3) May/June: 3.

"TMDL Status in the Southeast." 2000. *ECOS: The Environmental Communiqué of the States* (Winter) 7 (1): 3, 16. Excerpted from Lisa Haskins, *Georgia and Southeast Environmental News,* September/October, 1999.

"TMDLs Finalized for Louisiana Rivers." 2002. *Environmental Laboratory Washington Report-LRP Publications* 13 (10) May 23.

"Tucson Saves Water With Law and Order and Education." 2000. *Arizona Water Resource.* Tucson: Water Resource Research Center, University of Arizona, July–August: 4.

Tennessee Valley Authority [TVA]. 1999. *TVA River Neighbors Special Report, 1999-River System Performance.* Knoxville, TN: TVA.

Tennessee Valley Authority [TVA]. 2002a. *Reservoir Operations Study* 1 (March). Knoxville, TN: TVA.

Tennessee Valley Authority [TVA]. 2002b. *Impact Evaluation on Water Supply: Reservoir Operations Study, Water Supply Fact Sheet,* March. Knoxville, TN: TVA.

Tennessee Valley Authority [TVA]. 2003a. *Reservoir Operations Study* 3 (April). Knoxville, TN: TVA.

Tennessee Valley Authority [TVA]. 2003b. *TVA's Reservoir Operations Study: Fact Sheet.* Available at www.tva.com/feature_rostudy/index.htm.

Tennessee Valley Authority [TVA]. 2004a. "TVA Board Approves Reservoir Operations Study Preferred Alternative." May 19. Available at www.tva.gov/news/releases/aprjun04/ros-rod.htm.

Tennessee Valley Authority [TVA]. 2004b. "TVA Water Supply Information," tva.gov/river/watersupply/index.htm.

University Corporation for Atmospheric Research [UCAR]. 1997. *Our Changing Climate—A Report to the Nation.* Boulder, CO: University Corporation for Atmospheric Research Joint Office for Science Support and the NOAA Office of Global Programs.

United Nations. 2006. "Both Rich and Poor Have Interest in Protecting Environment, Promoting Sustainable Development, Secretary General Says." U.N. Press Release SG/SM/8239 ENV/DEV/637, May 14. Available at www.un.org/News/Press/docs/2002/sgsm8239.doc.htm.

United Nations Development Programme [UNDP]. 2004. Freshwater Country Profile: Hungary. Available at www.un.org/esa/agenda21/natlinfo/countr/hungary/index.htm.

United Nations World Water Assessment Programme [UNWWAP]. 2003. *Water for People, Water for Life: The United Nations World Water Development Report.* Barcelona, Spain: United Nations Educational, Scientific, and Cultural Organization (UNESCO) and Berghahn Books.

United Nations Division for Sustainable Development. 1999. *Intercountry Cooperation for Shared Water Resources Development.* New York: United Nations. Available at www.un.org/esa/sustdev/success/coopwrd.htm.

Upper Mississippi River Basin Association [UMRBA]. 1993. *Position of the Upper Mississippi River Basin Association on Flood Response and Recovery after the 1993 Flood.* St. Paul, MN: UMRBA, September.

U.S. Army Corps of Engineers. 1996. *ACF Draft Environmental Impact Statement.* Available at www.sam.usace.army.mil/pd/ACTACFEIS/act-draft.htm.

U.S. Bureau of Reclamation. 1948. *Boulder Canyon Project Final Reports. Part I: Introductory, General History and Description of Project.* Boulder City, NV: U.S. Bureau of Reclamation, Department of the Interior.

U.S. Bureau of Reclamation. 1957. *Colorado-Big Thompson Project, Vol. 1. Planning, Legislation, and General Description.* Denver: U.S. Department of the Interior.

U.S. Bureau of Reclamation. 2005. "Mission Statement." Available at www.usbr.gov/main/about/mission.html.

U.S. Department of Agriculture [USDA]. 2000. *Preparing for Drought in the 21st Century.* Washington, D.C.: National Drought Policy Commission, May.

U.S. Department of Agriculture Forest Service. 2000. *Water and the Forest Service.* Policy Analysis Staff, FS–660. Washington, D.C.: USDA, January.

U.S. Department of Justice. 1982. "Memorandum for Carol E. Dinkins, Assistant Attorney General, Land and Natural Resources Division." *Federal "Non-Reserved" Water Rights.* Washington, D.C.: Department of Justice, Office of Legal Counsel, June 16.

U.S. Department of the Interior. 1979. *Decisions of the Department of the Interior-Federal Water Rights of the National Park Service, Fish and Wildlife Service, Bureau of Reclamation and the Bureau of Land Management.* Washington, D.C.: Office of the Solicitor, U.S. Department of the Interior, June 25.

U.S. General Accounting Office [GAO]. 1981. *River Basin Commissions Have Been Helpful, But Changes Are Needed.* Report to the Congress of the U.S. CED–81–69. Washington, D.C.: GAO.

U.S. General Accounting Office [GAO]. 2002. *Water Quality: Inconsistent State Approaches Complicate Nation's Efforts to Identify Its Most Polluted Waters.* GAO–02–186, January 11. Washington, D.C.: GAO.

U.S. Geological Survey [USGS]. 2002. *Does Land Use Affect Our Streams? A Watershed Example from Gwinnett County, Georgia, 1998–2001.* Atlanta, GA: USGS Water-Resources Investigations Report 02–4281, December.

U.S. National Water Commission [NWC]. 1972. *Water Resources Planning: Consulting Panel on Water Resources Planning.* Washington, D.C.: NWC.

U.S. Water News. 1997. "Loss of Trees in Atlanta Area Produces Increased Stormwater Costs."

U.S. Water News. 2002. "Interior Secretary Cuts California's Share of Colorado River Water." December.

U.S. Water News. 2003a. "Georgia, Alabama, Florida Governors Sign Understanding Agreement." August. Available at uswaternewsonline.com/archives.

U.S. Water News. 2003b. "Policy Makers, Activists Disagree over Privatization of Water." April. Available at www.uswaternews.com/archives/arcglobal/3polmak4.html.

U.S. Water Resources Council [WRC]. 1968. *First National Assessment: The Nation's Water Resources.* Washington, D.C.: Government Printing Office.

U.S. Water Resources Council [WRC]. 1978. *The Nation's Water Resources, 1975–2000, Volume 1: Summary, 2nd National Water Assessment.* Washington, D.C.: Water Resources Council, December.

Verbruggen, H., and O. Kuik. 1991. "Indicators of Sustainable Development: An Overview." In *In Search of Indicators of Sustainable Development,* ed. O. Kuik and H. Verbruggen, 1–6. Norwell, MA: Kluwer Academic Publishers.

Vogel, Cathleen C. 1998. "Central and Southern Florida Project Comprehensive Review Study: Road Map or Road Block for the Future? A Case Study In Water Resource Planning in the Age of Ecosystem Management." *Water Resources Update* 11 (Spring). Universities Council on Water Resources.

Voight, William, Jr., 1972. *The Susquehanna Compact: Guardian of the River's Future.* New Brunswick, NJ: Rutgers University Press.

Volkman, John M. 1992. "Making Room in the Ark: The Endangered Species Act and the Columbia River Basin." *Environment* 34 (4).

Volkman, John M. 1996. *A River in Common: The Columbia River, the Salmon Ecosystem, and Water Quality.* Denver: Western Water Policy Review Advisory Commission.

Wade, William W., 1998. "California Water Supplies: Problem Solving through the 20th Century." Presentation to the Southeast Water Resources Management and Supply Conference, Chattanooga, Tennessee, August 26.

Wangsness, David J. 1997. *The National Water-Quality Assessment Program: Example of Study Unit Design for the Apalachicola-Chattahoochee-Flint River Basin in Georgia, Alabama, and Florida, 1991–97.* Atlanta: USGS Open Site Report 97-48, National Water Quality Assessment Program.

Ward, Evan R. 2003. *Border Oasis: Water and the Political Ecology of the Colorado River Delta, 1940–1975.* Tucson: University of Arizona Press.

Ward, Ken, Jr. 2002. "Court Upholds West Virginia Environment Department's Water Pollution Limits." *Charleston Gazette,* July 3.

Warren, Mark E. 1999. "Conclusion." *Democracy and Trust,* ed. Mark E. Warren, 346–360. Cambridge, England: Cambridge University Press.

Warren, David R., G. T. Blain, F. L. Shorney, and L. J. Klein. 1995. "IRP: A Case Study From Kansas." *Journal of the American Water Works Association* 87 (6) June: 57–71.

Watson, Robert T., Marufu C. Zinyowera, Richard H. Moss, and David J. Dokken, eds. 1996. *Climate Change 1995: Impacts, Adaptations, and Mitigation of Climate Change: Scientific-Technical Analyses.* Contributions of Working Group II to the Second Assessment Report of the Intergovernmental Panel on Climate Change. Published for the IPCC. Cambridge, England: Cambridge University Press.

Weimer, D. L. and A.R. Vining. 1999. *Policy Analysis: Concepts and Practice.* 3d ed. Englewood Cliffs, NJ: Prentice-Hall.

Weiss, Rick. 2003. "Threats Posed by Water Scarcity Detailed: UN Report Warns of Looming Crisis." *Washington Post,* March 5.

Wells, A. 1994. *Up and Doing: A Brief History of the Murray Valley Development League, Now the Murray Darling Association, from 1944 to 1994.* Albury, Australia: Murray Darling Association.

Werblow, Steve. 1999. "North Carolina Producers Cut Pollutants as Livestock Industry Grows." *Partners: Conservation Technology Information Center* 17 (1) January/February: 8.

Wessel, Hans. 1997. "Managing the River Rhine and its Basin." In *Environmental Law and Policy in the European Union and the United States,* ed. Randall Baker, 219–230. Westport, CT: Praeger Publishers.

Western, David, and R. Michael Wright. 1994. *Natural Connections: Perspectives in Community-Based Conservation.* Washington, D.C.: Island Press.

Western Water Policy Review Advisory Commission. 1998. *Water in the West: Challenge for the Next Century.* Springfield, VA: National Technical Information Service, June.

Weston, R. Timothy. 1984. "Delaware River Basin: Courts vs. Compacts." Paper presented at the ASCE-Spring Convention, Symposium on "Social and Environmental Objectives in Water Management: The Court as Water Managers." Atlanta, Georgia, May 16.

Weston, R. Timothy. 1995. "Delaware River Basin-Challenges and Successes in Interstate Water Management." Paper presented at the ASCE Water Resources Engineering Conference, San Antonio, Texas, August 17.

Weston, T. R. 1999. "Interstate Water Rights and River Basin Compacts in the East." Unpublished manuscript. Harrisburg, PA: Kirkpatrick and Lockhart, LLP.

Wetland Initiative. 1994. *Reinventing a Flood Control Strategy.* Chicago: Wetland Initiative.

Wheeler, William B., and Michael J. McDonald. 1983. "The 'New Mission' and the Tellico Project, 1945–70," pp. 167–193, in Erwin C. Hargrove and Paul K. Conkin, Editors, *TVA: Fifty Years of Grass-roots Bureaucracy.* Urbana: University of Illinois Press.

Whetzel, Carolyn. 2002. "Bond Legislation Approved by Voters to Authorize $3.4 Billion for Water Programs," *Environment Reporter* 33 (45) November 15: 2474.

White, Gilbert. 1977. "Comparative Analysis of Complex River Development." In *Environmental Effects of Complex River Development,* ed. Gilbert White, 1–21. Boulder, CO: Westview Press.

White, Gilbert F. 1994. "A Perspective on Reducing Losses from Natural Hazards." *Bulletin of the American Meteorological Society* 75 (7) July: 1237–1241.

Wilkinson, Charles F. 1992. *Crossing the Next Meridian: Water, Power, and the Future of the American West.* Washington, D.C.: Island Press.

Williams, John Page. 2000. *Another Side of the TMDL Discussion.* Chesapeake Notebook, 2–2000. Available at www.cbf.org.

Wilson, Robert. 2003. "Birth of a Dam." *Knoxville News Sentinel,* September 28: A1, A16–19.

World Bank. 1993. *Water Resources Management: A World Bank Policy Study.* Washington, D.C.: World Bank.

World Bank. 1996a. "The Environmental Dimension in Water Resources Management." *Environment Matters: Annual Review.* Washington, D.C.: World Bank.

World Bank. 1996b. "Strategically Managing the World's Water." *Environment Matters: Annual Review.* Washington, D.C.: World Bank.

World Bank. 2003. *Environment Matters: Annual Review.* Washington, D.C.: World Bank.

World Civil Society Forum. 2002. "Strengthen the Role of Civil Society in International Cooperation." Geneva, Switzerland. Available at www.worldcivilsociety.org/pages/164.

World Resources Institute [WRI]. 1995. *World Resources, 1994–5.* New York: Oxford University Press.

World Resources Institute [WRI]. 1999. *Resources at Risk; Water-Critical Shortages Ahead? World Resources 1998–99.* WRI, www.wri.org/wr-98-99/water2.htm.

World Resources Institute [WRI]. 2002. "Earthtrends: The Environmental Information Portal." Available at earthtrends.wri.org/maps_spatial/maps.

World Summit on Sustainable Development. 2002. Civil Society Secretariat: Johannesburg, South Africa. Available at www.worldsummit.org.za.

Worster, Donald. 1985. *Rivers of Empire: Water, Aridity, and the Growth of the American West.* New York: Pantheon Books.

Worster, Donald. 2001. *A River Running West: The Life of John Wesley Powell.* New York: Oxford University Press.

Wright, D. 1978. "The River Murray: Microcosm of Australian Federal History." In *Federalism in Canada and Australia: The Early Years,* ed. B. W. Hodgins et al., 277–286. Canberra, Australia: Australian National University Press and Wilfred Laurier Press.

Wright, Kenneth R., ed. 1998. *Water Rights of the Eastern United States.* Denver, CO: American Water Works Association.

Yin, Robert K. 1984. *Case Study Research: Design and Methods.* Beverly Hills, CA: SAGE.

Yoffe, Shira B., and Brian S. Ward. 1999. "Water Resources and Indicators of Conflict: A Proposed Spatial Analysis." *Water International* 24 (4) December: 377–384.

Zahodiakin, Phil. 2001. "EPA Delays TMDL Revisions." *Pesticide and Toxic Chemical News* 29 (52) October: 16.

Zakharov, Vladimir M., ed. 2001. *Regional Environmental Policy-Summary.* Moscow, Russian Federation: Center for Russian Environmental Policy.

Zoreda-Lozano, Juan J., and Victor Castaneda. 1998. "Critical Issues in Urban Technologies for Sustainable Development: The Case of Water Infrastructure in Mexico City." *Policy Studies Review* 15 (2/3) Summer-Autumn: 157–169.

Legislation

Clean Water Act. 1972. As amended. Title 33 U.S.C. §§ 1251–1387.

Delaware River Basin Compact. 1961. P.L. 87-328, 75 Stat 688.

Endangered Species Act. 1973. Title 33 U.S.C. § 403; 37 CFR, pt. 322.

Federal Power Act. 1920. Title 16 U.S.C. §§ 791–828c and 18 CRFR, pts. 4, 16.

Fish and Wildlife Coordination Act. 1958. Title 16 U.S.C. § 661. PL 85-624.

Joint Resolution Granting the Consent of Congress to the Apalachicola-Chattahoochee-Flint River Basin Compact. 1997. U.S. House of Representatives, 105th Congress, 1st Session.

National Environmental Policy Act. 1969. Title 33 U.S.C. §§ 401–426. 40 CFR, pt. 130.

National Park Service Organic Act. 1916. Title 16 U.S.C. § 1.

Pacific Northwest Electric Power Planning and Conservation Act. 1980. Title 16 U.S.C. § 839b(h).

"Proposed Rule to Withdraw the July 2000 TMDL Rule." 2002. Washington, D.C., EPA, December 20.

Tennessee Valley Authority Act. 1934. Title 16 U.S.C. 831 § 22.

Water Quality Standards Regulation. 1998. 63 Fed. Reg. 36742.

Wild and Scenic Rivers Act. 1976. Title 16 U.S.C. §§ 1271–1287. 82 Stat. 906.

Judicial citations

Arizona v. California. 373 U.S. 546, 565 (1963).

California vs. U.S. 438 U.S. 645, 648–668 (1978).

TVA vs. Hill. 437 U.S. 153 (1978).

United States v. New Mexico. 438 U.S. 696 (1978).

Winters v. U.S. 207 U.S. 564 (1908).

Index

Page numbers followed by *f* refer to figures; by *n* to notes; and by *t* to tables.

David Lewis Feldman is the head of the Department of Political Science at the University of Tennessee. His research focuses on comparative environmental and energy policy, water resources management, and ethics and public policy. Among his many publications are *Water Resources Management: In Search of an Environmental Ethic* (Johns Hopkins, 1995), *The Energy Crisis: Unresolved Issues and Enduring Legacies* (Johns Hopkins, 1996), and *Global Climate Change and Public Policy* (Nelson-Hall, 1994). Feldman is the 2001 recipient of the *Policy Studies Organization* Interdisciplinary Scholar Award and has served as editor of the *Review of Policy Research* and as symposium coordinator for the *Policy Studies Journal.* Feldman served for many years as a faculty member at the University of Tennessee–Knoxville and is a professor and the chair of the Department of Planning, Policy, and Design at the School of Social Ecology, University of California–Irvine. He also helped draft Tennessee's Inter-basin Water Transfer Act (2000) and the state's Water Supply Information Act (2002). He has testified before Congress on water policy and is currently undertaking research, in cooperation with Greenpeace, on the growth of civil society and environmental values in Russia.